D0068990

Slavery in the South

Slavery in the South

A State-by-State History

Clayton E. Jewett and John O. Allen

Foreword by Jon L. Wakelyn

GREENWOOD PRESS
Westport, Connecticut • London

E
441
.J49
2004

Library of Congress Cataloging-in-Publication Data

Jewett, Clayton E.
   Slavery in the South : a state-by-state history / Clayton E. Jewett and John O. Allen ; foreword by Jon L. Wakelyn.
       p.   cm.
   Includes bibliographical references and index.
   ISBN 0–313–32019–5 (alk. paper)
   1. Slavery—Southern States—History.   2. Slaves—Southern States—Social conditions. 3. African Americans—Southern States—Social conditions.   4. Southern States—History. 5. Southern States—Race relations.   6. Slaves—Southern States—Biography.   7. Southern States—Biography.   I. Allen, John O.   II. Title.
   E441.J49   2004
   306.3'62'0973—dc22   2003060004

British Library Cataloguing in Publication Data is available.

Library of Congress Catalog Card Number: 2003060004
ISBN: 0–313–32019–5

First published in 2004

Greenwood Press, 88 Post Road West, Westport, CT 06881
An imprint of Greenwood Publishing Group, Inc.
www.greenwood.com

Printed in the United States of America

The paper used in this book complies with the Permanent Paper Standard issued by the National Information Standards Organization (Z39.48–1984).

10 9 8 7 6 5 4 3 2 1

Contents

Foreword

In this succinct survey of American slave states, Clayton E. Jewett and John O. Allen have produced a splendid volume filled with pertinent factual and human interest information with inclusion of the voices of the slaves themselves. This reference covers slave life from the colonial period until the Civil War as well as the slave's role in ending slavery during the Civil War and that most important period of black life during the Reconstruction of the nation. The authors conclude with the rise of segregation and the laws of oppression, acquiesced by the North, as Southerners attempted to roll back the gains of freedom. By covering the development of slavery within all the Southern slave colonies and states, the authors have made an important contribution to the history of slavery. In doing so, they have done the academic profession and the many students who will read this volume an outstanding service.

The work is divided into separate chapters on each of the Southern slave colonies that became slave states after the Revolution. A splendid timeline covers all pertinent and necessary material needed for the reader to grasp the development of a slave society. In the colonial world, for example, Jewett and Allen date the important events of the countries that first brought slaves to the New World. Alabama slavery is dated from the French settling along Mobile Bay in 1737. Also listed are dates of slave codes so that one is able to see immediately how slavery was deepened by law in each of the colonies and states. The culpability of the colonies and states in making slave society is shown in these timelines. One sees, then, the migration of slavery westward into the fertile lands of the southwest that made the cotton belt and thus condemned the slaves to hard agricultural labor for their white masters. Most important, the timelines also include the story of slave resistance in each of the colonies and states. Slave activity in the Civil War and dates of resistance and freedom are also included. Lastly, the reader is given a quick factual introduction by date of the activities of ex-slaves during Reconstruction and the resistance of the freed people to the deepening laws of prejudice and physical violence perpetrated on them. The general timeline and the timelines in each chapter are thus useful introductions to slave society and life.

The authors also include statistical information on the growth of slavery in each of the states by decade from 1790. Instantly the reader is made aware of how many slaves lived in each of the Southern states at any one time. For those interested in the rise and fall of slave life in the Southern states, and in comparing growth and decline by southern region, the authors' factual information is most interesting. Thus, why Delaware lost slaves and contact with the lower South, why border slave states did not join the southern Confederacy, and why the lower South was so devoted to protecting slavers and detecting slave insurrection can easily be deduced from these facts. The authors' interregional data prove the power of slave population movement turn effect change within slave states. Appendices providing the number of slaveholders in each state in 1860 as well as important economic statistics on slavery add to the usefulness of Jewett and Allen's timeline tracing the rise and fall of slave society.

Most important in this volume are the profiles of slavery in the individual states. Topics develop the origins of slavery, the early days of colonial slave life, the great western land movement that included slaves, and the importation of slaves into each colony and state. Slave sales and slave traders are vividly depicted as the gains in profit from slave dispersal brutally divided slave families. The discussions of slave lives, work, and culture include thoughtful and concise bibliographies that offer the most current and pertinent information available on those in captivity. The living conditions of the slaves, even to the types of their housing, are included. That slaves resisted their condition of servitude shows that their collective values and personal dignity served them well in handling the horrors of their condition. In addition, the authors make an important contribution to the study of slavery by showing how slaves lived in an urban world. The necessity of whites to hire out slaves for profits also gave slaves the opportunity to mingle with their own people, to achieve a kind of independence, and no doubt contributed to their ability to claim freedom for themselves during the Civil War.

The sections on slave culture confirm the meaning of resistance. Slaves spoke out about their plight and the authors quote them in this volume. In the choice of pertinent slave voices, the reader is able to grasp much of the life of slavery. The authors also explore religion as a force that allowed slaves to create a separate existence from whites. The authors frequently quote slave songs and tales, allowing the reader to learn much about what slaves thought and felt. Most important, the authors enter the historical fray on the subject of slave family life. While Jewett and Allen write that family life was different in the many regions of slave population, they make much of the centrality of family life as defining slave society and culture. From patterns of family work to family resistance, the importance of slave childraising is stressed to allow readers to understand how slaves developed their own culture and resisted white oppression. Indeed, the authors show how a separate slave culture developed within white-controlled society.

The final sections on slave behavior during the Civil War, the freed people during Reconstruction, and the dignity of resisting the horrors of violent legal segregation at the end of the nineteenth century and after build on the authors' reading of how slaves handled their condition. For black escapees and fighting men, the story of the war is one of courage and learning more about freedom. The authors show that the Northern military did not always treat their black allies with respect. The authors are familiar with the war's *Official Record*, and they make much use of it to allow the slave resistors to tell their own military story. Likewise, the activity of ex-slaves in reconstructing themselves is told vividly. African Americans in politics and at work made a new life of dignity and even economic independence. That story of their wartime and postwar courage is perhaps one of the finest in this country's long history. But the history of the slave states ends on a sour note. State by state, the ex-slave South passed laws of segregation. The North acquiesced in segregation with the passing of the Plessy laws creating the lie of separate but equal facilities for the freed people. Yet this book's great effort to show how African Americans dealt with diversity holds out hope for the reader that segregation and prejudice in the twentieth century might, through the efforts of the African Americans themselves, give way to true freedom in the twenty-first century.

Jon L. Wakelyn
Kent State University

Preface

Recently, while teaching in Texas and Washington, D.C., we asked our students to tell us everything they knew about the Southern system of bonded labor. The students offered similar responses. Generally outspoken, our classes sat largely silent and offered answers such as "It was wrong," "Slaves were treated poorly," and "It couldn't have been that bad, they were fed." Perhaps clouded by oral recollections of their parents' experiences with the civil rights campaigns and the culture clashes of the 1960s, by a sometimes questionable secondary education system, and by the images provided in Hollywood productions and other media, many of their answers were apparently based upon myths and misinformation. Today, slavery, the "peculiar institution," is once again a topic of contention as politicians and interest groups argue about and explore the possibility of reparations for slavery. While it is not our intention to become involved in such matters, one wonders to what extent our children and our politicians understand the system of labor that defined so much of this country for so many years and still stands at the center of so much political and social debate. While a great deal of work by prominent historians appears on the subject of slavery, a comparative summary of the slave states does not exist, and it is this gap that our work seeks to fill. *Slavery in the South: A State-by-State History* offers high school and community college students, undergraduates, and other interested nonspecialists an informative summary of the slave experience in each individual slave state and a synthetic sketch of enslaved African Americans for each jurisdiction that still embraced the slave system at the onset of the American Civil War.

We have employed a topical approach within a chronological framework. Each illustrated chapter tackles a specific slave state. For each jurisdiction, we seek to explore and summarize the following broad topics: the genesis and growth of slavery, the economics of the peculiar institution, the life of free and enslaved blacks, the legal codes that defined the institution and affected both whites and blacks, the black experience during the Civil War, and the freedmen's struggle during Emancipation and Reconstruction.

We believe that each state's experience with slavery, although similar, also included numerous events and instances that created distinct stories. Each state had a unique chronicle of laws, rebellions, customary practices, and recollected vignettes regarding relationships among slaves, free blacks, white slave owners, and white non-slave-owners. For example, some areas like the Chesapeake Bay region (Maryland, Virginia, and Delaware) had a longer exposure to slavery during the colonial era than during the period between the American Revolution and the Civil War. In some states, slave patrols, "the patterollers," were present in every county and town; in other states, such patrols were not regularly employed. Thus, the history of slavery in each state is a story based on the unique events that took place within its jurisdictions and is a chronicle of the relationships and interactions between its blacks and whites. Thus, an approach organized by state and by categorical topic allows the reader to see the similarities and the differences and reach comparative conclusions.

For each state, we attempted to outline the particular landmark events that largely characterized slavery in that jurisdiction from its inception to its demise. Besides a timeline of important national events relating to slavery, each chapter opens with a chronological timeline of slavery that lists important dates and events specific to that state and more fully explored in the text of the chapter. The timelines are followed by tables that provide statistics on slave and free black populations in each state before 1860 and the rise or fall in state slave populations by decade through 1860. Particular chapters also contain other tables, both in the open statistical summaries and in text, relating to a statistical compilation specific to that state. Appendices at the end of the book include a table listing the number of slaveholders in each state in 1860, the dates of admission and (where applicable) of secession and readmission for each state, and pertinent economic statistics related to antebellum slavery. A detailed person and subject index provides additional access to information in the chapters.

We drew primarily on state-focused studies to create our summary sketches, although we also used more general seminal studies that included specific examples about the state in question. For example, *Freedom: A Documentary History of Emancipation*, a compilation edited by Berlin, Reidy, and Rowland on the black Union soldiers and the United States Colored Troops, provided substantial details about individual incidents that occurred in most Southern and border states. Furthermore, we included in this reference excerpts drawn from collected volumes of slave narratives. In this regard, the material developed by George Rawick was especially useful. In-text citations to the sources used are provided in parentheses at the ends of paragraphs; each citation is correlated with a full bibliographical reference found at the end of the chapter. The simplified in-text notations indicate the last name of the author or editor, the year of publication, and the relevant pages. Besides listing the reference works used for that state's summary, the concluding bibliographies also provide relevant Web sites.

REFERENCES

Berlin, Ira, Joseph P. Reidy, and Leslie S. Rowland, eds. 1982. *Freedom: A Documentary History of Emancipation, 1861–1867,* Series II, *The Black Military Experience.* New York: Cambridge University Press.

Rawick, George P., ed. 1972. *The American Slave: A Composite Autobiography.* 19 vols. Westport, Conn.: Greenwood Press.

Acknowledgments

This project would not have been possible without the aid and encouragement of others. We greatly appreciated the ideas and comments cordially offered by L.R. Poos, the Dean of Arts and Sciences at the Catholic University of America. We would like to thank John Wagner of Greenwood Press for his careful reading of the manuscript and his encouragement and cooperation on this project. We also owe a debt of gratitude to Jon L. Wakelyn, our mentor and friend, whose patience and guidance know no bounds. In addition, we thank our students at Austin Community College and the Catholic University of America, who offered thought-provoking questions and painstakingly listened to our lectures on the subject. Finally, we thank our friends and family members, who put up with us on a daily basis and offered their unyielding encouragement. Any mistakes of information or grammar we claim as our own. We hope that this reference work will prove a useful educational tool for students, energizing their thirst for knowledge and assisting in their growth into productive members of society.

Introduction

According to the historian Edmund S. Morgan, "Slavery is a mode of compulsion that has often prevailed where land is abundant" (1975, 296). White European settlers came to the New World complete with an ethnocentricity that incorporated the belief that land was plentiful and theirs to claim. While the former was true, the falsity of the latter would cause generations of turmoil, with repercussions to this day. Nevertheless, with land in European hands, the need and desire for labor quickly followed. In the formation of this country, the need for labor to exploit the land has been seen to be colorblind (Kolchin 1993, 7). Landowners seeking profits to improve their lot in society simply required hands to work the soil. This general demand for laborers was initially filled by indentured servants: whites who agreed to labor contracts with explicit terms, conditions, and time limitations in return for payment of passage to the New World. With Great Britain having its own economic difficulties, exacerbated by the English civil wars as well as by a spurt in population growth, white labor proved readily available. Additionally, indentured servants were less expensive than bought slaves. This especially held true in light of the high mortality rates in the Chesapeake colonies through the 1660s. It simply made good economic sense to use indentured servants acquired at a lower initial cost. As the availability of white indentured servants declined, in part due to the horrible conditions in Virginia, and as initial mortality rates dropped, landowners increasingly turned to purchasing slaves, either individuals transported directly from Africa or blacks of African descent brought from the Caribbean. In this way, the framework and structure for black slavery was established in the colonial era.

The turn to slavery, though, appeared to be almost a natural evolution. The legal system recognized the right of Europeans to own non-European human chattel as early as the late sixteenth century, and African slavery already existed in other parts of the world. In the early seventeenth century, the Dutch and Portuguese were at odds, with the Dutch taking over much of the Portuguese empire and the trade that came along with it, including the trade in slaves. The Dutch purchased Virginia tobacco and thus were the initial suppliers of human chattel for the Virginia system of slave labor. In the colonial settlements that eventually emerged as the United States, slavery was simply an extension of a labor system that existed elsewhere—spreading from the Mediterranean to the Atlantic Islands to the West Indies and Barbados and into Virginia and the American colonies. The switch, however, from indentured servitude to that of slave labor also involved other factors. In the late seventeenth century, England's economy rebounded, its political turmoil diminished, and its population pressures abated. These changes led to a decrease in the ready supply of indentured servants. However, in the colonies the demand for agricultural workers increased apace. In turning to African slaves as a labor source, colonial officials and assemblies made sure that black slaves would have a different legal status from white indentured servants. In virtually all the colonies, one of the first laws regarding slavery enacted by the local assembly specified that baptism into Christianity did not confer freedom. African slaves and white indentured servants would always be different forms of property (Morgan 1975, 158–180; Morris 1996, 40–44, 66).

Generally, slavery in the American colonies, and later in the United States, flourished in areas that could effectively grow a staple cash crop that required continuous labor throughout the calendar year. During the colonial era, the primary slave regions included the Chesapeake, where farmers and planters grew tobacco, and the Carolina coastal regions, whose agriculturists harvested rice and indigo. In later antebellum days, tobacco, rice, hemp, sugar, and, most prominently, cotton fulfilled these conditions. Wherever these characteristics did not appear or had disappeared, slavery quickly became a marginal aspect of the local economy and society. Delaware offers a good example. In the colonial era, Delaware slave owners profitably grew and marketed tobacco as part of the greater Chesapeake economy. During these years, slaves formed a significant part of the population and the social system. However, as tobacco declined as a viable crop alternative in Delaware, so too did the slave population.

Throughout the antebellum era, the typical yearly carrying cost for slaves was roughly twenty dollars to thirty dollars; the actual cash outlays were often ten dollars or less. If a slave, when combined with others on a labor gang, grew and harvested crops that averaged on the market two hundred dollars to four hundred dollars per worker, the slave owner could clear a substantial cash profit, even if all of his workforce could not be employed, such as the elderly, the infirm, and the young. Thus, when crop prices were robust, a well-run slave plantation growing rice, hemp, sugar, tobacco, or cotton would generate substantial economic returns. Therefore, an important aspect of American slavery would always be the profitable economic exploitation of African American slave labor (Fogel 1989, 17–113).

As written by Thomas Jefferson, the opening paragraphs of the Declaration of Independence state, "We hold these truths to be self evident: That all men are created equal; and endowed by their Creator with certain unalienable rights; among these are life, liberty, and the pursuit of happiness." However, blacks in the colonial New World were anything but free and equal. Nevertheless, they played a significant role in the American Revolution. In some cases, they fought, but, more important, blacks made it possible for whites to gain their freedom from Great Britain. Without bonded labor, whites would not have had the hands to produce the tobacco necessary to successfully bargain with France and to secure French intervention in the conflict. Thus, black slave labor contributed to American freedom. Not only, as Morgan points out, is this one of the greatest paradoxes in American history but it also is one of the grossest hypocrisies in our nation's past (Morgan 1975, 386–387). Whites understood all too well the complexity of the situation; they had fought and won a war for liberty and freedom, yet were denying the same to hundreds of thousands of blacks. Thus, whites constantly worried about the possibility of slave revolts.

Prior to the Revolution, slave conspiracies were a real threat, more than we will ever know, since many slave owners diligently suppressed much of the information regarding such plots. Slave revolts, as historian Sylvia Frey reveals, not only were a product of the slave environment, but also stemmed from a legacy of military traditions brought from Africa (Frey 1991, 45–80). Rebellion was simply an extension of the African heritage brought to the surface by the colonial struggle with Great Britain. Most American political leaders consciously chose to ignore the relationship between political slavery to Great Britain and the enslavement of Africans for their own economic well-being. This connection, however, was not lost on free or enslaved blacks in the colonial world. Although slaves were illiterate, so was a huge segment of the white population. Furthermore, in an era where cultural values were transmitted orally—for both blacks and whites—slaves had some knowledge of the revolutionary ideology employed by whites in their struggle against the Crown. While enslaved blacks could not evoke the arguments of Locke, Trenchard, Gordon, or Paine, they did understand in simple terms that their masters were fighting for their own freedom from political and economic enslavement by Great Britain. Furthermore, they understood their status as slaves: forever bound in perpetual servitude by the laws of society. The irony and the hypocrisy were all too glaring. As the turmoil of the crisis developed, slaves were caught up in the drama of the revolutionary era and learned their lessons well. They too protested their enslavement in numerous ways.

Boston slaves, for example, sent petitions for their freedom to the colonial assembly. In addition, when the Sons of Liberty marched about with shouts of liberty, protesting against the injustice of the British government and the system of taxation, blacks emulated whites. In some instances, they too took to the streets and yelled for freedom and justice, not from Great Britain, but from the confines of a labor system that denied them their dignity and freedom on a daily basis. Slaves revolted against their masters in small ways on a daily basis. Such emulation sent shock waves down the spines of colonial whites. In retrospect, it is a wonder that slave rebellion was not more pronounced during the American Revolution.

The fallout from the Revolution's aftermath largely created the political geography that remained current until the Civil War. The widespread dissemination of natural rights rhetoric caused the public's perception for the justification of slavery to weaken in regions where it offered few economic advantages or where it had not become deeply entrenched. North of Delaware and Maryland, state assemblies proscribed the peculiar institution or adopted rules that permitted gradual emancipation. By 1800, all these states had taken steps to eradicate slavery in their jurisdictions. In the three Chesapeake states, Delaware, Maryland, and Virginia, revolutionary era slave owners, deeply influenced by the ideas of human and natural rights, unleashed a wave of enslaved African Americans by using large-scale manumissions and contractual emancipations. These free blacks dramatically altered the human landscape in the region. Large numbers would henceforth live in this area and, in Delaware, would significantly outnumber slaves. Additionally, the newly inaugurated national government set boundaries on slavery's limits. The 1789 legislature accepted the earlier Northwest Ordinance, which proscribed slavery in lands north of the Ohio River. Moreover, the compromises that led to the acceptance of the Constitution and to the implementation of a newly defined United States barred slave importations after 1807. Therefore, the founders effectively limited the reach of the slave system in creating the newly organized nation (Frey 1991, 206–241).

Thus, three trajectories of assumptions about slavery had been set in motion. In the North, slavery disappeared. A small vocal minority spoke out vehemently against its evils and promoted complete abolition throughout the entire United States. In areas of the Upper South that bordered the North, large numbers of free blacks and hired-out slaves joined enslaved African Americans as important components in the population. The resulting politics led many whites to be as concerned about the status of free blacks as about slavery itself. A more typical understanding here held that slavery was a necessary evil and an important element in managing race relations. Finally, the more southern slave states recovered from the severe dislocations of the revolutionary years and soon came to believe that slavery was a positive contributor to the economy and to the social fabric of society. After the innovation of successful cotton gins made upland cotton a viable cash crop, chattel slavery offered the primary way to exploit land for profit. These three assumptions and geographical trajectories moved westward with the expanding population and largely held sway until the Civil War.

Although during the antebellum era the particulars of slavery varied over time and place, historians have generally viewed the master-slave aspect of the peculiar institution as being either paternalistic or capitalistic. To view the system of bound labor as paternalistic is to focus on the reciprocal relationship between masters and slaves. Slaveholders defended their ownership of human property and upheld a paternalistic view, believing they were doing well for the slaves, that they were providing a better living condition than the slaves would have had in Africa or other places of origin. Historians, such as Eugene Genovese, studying the records of larger plantations, have also argued that the masters' treatment of their property endorses such a view. However, on a deeper level, Genovese argues that the slaveholding elite relied upon the institution and demanded loyalty from their slaves as a means for the owners to curb their own harsh tendencies. In a manner of speaking, the institution of slavery allowed whites to impose order on a society that was often uncertain and unstable. Slaves also, argues Genovese, had a role in supporting the paternalistic nature of slavery. Their acceptance of what Genovese calls the "aristocratic ethos," accepting an authority figure who "simultaneously protects and abuses, nourishes and punishes," is evidence of the reciprocal nature of the relationship. In addition, slaves held certain expectations of their owners. For example, slaves often gave small gifts of food to the owner when the owner visited the slave quarters. Likewise, slaves expected the owner to return the act of kindness in some manner. This view also carried over into the work environment where slaves expected special privileges, such as passes, for their hard work in the field. Finally, historians have pointed to the legal codes that not only reflected, but also cemented the paternalist nature of the slave system. For example, in every slave state, laws declared to some degree that owners must provide for the basic necessities of their slave property. Likewise, the legal system restricted slave activity, deeming certain and specific actions a violation of the law requiring punishment. The law "constituted a principal vehicle for the hegemony of the ruling class." In general, then, to view the slave system as paternalistic, and the relationship as reciprocal, is to view both the owners and the slaves as benefiting from the institution of slavery, where both parties extracted what they wanted and needed from the other in a symbiotic relationship (Genovese 1972, 26, 91, 120).

Not all historians agree on emphasizing the paternalistic nature of the slave system. Some historians emphasize the capitalistic nature of the peculiar institution. Slavery allowed those who had built up large estates, and those who aspired to do so, to maintain their economic standing. As the market economy dictated, Anglos began to rely on slavery to meet the European demand for tobacco and cotton. Historian James Oakes reveals that "the demand for slaves grew in complex relation to the rising demand for consumer goods." Thus, according to Oakes, what clearly separates New World slavery from ancient slavery is that the institution was tied to capitalism and in many ways "was itself the servant of the driving force of capitalism" (Oakes 1990, 52). To view the peculiar institution as capitalistic is therefore to view slaves as cogs in the machinery, as a means to an end—profit. Thus, slave owners did not necessarily care for the welfare of their human chattel, but instead provided the basic necessities as a means to keep their labor force working for the master. Nevertheless, the value of each individual slave as a human commodity generally increased throughout the antebellum era. The economic value of human chattel led at least some owners to take pains with the health and hence the market value of their human property. Additionally, slaveholders sold or transported over 750,000 enslaved African Americans from the Upper South and the older slaveholding states to the Gulf states in the antebellum era (Tadman 1989, 12).

In many ways the historical debate between the paternalists and capitalists is somewhat mute; slaves did not have their freedom. The paternalistic nature of the system required owners to eradicate any vestige of slave independence and keep the slaves as perpetual children dependent upon their master. Likewise, the capitalistic nature of the system required slaves to submit to a life that was undeniably harsh and commonly arbitrary. Whether in the cotton fields of Mississippi, the tobacco fields of Virginia, or the rice swamps of South Carolina, slaves woke well before sunup, toiled under harsh conditions with the constant threat of the lash, and worked until past sundown. Their private lives were intruded upon, they were physically and sexually abused, and they were often torn from loved ones through slave sales. This system of forced labor allowed whites to exploit the land, and their laborers, for profit (Kolchin 1993, 99–100).

If slaves worked hard and did their job, however, they might escape punishment or might be looked favorably upon and extended a privilege or a pass to visit a loved one. This of course depended solely upon the character and the mood of the owner. For slaves who directly disobeyed their owners or the overseer, the lash was the most common form of punishment. More likely than not, local laws dictated the precise number of lashes for each offense. In some areas, slaves not only were whipped, but also branded or mutilated, especially to discourage them from running away. Cutting off an ear served as a constant reminder to the slave and the slave community of the consequences of serious transgressions. For the most heinous crimes, such as murder, slaves suffered execution. Local laws and customs also dictated this. In many places, an execution was carried out by hanging; in some areas, even well into the antebellum era, slaves were burned to death.

However, to view the peculiar institution as uncontrollably forbidding is to neglect the spirit and tenacity of humanity. According to historian Lawrence Levine, slaves created their own worldview complete with a living and vibrant culture that allowed them to transcend the restrictions of their environment. Slave songs allowed slaves to "voice criticism as well as to uphold traditional values and group cohesion." The spirituals that slaves incorporated into their daily lives allowed them to transcend their environment, as they looked back to the past, to patriarchal figures for guidance, and upward toward heaven for comfort and freedom. The tales they told their children also helped reinforce their history and the importance of family ties, obligations to parents, and God. These things the master could not take from them. The oral nature of this culture, which drew upon the past and the present and varied over time and space, was instrumental in keeping "legal slavery from becoming spiritual slavery" (Levine 1977, 6, 32, 80).

The 1840s represented an era of growth, optimism, and expansion. During this period, the United States annexed Texas and acquired Oregon, New Mexico, and California. This was also a time of fear of the black population. This fear provided much of the impetus for American expansion. For Northerners, racial anxiety over the potential influx of free blacks allowed them to accept westward expansion as a means to disperse the black population. This would, in turn, distance the border states from the peculiar institution and, in many minds, lead to the eventual demise of slavery. For Southerners, the fear of abolition that threatened the institution of slavery provided the impetus for expansion. For them, westward expansion provided an opportunity for more land, the expansion of slavery, and additional economic gains. They viewed westward expansion as the only viable means to safeguard their economic investment. The concern over westward expansion, with the place of blacks in society at the center of the debate, fueled the political division between Whigs and Democrats. For the most part, Whigs refused to accept westward expansion as the solution to their fear of a growing and encroaching black population. Democrats, on the other hand, generally supported annexation of western territory as a means of securing the institution of slavery and warding off the threats of abolitionism. Thus, the conflicting political assumptions about slavery in the 1840s and 1850s, hammered out over the status of the newly acquired western lands, resonated throughout the voting population and with the politicians who sought to win elections (Hietala 1985, 10–54; Morrison 1997, 1–10).

This disagreement over the extension of slavery into the lands acquired from Mexico threatened to rip the nation asunder in 1849 and 1850. In this, the first secession crisis, Henry Clay and other Jacksonian politicians worked out a package of enactments that together passed into history as the Compromise of 1850. California entered the Union as a free state. Congress proscribed slave trading within the District of Columbia. The enforcement provisions of the Fugitive Slave Law were strengthened. For a few years, slavery as a political issue was somewhat removed from the front burner (Morrison 1997, 96–126).

The competition between pro-slavery and abolition forces reopened the old sectional wounds when Senator Stephen A. Douglas pushed through the Kansas-Nebraska Act in 1854. This legislation canceled out the Missouri Compromise of 1820, which had geographically defined the jurisdictions that could legally include slaves. The whole issue of whether a newly organized western territory would be slave or free was thrust upon the electorate through Douglas's doctrine of "popular sovereignty." The newly organized western territories would vote to be slave or free. The contest in Kansas created a bloody guerilla war and introduced the figure of abolitionist John Brown to the American public. Slavery in the western territories again became a major political battleground among voters and politicians who opposed slavery, who supported slavery, and who wanted to keep the peace. By 1854, the nation was on the verge of political turmoil. The role of slavery in the west would cause the demise of the Whig Party and instigate the failure of the second American party system (Morrison 1997, 126–156; Hietala 1985, 10–54).

As slavery became entrenched in the Southern states, an ideology of free labor emerged in the North. This emergence is not surprising considering that from the American Revolution on, Northern society designed to abolish slavery. From the Quaker petitions to the Northwest Ordinance of 1787, and the abolitionist preachers of the 1830s to the birth of the Republican Party in the 1850s, Northerners came to view slavery as the antithesis to a well-ordered society based upon constitutional principles. A component of this ideology, as historian Eric Foner reveals, involved the fear of a slave power. This fear was based upon the belief that a conspiracy existed among Southern slaveholders and politicians to seize the reigns of government and pervert the American Constitution by forcing slavery upon the nation, passing trade laws favoring slaveholders, and, even worse, reopening the trans-Atlantic slave trade (Foner 1995, ix–xxxii). With a history of struggle over the admittance of slaves and the issue of slavery in the west, along with such incidents as "Bleeding Kansas" and "Bleeding Sumner," it is no surprise that an opposing ideology emerged that would shape Northern society, would lead to the disintegration of the Northern system of party politics, and would move the United States one step closer to a full-scale civil war. The Republican Party, however, was not the immediate beneficiary of the Kansas-Nebraska Act and the subsequent cycle of events. Historian Tyler Anbinder contends that antislavery sentiment was an integral component in the success of the Know-Nothing Party, one of the precursors of the Republican Party. Although the national party platform backed presidential candidate Millard Fillmore and his support of the Kansas-Nebraska Act, Northern Know-Nothings generally repudiated both Fillmore and the 1855 party platform supporting the Kansas-Nebraska Act. The antislavery sentiment of the northern wing of the party most likely originated from the members antagonism toward Catholics and Irish who supported the peculiar institution. The sectional split and demise of the Know-Nothing Party over the issue of slavery gave rise to the Republican Party in the North. This party, unlike its predecessors, made no attempt to create a southern wing or to reach a political compromise with Southern politicians. Thus, with the birth of the Republican Party, the nation's electorate was confronted with overt sectionalism and with politicians who appealed to only one geographical region. In 1860, the election to the presidency of the Republican candidate, Abraham Lincoln, who did not appear on the ballot in over 90 percent of slave state precincts, became the instigating event in sectional dissolution; the last straw of the American political party system was broken. Led by South Carolina, the slave South bolted from the Union and precipitated a civil war (Anbinder 1992, 220–245).

When the bells of secession rang across the Southern states, slaveholders tightened their grip on the peculiar institution and signaled their willingness to die for what they believed was their natural right to the pursuit of happiness through individual, private property ownership and economic profit. The Civil War represented more than a battle between the forces of industrialism and agrarianism, extended beyond ideological minds of Northern and Southern leaders, and was more significant than a generation of any politicians could manage. The Civil War represented a conflict within capitalism with slavery as the focal point of dispute. For free and enslaved blacks, the Civil War represented a turning point in racial and labor relations.

Free blacks viewed the Civil War with suspicion and trepidation. Many free Southern blacks wished to support the Union cause. Nevertheless, it would not be until the Second Confiscation Act in 1862 that the Union would begin to organize blacks into militia companies. The government's prior refusal to do so was a reflection of President Lincoln's desire not to disrupt the institution of slavery in border states that had not seceded, especially Kentucky. The Union's decision to use black soldiers was a strategic move. It undercut the Southern labor supply system and allowed the Union to employ forces already present in the area, to cut transportation costs, and to maintain the Northern system of labor by not drafting white factory workers.

Free blacks in the South fought for the Union cause to exact revenge against Southern whites; some were nobler in their cause, seeking to free their enslaved kinfolk. Ironically, free blacks also fought for the Confederacy. They did so to drive Union forces out and protect their own property—not only in terms of improved acreage, but also in terms of property ownership of human chattel.

While slaves might not have fully understood the conflict at hand or its ramifications, they did understand the fear that swept across the Southern cotton and wheat fields. With the onset of the Civil War, many masters in the border states took their bondsmen and fled to the Appalachian Mountains or further south. Slaves witnessed first hand the fear on their masters' faces, which immediately transformed the relationship. In 1862, the Confederate States of America passed the Conscription Act, and the Confederate government began to conscript slaves into the war effort to build fortifications and to work as general laborers, nurses, and cooks. In some cases, slaves even fought next to whites due to the exigency of war. The conscription of slaves for the war effort proved problematic for Southern whites who balked at governmental control of the labor force. Whites across the South railed against the government's attempt to seize their property, causing them to flee from the manacles of the Confederacy.

African Americans marched with both armies. Most officers in the Confederate regiments carried along black body servants on campaigns. Some of these blacks eventually escaped to the Union forces and freedom. Others remained with the rebel ranks. Likewise Union officers also used black camp servants. Both sides employed black laborers to build fortifications and dig trenches. The primary difference between the two sides had to do with pay. The Confederates used impressed slaves for sixty or one hundred twenty days at a time. The Union army generally paid its laborers a wage.

The implementation of the Emancipation Proclamation in January 1863 turned a war for union into a war for freedom. By the summer of 1863, the federal army began enrolling black soldiers into its regiments. Wherever the Union army overran Confederate territory, escaping slaves joined the ranks. Large numbers from the nonseceded border states also enlisted. Overall, approximately 179,000 African Americans served in the Union military forces. When Union armies marched through the South in 1864 and 1865, participating black regiments, organized as United States Colored Troops, became agents in the liberation of Southern slaves. Nothing spoke more convincingly about the changed circumstances than former slaves, now adorned with the "blue suit" and carrying weapons, guarding captured Confederate ex-slaveholders. The "bottom rail" had been moved to the top (Berlin 1982, 1–35).

Abraham Lincoln signed the Emancipation Proclamation in the autumn of 1862 and the enactment went into effect on January 1, 1863. In no way, however, were Southerners bound by it since they had created their own nation with their own president and Congress. Emancipation for slaves arrived at a slow pace and depended purely on Union military presence during and after the Civil War (Litwack 1979, 172–173).

There were many areas, especially in Texas, where the war never reached and Union occupation was nonexistent. Additionally, after the war, the Union army could not patrol every single area of the South during military occupation. The geographical size of the South made this a virtual impossibility. In addition, the prevailing view of whites, that blacks were property to be owned, and the white unwillingness to dismantle the foundation of their economic, social, and political system kept many slaves in chains well after the end of the military conflict. Some whites, however, accepted emancipation, viewing it as an immediate relief to their war-torn condition. No longer were they responsible for their bondsmen's general welfare, and now they were able to hire black labor at little cost.

The black reaction to emancipation was mixed and cannot be easily characterized. Some newly freed slaves did not even understand what emancipation meant. Many simply and quickly picked up and went on a search for loved ones, a journey that sometimes took decades. Other freedmen were quick to renew their marriage vows and legalize their union before a preacher and the eyes of the law. Still others wandered about from place to place, seeking work, while some chose to stay on the farms and plantations they had always known. Regardless of their specific path, blacks everywhere had a basic choice to either challenge or submit to the traditional code of racial etiquette. Herein lay the struggle of the Reconstruction era.

After the Civil War, the United States entered another experimental period of nation building. What, after all, did it mean to reconstruct the Union? Politicians were embarking on an endeavor with no design precedents as they attempted to transform a slave society into a free labor society. As such, heated political debate lasted for years and pitted Southerners against Northerners, Northerners and Southerners against themselves, and Congress against the president. Despite the political wrangling, Reconstruction gained a more radical tone as the North passed significant legislation to aid the freedmen and restore the Union. Although the Emancipation Proclamation began the process of freedom, it would not be until the Thirteenth Amendment, abolishing slavery in the United States, was ratified in December 1865 that the process of reconstruction could officially begin. Congress followed the Thirteenth Amendment with four additional and significant pieces of legislation. In March 1866, Congress passed, over President Andrew Johnson's veto, the Civil Rights Act, which defined all persons born in the United States as American citizens with equal rights. The Civil Rights Act of 1866 would provide the foundation for the Fourteenth Amendment, ratified in 1868, which strictly prohibited the states from depriving any citizens of their rights and liberties. In addition, the Fourteenth Amendment prohibited all Southern rebels from holding state or federal office. With these amendments in place, Reconstruction took a more radical turn when Congress passed the Reconstruction Acts of 1867, which divided the South into five military districts, each to be controlled by a military commander. Furthermore, it established that Southern states could only be readmitted into the Union once they wrote and ratified a new state constitution, ratified the Fourteenth Amendment to the United States Constitution, and provided for black male suffrage. The right for freedmen to vote was a significant concern for the radical proponents of Reconstruction. As such, Congress passed the last significant piece of Reconstruction legislation in 1869—the Fifteenth Amendment, ratified in 1870. The Fifteenth Amendment theoretically guaranteed black males the right to vote. It prohibited any state from denying suffrage to any person based upon "race, color, or previous condition of servitude" (Kolchin 1993, 209–211).

The black experience during Reconstruction would be shaped in part by the freedmen's own expectations and by white reaction to legislation. For freedmen, emancipation brought with it the hope of education and landownership. In March 1865, Congress established the Bureau of Refugees, Freedmen, and Abandoned Lands to carry out this expectation. Nevertheless, this bureaucratic system was no match for ingrained Southern white supremacy. White opposition to black education and landownership represented the rampant fear among whites of economic competition from blacks and the subsequent erosion of white supremacy.

The Freedmen's Bureau was successful, however, in helping blacks receive payment for work contracted for by white employers, often their former masters. It was less successful in helping the newly freed slaves gain access to land and in creating economic opportunities. Moreover, the Freedmen's Bureau was able to establish numerous schools across the South, including a number of the original historic black colleges such as present-day Howard University in Washington, D.C. Nevertheless, the vast majority of these schools were in the more urbanized areas of the South, and the bulk of the black population lived in the more rural area. By 1870, less than 10 percent of blacks over the age of twenty achieved literacy; the institution of slavery had not prepared blacks to live the reality of an emancipated life (Ransom and Sutch 1977, 15–39).

Blacks thus were trapped and victims of the Southern agricultural system. They were forced into wage labor contracts on the plantations. The new system of agricultural wage labor mirrored that of slavery—complete with gangs, overseers, slave quarters, and punishment. In addition, vagrancy laws requiring blacks to work or face fines, jail terms, and forced work made it impossible for freedmen to protest the system.

The period of military occupation and congressional reconstruction opened a glimmer of light into the possibilities of black citizenship. The Union army prevented blacks from being intimidated at the polls, and African American legislators began appearing in statehouses and in the federal congress. This golden period, however, lasted only a few years. As soon as most of the Southern states had complied with the Reconstruction

Acts and had been duly readmitted, white politicians openly conducted campaigns to take back political power from blacks and the Republican Party in the former slave states. This process was typically called "redemption." White Democrats used intimidation, violence, threats, fraud, and deceit to regain statehouse control. Once in power, most former slave state legislatures passed voter registration laws, such as "poll" taxes and "literacy" tests, that acted to limit black political participation. After 1875, the number of African American delegates dropped precipitously in most Southern states. In 1877, the last federal troops left the South and the final two states, South Carolina and Louisiana, were completely "redeemed." Next, lily-white legislatures proceeded to pass "Jim Crow" segregation laws. A racially bifurcated society emerged and in it blacks enjoyed only limited economic, political, and legal rights. The full advantage of complete legal citizenship for African Americans had to await the civil rights struggles of the mid-twentieth century (Foner 1988, 512–587).

REFERENCES

Anbinder, Tyler. 1992. *Nativism and Slavery: The Northern Know Nothings and the Politics of the 1850s*. New York: Oxford University Press.

Berlin, Ira, Joseph P. Reidy, and Leslie S. Rowland, eds. 1982. *Freedom: A Documentary History of Emancipation, 1861–1867*, Series II, *The Black Military Experience*. New York: Cambridge University Press.

Fogel, Robert W. 1989. *Without Consent or Contract: The Rise and Fall of American Slavery*. New York: W.W. Norton.

Foner, Eric. 1995. *Free Soil, Free Labor, Free Men: The Ideology of the Republican Party before the Civil War*. New York: Oxford University Press.

———. 1988. *Reconstruction: America's Unfinished Revolution, 1863–1877*. New York: Harper & Row.

Frey, Sylvia R. 1991. *Water from the Rock: Black Resistance in a Revolutionary Age*. Princeton: Princeton University Press.

Genovese, Eugene D. 1974. *Roll, Jordan, Roll: The World the Slaves Made*. New York: Pantheon Books.

Hietala, Thomas R. 1985. *Manifest Design: Anxious Aggrandizement in Late Jacksonian America*. Ithaca: Cornell University Press.

Kolchin, Peter. 1993. *American Slavery, 1619–1877*. New York: Hill and Wang.

Levine, Lawrence W. 1977. *Black Culture and Black Consciousness: Afro-American Folk Thought from Slavery to Freedom*. New York: Oxford University Press.

Litwack, Leon F. 1979. *Been in the Storm so Long: The Aftermath of Slavery*. New York: Random House.

Morgan, Edmund S. 1975. *American Slavery, American Freedom: The Ordeal of Colonial Virginia*. New York: W.W. Norton & Company.

Morris, Thomas D. 1996. *Southern Slavery and the Law, 1619–1860*. Chapel Hill: University of North Carolina Press.

Morrison, Michael A. 1997. *Slavery and the American West: The Eclipse of Manifest Destiny and the Coming of the Civil War*. Chapel Hill: University of North Carolina Press.

Oakes, James. 1990. *Slavery and Freedom: An Interpretation of the Old South*. New York: Knopf.

Ransom, Roger L., and Richard Sutch. 1977. *One Kind of Freedom: The Economic Consequences of Emancipation*. New York: Cambridge University Press.

Tadman, Michael. 1989. *Masters, Traders, and Slaves in the Old South*. Madison: University of Wisconsin Press.

Timeline of Significant Events

1522: First Spanish importation of slaves from Africa to America

1619: First Africans arrive in Virginia

1660: English colonies begin legal establishment of slavery

1700: Beginning of extensive slave importations into the English colonies from Africa

1720: Blacks begin to outnumber whites in South Carolina

1750s: Quakers campaign against slavery

1753–1763: French and Indian War results in the expulsion of the French from most of North America

1775, April 19: Revolutionary War officially begins with the Battles of Lexington and Concord

1776, July 4: United States officially declares its independence from Great Britain

1778, July 9: Continental Congress approves the Articles of Confederation

1780: Massachusetts and Pennsylvania abolish slavery

1783, September 3: Treaty of Paris is signed by Great Britain and the United States, officially ending the Revolutionary War and recognizing the United States as a sovereign nation

1787, September 28: Continental Congress sends the new Constitution to the states for ratification

1789, April 30: George Washington is sworn in as first president of the United States

1791, December 15: Bill of Rights (containing the first ten Amendments) is ratified by three-fourths of the states and becomes a part of the U.S. Constitution

1793: Eli Whitney invents the cotton gin

1800, December 12: Washington, D.C., becomes the official capital of the United States

1803, April 30: United States purchases the Louisiana Territory from France for $15 million

1808: Federal ban on the importation of slaves takes effect

1812, June 18: United States declares war on Great Britain, beginning the War of 1812

1814, December 24: United States and Great Britain sign the Treaty of Ghent, ending the War of 1812

1820: Missouri Compromise bars the extension of slavery north of the southern border of Missouri, which is admitted to the Union as a slave state

1822: Liberia is founded as an African colony for American blacks; Denmark Vesey's planned slave revolt is uncovered

1830: White churches initiate missions to slaves

1831: Nat Turner's slave revolt is quelled in Virginia

1846, May 8: Mexican War begins with the Battle of Palo Alto
       May 13: United States declares war on Mexico

1848, February 2: Mexico and the United States sign the Treaty of Guadalupe Hidalgo, ending the Mexican-American War and ceding Mexican territory, including Texas, New Mexico, and California, to the United States

1850: Compromise of 1850 is passed in an attempt to resolve the dispute over the extension of slavery into territories won from Mexico—among other things, the measure provides for California's admission to the Union as a free state and for passage of a new Fugitive Slave Act requiring the return of escaped slaves

1854: Kansas-Nebraska Act repeals the Missouri Compromise

1857: Supreme Court renders the Dred Scott decision

1861, February 4: Confederate States of America is formed

February 18: Jefferson Davis of Mississippi is sworn in as president and Alexander Stevens of Georgia as vice president of the Confederate States of America

March 4: Abraham Lincoln is inaugurated as sixteenth president of the United States

March 11: Confederate Congress adopts a Constitution

April 12: Confederate forces assault Fort Sumter in the harbor of Charleston, South Carolina

May 6: President Lincoln declares a state of insurrection in the Southern states

May 21: Richmond, Virginia, becomes the official capital of the Confederate States

1862, September 22: Lincoln issues the Emancipation Proclamation freeing slaves in territories under Confederate control

1863, January 1: Emancipation Proclamation takes effect

1865, February 1: Congress passes the Thirteenth Amendment abolishing slavery

March 4: Lincoln is inaugurated as president for a second term

April 9: Robert E. Lee's Army of Northern Virginia, the primary Confederate field army, surrenders at Appomattox Courthouse in Virginia, effectively ending the Civil War

December 18: Thirteenth Amendment is ratified

1866, June 16: Congress passes the Fourteenth Amendment guaranteeing citizenship to the former slaves and threatening states with a loss of representation if they denied freedmen the vote; race riots engulf Memphis and New Orleans

1868, July 23: Fourteenth Amendment is ratified

1870, March 30: Congress passes the Fifteenth Amendment guaranteeing freedmen the right to vote

1877, March 5: Republican Rutherford B. Hayes is sworn in as nineteenth president of the United States after the disputed election of 1876; Reconstruction ends

Alabama

TIMELINE

1737: French settlers along Mobile Bay begin importing slaves

1763–1783: English administer the Mobile Bay region as part of West Florida; English officials promote the slave trade

1766: West Florida Assembly passes slave codes

1776–1783: Slaveholding Loyalists flee the American Revolution and carry slaves to Mobile Bay

1783–1813: Spanish govern the Mobile Bay region

1813: Americans capture Mobile

1814: General Andrew Jackson's frontier army defeats the Creeks

1814–1835: Indian land cessions totally remove the Creeks, Choctaws, Chickasaws, and Cherokees from Alabama

1815–1830: Alabama land rush is heightened by slaveholders from Virginia and the Carolinas

1819, December 14: Alabama is admitted to the Union as a slave state

1820–1840: Over 150,000 enslaved African Americans are brought into Alabama

1832: Alabama Legislature ends attempts to limit the slave trade

1861, January 11: Alabama secedes from the Union and joins Confederacy; Montgomery serves as Confederate capital from February until June

1861; Mississippi Senator Jefferson Davis is elected first (and only) president of the Confederate States of America

1863: Alabama African Americans begin enlisting in the Union army

1864: Fort Pillow Massacre—Confederates kill Union African American soldiers after they surrender

1865, May 2–9: Remaining Confederates in Alabama surrender; slavery is ended

1868, June 25: Alabama is readmitted to the Union

1870: Ku Klux Klan terror appears in Alabama; Democrats win state elections by using intimidation, lynching, and threats of violence

1870–1900: Alabama African Americans lose political, economic, and social rights

1881–1915: Booker T. Washington serves as president of Tuskegee Institute

Slave and Free Black Population

Census Year	Slave Population	Population Percentage	Free Black Population	Population Percentage
1820	41,879	33	571	under 1
1830	117,549	38	1,572	under 1
1840	253,532	43	2,039	under 1
1850	342,844	44	2,265	under 1
1860	435,080	45	2,690	under 1

**Net Slave Entries and Exits, by Decade
(Tadman 1989, 12)**

1810–1819: + 35,500	1840–1849: + 16,532
1820–1829: + 54,156	1850–1859: + 10,752
1830–1839: + 96,520	

ORIGINS OF SLAVERY

European settlers in the Mobile Bay region purchased slaves from English ship captains as early as 1737. Although Spanish explorers first trekked across what would become Alabama, French pioneers became the first Europeans to establish permanent settlements near the current location of Mobile from 1702 to 1711. Although the French government attempted to discourage slavery in this part of Louisiana, newcomers demanded the right to use slaves to clear land and to grow crops. By the time control of Mobile Bay passed to the British in 1763 at the end of the French and Indian War (Seven Years' War), African slaves had already become an acceptable and, according to the residents, a necessary element in society.

From 1763 to 1783, the English administered the area as the province of English West Florida and accelerated the importation of slaves. Because the British government earned a ten-shilling tax on every slave imported into the province, colonial officials encouraged the slave trade. Thus, British captains sailed English slave ships from Africa and the Caribbean into Mobile Bay and hawked their human cargo to farmers and plantation owners along the lower Alabama and Mobile rivers. These settlers purchased so many bonded Africans that, by the turn of the nineteenth century, slaves comprised half the population along the rivers. Additionally, many slaveholding Loyalists from Virginia and the Carolinas, seeking to escape the ravages of the internecine guerilla war that engulfed the southern colonies during the last years of the Revolution and to escape as well any patriot retribution, added their human chattel to the Mobile Bay population (Sellers 1950, 6–8).

COLONIAL SLAVE CODES

Four large Native-American tribes—Creeks, Cherokees, Choctaws, Chickasaws—limited European settlement in what would become Alabama to the area surrounding Mobile Bay and along the lower Mobile and Alabama rivers until 1814. As part of the Treaty of Paris that ended the American Revolution, the British turned over control of the region to the Spanish who loosely administered the region from 1783 to 1813.

In 1766, the British West Florida Assembly, which included the Mobile Bay region, enacted a series of slave laws that held force throughout the colonial years and underlay the slave rules later adopted by the new state of Alabama. These enactments included the following provisions: baptism of enslaved Africans did not confer freedom; a slave had to carry a pass when more than two miles from his master's residence or be subject to arrest and punishment; any black without a pass was assumed to be a runaway and subject to arrest, incarceration, and punishment; and, a slave could not carry firearms away from his owner's residence without written permission. Additionally, slaves could not own property, including livestock. Moreover, merchants could not sell whiskey to slaves without their owners' permission. Violations resulted in public whippings ranging from fifty to five hundred lashes.

African American slaves and their white owners also received different levels of punishment for violent crimes. A white murdering a slave could be fined up to one hundred pounds; however, a slave committing violence (not necessarily resulting in death) against a white could be executed. Although the assembly allowed manumissions, the grantor was required to deposit one hundred pounds to offset any costs incurred by indigent free blacks. Rules for manumission and emancipation continued to be so strict throughout Alabama's antebellum era that free blacks remained a very insignificant segment of the population, as noted in the introductory summary of slavery (Sellers 1950, 10).

ALABAMA LAND RUSH

Native Americans controlled 80 percent of present-day Alabama at the onset of the War of 1812; however, American settlers, real estate speculators, and cotton planters already had turned envious eyes onto the Indian lands at this time. As soon as the opportunity arose, Americans seized the bay region from Spain hoisting the Stars and Stripes over Mobile on April 13, 1813.

An Indian war erupted later that year when the Creeks responded to white incursions by wiping out a settlement near Tensaw. Retaliation followed in 1814; General Andrew Jackson led a mostly backwoodsman force that defeated a Creek army, commanded by Red Eagle, at Horseshoe Bend. The ensuing peace treaty, ending the conflict, required the Creeks to surrender the entire central and southern sections of present-day Alabama. This agreement opened up agriculturally rich, new areas for settlement (Abernethy 1965, 24).

Immediately, pioneers stampeded onto the virgin lands. Most came from other Southern states and hoped to apply slave labor to cotton production. The invention of the cotton gin by Eli Whitney in the 1790s had led to the intensive development of very profitable cotton plantations in the Carolinas and Georgia. Slave owners moving to Alabama hoped to exploit land and labor in a similar way to extract riches from cotton cultivation. Additionally, the newly opened central region of Alabama included part of the "black belt": an expanse of very rich soil that yielded large harvests and high-quality cotton crops. Many newcomers rapidly made fortunes while other more modest farmers nevertheless found profits producing cotton with slave labor.

The Alabama region, initially administered as part of the Mississippi Territory, grew so quickly that within two years, by March 1817, the U.S. Congress created a separate Alabama Territory. At this time the total population in the new jurisdiction numbered about twenty thousand white settlers who then owned ten thousand enslaved African Americans. Within two more years, the population jumped to more than a hundred thousand, including more than thirty thousand slaves (Sellers 1950, 18).

Moreover, throughout the antebellum years, the enslaved population continued to increase at a faster rate than the white population. By 1860, as the opening summary indicates, slaves comprised 45 percent of the population. Farmers and planters bought, brought, or transported into Alabama large numbers of enslaved African Americans throughout these four antebellum decades. From 1820 to 1840, slave traders and settlers carried more than one hundred fifty thousand bonded blacks into the Alabama jurisdictions. Following up on the large Creek cession, the U.S. government, from 1814 to 1835, negotiated Indian treaties that gradually extracted all Alabama lands from Native American Tribes. Each additional land cession led to a mini–land rush as new areas became available for settlement (Tadman 1989, 12; Abernethy 1965, 24–25).

The saga of Samuel Townsend offers a chronicle of the financial possibilities available in antebellum Alabama. Townsend migrated to the Tennessee River valley, in the northern part of the state, from Lunenburg County, Virginia, during 1819. His ancestors had participated in the French and Indian Wars, the Revolution, and in the War of 1812. They included modest slaveholders familiar with Virginia's slave-based tobacco culture. Townsend, soon followed by his brother Edward, brought with him his human chattel and settled in Hazelgreen, intent on growing cotton. By the time of his death in the late 1850s, Townsend owned eight different plantations worth over a quarter of a million dollars, as well as 195 enslaved African Americans. In a similar fashion, during the 1820s and 1830s, whites from the older slave states, especially Virginia and the Carolinas, flooded the region and sought to employ their underused slave gangs by transferring their operations to the good cotton lands of Alabama (Sellers 1950, 28; Blassingame 1977, 639–655).

SLAVE SALES AND SLAVE TRADERS

While many farmers, planters, and speculators carried their human chattel with them when moving to Alabama, others bought bondsmen from the slave-dense Upper South regions, especially Virginia. Moreover, many slaveholders, like Samuel Townsend who already resided in the new regions with slaves brought from Virginia (nicknamed the Old Dominion), sought to add to their enslaved workforces. Being sold to slave traders, speculators, or to a landowner moving out of the area was the most soul-rending experience most African Americans endured, other than bodily punishments.

Ex-slave Ben told interviewer Mary White Ovington in 1910 that every fall slaves would be sold just like cattle. Slaveholders would drive them from place to place as if they were mules or horses. Families would be split: children from mothers, husbands from wives. Those who had been sold never knew what to expect, what type of new master they would encounter.

Ex-slave Kitty told Ovington, "The hardest part of those days was being sold. It don't seem as though you could bear it. When I was sold away by the speculators it seemed like I grieved to death. I had a good mother and sisters and brothers, but one morning they took me off and I never seen one of them again" (Blassingame 1977, 534–536).

When Samuel Townsend sought to increase his labor force, he went back to Virginia and bought slaves from his Lunenburg County neighbor, William Blackwell, as well as from traders in Richmond. This movement of slaves from the Upper South to the Gulf states offered fertile ground for profitable speculations. Thousands of slaves born in Virginia ended up in Alabama during the 1820s, 1830s, and 1840s (Sellers 1950, 141–142; Tadman 1989, 12).

Coffles of slaves moved overland from Virginia and the Carolinas each fall taking about six weeks to reach Montgomery, Alabama's largest slave sale site. Blacks shuffling along encumbered by foot irons and chains were a common sight on the roadways in the 1820s, 1830s, and 1840s. After railroads connected Montgomery with the Upper South slave marts, particularly during the late 1850s, more traders and speculators began using this form of transportation to move their human cargo (Sellers 1950, 150–154).

Profits for slave dealers could run into the thousands of dollars. Peter Stokes of Virginia regularly carried a coffle of twenty or so enslaved blacks from southern Virginia to Alabama. He prided himself on his expertise at being able to sell slaves. He wrote back to Virginia to his cousin and partner, William Haynie Hatchett, that he had been able to sell slaves in Alabama when other dealers could not. He disclosed that he had cleared more than two thousand dollars in profits and still had more slaves to sell. Interestingly, neither Hatchett nor Stokes incurred any social opprobrium back home in Virginia for engaging in slave trading.

Moreover, Alabama earned taxes from the trade. Beginning in 1842, all slave traders had to pay a yearly license fee (fifty dollars) and one or two cents for each slave bought or sold. These tax rates were raised in 1845 and in 1847. All payments went into a special fund that the state used to reimburse slave owners whose human property had been put to death for committing capital crimes (Sellers 1950, 177).

From 1826 until 1832, the Alabama legislature attempted to limit and regulate slave trading; however, the various laws were served more by their breach than by their observance. In 1832, the state in essence gave up and slave trading boomed from that year to 1837 and again from 1845 to 1860. In 1851, Governor Henry Collier offered a statute that would ban interstate slave trading in Alabama; however, this bill received tepid support and did not pass. There was little opposition to slave trading in Alabama during the 1840s and 1850s (Sellers 1950, 190).

SLAVE LIFE

Most slave housing consisted of huts or cabins. Some bondsmen used the original cabins that the white family had lived in as pioneers. These typical huts had one or two rooms with one fireplace raised a foot or two above the ground. Some planters built houses using a common wall that divided two-family residences. The entrances to these dual huts were sited at the opposite ends of the building. Beds were normally frames built into the walls filled by mattresses stuffed with straw or corn shucks. Few Alabama slaves had the use of sheets, though most covered themselves with homemade quilts sewn together from rags. A homemade chair or table completed the furniture ensemble. Families or extended family groups lived together in these cabins with the average hut holding five or six persons, though owners squeezed more in if children were numerous in the family. Most planters and farmers also built outhouse privies for their enslaved African Americans, but not all did so. Generally called slave "quarters," these huts were grouped behind or beside the "big house," forming a small village when combined with the other farm outbuildings: the kitchen, corncrib, smokehouse, and washhouse (Sellers 1950, 86–87; Blassingame 1977, 657, 669).

The primary food for slaves consisted of smoked, salted pork and cornmeal. Most owners allowed their enslaved blacks from three to five pounds of pork a week along with a peck of cornmeal. Additional portions of buttermilk, sweet potatoes, and molasses often accompanied the basic ration. Most slaves also kept family vegetable gardens that they tended on their day off, Sunday. Many augmented these victuals with fishing and trapping. The noon meal, called dinner, was the largest of the day and was carried out to the field gangs in buckets by the younger children. The evening meal, supper, generally was prepared in the family hut fireplace. Additionally, stealing food from owners constituted the most commonly committed offense, one that typically resulted in punishment, such as whipping with a leather lash (Hamilton 1977, 62–63).

Owners typically treated their enslaved minions to additional food during hog-killing time and over the Christmas break when no one worked. The week between Christmas and New Year was virtually the only time of the year that slaves could drink whiskey or fruit wines without being subjected to whippings. In Alabama, farmers killed hogs in January because they had to wait for near-freezing weather. Cold temperatures prevented the pork from spoiling while the hogs were slaughtered and the meat was prepared to be salted, smoked, and cured. Slave families received the extras that were not preserved: chitterlings, organ meats, ears, tail, and lites (lungs) (Sellers 1950, 90–91).

Slaves generally received clothes twice a year, in the spring and in the autumn. Winter clothes were typically made of coarse lindsey-woolsey cloth, a woven textile consisting of linen and wool, as were their blankets. Warm-weather clothes were made from a variety of inexpensive cotton cloths, many woven in the textile mills of New England. An enslaved black male would usually receive the following in a year: one wool coat and vest, one pair of wool pants, three shirts, two pairs of cotton pants, one pair of shoes, three pairs of socks, and one hat. A woman would get one lindsey-woolsey cloak and cape, one lindsey-woolsey dress, two cotton dresses, three sets of underwear, three pairs of cotton stockings, one pair of shoes, and one hat. Children's clothes were similar, though many owners often had the plantation seamstress make their underwear out of old flour sacks. Additionally, children and most men wore homemade straw hats during the summertime (Sellers 1950, 103).

Most adult slaves in Alabama worked in the fields. Old folks and children fed the chickens, took care of the livestock, and toted water and lunch to the field hands in pails. As many as three-quarters of the women on the larger plantations labored in the fields on work gangs. The primary crops were cotton and corn. Field preparation began in February, and all the cotton and corn had typically been planted by May. The work gangs then plowed and hoed all the fields on a continuing basis to prevent weeds from overtaking the planted crops. John Hartwell Cocke's overseer on his plantation in Greene County wrote in 1847 that by the middle of June his slave force had plowed the cotton twice and hoed it through three times. They had likewise plowed the corn three times and hoed it twice. Corn and cotton were harvested from the middle of September to the middle of December, with cotton picking requiring the greater and longer effort. Cocke's Alabama plantation in 1847 produced forty five-hundred-pound bales of cotton (Blassingame 1977, 65).

Most of the larger farmers and planters used overseers. Some substituted slave drivers for overseers and some used drivers in addition to overseers. The field slave drivers were responsible for setting a reasonable pace that got the tasks accomplished but allowed everyone on the work gang to make it through the day.

Work discipline was maintained with the lash. George Skipwith, John Hartwell Cocke's Greene County overseer, wrote to his employer in 1847 that "he had worked the people but not out of reason." He had "whipped none without a cause." He then listed the reasons. He had lashed Sukey five times for slow work. He lashed Isham twice for covering up cotton plants with plowed dirt. An entire seven-person work gang received ten "licks" for slow work. He subjected Evlyann to ten lashes for a lost hoe. Additionally, he had a face-to-face confrontation with Robert, who spoke back to him. He noted that he had whipped Robert "pretty good" (Blassingame 1977, 65–66).

RUNAWAYS AND PATTEROLLERS

Because most of the slave-dense "black belt" counties and the fertile river valleys were located in Alabama's interior, runaways attempting to get north to freedom were less of a problem than in the Upper South border slave states. Most Alabama runaways were men who sought escape from their owners for three primary reasons: they had recently been sold, transported, and separated from their families; they had been subjected to a period of ill treatment; or, they had just committed a crime or offense against their owner and feared the repercussions. A typical advertisement for an Alabama runaway follows:

> **$200 Reward**
> Ranaway [*sic*] from the subscriber in Tallapoosa County. . . . Two Negro men between 30 and 35. One a mulatto, named Armistead, six feet . . . wears whiskers, reads well, perhaps can write, is a blacksmith, a Methodist preacher. The other is a black man, Rob or Robin, five feet six or eight, one of his big toes is off, has a scar across his chest. (Seaborn J. Thomas)

Armistead's attempt to escape his owner followed directly upon the heels of the theft of a substantial amount of money, one thousand dollars, from Seaborn Thomas. More than likely, the literate preacher planned to try to escape and then absconded with the cash so that he had the wherewithal to try to get to freedom. Most runaway ads had individual descriptions of the escaped slaves, which included specific marks, scars, or injuries that reflected the slaves' past experiences and how they had been previously disciplined (Sellers 1950, 266–270, 279).

While some enslaved African Americans attempted a permanent escape, other Alabama bondsmen simply took a "vacation in the woods." These events generally followed periods of mistreatment. Black women especially, who did not wish to leave children or old folks behind, occasionally took to the woods to allow their anger to cool after an unpleasant episode with their master or mistress. After a few days, they would generally return. Their punishment usually entailed a number of lashes. William Dunbar noted that Bessy ran away and was caught. Dunbar kept her in irons for four days and administered twenty-five lashes. Ketty ran away but returned after spending a few nights in the woods without food or shelter. Because she returned of her own volition, Dunbar lashed her only a few times and did not administer additional punishments. Two others who had run off before received a more severe chastisement. They were placed permanently in foot chains to limit mobility and subjected to five hundred lashes administered in five separate whippings (Sellers 1950, 13).

The physical methods used by whites to compel obedience, to maintain work discipline, to preserve authority, and to render punishment meant that most Alabama African American slaves had various scars and distinguishing marks on their bodies. These legacies more than any other item indicated that physical force and physical punishment were an integral component in keeping the slave system functioning, at least from the owners' perspectives.

Slave patrols comprised the primary enforcement mechanism used in Alabama. Generally each county assigned patrols for every magisterial district within its jurisdiction. These patrols were responsible for checking passes, particularly after dark, and getting offenders back to their rightful owners. Some slave patrols made use of dogs to find and chase runaways (Sellers 1950, 286).

The African American slaves called the whites who served on the slave patrols "patterollers." These men were the bane of black existence, causing fear, terror, and, if caught without a pass, whippings. The Alabama black folks sang a jingle—"Run, Nigger, Run/the Patteroller Ketch you Jus' 'Fo Day"—that captured the essence of the hardships that the slave patrols meted out. Sarah Fitzgerald remembered, "You know about the patterollers . . . they were white folks who went around at night and caught slaves when they went off the home place and if they didn't have no pass, they'd beat them and run them back home." Henry Baker recollected that if "blacks didn't come home when their passes were out, they got a whipping just the same because the patterollers were always ready. If a man had a wife on another place and he went to see her with a pass, if he stayed overtime, he got whipped" (Blassingame 1977, 641, 656).

In a few instances, small groups of runaways coalesced into a virtual "maroon" community. For example, two dozen or so escapees from slavery hid out in the Cypress Swamp in Montgomery County. They got by through trapping, fishing, and surreptitiously stealing food at night from the smokehouses and corncribs of local slave owners. Eventually a slave patrol posse caught up with the Cypress Swamp maroons and dispersed the band. They killed a number, hanged others, and returned the remainder to their lawful owners after severe whippings (Sellers 1950, 283).

SLAVE CODES

Alabama's slave codes derived from statutes that had legal jurisdiction during its colonial and territorial past. Alabama law specifically banned owners from teaching enslaved African Americans reading and writing, though this provision was not always enforced. As noted, some slaves were literate and this often became a distinguishing idiosyncratic characteristic.

County justices of the peace oversaw local law enforcement and conducted trials for individuals who had committed minor breaches of Alabama statutes. Slaves who had committed minor crimes, most often petty theft, fell within this jurisdiction. The justices also handed out punishment for these misdemeanors and minor felonies, meting out up to one hundred lashes as the sentence for a slave who committed violations. More substantial thefts or more serious noncapital crimes could incur branding as a punishment. Owners had to pay the court costs for more serious offenses, and if they chose not to do so, the offending slave, after being whipped and branded, would be sold with the sale proceeds used to cover the trial expenses.

Capital crimes, including those committed by slaves, were tried by circuit courts. Whites comprised the twelve-man juries that heard these cases and decided on the verdict. Moreover, two-thirds of every jury hearing a case involving a slave accused of a capital offense had to be slaveholders. Slaves were required to have legal counsel. If the slave's master refused to provide for an attorney, the sheriff would collect ten dollars from the owner, and the court would appoint an attorney.

Slaves were not offered any charge other than first degree murder. Slaves accused of taking a life could not be charged with murder or manslaughter by degrees. Also, self-defense could not be used as exculpatory evidence especially when involving the slave and his or her owner. "When a slave in a personal conflict with his master, resists his authority by physical force, and in that resistance kills his master, he cannot reduce the crime from murder to manslaughter, by showing that, in the commencement of resistance, he had no designs to take a life" (Sellers 1950, 222).

Attorneys for slaves convicted of capital crimes could appeal to the Alabama Supreme Court, though few verdicts were reviewed and even fewer overturned. A slave convicted of a capital crime was given a thirty-day waiting period before execution unless the charges specified that the guilty party engaged in conspiracy, insurrection, or rebellion. In these cases, executions immediately followed the handing down of the verdict.

Slave owners deprived of their human property due to a slave's execution were repaid one-half the fair market value of the bondsman at the time of his or her trial. These recompensatory funds were taken from taxes collected from slave traders. Thus, while the slave lost his or her life, the slave owner received monetary compensation.

Slaves could render testimony against other slaves or against free blacks at trials and hearings but could not speak out against whites. After 1841, free blacks and African American slaves took the same oath before testifying as whites did. Slaves convicted of committing perjury had a "p" branded on their hands and received thirty-nine lashes. Before 1841, punishment for perjury by a black bondsman could also include having one's ears nailed to a pillory and then cut off.

Although Alabama passed a number of laws regarding slave welfare, few violations of these rules were prosecuted, since slaves could not testify against their white owners. The few cases that reached trial involved very public, very visible abuses. For example, Henry Hall was accused of whipping a slave to death by subjecting his human chattel to a two-hour public lashing. He was convicted, paid a five hundred dollar fine, and spent two months in jail.

The code of Alabama conferred on the owner of slaves or a designee the absolute right of correction. According to the Alabama Supreme Court, the master, owner, overseer, or hirer largely determined what was reasonable punishment and what was reasonable treatment. Thus, only exceptionally flagrant public violations drew any legal attention (Sellers 1950, 213–232).

SLAVERY AND TOWNS

While most of Alabama's enslaved African Americans lived and worked on farms and plantations, a smaller number resided in the towns. Here too slave life was severely circumscribed. Patterollers enforced curfews. In Mobile, slaves had to have a written pass to be out after eight in the winter and nine in the summer. The towns also included most of Alabama's hired-out slaves (Sellers 1950, 232).

Owners contracted with hirers to have their bondsmen work for someone else for a designated period of time (typically a year) and for an agreed-upon wage. Many of the enslaved tradesmen and workers along the rivers and in the Alabama towns were hired-out slaves. Most towns required hired-out slaves to be registered so that they could be accounted for. For example, in Huntsville during 1834, the following hired-out slaves were registered:

Owner	Slave	Hire Price
A.I. Withers	Tim	$125
William McKay	George	$120
John Robinson	Levi	$125
I.R.B. Edwards	Pepper	$101
I.R.B. Edwards	Wat	$127
George Connally	2 Boys	$216
George Fearn	Nelson	$105

As a rule of thumb, the annual hire price for a slave approximated 10 percent of the bondsman's sale price on the auction block. Hired-out slaves who had skills such as blacksmithing or carpentry commanded higher annual contracts (Sellers 1950, 210).

The freest slaves in Alabama included those African Americans who hired out their own time. They made their own living arrangements, remitted the annual fee required by their owners, and kept the remainder. They had few restraints other than curfews and restrictive laws regarding drinking, congregating, and owning property. Some saved enough money to buy their own freedom. Taking this step in Alabama was a large one, however, since all newly freed blacks were legally required to leave the state. Hence, a hired-out slave purchasing his or her freedom had to consider family circumstances when making these choices. Many of the barbers, porters, and waiters on the riverboats were hired-out slaves (Sellers 1950, 193–211).

The liberties that hired-out slaves enjoyed worried many white towns-people. They did their best to circumscribe these opportunities and to maintain their oversight and control over these minions. They went so far as to bar free black sailors entering Mobile Bay from leaving their ships or coming into Mobile to seek refreshments. They did not want hired-out slaves to be contaminated or stirred up by black men from the northern United States (Franklin 1947, 218).

RELIGION, MUSIC, AND FAMILY LIFE

Alabama's enslaved African Americans created a life for themselves in spite of the inherent brutalities of the slave regime. They especially enjoyed music, family life, and religion. The most difficult times for individuals resulted from the forced rupture of families and the interruption of regular family life caused by slave sales.

One former slave told Mary White Ovington that she had been sold in North Carolina. She had four children but all were left behind except the baby. "That nearly broke my heart." Sales split mothers and children, husbands and wives, and provided the underlying cause for much grumbling and discontent (Blassingame 1977, 539).

Sharing family life and enduring the hardships of the slave experience drew families closer together and provided buffers that helped ward off the more brutal aspects of the institution. Families were close. Getting back to one's family was a major reason for running away. At the end of Civil War with the advent of emancipation, reuniting families became the first and foremost undertaking by many new freedmen and freedwomen.

James Fischer recalled, "I heard no more from my mother, till I received the following from sister Ellen, enclosing a lock of our mother's hair: 'Brother, our best friend is gone. I have lost my mother. Lost in sorrow, I scarcely know where to look, or what to ask. Thank God, I have a brother and sister living; and to them I must look more than I have done hereto-fore. Sister Elizabeth is with me'" (Blassingame 1977, 235).

Music and its allied activities formed one of the favorite amusements allowed to slaves. Sarah Fitzgerald remembered, "When I commenced courting I had plenty of fellars . . . all I cared for was dancing, going to big candy pullings, and plenty of music. We had colored fiddlers . . . my cousin and brother-in-law were fiddlers and my uncle was a banjo picker . . . we sure had a good time."

Courting had its difficulties. Sarah continued, "[I]f a boy wanted to court a gal he had to get his Master to write a letter for him and then the gal's Mistress had to read the letter to her and write the boy back." Other dangers also interfered. "If a boy wanted to take a gal somewhere to church or to a hot supper or frolic, both of them had to have passes. If they didn't, the patterollers caught them, beat them, and run them back home" (Blassingame 1977, 643–644).

Henry Baker remembered that in Alabama a favorite game was called "town ball," an early form of baseball. "The way we played town ball was we had bases and we run from one base to the other, if the runner was hit with the ball he was out. We always made the ball out of cotton and rags." They had contests with blacks from other plantations and the white kids played as well (Blassingame 1977, 657).

The most universal form of social interaction for bonded African Americans involved going to church. Slave owners generally supported slave church attendance because baptism did not confer any additional liberties. Moreover, in some instances, Christianity could assuage some of the feelings of anger and help the enslaved accept their lot in life, or so the masters reasoned. Churches generally were integrated, with the balconies being reserved for black members. Furthermore, some churches held services for blacks in the afternoon after the whites met in the morning.

Blacks formed 60 percent of the communicants at Center Ridge Presbyterian Church in Dallas County. The Presbyterian pastors in Alabama regularly preached to slaveholders about the need for religious education for their human chattel. Some masters offered more Christian education than others. Moreover, the Episcopal bishop of Alabama averaged baptizing one hundred African Americans a year for the fifteen years from 1845 to 1860. Additionally, the first baptism recorded in St. John's Catholic Church in Tuscaloosa was for Martha, a slave of a Mrs. O'Neil (Sellers 1950, 313–324).

The Baptists and the Methodists, however, made the primary inroads for converting blacks to Christianity. The First Baptist Church in Montgomery had three hundred white members and six hundred blacks. The pastor, I.T. Tichenor, noted that he had baptized more than five hundred blacks during his fifteen-year ministry. The African Americans belonging to First Baptist had their own preacher, their own deacons, and their own services, with Tichenor providing general oversight.

Baptists also aided some communities in opening separate black churches. Huntsville had an all-black church, the Huntsville African Baptist Church, as early as 1820. This church had seventy-six members in 1821 and more than two hundred fifty members twenty years later. The Cotton Fort African Church had one hundred forty members in 1840. Its pastor was a slave named Lewis whose owner was a Mr. Jamieson of Talledega (Fleming 1906, 247; Sellers 1950, 300).

The Methodists began missions to enslaved African Americans as early as 1831. In 1854, a third of Alabama's Methodist Church membership, more than nineteen thousand, were blacks. The most famous black Methodist preacher of the antebellum years was Jim Lewis whose owner, Edgar Swoop, also worked as a minister (Sellers 1950, 301–308).

Sarah Fitzgerald remembered that the slave owners wanted their slaves to go to Sunday School and church and to learn the catechism so that they would mind and behave better; however, the blacks wanted to go to all black religious gatherings so that they could better express themselves. To get passes so that the patterollers would not pester them, they often went to white church services and then had a meeting later in the day after most whites had left. "My aunt use to tear loose in church and shout, my she sure could shout" (Blassingame 1977, 643).

The better masters in Alabama allowed their minions enough personal space to develop a family life and the chances to enjoy church services, music, games, and some social gatherings. These outlets prevented slave life from becoming completely unbearable and gave slaves from neighboring plantations the opportunity to get to know one another. These social occasions played an important role in determining courtship and marriage possibilities.

THE CIVIL WAR, BLACK TROOPS, AND EMANCIPATION

Slaveholders and pro-slavery positions dominated antebellum Alabama. Thus, the Yellowhammer state quickly followed South Carolina's lead and seceded on January 11, 1861. The Deep South and Gulf states then met in Montgomery in February 1861 to form the Confederate States of America. Alabama's capital served as headquarters for Jefferson Davis's new government until he transferred the seat of authority of the nascent nation to Richmond later in the spring.

Because Alabama was not overrun by the Union army until very late in the war, and because the state had a limited coastline, the interior became a place of refuge for slaveholders trying to hang on to their human property. The stresses and strains of the war effort as well as the ongoing turmoil resulting from large-scale population shifts gave some African American slaves better bargaining chips to negotiate more personal freedoms. Additionally, some farm and plantation owners altered their planting schedule and grew more foodstuffs. Alabama slaves were impressed, generally for sixty days at a time, to construct fortifications around Mobile and on the railroads running out of Tennessee. Others were taken to munitions factories and labored making arms and ammunition for the Confederate armies.

In the autumn of 1863, as a result of the implementation of the Emancipation Proclamation that took effect January 1, 1863, and other federal programs designed to organize black troops to fill the ranks, Union officers began widespread recruiting among African Americans in the Mississippi valley. The proximity to federal armies and gunboats helped officials form numerous black regiments from Mississippi and Louisiana. Black troops from Alabama were far less common (Berlin 1985, 266, 680–682, 717, 756–758).

Although Alabama included more than eighty-four thousand African American males between the ages of eighteen and forty-five, the prime military service years, only about five thousand joined the Union army. Those who did had to avoid Confederate outposts, rebel cavalry, partisan bands, and patteroller patrols to get to enlistment offices. Eventually, the Union adjutants formed most of the black soldiers from Alabama into four units: a heavy artillery regiment, a cavalry regiment, and two regiments of United States Colored Troops (USCT) infantry. The heavy artillery unit eventually received designation as the Sixth United States Colored Heavy Artillery. The cavalry became part of the Third United States Colored Cavalry and the black Yellowhammer infantry, originally called the First and Second Alabama Infantry (African Descent), became the Fifty-fifth and One hundred-tenth United States Colored Infantry (Berlin 1985, 12).

These Alabama black troops generally served in the Mississippi valley and occupied important military objectives that had been taken from the rebels. They were stationed in fortifications around Memphis, Natchez, and Fort Pillow. Moreover, the Alabama Cavalry unit distinguished itself late in 1864 in a frontal attack across the railroad bridge spanning the Big Black River.

The Heavy Artillery unit, however, was the victim of one of the most talked about massacres of the war. This unit had recently been sent to reinforce Fort Pillow against Confederate raiding parties. A Confederate force commanded by Major General Nathan Bedford Forrest surrounded the fortifications, demanded a surrender, which was refused, and commenced attacking. After a six- to seven-hour struggle the rebels, present in overwhelming force, overran the Union positions. When many of the black troops attempted to surrender, some were shot even after throwing down their arms and raising their hands. Forrest and his Confederates denied the commission of a massacre, but testimony of those present leaves little doubt as to what happened (Glatthaar 1990, 157).

The Official Records of the War of the Rebellion included these testimonies and reports: Philip Young of the Sixth United States Colored Heavy Artillery stated that he saw at least one hundred black soldiers shot as they attempted to surrender. He was told that he would be executed later after the Confederates retreated. Jacob Wilson testified that his unit was overpowered after hours of hard fighting and driven down the bank from the fort. The men threw down their arms trying to surrender. He said that many, including William Morgan, Reuben Jones, William Lincoln, Samuel Tangesley, and Charles Cross, were shot after they had given up. Major General Stephen Hurlburt in his official report noted that a Confederate force directed in person by Bedford Forrest attacked Pillow and carried the works around 3:00 P.M. "After resistance had ceased, and in gross violation to all honorable warfare, the Confederates butchered in cold blood the prisoners and wounded."

Other Alabama black soldiers in different units also had traumatic war experiences. Joseph Howard was captured by Confederates near Athens, Alabama, in September 1864. Rebel soldiers took all his personal possessions and marched him overland to Mobile. There he had to work digging fortifications with impressed slaves. He said that Confederates enforced work discipline through whippings with a lash and fed him poorly with corn bread and mule meat. After the federal navy under Admiral Farragut captured Mobile Bay, Howard escaped to a Union gunboat and was allowed to return to his army unit in Nashville (Berlin 1985, 591–592).

In the spring of 1865, the United States Colored Troops became an army of liberators as they joined in the march from Mobile to Montgomery. As the Union soldiers passed along the roadways, they were cheered and greeted with songs and dancing by former Alabama slaves as white ex-slaveholders sullenly looked on. Nothing could more emphatically demonstrate the application of the Emancipation Proclamation than United States colored regiments marching through the heart of Alabama.

Henry Baker remembered that when the African Americans living with him on the Harris place heard that they were free, they all got together with other just-freed slaves from the area and held a prayer meeting. They thanked the Lord for deliverance and old Aunt Roney sang, "Thank God we all is free" and "Let Every Day Be Sunday."

"We certainly were happy in those days . . . after the Surrender. We sung, we prayed, and we preached. You should of seen them shaking hands and hollering, 'Thank God my children can come with me to Church and no patterollers have to run after them'" (Blassingame 1977, 660–661).

RECONSTRUCTION

Putting families back together and reuniting long separated members formed the first task most newly freed blacks attempted. The Alabama legislature of 1865–1866, still completely white, passed legislation declaring that all slave marriages would be recognized as valid. Sarah Fitzgerald remembered, "You see after the war closed all the colored were looking round for their own folks. Husbands looking for their wives, and wives looking for their husbands, children looking for parents, parents looking for children, everything sure was scrambled up in those days" (Donald 1952, 59; Blassingame 1977, 644).

The Freedmen's Bureau, in the years immediately following the collapse of the Confederacy, quickly became the most important federal agency helping the new freedmen and freedwomen; however, the bureau in Alabama suffered shortages in funding and staffing. The largest contingent in Alabama at any one time numbered only twenty. The bureau tried to help freedmen bargain effectively for wages but noted widespread violation of labor agreements. Bureau agents were effective in some cases at getting back wages paid to freedmen for work already completed. Most white Alabamians whenever possible, however, generally thwarted the agency in its efforts. The Southern Homestead Act opened up the remaining public land in Alabama for sale. Freedmen had a six-month window to process land claims, since most Alabama whites (those who had supported the Confederacy) were initially prohibited from filing until July 1867 (Foner 1988, 143; Fleming 1906, 266–267).

Most of Alabama's new freedmen, however, were far from assertive and simply wanted to get on with life and enjoy their new liberties. Thomas Lee, a former slave, noted, "I have no desire to take away the rights of the white man. All I want is equal rights in the Court House and equal rights when I go to vote." Nevertheless, by the late 1860s, the Ku Klux Klan had reared its ugly head in the state (Foner 1988, 324, 342).

Outbreaks of violence accompanied the elections of 1870. In Sumter County, the Klan, or at least a band of whites, murdered Richard Burke, a leader of the Loyal League and a legislator who advocated freedmen's rights. In October 1870, armed white men broke up a Republican Party campaign rally in Greene County killing four blacks and injuring fifty-four more. In the Tuskegee area, nearly every black church and school was burned that fall. At the same time, the Klan lynched William Luke, a white teacher in a black school at Cross Plains, along with four African American freedmen. Even though witnesses identified the perpetrators, a grand jury failed to pass down any indictments. In Blount County,

In a scene typical of postwar Alabama and other Deep South states, a family of freed slaves continues to live in former slave quarters. (Library of Congress.)

veterans of the Union army formed the "Anti–Ku Klux," which threatened the Klansmen with reprisals and ended local violence. A Democratic victory in state elections became the political fruits of these physical assaults and of the widespread intimidation of blacks attempting to vote (Foner 1988, 426–442).

From 1870 to 1877, Alabama blacks and the local Republican Party gradually lost the "peace." In the courthouse and at the ballot box, whites supporting the Democratic Party gradually regained political and legal power. In 1870 during the violence, a freedwoman was assaulted and beaten by a gang of white men. She attempted to bring suit. The local judge, having jurisdiction over such offenses, required her to raise $16.45 to cover court costs before he would hear her complaint. She raised the money; however, after hearing testimony, the judge refused to charge the offenders, ordered the woman to drop all charges or go to jail on contempt charges and be subject to a whipping. Black groups and white advocates tried to get laws enacted that would require at least some blacks on a jury whenever an African American was tried; however, they never succeeded (Foner 1988, 421, 539).

The state government, elected through intimidation in 1870, gradually expanded its base by enacting legislation that granted amnesty for virtually all white males in 1871 and 1872. This revived the Democratic Party electorate, and by 1875, the white supremacists could count on winning the majority of Alabama's elections. Later in the 1880s and 1890s, the Alabama legislature passed a series of laws that disenfranchised large percentages of Alabama's African Americans. These rules contained provisions with grandfather clauses that allowed most whites to be automatically eligible for voter registration but demanded additional requirements of the vast majority of blacks. Would-be black voters had to pay poll taxes in cash and also had to be able to read any section of Alabama's Constitution, explain what that segment meant, and describe the implications of the recited statutes. White registration officials passed judgment subjectively on whether the constitutional explanations were sufficient to allow any individual African American the opportunity of voting (Franklin 1947, 328–340).

By 1900, Alabama included 181,000 black males of voting age in its population but only 3,000 were registered to vote. Moreover, during the last two decades of the century, African American lynchings grew in frequency and the legislature enacted Jim Crow laws that defined legal segregation. By the turn of the twentieth century, Alabama blacks lived in a racially bifurcated society and struggled with intimidation, physical violence, and biased courts. Most still resided in the "black belt" and river valley agricultural districts, eking out livelihoods as sharecroppers and tenant farmers (Franklin 1947, 340, 439).

AFRICAN AMERICAN LEGISLATORS

Unlike states such as Mississippi and South Carolina, which also contained a large percentage of blacks among their populations, Alabama had relatively few African American officials elected during Reconstruction. Some served in both the state House and state Senate but they were not numerous enough to create an influential voting bloc. They helped pass the ratification of the Fourteenth and Fifteenth Amendments that should have guaranteed African Americans economic and political rights but were later rendered ineffective by Supreme Court rulings, especially the famous *Plessy v. Ferguson* case that allowed legal segregation under the definition of "separate but equal." The few black legislators, nevertheless, supported the passage of enactments that set up a public school system for Alabama. Eventually this resulted in the founding of a number of historically black colleges to top off a segregated educational system (Franklin 1947, 318–320).

Three African Americans did represent Alabama in the U.S. House of Representatives during the 1870s. These three, Benjamin Sterling Turner, James T. Rapier, and Jeremiah Haralson, served consecutive terms from 1870 to 1876.

Turner, a former illiterate slave, became Dallas County tax collector in the early days of Reconstruction and also served on Selma's city council. He was in Washington, D.C., from 1871 to early 1873 representing an Alabama House district. Turner voted in Congress to enact legislation that called for white "loyalty" oaths and desegregated public schools. He also voted for the civil rights acts that were proposed at this time.

James T. Rapier was born in Lauderdale County in 1837 into a free black family. His father sent him to Buxton, Ontario, Canada, a refuge for escaped slaves and free blacks, to get an education. After the war, Rapier organized the first black labor union in the United States, the Labor Union of Alabama, which lasted from 1871 to 1877. His brother was the first African American admitted to the medical school at the University of Michigan and earned an M.D. degree from there in 1864. Rapier represented the Montgomery district from 1872 to 1874. On his way from Montgomery to Washington, D.C., Rapier was not allowed to sit in first-class seating due to his race, regardless of his elected position. He was defeated for re-election in 1874 by Jeremiah Haralson, a self-educated former slave (Hamilton 1977, 71–77).

BOOKER TALIAFERRO WASHINGTON

Booker T. Washington became the best-known Alabama African American in the latter part of the nineteenth century after he organized Tuskegee Institute in 1881. He served as the president and the guiding light of the school until his death in 1915.

Washington had been born a slave in Franklin County, Virginia, in 1856.

After emancipation, his family moved to the Kanawha valley of West Virginia. He attended a mission school there but largely educated himself. Later, he studied at Hampton Institute, which he used as a model when he set up Tuskegee.

Washington promoted black self-sufficiency through education. He believed that learning trades as well as academic subjects would enable African Americans to survive in the white-dominated world. He also promoted extension classes and services for rural blacks in Alabama and promoted the National Negro Business League.

At the time of his administration of Tuskegee, he was widely recognized and applauded and became a leading role model for many young black men of this era. He, however, also attracted a great deal of scorn, skepticism, and criticism from other educated African Americans who balked at being relegated to a second-class industrial-vocational education. To them, Washington failed as a leader when he refused to confront the white politicians of Alabama on the injustices then occurring every day in the state. Washington's many speeches also indicated that on certain occasions he was willing to conform to white supremacy. The methods and rules he used to administer Tuskegee, as well as his appeasement of white leaders, has led to Washington becoming a controversial figure in African American history (Smock 1988, 3–24; Madaras 2000, 144–169).

REFERENCES

Abernethy, Thomas P. 1965. *The Formative Period in Alabama, 1815–1828*. University: University of Alabama Press.

Berlin, Ira, Joseph P. Reidy, and Leslie S. Rowland, eds. 1985. *Freedom: A Documentary History of Emancipation, 1861–1867*, Series II, *The Black Military Experience*. New York: Cambridge University Press.

Blassingame, John W., ed. 1977. *Slave Testimony: Two Centuries of Letters, Speeches, Interviews, and Autobiographies*. Baton Rouge: Louisiana State University Press.

Donald, Henderson H. 1952. *The Negro Freedman: Life Conditions of the American Negro in the Early Years after Emancipation*. Repr., New York: Cooper Square, 1971.

Fleming, Walter L., ed. 1906. *Documentary History of Reconstruction*. Cleveland: Arthur Clark.

Foner, Eric. 1988. *Reconstruction: America's Unfinished Revolution, 1863–1877*. New York: Harper & Row.

Franklin, John Hope. 1947. *From Slavery to Freedom: A History of Negro Americans*. New York: Knopf.

Glatthaar, Joseph T. 1990. *Forged in Battle: The Civil War Alliance of Black Soldiers and White Officers*. New York: Free Press.

Hamilton, Virginia Van der Veer. 1977. *Alabama*. New York: W.W. Norton.

Madaras, Larry, and James M. SoRelle, eds. 2000. "Did Booker T. Washington's

Philosophy and Actions Betray the Interests of African Americans?" In *Taking Sides: Controversial Issues in American History,* Volume II, *Reconstruction to the Present.* Guilford, Conn.: McGraw-Hill.

Sellers, James B. 1950. *Slavery in Alabama.* University: University of Alabama Press.

Smock, Raymond W. 1988. *Booker T. Washington.* Jackson: University Press of Mississippi.

Tadman, Michael. 1989. *Speculators and Slaves: Masters, Traders, and Slaves in the Old South.* Madison: University of Wisconsin Press.

WEB SITES

Alabama Slave Code of 1833: http://www.wfu.edu/~zulick/340/slavecodes.html

Alabama Supreme Court and Slaves: http://www.lib.auburn.edu/archive/aghy/slaves.htm

Booker T. Washington: http:// www.spartacus.schoolnet.co.uk/USAbooker.htm

Central Alabama Slave Narrative: http://xroads.Virginia.edu/~UG99/brady/Albama.html

Macon County Slave Narrative: http://www.dollsgen.com/slavenarratives.html

Arkansas

TIMELINE

1790s: First slaves enter the territory that will become Arkansas

1803: Louisiana Purchase—the United States buys Louisiana from the French, a territory that includes all of present-day Arkansas

1819: Arkansas becomes a territory

1836, June 15: Arkansas enters the Union as a slave state

1861, May 6: Arkansas secedes from the Union

1862: Southern Homestead Act is passed by Congress

1864: Society of Friends (Quakers) organizes efforts to aid freed blacks

1865, May: Civil War and slavery end in Arkansas
June: Major General John W. Sprague opens the Freedmen's Bureau in Arkansas

1866: Over 4,000 African Americans receive sharecropping contracts in Phillips County

1868, June 22: Arkansas is readmitted to the Union
Autumn: Widespread violence occurs before the presidential election of 1868

Slave and Free Black Population

Census Year	Slave Population	Population Percentage	Free Black Population	Population Percentage
1820	1,617	11	59	under 1
1830	4,576	15	141	under 1
1840	19,935	20	465	under 1
1850	47,100	22	608	under 1
1860	111,115	24	144	under 1

Net Slave Entries and Exits, by Decade (Tadman 1989, 12)

1810–1819: +1,000	1840–1849: +18,984
1820–1829: +2,123	1850–1859: +47,443
1830–1839: +12,752	

ORIGINS OF SLAVERY

Slaves first appeared in Arkansas in the late eighteenth century, introduced to the region first by the French and then by the Spanish. In 1798, approximately fifty-six slaves lived in the Arkansas region. This increased to one hundred thirty-six slaves by 1810. Although many Anglo settlers moved into the region with their slaves after the War of 1812, it would not be until after Arkansas officially became a territory in 1819 that slavery began to take hold and become the foundation of Arkansas society (Bolton 1998, 125–126).

Before 1840, slaves made up only a small proportion of the total population. After 1840, though, slaves constituted 20 percent or more of the population. This percentage continued to increase until the Civil War crisis. By 1860, slaves constituted more than 24 percent of the population. Nine percent of the slave owners in the state held twenty-five or more slaves, approximately 46 percent of all slaves. As the number of slaves in Arkansas increased, slavery became geographically concentrated in the Delta and Gulf coastal plain regions. Several counties in these regions counted slaves as high as 75 percent of their total population. Six counties in these regions held 50 percent of the state's entire slave population.

The existence of slave labor during the antebellum period and the increasing reliance upon slavery helped to ensure the economic survival of Arkansans until the cotton economy took full hold. As elsewhere, slaves existed as a valuable commodity in Arkansas. In the 1820s, the average price for a slave was approximately $380. This rose to $485 in the 1830s and $627 in the 1850s. Prices varied, of course, depending on the age, gender, skills, and physical ability of a slave. Generally, skilled slaves and field hands brought the highest prices. It was common, in some areas, for a skilled slave to cost between two thousand five hundred and four thousand five hundred dollars. The high value of the bondsmen ensured that only the more prosperous individuals in Arkansas would enter the slaveholding ranks. As slavery became concentrated among a minority of the white population, this served to define the slave environment specifically and Arkansas society in general (Bolton 1998, 127–129; Lovett 1995, 305–306).

SLAVE LIFE

During the early antebellum era, Arkansas bondsmen did not live the life of plantation slaves common in other states, but rather aided their masters in eking out an existence as subsistence farmers, cultivating corn and vegetables, and tending hogs and cattle. Their working environment in these early times, the pioneer years, ensured slaves a measure of equality. Masters and their chattel ate together, slept together, and worked side-by-side each day. The physical separation between the two did not begin until after the completion of both the master's house and the slave's cabin. This event signaled the end to the more egalitarian pioneer days and the onset of the more typical master/slave relationship (McNeilly 2000, 124, 131).

After 1840, with the growth of the cotton economy, the majority of slaves in Arkansas lived on plantations. The cotton culture dictated their work and life. Slaves cleared the land, plowed, planted seeds, maintained the fields, and picked and ginned cotton. The process began in January and lasted through October. Work, though, was not limited to cotton production. Slaves kept busy cultivating subsistence crops and tending sheep, cattle, and hogs. Regardless of the size of the farm or plantation, slave owners in Arkansas expected slave children to work. They performed household chores, gathered wood, gathered berries and pecans for sale, tended to the livestock, and hauled water and food to the fields where their parents worked. Women too worked in the fields and helped the master's wife with cooking and laundry (Bolton 1998, 130; McNeilly 2000, 140).

Not all slaves worked as field hands. Slaves escaped the cotton fields by learning skills, such as blacksmithing or carpentry. Other slaves earned their master's favor and received promotion to drivers, teamsters, or housekeepers. Though the vast majority of slaves lived on farms and plantations, a minimal slave population did exist in various towns. In 1860, approximately three thousand eight hundred slaves lived in urban areas. Their environment was not as restrictive as the farm or plantation. Urban slaves worked as bricklayers, carpenters, plasterers, stonemasons, blacksmiths, and domestic servants.

Another typical aspect of Arkansas slavery was the practice of hiring out slave labor. Whether a master was a subsistence farmer or a larger plantation owner, the hiring out of slaves was a common practice. Owners hired out their bondsmen not only to gain an additional source of income, but also to aid their neighbors during cultivation and to assist the government in completing public works projects. Some masters even permitted their slaves to hire themselves out to earn money. In very rare cases, some slaves earned enough to buy time off from work. There too are instances in which some slaves saved enough to purchase their own freedom, although this proved rare in Arkansas, as the small free black population denotes (McNeilly 2000, 142, 147, 149; Moneyhon 1994, 47).

Not only were the working conditions of Arkansas slaves characteristic of Southern society, so too were their living conditions. Slaves generally lived in small one-room cabins. These cabins contained one window, one door, and one bed bolted to the wall. Slaves supplied any additional furniture they desired. The slave diet consisted mainly of pork and corn. Each chattel typically received three to five pounds of cured salted meat as well as a peck of cornmeal each week. Owners often supplemented this with portions of other meats, including game, and some owners also distributed rations of molasses, sweet potatoes, and buttermilk. Some slaves received permission to tend their own vegetable gardens. Though blacks were prohibited from possessing firearms, the law was hardly enforced because owners and slaves alike relied on hunting and fishing to supplement their diet. Owners did believe in clothing their slaves, yet provided them with the bare minimum. Arkansas slaves were clothed primarily in osnaburg cotton. Some masters, however, gave servants their own worn-out clothes. Children often wore just a plain cotton shirt. Gracious masters might be generous at Christmastime and other holidays by giving their slaves hand-me-down clothes (Moneyhon 1994, 64).

Though they existed at just the subsistence level, slaves believed that they were entitled to the basics of life—adequate food, clothing, medical treatment, and time off—as the privileges of hard work. In Arkansas, slaves protested their harsh treatment and working conditions by running away. Some slaves would disappear for only a few days, while others sought freedom. Only in rare cases did slaves turn on their masters or overseers and inflict injury or death. In those cases, slaves were promptly punished and hanged. Unlike other slave states, Arkansas did not witness a major slave revolt. Thus, protest was generally an individual undertaking (Bolton 1998, 135; McNeilly 2000, 137, 144).

Owners used a variety of methods to maintain control over their slaves to ensure hard work and successful production. Slaves generally lived in a harsh environment and were kept under control by violence, slave patrols, and black codes. Most often, masters whipped their slaves to instill discipline and obedience. Fear of the lash proved a successful incentive for bondsmen to work. Unruly slaves would find themselves staked to the ground, face down. The owner or overseer would then take a whip or lash and beat the slaves until he believed he had drawn enough blood. In addition, some masters even added insult to injury, as well as additional pain, by rubbing salt into the fresh wounds of the slave. While this might have aided the healing process in the long term, the immediate result was excruciatingly painful. Not all masters resorted to the whip. Some masters withheld privileges and forced their troublesome slaves to work on holidays. On the other hand, some used small rewards, such as providing days off, for those who picked the most cotton (Moneyhon 1994, 69; Bolton 1998, 132).

Despite the confines of the peculiar institution, slaves did maintain a degree of control over their own lives. This appeared most evident in matters of religion. The Methodist, Baptist, Presbyterian, and Episcopalian churches all attempted to evangelize the slaves in Arkansas. White Christianity emphasized the virtue of obedience to the master and warned against stealing, laziness, and drunkenness. While many slaves did attend church and adhered to one of these denominations, they took only what they wanted from white Christianity and blended it with their own rituals and beliefs. This varied from plantation to plantation depending on the African roots of the slaves. Their religious culture was vibrant, consisting of music, dance, preaching, and magic. Superstition, for example, played an active part in slave religion. Some slaves and freedmen believed that to prevent a man and wife from separating, a person should wrap a rabbit's forefoot, a piece of loadstone, and nine hairs from the top of the head in a red flannel and bury it under the front door steps. Slave religion also stressed eventual freedom and served as a form of education for many slaves. Not all masters, though, allowed their slaves to attend church, and the harsher owners even forbade all religious functions. This, however, did not stop the slaves from gathering in the woods at night to perform their own religious rituals (Rawick 1972, 2:7; Bolton 1998, 136–137; McNeilly 2000, 151).

Slaves found comfort and escape not only through religion, but also in the family. Although the law did not recognize slave relationships, oftentimes masters did and encouraged them, and that is what mattered. Slaves chose mates from their own or adjoining farms or plantations. On many plantations, slaves performed the ritual of broom jumping to signify their union. In many cases, the master presided over the marriage of his slaves. For example, Harriett McFarlin Payne, an ex-slave, recalled, "When two of de slaves wanted to get married, they'd dress up nice as they could and go up to the big house and the master would marry them. They'd stand up before him and he'd read out of a book called the 'discipline' and say, 'Thou shalt love the Lord thy God with all thy heart, all thy strength, with all thy might and thy neighbor as thyself.' Then he'd say they were man and wife and tell them to live right and be honest and kind to each other. All the slaves would be there too, seeing the 'wedden'" (Rawick 1972, 10:302).

Depending on the character of the owner, some slave marriages lasted for many years, while others were broken up through slave sales. As in most places, the union between slaves became subject to interference by the master. Slaves were helpless to defend their spouses against physical punishment and sexual advances. In addition, owners were not bound by law to keep families together, and often they sold slave children simply to pay off debts. While they might have acknowledged slave relationships, many owners did not respect them. Nevertheless, the existence of slave marriages and slave families led to the creation of kinship networks and served to cement relationships throughout the larger slave community. This was vital for slaves; it gave them a measure of control over their own lives, and kinship networks provided a fundamental part of slave culture that allowed bondsmen to transcend their restrictive environment (Moneyhon 1994, 68; McNeilly 2000, 151).

FREE BLACKS

Before the 1850s, Arkansas did provide for the manumission of slaves, and though not numerous, free blacks did live in the state. Although the prevailing racial code frowned on interracial marriage, some wealthy planters, such as Elisha Worthington, did take a black wife and raised mulatto children. The majority of free blacks in Arkansas were mulatto, suggesting that their relationship with the owner was a significant cause for their freedom. Most manumissions, though, occurred when the master died and willed that his slaves should be set free upon his death. In some cases, owners came to find the institution of slavery distasteful and set their slaves free. After 1850, as the political crisis over slavery deepened and the number of free blacks increased in the state, law prohibited owners from manumitting their slaves. Whites viewed free blacks as a threat to the peculiar institution, and during the 1850s, the free black population decreased in Arkansas. By 1860, the Arkansas legislature had passed a bill requiring all free blacks to leave the state or be subject to forced slavery (Gatewood 1991, 7–8; Bolton 1998, 139; Lovett 1995, 308).

THE CIVIL WAR

During the Civil War, many blacks fled as Union forces overran Arkansas. Even at the beginning stage of the crisis, many owners took their slaves and moved to Texas. One ex-slave recounted as a child, "I 'member when they said the Yankees was comin' the boss man put us in wagons and runned us to Texas. They put the women and chillin in the wagons but the men had to walk" (Rawick 1972, 10:25).

Countless slaves also served the Confederate cause in some capacity during the Civil War. One ex-slave, Pate Newton, recalled that when the war came, his master sent him into the army to take care of Colonel Bashom's horses. Pate was about eleven or twelve years old at the time. Women too were forced to aid the war effort. Annie Page recalled, "I used to help spin the thread to make the soldiers' clothes." Numerous other slaves, however, fled and joined the Union army. Blacks were placed in designated camps, on safe farms, and forced to work for the Union cause where many received wages for their labor. They worked on military installations, on riverboats, served as drivers, cooks, servants, nurses, and general laborers. Some slaves even obtained permission to lease out their own land, refusing to work for whites as they had during slavery. Fighting against the Confederate army and whites that had enslaved them, though, blacks faced numerous atrocities. In one instance, Confederate forces killed more than eighty black soldiers at Poison Springs, and similar situations occurred elsewhere in the state. Although Arkansas experienced political and economic chaos during the Civil War, slaves were still forced to abide by the laws and constraints of society and remained somewhat cautious about their activities. Any slave caught roaming the area without a pass was taken into custody and whipped. One ex-slave recalled, "Corse if they ketch you out without a pass they'd beat you nearly to death and tell you to go home to your mother" (Lovett 1995, 313–315; Finley 1996, 2; Rawick 1972, 10:25, 216–217, 235).

RECONSTRUCTION

After the Civil War, freedmen had a tendency to move and relocate in the vicinity of other blacks. The vast majority of freedmen moved to the southern and eastern counties of the state. In fact, in every southern and eastern Arkansas county, the population contained at least 25 percent blacks. In some cities, such as Arkadelphia, Fort Smith, and Van Buren, blacks constituted well over 70 percent of the population (Finley 1996, 24–25).

For most blacks, Reconstruction was a period in which they searched for and defined their own identities. The strengthening of kinship networks emerged as a vital component of this process. While blacks faced a difficult time maintaining marital ties and family relationships during slavery, the Freedmen's Bureau in Arkansas supported marriages and the rejoining of kin as a means to uphold social order in a chaotic period, and freedmen earnestly searched for loved ones previously sold away. This did not mean the family went without assault. Many bureau agents, adhering to racist ideas, believed that black women were still to be used for sexual gratification, and many cases exist where agents sexually exploited them (Finley 1996, 34–36, 40).

Religion also served a critical role in this process of identification. Throughout the state, blacks formed their own congregations and worshipped as they pleased. In some areas, they built new churches; in other areas, they turned abandoned white schools into places of worship. Furthermore, religious organizations, with the help of the Freedman's Bureau, emerged active in aiding the plight of blacks. For example, beginning in 1864, the Quakers established orphanages and schools for black children. Many blacks in Southland, for example, joined the Society of Friends, attracted by the emotional preaching and efforts at social and economic welfare. Their task at forging their own religious communities, however, often met with assault. The effort of some religious organizations went against the grain of mainstream white society, and groups such as the Friends became the target of the local Ku Klux Klan. In many areas throughout the state, blacks were beaten and whipped on their way from church; and in some areas, whites were guilty of burning black churches (Kennedy 1991, 116–117, 130–131; Finley 1996, 52–53).

Despite the harsh social conditions in postwar Arkansas, many blacks found a political voice after the war by joining the Union League, an organization aimed at raising the political consciousness of blacks by holding meetings, rallies, and encouraging freedmen to register to vote. In some areas, political enthusiasm ran high and a vast majority of the freedmen voted. Nevertheless, more often than not, whites manipulated the vote in some manner. One ex-slave recalled, "Lord! I don't know how many times I ever voted. I used to vote every time they had an election. I voted before I could read. The white man showed me how to vote and asked me who I wanted to vote for." White control of the black vote undoubtedly led to widespread manipulation and fraud (Finley 1996, 55; Rawick 1972, 10:48).

When it came to politics and voting, splits in the black community also hampered the black political voice in Arkansas. A freedman in Miller County, Arkansas, Doc Quinn became very influential among other blacks. Quinn recalled, "Not long after de negroes wuz freed, I took 86 ob dem to the votin' place at Homan and voted 'em all straight Democratic." Quinn's activism outraged local Republicans, and while on his way home from voting, two men jumped Doc Quinn and hanged him from a tree. He was rescued by the election officers that just happened to be traveling down the road. "Iffen dey had known how to tie a hangmans knot," Quinn said, "I wouldn't be here to tell you about it." In many areas, the enthusiasm for exercising a political voice became tempered by violence. As in other states, the Ku Klux Klan operated as a formidable force in keeping blacks away from the ballot box. The use of violence through beating, whipping, and lynching served as an effective means to discourage blacks from exercising their political freedom. Nevertheless, northern elite blacks had moved into Arkansas to take advantage of the political turmoil and many

This drawing by A.R. Waud shows a former slave casting his first vote. (Library of Congress.)

served in politics. Through their efforts, and the efforts of black voters, Arkansas passed civil rights legislation in 1868 and 1873. By 1873, twenty blacks held seats in the Reconstruction legislature of Arkansas, and many blacks served at the county and local level as judges, sheriffs, and justices of the peace (Rawick 1972, 10:6:2; Lovett 1995, 334–335).

During Reconstruction, economic freedom emerged as the most serious objective facing freedmen. The Freedmen's Bureau, headed by Oliver Otis Howard, began work in Arkansas immediately after the Civil War to aid the plight of ex-slaves. The Freedmen's Bureau, however, was wrought with racism, paternalism, and a commitment to racial hierarchy. This ideology led bureau agents to formulate a work ethic for freedmen that defined the actions of the bureau. In the bureau's view, blacks might be free, but they had to work and take responsibility for their own freedom (Finley 1996, 22–23).

To this end, the Freedmen's Bureau instituted the sharecrop system for blacks. The bureau had the responsibility of placing blacks in those areas that needed labor and it oversaw labor contracts. In Phillips County, in

1866, for example, more than four thousand blacks obtained sharecropping contracts. There is, though, no easy way to stereotype the economic plight of blacks after the Civil War. In some cases, the bureau achieved success at brokering favorable contracts for blacks. Some black males earned as high as sixty dollars and as little as five dollars per month, averaging seventeen dollars per month. Women earned as much as forty dollars and as little as five dollars per month, averaging twelve dollars per month. In some areas, though, labor contracts between blacks and whites virtually resurrected the institution of slavery. In these instances, landowners contracted black labor for the cost of food, clothing, and medical care, but not for money or a share of the crop. The Freedmen's Bureau was corrupt and, more likely than not, simply took bribes from white landowners for the supply of cheap black labor. Most blacks were never even paid money, but instead worked for the necessities of life. In these cases, the freedmen were sometimes worse off than they were during slavery. Not all blacks entered simple labor contracts, however. Many worked out sharecropping arrangements with white landowners. Here too no set arrangement existed. While bureau agents attempted to monitor planters to ensure the economic well-being of the freedmen, it was a virtually impossible task. In some areas, the bureau succeeded, in other areas, it completely failed. Moreover, in some instances, especially in the frontier regions of the state, blacks were kept in slavery well into 1867.

Many blacks in the state received hope when Congress passed the Southern Homestead Act in 1862. This opened nine million acres of public land in Arkansas that allowed individuals to purchase eighty-acre tracts. The bureau encouraged blacks to purchase their own land. Although many troubles, such as falsified land claims, duplicate claims, and land stealing by individuals and the railroad, made the process difficult, hundreds of free blacks did become landowners. Although most blacks continued in the same occupation, farming the land, they did so under their own work ethic. To many, freedom meant working when they wanted to and playing when they wanted to. They refused to adhere to the antebellum work discipline forced upon them by whites. This is not to say that the freedmen farmers were lazy, just that they worked at the pace they wished and took time to enjoy their freedom with the pursuits of leisure activities, such as fishing, hunting, singing, and dancing (Lovett 1995, 316–317; Finley 1996, 73–76).

Although there were many success stories, there were just as many horror stories. Violence plagued post–Civil War Arkansas. Blacks suffered physical abuse for minor legal and social infractions. Scores of black men and women were beaten and whipped, sometimes for no reason. The beatings they suffered were of the most violent nature. During slavery, whites were careful not to beat their slaves too much or maim them in any way due to the fear of flight and damage to their slave property. After the war, however, whites were not constrained in their violence, and numerous black men and women were beaten to death with the whip. After the Civil War, times were tough for most freedmen in Arkansas. One ex-slave, Charlie Morris, best summed it up: "Some of the colored folks better off free and some not. That's what I think but they don't" (Rawick 1972, 10:220).

REFERENCES

Bolton, Charles S. 1998. *Arkansas, 1800–1860: Remote and Restless*. Fayetteville: University of Arkansas Press.

Boyett, Gene W. 1992. "The Black Experience in the First Decade of Reconstruction in Pope County, Arkansas." *Arkansas Historical Quarterly* 51 (Summer).

Finley, Randy. 1996. *From Slavery to Uncertain Freedom: The Freedmen's Bureau in Arkansas, 1865–1869*. Fayetteville: University of Arkansas Press.

Gatewood, Willard B. 1991. "Sunnyside: The Evolution of an Arkansas Plantation, 1840–1945." *Arkansas Historical Quarterly* 50 (Spring).

Higgins, Billy D. 1995. "The Origins and Fate of the Marion County Free Black Community." *Arkansas Historical Quarterly* 54 (Winter).

Kennedy, Thomas C. 1991. "The Rise and Decline of a Black Monthly Meeting: Southland, Arkansas, 1864–1925." *American Historical Quarterly* 50 (Summer).

Lovett, Bobby. 1995. "African Americans, Civil War, and Aftermath in Arkansas." *American Historical Quarterly* 54 (Autumn).

McNeilly, Donald P. 2000. *The Old South Frontier: Cotton Plantations and the Formation of Arkansas Society, 1819–1861*. Fayetteville: University of Arkansas Press.

Moneyhon, Carl H. 1994. *The Impact of the Civil War and Reconstruction on Arkansas: Persistence in the Midst of Ruin*. Baton Rouge: Louisiana State University Press.

———. 1999. "The Slave Family in Arkansas." *Arkansas Historical Quarterly* 58 (Spring).

Rawick, George P., ed. 1972. *The American Slave: A Composite Autobiography*. Westport, Conn.: Greenwood Publishing Company.

WEB SITES

African American Experience: http://www.aristotle.net/persistence/index.html

Heritage of Slavery: http://www.arkansasheritage.com/peoplestories/africanamericans

Jefferson County: http://freepages.genealogy.rootsweb.com/~ajac/arjefferson.html

Pike County: http://homepages.rootsweb.com/~xrysta/research/blacks.html

Resources: http://arkedu.state.ar.us/africanamerican/arkres.html

Delaware

TIMELINE

1639: Black Anthony is carried to New Sweden becoming the first African to reside in what is to become Delaware

1680–1740: Tobacco planting flourishes; many slaves are taken to Delaware from Maryland and Virginia

1700–1726: Delaware Assembly establishes separate courts and laws for all African Americans

1750–1800: Era of manumissions—many slaves are freed

1776: Delaware bans slave importations

1787, December 7: Delaware enters the Union; Delaware proscribes the entire slave trade, both imports and exports

1800–1830: Era of "slave-napping" involves the infamous Patty Cannon

1812: Free blacks establish the African Union Methodist Church

1845–1861: Underground Railroad flourishes in the Wilmington area; Thomas Garrett and Harriet Tubman aid hundreds of escaped slaves

1873: Delaware enacts the poll tax requirement for voters

1880s: Delaware Assembly and local governments pass numerous "Jim Crow" segregation laws

Slave and Free Black Population

Census Year	Slave Population	Population Percentage	Free Black Population	Population Percentage
1790	8,887	15	3,899	7
1800	6,153	9	8,268	13
1810	4,177	6	13,136	18
1820	4,509	6	12,958	18
1830	3,292	4	15,855	21
1840	2,605	3	16,919	22
1850	2,290	3	18,073	20
1860	1,798	2	19,829	18

**Net Slave Entries and Exits, by Decade
(Tadman 1989, 12)**

1790–1799: − 4,523	1830–1839: − 1,314
1800–1809: − 3,204	1840–1849: − 912
1810–1819: − 817	1850–1859: − 920
1820–1829: − 2,270	

ORIGINS OF SLAVERY

In November 1637, two ships from Gothenburg, Sweden, loaded with cargo and passengers, embarked for North America. This expedition, headed by a former Dutch colonial official, established a colony along the Delaware River known as New Sweden. Although the two vessels, the *Kalmar Nyckel* and the *Vogel Grip* (also known as the *Grippen* or *Griffen*), sailed under the Swedish flag and transported Swedish colonists, most of the crew, the cargo, and the financing originated with the Dutch. After delivering these new inhabitants to North America, the *Griffen* left the Delaware to look for trading opportunities with the Virginians farther south. The settlers and the English officials along the rivers of the Chesapeake Bay rebuffed these Dutch/Swedish overtures, and the crew and the captain of the vessel headed for the West Indies looking further afield for profitable possibilities or for an unwary Spanish merchant galleon, hopefully loaded with treasure. Unfortunately for the mariners, salivating for a rich prize, this journey generated no tangible returns; however, the mostly Dutch crew, experienced in the slave trade, acquired a native African while resupplying among the islands. They carried along an individual known by the sailors as "Black Anthony" to the Delaware colony on their return trip. Thus, in April 1639, Anthony became the first person of African heritage to reside in what would become the state of Delaware (Hoffecker 1977, 90; Munroe 1978, 16–18; Essah 1996, 9).

Anthony and the African Americans who followed him, both those enslaved and those liberated, played a substantial role in the development of Delaware throughout the eighteenth and nineteenth centuries. During the antebellum years, free and unfree blacks made up between 20 and 25 percent of the state's total population as the opening summary chart demonstrates. Moreover, the status of these individuals, descendants of forcibly imported Africans, became and remained a central social and economic issue that divided the state politically for a century. Southern Delaware—Sussex County and the southern half of Kent County—always contained more African Americans during these years than the northern half of the state, and the politicians from these districts effectively blocked all attempts to give freed blacks equality with whites—legally, socially, or politically. Even though the successful passage of the Thirteenth Amendment ended chattel slavery in December 1865, the Delaware Assembly refused to ratify this document until 1901.

THE COLONIAL ERA

Early settlers eventually brought moderate numbers of Africans and African Americans into the colony to work the fields along the Delaware River and its tributaries. This resulted from an effort first by Swedish and Dutch colonial administrators and later by the British to replicate the financial successes of the Chesapeake Bay settlements by developing a tobacco economy. In Virginia and Maryland, exported leaf provided cash that paid for land and monetarily supported colonial officials, ministers, and other administrators. The exported tobacco and the goods imported by well-to-do planters offered excellent opportunities for merchants and traders. Additionally, the ships supported the merchant marine by offering employment to hundreds of sailors engaged on the trans-Atlantic voyages. Thus, a cash crop like tobacco greatly enhanced the mercantilist economy of a European "Mother Country," as well as the subsidiary North American colony, and met the standards of the system of "mercantilism" whose tenets dominated that era's understanding of political economy.

Beginning in 1642, Sweden officially granted the Delaware colony, New Sweden, a tobacco monopoly. The Swedish colonial governor, John Printz, aggressively promoted tobacco planting and additionally purchased hogsheads of leaf from Chesapeake Bay planters for export. Dutch traders soon began to sell slaves to would-be planters to drain the swamps, to clear the land, and to cultivate the plant.

When the Dutch took over the management of the colony along the lower Delaware River in 1655, their officials continued to emphasize tobacco as a cash crop. Additionally, the Dutch established officially sanctioned tobacco warehouses to provide storage space for planters, to ease the task of collecting and loading the hogsheads for shipping, and, not incidentally, to make the collection of taxes less difficult. The Dutch continued to supply the farmers and planters with an enslaved African workforce paid for with tobacco proceeds.

England furthered the development of this tobacco economy when Delaware passed to the English Crown after the short Anglo-Dutch War of 1664. English officials representing the Duke of York, the future King James II, offered Delaware's prospective settlers the same land terms as did the Calverts of Maryland. As the acreage along the Chesapeake Bay became occupied or drained of fertility by the nutritionally greedy tobacco plant, numerous Maryland planters acquired land in what would become Delaware and moved there with their enslaved workers. The majority of these Marylanders settled in Sussex County and in the southern portions of Kent County not far from the borders of their original homesteads (Munroe 1978, 21–74).

The tobacco cash-crop economy flourished along the banks of the southern and western regions of the Delaware River from the 1670s until the 1740s. Farmers planting tobacco acquired enslaved Africans to grow and harvest their crops or brought along their human chattel when moving to Delaware from Maryland. Especially in the southern half of the colony, a full-blown plantation economy evolved. Pounds of tobacco enumerated wages, salaries, taxes, and clergy compensation. Large farms, in excess of five hundred acres and manned by toiling enslaved blacks, dotted the landscape. Almost all of the ancestors of the African Americans living in Delaware during the antebellum years arrived to work on lands in what would become the state's three counties during this era, the age of the tobacco plantation economy, which extended from the 1670s into the late 1740s (Munroe 1978, 94).

Many of these human chattel, transported from Chesapeake farms and plantations, already needed to be classified as African Americans because many had been born on the North American side of the Atlantic. Others, however, entered the colony by means of slave sales taking place in Baltimore, Annapolis, Wilmington, New York, or Philadelphia. These native Africans had been ripped from their homes and villages, herded into pens along the West African coast, and then packed onto "slavers" that conveyed these individuals across the Atlantic along the infamously cruel "middle passage." Slave traders crammed the Africans into the bowels of their ships. These pestilential floating prisons, bereft of any rudimentary type of sanitation, conveyed from two hundred to four hundred human souls at a time as human cargo (Munroe 1978, 152).

Mortality aboard ship sometimes eliminated a quarter or more of the human payload, though the death rate for slaves transported averaged 16 percent for the entire Atlantic slave trade period. Eighty to ninety percent of this mortality resulted from disease and the rampant infections ensuing from the abominably filthy conditions. Most of the Africans brought to North America by Dutch and English slave traders came from the West African regions along the Gulf of Benin and the Bight of Biafra, present-day Nigeria (Curtin 1969, 224–225, 248, 277).

SLAVE CODES

In the first years of the colony, Africans transported to Delaware or African Americans carried into Delaware from the Chesapeake lived in an undefined legal state, somewhere between total enslavement and indentured servitude. Following the lead of Maryland and Virginia, Delaware officials began enacting slave codes in the 1680s. These laws confirmed the legal rights of whites of European heritage to hold individuals of African descent as slaves and effectively differentiated white indentured servants from enslaved Africans in the statutes (Essah 1996, 10).

In 1700, the Delaware Assembly passed a series of laws that set up a trial system to adjudicate African Americans, both free and enslaved. These courts consisted of two justices of the peace joined by six other "respectable" white citizens. Capital offenses included murders, homicides, burglaries, and rapes. Attempted rape of a white female could result in the castration of the offending black man; in 1726, the legislators reduced this penalty to four hours in the public pillory. A slave owner received reimbursement at government expense for any enslaved African American executed. These laws also proscribed any interracial liaisons "to ensure the preservation of virtue and chastity among the people . . . and to prevent . . . the sins of adultery and fornication."

The legal system as well as the society at large rigorously subjected black male/white female relationships to greater scrutiny than white male/black female unions. These rules relegated any mulatto child born of a white mother to indentured servitude until the age of thirty-one. Any mulatto child born of a bonded African American female automatically became a slave and the human property of the owner of the enslaved woman (Essah 1996, 33–35).

In addition to installing a judicial system that treated blacks and whites differently, the residents further circumscribed the lifestyle of African Americans by requiring blacks to obtain passes. Slaves could move about the countryside legally only after their owners issued them written permission slips. Any black without a pass would be incarcerated and investigated. These rules caused numerous hardships among many African American families. Because most slaves lived on relatively modest-sized farms and plantations, many men took "broad" wives who resided at other locations. This "pass" system effectively placed the frequency and timing of family get-togethers in the hands of the slave owner, who used this circumstance to enforce compliance and levels of labor expended. Most men visited their families on Saturday night, staying over until Sunday evening (Curtin 1967, 42).

COLONIAL ERA SLAVE LIFE

The typical workweek in Delaware and in the Chesapeake ran from Monday morning until noon Saturday; the workday extended from sunup until sundown, except in periods of inclement weather. Slaves generally had Saturday afternoon and all day Sunday as their own time. Otherwise, slaveholding farmers attempted to keep them fully occupied. For field hands, tobacco cultivation provided a year-round list of chores with enough time left over to see to the wheat, corn, and forage crops. Taking care of tobacco tended to be tedious and repetitious, rather than heavily burdensome. Monotonous tasks, especially walking along the rows of the tobacco plants pulling off green horned worms, consumed many summer days. The young and the old managed the livestock, the poultry, and the vegetable garden. A number of the enslaved African American women generally worked in the house as domestics, maids, or cooks. The size of the plantation and the number of slaves thereon determined how many workers could be relieved of field tasks to see to the household chores.

By the late colonial times, most slaveholders in Delaware adhered at least nominally to the Church of England, and the Anglican clergy made some attempts to baptize black children. By the 1770s, most African Americans in Delaware had become acquainted with Christianity, had often received some rudimentary instruction or catechism, and had a cursory knowledge of a number of Bible stories. Baptism and membership within the Christian community, however, did not alter the enslaved status of Delaware's human chattel nor advance the civil rights of its free blacks (Munroe 1978, 170).

THE REVOLUTIONARY ERA

From the 1740s until the turn of the nineteenth century, many Delaware slaveholders rethought their commitment to the validity and the viability of the slave system. Thus, in Delaware in 1730, the typical African American toiled as a slave; however, by 1800, more Americans of African heritage claimed status as free blacks. This change in station resulted primarily from three trends: financial, ideological, and religious. The decades that encompassed the American Revolution and the installation of a new national government became in Delaware an "era of slave manumissions" (Essah 1996, 36).

The economy changed from the 1740s onward when almost all the farmers along the Delaware River and its tributaries switched from cultivating tobacco to growing grains. By the 1770s, tobacco as a crop had largely disappeared. These decisions followed a steep decline in leaf returns, resulting both from lower prices and also from lesser yields, as the tobacco plant sucked the nutrients from the tidewater soils and fertility declined precipitously. While tobacco required year-round labor, wheat and corn necessitated toil only twice a year, at planting and at harvest. Slave owners felt economically encumbered by having to provide for underemployed African American slaves. Many began to manumit their excess redundant workers (Essah 1996, 37).

The second trend convincing slaveholders to seriously consider manumission flowed from the pervasive use of vibrant liberal, enlightened, and natural rights rhetoric during the years engulfed by the American Revolution. Politicians, statesmen, lawyers, and pamphleteers all employed language emphasizing individual freedoms and human rights. Thomas Jefferson's phrase: "all men are created equal, that they are endowed by their Creator with certain inalienable rights" sounded a clarion call in all who questioned the legitimacy of enslaving human beings in perpetual bondage. For owners unable to reconcile slavery and the rights enumerated and included in the new state constitution, manumission appeared as a rational option; that the economic benefits of slave ownership had declined also helped. Slaveholders influenced by this enlightened rhetoric and philosophical reasoning often chose the Fourth of July as the manumission date for their chattel (Essah 1996, 40, 86).

Moreover, the Delaware legislature allowed bondsmen to serve in lieu of masters in the Continental army and in the local militia. Masters often promised freedom for service and many former slaves entered the ranks of free blacks through successful military participation. In addition, Delaware's revolutionary era constitution (1776) prohibited importation of enslaved Africans. Furthermore, in 1787, the Delaware Assembly passed laws that proscribed all out-of-state slave sales. This effectively barred traders from buying Delaware slaves for sale farther south and ended the practice of raising and selling slaves for profit (Hoffecker 1977, 160).

Two religious denominations responded to the natural rights rhetoric and the trend toward more enlightened political philosophy by adopting antislavery tenets and by advocating manumission for its communicants who held bonded African Americans. Significant Quaker opposition to slavery emerged in the late 1750s, and in the independence year of 1776 the Society of Friends mandated that all members attending its meetings must free their slaves to remain in good standing within their congregations (Essah 1996, 41).

Warner Mifflin, who grew up in a tidewater Virginia slave-owning family and subsequently moved onto land near Camden in Kent County, decided to free all his numerous slaves. He even compensated the freshly liberated blacks for their former services. He soon began to journey around the Delaware countryside speaking passionately at Friend's meetings about the evils of owning slaves. A Kent County neighbor of Mifflin, John Dickinson, also freed his many slaves during the Revolutionary War years. By 1792, 123 Quakers had manumitted more than 450 African Americans. As these examples indicate, the Society of Friends' antislavery campaign produced the greatest impact in the farm county of Kent, the centermost of Delaware's three counties (Hoffecker 1977, 92–93).

Likewise, the Methodists of Delaware joined their brethren in Philadelphia and the neighboring Quakers by speaking out in opposition to human chattel slavery. Their campaign also resulted in numerous manumissions in Kent and New Castle counties as well. In 1790, Anna White of Kent noted in her manumission decree, "being sensible that it is not only contrary to the principles of justice and humanity, but likewise to the sacred law of God, to hold Negroes in perpetual bondage" and immediately freed Candice and promised to free the four-year-old Zava at age twenty-one. Many manumissions called for freedom in the future at a certain age or date. America Rogers of Sussex County freed George out of the conviction that "Liberty is the Right of all human creatures and Especially Natural born citizens of these United States of America" (Essah 1996, 66–67).

Thus, the decline in the tobacco economy, combined with the enlightened rhetoric used by the political and religious reformers, provided the impetus that created dramatic shifts in the status of Delaware's African Americans. These initial waves of manumission spread most noticeably through Kent and New Castle counties, but had less of an immediate impact in Sussex County. In Sussex County, the southernmost of the three counties, farmers had completely embraced the concept of plantation slavery as a form of economic and social organization. Here on large isolated farms bordering Maryland, Delaware slavery lingered the longest. By the early 1800s, only in Sussex County did more African Americans live as slaves than as free blacks. During the Early National Era (1790–1820) and continuing throughout the antebellum years (1820–1860), the number of slaves counted in the decennial census dropped precipitously (see summary chart), while the population of free blacks grew in proportion. Therefore, the major quest for African Americans in Delaware up through the Civil War lay not in a debate over slavery, still legal yet well on its way to disappearing, but rather in the attempts by blacks to gain full political citizenship and to achieve legal and economic equality. These struggles in Delaware foreshadowed the difficulties blacks confronted in the post-Reconstruction South.

SLAVE SALES

The ban on all types of slave trading circumscribed the alternative choices of masters who sought to exploit the market for enslaved labor by selling slaves south for profit; however, two exceptions existed in the Delaware law. These loopholes created the legal road that led several thousand African Americans into continued enslavement outside the boundaries of Delaware. Historian Michael Tadman estimated that nearly eight thousand bonded Delaware blacks left the state between 1790 and 1810, while a lesser number continued to leak out of the state throughout the antebellum years (Tadman 1989, 12).

These bans declared that any slave owner selling all of his land and permanently moving out of Delaware could take his human chattel along. Numerous Sussex County and Kent County masters selected this option and moved to lands farther south within the slave states that were more amenable to slave-based agriculture. The second loophole that contributed to the exodus of Delaware's enslaved blacks proclaimed that owners of land in both Delaware and Maryland could move slaves back and forth without breaking the law. Using this method, a master in Delaware could sell a slave to a landowner in both states and that individual could take the enslaved African American to his Maryland property where no bans existed on sales farther south. This somewhat circuitous, though legal, path allowed certain slave owners to pocket gains on slaves sold to areas where prices for human chattel greatly exceeded the returns available in Delaware.

Furthermore, unscrupulous individuals used two illegal methods to secure, for personal gain, the capital value attributed to each bonded black. The first method entailed surreptitiously carrying or smuggling slaves across the Maryland border and transferring title there. The rural countryside of southern Delaware, bordering Maryland, combined with the largely pro-slavery populace therein, offered little risk of disclosure to the willing participants.

The second method proved much more vile. Kidnappers would snatch unwary African Americans, especially free blacks, from their homes or while they walked along the roadside and would carry these unfortunate individuals across the border into Maryland and then along the Nanticoke River to the Chesapeake Bay. After traveling down the bay to southern Virginia or northern North Carolina, the slavenappers could present their captures to a county court. Because no one locally would know about or would verify the black person's free legal status, and because the offenders would destroy all evidence of the African American's prior freedom, the court would then declare that person a slave and then issue the appropriate papers. Subsequently, the smugglers would legally sell this individual to an unsuspecting slave owner who then had a valid bill of sale for the former free black. Because the smugglers did not have to originally buy the black, only pay for transportation and any bribes, the profits from these transactions proved quite high. This villainous form of commerce flourished in the early 1800s.

The most notorious slavenapper was one Patty Cannon. She bought a house that fortuitously straddled the Maryland/Delaware border. Next, she hired numerous accomplices to steal an unwary slave or an unsuspecting free black and then spirited that individual down her pipeline for sale farther south. Officials finally collared her in 1829 after thirty years of nefarious activities (Shields 1990).

FREE BLACKS

In addition to avoiding any stray slavenappers, most African Americans, more than any other goal, desired treatment in the eyes of the law equal to that of white citizens. In the nineteenth century this was not to be. Free blacks in Delaware occupied a twilight legal status between abject slavery and full freedom. Laws enacted by the all-white assembly delineated the limits of black freedom and carefully circumscribed individual liberties.

Moreover, in the most populated areas in northern Delaware, slavery scarcely existed by 1840. Wilmington, unlike Baltimore, Washington, or Richmond, counted few enslaved domestics and no bonded industrial workers. The many free blacks here and throughout the state abided by laws applicable only to people of color (Essah 1996, 52).

The legislature in 1826 passed a law that required all free African Americans to carry passes. In 1832, following the Nat Turner insurrection in Virginia, Delaware's elected delegates enacted legislation that prohibited free blacks from carrying firearms unless they first obtained a permit that had to be endorsed by five white men. In addition, no gathering of free blacks of a dozen or more could take place in the evening without at least three whites present. Statutes approved in 1839 specified different sentencing guidelines covering identical crimes and offenses for blacks and whites. In 1849, the assembly passed vagrancy and vagabond laws that allowed local county and town authorities to hire-out any "idle" free blacks on the best terms available. Legally, free blacks could neither vote nor hold office, and they had to stay at least a half a mile away from polling places on election days. The campaign to win full rights continued throughout the entire nineteenth century (Essah 1996, 110–117).

SLAVE AND FREE BLACK LIFE

After the American Revolution, the Methodist Church quickly became the single most important social institution for Delaware's black population. The famous Methodist cleric, Francis Asbury, often included African American exhorters among his preaching entourage, including the well-known "Black Henry" Hosier. Additionally, Methodists permitted blacks to preach, to attend divine services, and to participate in church activities; however, membership groups relegated African Americans to balconies and galleries for seating, while local by-laws prevented any free blacks from voting or from holding any congregational office. To counter these limitations, free black religious leaders began organizing their followers into separate congregations with separate facilities. This eventually resulted in the founding of two new distinct church denominations (Munroe 1978, 193–194).

In 1805, a group of free blacks split from the Asbury Methodist Church in Wilmington to form the Ezion Church. In 1812, members of this church led by Peter Spence and William Anderson, both African American lay preachers of some repute, organized a conference of black churches, the African Union Methodist Church. This became the first black-controlled incorporated body in Delaware. Each autumn, beginning in 1813, this conference held a meeting that attracted free blacks from all over Delaware and eventually from the rest of the Delmarva Peninsula. Masters and employers in this area began giving hired-out slaves these days off as well, and in a few years, the African Union Methodist Convention emerged as the largest social event for blacks in the region: a time for sermons, singing, praying, and socializing (Hoffecker 1977, 97–98).

The African Methodist Episcopal (A.M.E.) Church emerged in Philadelphia for the same reasons. Both of its founding fathers, Richard Allen and Absalom Jones, grew up as slaves in Delaware: Allen, near Dover in Kent County, and Jones in Sussex County. Additionally, Richard Allen became the first A.M.E. bishop. He later published his life story that showed how he and his brother worked as hired-out slaves and eventually purchased their freedom. Allen learned about Christianity by attending Sunday school for blacks in the fields and under the trees. He subsequently, after obtaining his freedom, worked his way around Delaware, New Jersey, and eastern Pennsylvania, cutting wood and driving mule teams during the weekdays, and teaching and preaching during the evenings and on Sundays (Allen 1960; George 1973).

African Americans in Delaware, however, had less success in organizing schools and other educational outlets. Although state law did not specifically deny free blacks access to education, white schools did not welcome African Americans and no provisions for separate venues existed. A number of poorly funded groups, often connected with churches or charities, originated in the antebellum years in futile attempts to fill this educational shortfall. Before the Civil War, historians estimate only two hundred to two hundred fifty blacks in the state received any formal education in any year. This represented 2 percent or less of the total black population. The African School Society, supported financially by the white abolitionist businessman Thomas Garrett, emerged in the 1840s, but lacked adequate resources to do much more than offer cursory learning to scant numbers. Access to and inclusion in a public school system on the same terms as whites remained a key black political objective until the 1950s (Essah 1996, 123–124).

THE UNDERGROUND RAILROAD

Thomas Garrett, in addition to attempting to help free blacks in Wilmington obtain rudimentary education, also provided the final stop within the eastern slave states for an Underground Railway network that carried escaped African American slaves to freedom from the tidewater areas of Virginia and North Carolina. This path reversed the route up the Chesapeake Bay previously used by Patty Cannon and other slavenappers earlier in the nineteenth century. Operatives and safe houses existed along the Nanticoke River that offered a path into Delaware from Maryland and Virginia. In Wilmington, Thomas Garrett smuggled the escapees across the last bridge within slavedom to the free jurisdictions of Pennsylvania. He surreptitiously transported his charges across the river by hiding them in the bottoms of wagons used by free black bricklayers moving bricks and workers from Wilmington to Philadelphia.

Using this strategy, Garrett aided more than two thousand African Americans in their journey toward freedom in the years preceding the Civil War. Because he made his living as a shoe factory owner, the escaping slaves always left his hiding places with a new pair of shoes. The most famous operative along this route, Harriet Tubman, enlisted Garrett's aid to help spirit three hundred slaves up this secret road to freedom. Garrett eventually paid a substantial economic price, however, for in 1848 officials cracked down on his activities and the resultant fines

The Underground Railroad, which flourished in and around Wilmington, Delaware, in the two decades before the Civil War, helped many slaves escape to freedom in the North and Canada. (Library of Congress.)

left the abolitionist in a reduced financial condition that no longer allowed him to support free black education as before (McGowan 1977; Bradford 1974).

THE CIVIL WAR

In the years just prior to the onset of the Civil War, Delaware voters split almost equally on the politics of slavery and on free black rights. The majority of the populace in Sussex County and in the southern half of Kent County consistently supported the Democrats, opposed any laws granting further equality to free blacks, and opposed all efforts to proscribe slavery. Many more citizens in New Castle County and in the northern half of Kent County, however, supported the Republicans and the limitations on slavery's expansion, and were more willing to consider additional freedoms for free blacks. Moreover, the representatives from the southern districts successfully blocked abolition bills in 1845, 1847, and 1849 (Essah 1996, 158).

Even though, in 1860, Delaware contained few slaves and fewer slaveholders, the polling returns declared John C. Breckenridge, the southern Democrat and pro-slavery candidate, the winner of the state's presidential electoral ballots. Historian Harold Hancock argued: "The Democrats won the election by playing upon the fears of Delawareans that the Republicans were enemies of slavery, believers in Negro equality, and dissolvers of the Union." As armed conflict approached, the state's Democratic senators, Willard Saulsbury and James A. Bayard, Jr., contended, "the South should be allowed to go in peace" (Hancock 1961, 37).

Pro-slavery groups in Sussex County, which contained 75 percent of the remaining slaves and slaveholders, spoke out in support of the newly formed Confederacy but made no overt attempts to carry Delaware into the ranks of that nascent nation. Just to make sure, President Abraham Lincoln's government, in early 1862, sent two companies of loyal Maryland troops to Dover where they peaceably disarmed the local militias from New Kent and Sussex counties to which rumor attributed pro-Confederate leanings (Hoffecker 1977, 179–182).

Nevertheless, President Lincoln hoped to use Delaware as a test case for gradual, compensated emancipation, which he prayed would end slavery in the border states that still adhered to the Union. The Democrats, however, gridlocked the Assembly and stalemated Lincoln's political overture. Moreover, the Emancipation Proclamation, which took effect on January 1, 1863, did not include slaves domiciled in these border states, still within the Union, under its purview. The few remaining Delaware slaves had to wait until December 1865, when a sufficient number of states ratified the Thirteenth Amendment, whose provisions finally outlawed slavery in all United States jurisdictions (Berlin and Rowland 1997, 95).

Even though Democratic politicians prevented the early demise of slavery, Delaware's men of eligible military age overwhelmingly voted for the Union by volunteering to join the federal forces in record numbers. Regardless of how they felt about slavery, the state's citizens enjoyed their heritage as the descendents of those who made Delaware the first state to ratify the federal Constitution. Eventually a greater percentage of Delaware's eligible men served in the Union army than those volunteering from any other state. Additionally, blacks from Delaware served in United States Colored Troops regiments that saw action at the Crater outside Petersburg, in the trenches bordering Richmond, and in the attack on Fort Harrison (Berlin, Reidy, and Rowland 1982, 12).

EMANCIPATION AND POSTBELLUM AMERICA

Because Delaware never seceded, its citizens never had to grapple with Reconstruction. Free blacks, however, continued their antebellum quest for greater equality and greater economic opportunity while continuing to build on the religious, educational, and charitable institutions that had their beginnings in the antebellum era. For white citizens, the single most jarring outcome of the war resulted from the passage of the Fifteenth Amendment that validated black voters. This, in one moment, increased the franchise by 20 percent. Democrats responded by successfully enacting poll tax requirements in 1873 to limit black participation. Delaware quickly adopted other Jim Crow legislation and eventually set up a dual school system topped by the black college Delaware State. From the 1870s to the 1950s, Delaware organized its politics, its legal system, its economy, and its culture on the Southern idea of segregation and the legal principal of separate but equal.

Although the African American citizens of Delaware escaped the worst of the Southern white backlash and the vigilante violence frequent in the years after Reconstruction, blacks in the state failed to achieve their quest for equality before the law, until the civil rights struggles of the 1950s and early 1960s finally ended legal segregation.

REFERENCES

Allen, Richard. 1960. *The Life Experiences and Gospel Labors of the Right Reverend Richard Allen*. New York: Abingdon Press.

Berlin, Ira, Joseph P. Reidy, and Linda Rowland, eds. 1982. *Freedom's Soldiers: The Black Military Experience in the Civil War*. London: Cambridge University Press.

———. 1974. *Slaves without Masters: The Free Negroes in the Antebellum South*. New York: Pantheon Books.

Berlin, Ira, and Leslie S. Rowland, eds. 1997. *Families and Freedom: A Documentary History of African American Kinship in the Civil War*. New York: The New Press.

Bradford, Sarah. 1974. *Harriet Tubman: The Moses of Her People*. Secaucus, N.J.: The Citadel Press.

Curtin, Philip D., ed. 1967. *Africa Remembered: Narratives by West Africans from the Era of the Slave Trade*. Madison: University of Wisconsin Press.

———. 1969. *The Atlantic Slave Trade: A Census*. Madison: University of Wisconsin Press.

Essah, Patience. 1996. *A House Divided: Slaves and Emancipation in Delaware, 1638–1856*. Charlottesville: University of Virginia Press.

George, Carol V. 1973. *Segregated Sabbaths: Richard Allen and the Rise of Independent Black Churches, 1760–1840*. New York: Oxford University Press.

Hancock, Harold B. 1961. *Delaware During the Civil War*. Wilmington: Historical Society of Delaware.

Hoffecker, Carol E. 1977. *Delaware: A Bicentennial History*. New York: W.W. Norton.

McGowan, James A. 1977. *Station Master on the Underground Railroad: The Life and Letters of Thomas Garrett*. Moylan, Pa.: Whimsie Press.

Munroe, James A. 1978. *Colonial Delaware: A History*. New York: KTO Press.

Shields, Jerry. 1990. *The Infamous Patty Cannon in History and Legend*. Dover, Del.: Bibliotheca Literoria Press.

Tadman, Michael. 1989. *Speculators and Slaves: Masters, Traders, and Slaves in the Old South*. Madison: University of Wisconsin Press.

WEB SITES

African Union Methodist Protestant Church History: http://www.aumpchurch. org/history.htm

Daniel J. Russell. History of the African Union Methodist Church: http://doc. south.unc.edu/church/Russell/menu.html

Harriet Tubman and the Underground Railroad: http://www.americaslibrary. gov/cgi-bin/page.cgi/aa/tubman

Underground Railroad in Delaware: http://www.lib.udel.edu/ud/spec/exhibits/ undrgrnd.htm

Underground Railroad Tour: http://www.dovermuseums.org/itineraries/ undergroundrr.htm

District of Columbia

TIMELINE

1792–1810: United States hires slaves to build the President's Palace (White House), the Capitol, and other government buildings in Washington

1800: District of Columbia appears as a legal jurisdiction encompassing all African Americans, slave and free, in the ceded areas of Virginia and Maryland

1820–1845: Owners sell sizable numbers of slaves at auction blocks in Alexandria

1835: Violence against free blacks in the District erupts during the Snow Riot

1846: Federal government retrocedes the Lower District to Virginia

1848: Drayton Affair—watermen who attempted to aid escaped slaves are apprehended

1850: Compromise of 1850 ends the slave trade within the District

1861–1865: During the Civil War, the District becomes a haven for refugees and "contrabands"

1862: District Emancipation Act frees all remaining slaves in the District

1863: First Regiment of United States Colored Troops (USCT) is mustered in

1866–1880: The Golden Age—the District becomes the focal point for African American intellectuals and culture

1867: Howard University, the historical black college founded in the District by the head of the Freedmen's Bureau, General Oliver Otis Howard, opens

1872–1895: Former slave and prominent abolitionist Frederick Douglass resides in the District

1873–1882: Father Patrick F. Healy, S. J., serves as president of Georgetown University

Slave and Free Black Population

Census Year	Slave Population	Population Percentage	Free Black Population	Population Percentage
1800	3,244	23	783	6
1810	5,395	22	2,549	11
1820	6,377	19	4,048	12
1830	6,119	15	6,152	15
1840	4,694	11	8,361	19
1850	3,687	7	10,059	19
1860	3,185	4	11,131	15
1870			43,404	33

**Net Slave Entries and Exits, by Decade
(Tadman 1989, 12)**

1800–1809: – 1,123	1830–1839: – 2,575
1810–1819: – 576	1840–1849: – 2,030
1820–1829: – 1,944	1850–1859: – 1,222

African Americans in the District of Columbia

Upper and Lower Counties	1800	1810	1820	1830	1840
Free Blacks					
Upper	400	1,572	2,758	4,604	6,499
Lower	383	977	1,290	1,548	1,862
Slaves					
Upper	2,072	3,554	4,520	4,505	3,320
Lower	1,172	1,841	1,857	1,614	1,374

ORIGINS OF SLAVERY

By a statute of Congress enacted on July 16, 1790, the District of Columbia emerged on the map as the outcome of a compromise brokered between the political disciples of Alexander Hamilton, the first Secretary of Treasury, and the partisans who followed the lead of Thomas Jefferson. Hamilton's friends agreed to support legislation that located the new federal capital on a site preferred by George Washington, as well as by Jefferson, in return for the latter's aid in passing financial laws promoted by Hamilton. Thus, the future center for American political deal making was itself essentially located by the expediency of a political deal.

The District officially appeared as a legal jurisdiction in December 1800, when all the individuals residing within its recently drawn boundaries fell under its new administrative authority. Both Maryland and Virginia contributed land and money. The initial District of Columbia contained not only a swath of Maryland, formerly parts of Prince George's and Montgomery counties, but also encompassed a land and financial cession by Virginia that included the bustling town of Alexandria, a rural segment that would eventually become Arlington County, and a financial payment of one hundred twenty thousand dollars. As the summary chart denotes, more than four thousand slaves and free blacks lived in the new Federal District, comprising almost 30 percent of the total populace. Throughout the antebellum years and into the 1870s, African Americans generally provided from a quarter to a third of the entire District population (Tremain 1892, 4–11).

SLAVERY AND THE LAW

At the time of the District's creation, the U.S. Congress passed legislation that stated that the current laws of Maryland and Virginia then in effect, governing and defining the legal status of African Americans and also circumscribing the rights of free blacks, would be valid in the new jurisdiction. Maryland law would be applied in the Upper County, formerly a part of that state, and Virginia law would hold forth in the Lower County, likewise formerly a part of that commonwealth. Furthermore, from 1808 forward to the Civil War years, a committee of Congress oversaw this federal jurisdiction. Southern congressmen always composed a majority of the membership and the committee always included at least one member from both Maryland and Virginia. This congressional oversight, weighted toward the Southern perspective, meant that the initial political assumptions and the legal framework in which the District would operate included a decidedly pro-slavery bias (Tremain 1892, 26).

Five separate municipalities initially made up this new federal entity. The Lower District, the segment of the new jurisdiction situated below the Potomac River, included Alexandria Town as well as a rural section, then called Alexandria County. The Upper District encompassed the town of

Georgetown; the newly built town of Washington City, the location of the new government buildings, the Congress, and the President's Palace; and the remainder of the Maryland cession organized as the County of Washington. Each area operated courts and applied local ordinances; these somewhat differed in reach and in application. Maryland law and Virginia law did not agree on all facets, and the Congress decided that in each region the rules of the ceded areas would be based on Maryland or Virginia statutes and precedents, respectively. Thus, the laws regarding African Americans and slaves varied depending on the jurisdiction. Additionally, that part of Washington County located across the Eastern Branch (or Anacostia River), soon to called Anacostia, followed a somewhat separate trajectory. This territory was physically cut off from the remainder of the District by the waterway and retained the characteristics of the southern Maryland region from which it had been withdrawn. Here tobacco planting persisted long into the antebellum era together with the enslaved minions who cultivated the plant. Anacostia would maintain primarily this rural character up to the Civil War. Thus, the African Americans who ended up as residents of the new federal city lived in a world that differed by locality. That part of the District in which they resided determined how they could be treated, which laws applied, and, for the majority, how they would live their work-a-day lives (Powell 1928, 199).

THE LOWER DISTRICT

On February 7, 1801, Congress enacted legislation that extended federal control over the town and the county of Alexandria. At that time, this former part of Virginia housed roughly a quarter of the new District's total number of inhabitants and, likewise, a similar percentage of its African American residents, as the summary chart denotes. In the early years of the new century, slaves outnumbered free blacks approximately three to one; however, by the 1830s, expanded volumes of manumissions and emancipations, as well as the increased sales of slaves to the south, equalized the ratio between free blacks and enslaved African Americans. In addition, as the summary chart indicates, the population below the Potomac River of those Americans of African origin increased less rapidly than the populace in the municipalities withdrawn from Maryland. While the region north of the Potomac sprouted government buildings and housed nomadic congressmen, the former Virginia areas retained their predominantly agrarian character (Powell 1928, 230; Provine 1990, x).

Because congressional will dictated that Virginia law would prevail in the Lower District, a plethora of statutes, some dating from as far back as the 1660s, became the legal framework and the precedents for the court decisions in this jurisdiction. Congress made no attempt to interfere with slavery or to ease the burdens placed on free blacks. These Virginia statutes defined slavery as applying only to those of African descent and declared that baptism into Christianity conferred no alteration of legal status. More enlightened revolutionary era legislation proscribed slave importations from overseas and also allowed owners the legal right to emancipate their human chattel. In addition, a variety of "Treatment Acts," dating from 1748, fined slave owners for excessive cruelty and for failing to provide their bondsmen with sufficient quantities of food and clothes; however, other laws prevented any African American from testifying against any individual white and largely negated these rules. Additionally, this legal system assumed that any black without a pass, document, or identification was a runaway subject to arrest and to incarceration. Furthermore, any African American refusing arrest could be killed with no legal consequences for the executioner. If jailed, a black had to provide evidence of freedom or be vouched for by a white citizen. Otherwise, these individuals could be sold into slavery to cover jail expenses. For example, in 1827, the Lower District circuit court, meeting in Alexandria, sold into slavery five African Americans who could not produce white references. The application of these rules greatly aided the nefarious slavenappers operating in Delaware and along Maryland's Eastern Shore (see chapter on Delaware; Bryan 1914, 140).

A further insult to those who decried the evils of the peculiar institution flowed from the large slave auction jails operating in Alexandria. As plantation agriculture throughout Northern Virginia shifted from tobacco to general farming and growing grains, slaveholders increasingly sold excess bondsmen to traders and slave owners in the Gulf states of the Lower South to toil in the expanding cotton fields. Thousands of African Americans passed across the Alexandria auction block that handled the slave trade for all of Northern Virginia. Slave traders estimated that from one thousand to one thousand two hundred enslaved African Americans were sold in Alexandria in 1834 alone.

As the case with most Virginia towns, Alexandria included free blacks, hired-out slaves, as well as slaves who resided in their master's house or on their owner's property. Most African Americans living in Alexandria worked as domestics or tradesmen. In rural Alexandria County, the majority labored on the general agricultural chores typical of that part of Virginia. The proclivities of the slave owner, rather than the application of the law, determined the ease or the severity of bondage for these individual blacks.

Some slaveholders, such as George Washington Parke Custis, who owned and managed the picturesque estate Arlington, which overlooked the Potomac Basin opposite the new government center, were considered benign and paternalistic masters. Washington Custis, a grandson of Martha Washington and an heir of the first president, manumitted the Custis slaves upon his death in the late 1850s. His son-in-law, Robert E. Lee, the future

Confederate general, was engaged in this legal work of slave emancipation at the Civil War's advent, and federal troops quickly occupied the old plantation turning the grounds into Arlington Cemetery. On the other hand, other masters enforced paternal authority among their human chattel and compelled labor with the aid of the whipping lash.

From the 1830s onward, halting the slave trade within the District of Columbia became a hot-button issue for the growing number of abolitionist groups opposing the peculiar institution. Fearful that the U.S. Congress would bow to the antislavery pressure groups and enact legislation that barred slave auctions within the District boundaries, pro-slavery Virginia Senator Robert M.T. Hunter drew up and promoted legislation that would permit the Lower District to be retroceded to Virginia. Hunter hoped to preserve Alexandria's slave mart as a prime outlet for the sales of African Americans from Northern Virginia to the Lower South. Hunter's efforts bore legislative fruit in 1846, and Alexandria, town and county, returned to become again part of Virginia. African Americans living there would join their fellow black Virginians in the struggle for equal rights and liberties. Moreover, Hunter's prophecy proved correct when Congress enacted legislation known to history as the Compromise of 1850. Slave auction sales were henceforth proscribed in the District of Columbia. In Alexandria, however, the laments of soon-to-be-separated black families continued to greet its denizens and visitors for another decade.

WASHINGTON CITY

Free blacks and hired-out slaves played a major role in the new District's initial creation. When Congress appointed Andrew Ellicott of Maryland to survey the new federal district boundaries, he in turn hired Benjamin Banneker, his free black neighbor and well-known astronomer and mathematician, to do most of the actual surveying. According to Banneker's journal, he ate his meals with the local slave families and often resided with them while laying out the boundaries. He especially befriended George and Sophia Bell who had a slave cabin near the confluence of the Eastern Branch (Anacostia) and the Potomac River (Hutchinson 1977, 17–19; Banneker's Almanac 1795, see Maryland References).

After Banneker and Ellicott measured out the boundaries of the nascent District in 1795, Congress appropriated money to begin the erection of the new government center. Hired-out slaves comprised the majority of the workforce, supplying the labor that built the Capitol and the White House, as well as the nearby taverns and boarding houses that were haphazardly thrown up to offer lodging to the itinerant congressmen and the small staff of full-time government employees who soon descended on the new capital. Slaveholders from Virginia, Maryland, and the outlying parts of the District received seventy-five cents a day for the use of their enslaved laborers. Owners agreed to furnish their hired-out slaves with one complete suit of clothes and a blanket, while the U.S. government supplied one full meal a day. Thus, the citadel of democracy and freedom was built (Hutchinson 1977, 21).

Slave owners, in Northern Virginia, in Southern Maryland, and in Anacostia and in Washington County of the District of Columbia, who might otherwise have sold their redundant human chattel south, now found that hiring out slaves as laborers to the government, or as domestics to congressional families living on Capital Hill or in Georgetown, provided good sources of incomes. Slave coffles shuffling through the District became a familiar sight. Some of these hard-working minions were eventually able to accumulate enough cash to purchase their freedom.

A number of the hired-out slaves used their free time to grow vegetables or to fish. They also trapped and dug up oysters and crabs. These goods were then sold in Georgetown, Alexandria, and Washington City. Sophia Bell, who had hosted the surveyor Benjamin Banneker and his party, marketed enough produce from her small garden to secretly save more than four hundred dollars. She used the money to buy her husband's freedom. A few years later, after her husband had accumulated enough from his wages, he purchased Sophia's freedom as well. Eventually they were able to free additional family members through a disciplined effort of saving and purchase. All told, the greater Bell family liberated about two dozen family members over the antebellum era through purchasing. Additionally, after acquiring their freedom, Sophia and her husband, George, opened up, with the aid of two additional free blacks, the first school for African Americans in the District in 1807 (Hutchinson 1977, 33–37).

The free black population within the District continued to increase as others followed the road taken by Sophia Bell and her family. Furthermore, the laws of both Maryland and Virginia allowed the legal emancipation of slaves by owners, and as these became the basis for District legal precedents, the number of manumissions climbed. By the 1850s, as the opening summary chart denotes, the free black population outnumbered the enslaved African Americans within the District by a three to one margin (Tremain 1892, 54).

As with the case of African Americans living in Delaware and in Maryland, the majority in the District lived as free blacks but did not enjoy full equality under the law. Although the District legal system included laws proscribing the kidnapping and sale of free blacks, this practice persisted, similar to the episodes in nearby Maryland and Delaware, into the 1830s. In most of the District, free blacks had to carry passes or documents to avoid arbitrary arrest. For example, Gilbert Horton, a free black from New York who often worked transporting cargo by wagon, traveled to the District in 1826 on business. Local police officers did not recognize him and locked him up as a runaway because he had no documents of identification on his person. He spent the summer in the Washington, D.C. jail until word could be sent and received that verified his legal status. During the intervening weeks, Horton was offered for sale by the District government to cover jail expenses. Fortunately for Horton, proof of his freedom arrived before a sales transaction could be completed (Tremain 1892, 43).

Additionally, for much of the antebellum era, free blacks had to abide by a 10:00 P.M. curfew. Furthermore, they had to apply to the mayor of Washington City or Georgetown for special permits if they wished to convene a meeting or sponsor a party. A free black wishing to move to the District had to present papers to the mayor's office that he or she was indeed free and that he or she had a job or occupation; this individual also was required to produce a list of family members. In general, throughout the years prior to the Civil War, free black liberties were carefully circumscribed by the white community (Tremain 1892, 52–54).

In response to the Nat Turner insurrection in neighboring Virginia, Georgetown enacted ordinances in October 1831 that banned the distribution of abolitionist tracts to African Americans. Suspicions about the incitement of slaves and of free blacks to insurrection led to the two-day, three-night "Snow Riot" of 1835. Reuben Crandall, M.D., who had traveled from New York to lecture on medicine, was arrested and tried for having antislavery newspapers in his luggage. A crowd gathered around the Georgetown jail to hurl insults at Crandall and quickly turned into a mob. The unruly denizens then moved into Washington City proper to Snow's Restaurant, a free black establishment. They proceeded to wreck the restaurant, to break the windows of neighboring African American churches, and to torch the houses of a number of free blacks. Marines and soldiers had to be deployed to keep order. White leaders in Washington City and Georgetown attempted to shift the blame onto the free blacks who, they contended, were "about to be incited" (Bryan 1914, 144–146).

Any individuals who interfered with slavery were also subject to prosecution. In 1848 for a few months, Daniel Drayton, a Chesapeake Bay waterman, successfully spirited a number of the District's enslaved African Americans to freedom. He was found out later that year and arrested along with seventy-six slaves, men, women, and children. Drayton suffered four years of incarceration, and most of the slaves were declared fugitives, sold to a Baltimore slave trader, and subsequently carried south (Bryan 1914, 384–385).

As a result of the Snow Riot, even the circumscribed liberties of free blacks came under attack by white Washingtonians. Residents in Georgetown complained that free blacks set bad examples for hired-out slaves. Nevertheless, in spite of white opposition, small groups of free blacks aided by some hired-out slaves gradually began setting up churches, schools, and neighborhoods for African Americans. Small congregations, such as the Allen African Methodist Episcopal (A.M.E.) Church in

Anacostia, organized help for destitute blacks and attempted to support attempts at providing education (Hutchinson 1977, 46–47).

While attempts to offer education for free blacks remained in its infancy during the late antebellum years, primarily due to insufficient funding, Dr. Charles Henry Nichols, the director of St. Elizabeth's Hospital, the government-run mental facility in Anacostia, began accepting black patients in 1852. Blacks, however, were shut out from buying lots in the new working-class housing development of Uniontown in the 1850s. The real estate developers used racial covenants in their deeds to deny any black the chance to acquire a housing lot among the newly arising buildings (Hutchinson 1977, 53–59).

Not all whites in the District, however, supported these efforts. From 1835 to 1850, Washington became a center for white and black activists who supported abolition. The slave trade in the District offered the primary target. That a slave auction block existed within sight of the Capitol and that slaves were held in the local jail awaiting their turn in this human sales mart enraged most abolitionists as well as many congressmen and officials from the northern areas of the country who did not necessarily agree with the programs or the methods of the antislavery forces. As noted, Congress eventually passed legislation as part of the Compromise of 1850 that ended this nefarious business.

While the country tumbled toward schism and war during the last antebellum decade, the number of African Americans living in slavery in the District declined as well. Most blacks in Washington had been manumitted and lived as free blacks with circumscribed liberties, while most of the remaining slaves were hired out. They paid part of their wages to their owner, but most made their own domestic arrangements. Slaves made up only 4 percent of the District's population in 1860 and only 20 percent of the African American residents.

The largest remaining slaveholders lived in Anacostia, across the river. Here G.W. Young continued to grow tobacco on two farms using sixty-nine enslaved blacks and overseers. He valued his land and slaves at seventy-four thousand dollars for the census taker in 1860. By contrast, the average American in 1860 had a net worth of two thousand five hundred dollars. George W. Talbert valued his slaves at more than fifteen thousand dollars, and Mrs. Margaret Barber owned more than thirty slaves, most of whom she hired out. These remaining vestiges of the older plantation economy of southern Maryland were not typical in the District, however. By 1860, most slaveholders owned from one to four slaves, most often domestics, and few African Americans in the District labored on farm chores. The vast majority worked as household servants or as tradesmen (Hutchinson 1977, 61–66).

In Georgetown, relationships between the races remained tolerant but separate. African Americans worshipped with whites at St. John's

Episcopal Church but used a special entrance and sat in the balcony separated from the whites below. The village also included the oldest African American congregation in the District, Mt. Zion United Methodist Church. Moreover, in the later antebellum years, Georgetown free blacks operated a very successful safe house as part of the Underground Railroad that was used to hide escaped slaves who were traveling north to freedom (Lesko 1991, 6–7, 14).

THE CIVIL WAR AND EMANCIPATION

After the secession of eleven Southern slaveholding states, the formation of the Confederacy, and the advent of a shooting war, President Abraham Lincoln proposed legislation to emancipate the remaining slaves in the District. He hoped that compensated emancipation would offer the loyal border states an acceptable path to abolition. Legislators from the Upper South areas who still followed the federal government initially rebuffed the plan that the president offered to Congress in the summer of 1861. Segments of the District's white population also opposed immediate emancipation (Tremain 1892, 90–91).

The *National Intelligencer* noted that slavery "was doomed to gradual extinction in the District anyway, and few people would have regretted it. It is only the sudden emancipation that disturbs the people of the District of Columbia and alarms the border states." The Congress meeting in the spring of 1862, however, overrode the objections of border state representatives. In April, compensated emancipation for the District passed in both houses. President Lincoln signed the enactment on April 16, 1862 and declared: "I have never doubted the constitutional authority of Congress to abolish slavery in the District and I have ever desired to see the Capital freed from the institution." The District's growing black population responded immediately upon hearing the news. Church bells rang out. African Americans dropped to their knees in the streets in prayerful thanks: "deliverance" (Tremain 1892, 94; Hutchinson 1977, 70–71).

Congress set up an Emancipation Commission to oversee owner compensation: a Baltimore slave trader evaluated each slave individually according to age, health, gender, and skills and reached his monetary verdict. All told, the Commission expended $993,406 as recompense for 3,100 slaves. The previously noted large slaveholders from Anacostia received hefty payments. The commission paid Margaret Barber $9,351; George Talbert $5,234; and G.W. Young $17,772. Young began immediately to build individual houses for his former slaves and offered them the opportunity to continue growing tobacco for him as sharecroppers (Hutchinson 1977, 71).

The advent of hostilities and the Union army occupation of parts of Northern Virginia offered many African Americans the opportunity to flee the bonds of slavery. On the Virginia Peninsula outside Fort Monroe, Union General Ben Butler declared that escaped slaves from supporters of the Confederacy would not be liable to be returned to their owners and would be held as confiscated property and "contraband" of war. Thus, slaves could legitimately leave their owners and be succored by the federal government and the Union army. Moreover, the District quickly became a safe haven for many "contrabands" from nearby Virginia counties that were crossed by the warring armies (Lesko 1991, 16).

Former slaves began working for the Union army as camp servants and as laborers, digging the entrenchments surrounding the nation's capital. African American women became laundresses and cooks for garrison troops. When the numbers of destitute contrabands residing in the District continued to increase, Congress enacted legislation to provide aid and sustenance for the newcomers. In March 1862, the federal government created the Contraband Department to register liberated or escaped slaves and to provide rations. A few weeks later, the government set up the Freedmen's Relief Association, which provided clothing, housing, jobs, and began organizing schools for the newly liberated. The association estimated that by early 1863 more than ten thousand freedmen had escaped to the District (Lewis 1976, 58).

Beginning in 1863, African Americans could directly take a hand in their own liberation. July 1862 legislation allowed the president the discretion of using black troops in militia levies. Furthermore, the formal enactment of the Emancipation Proclamation in January 1863 sanctioned the mustering of African Americans into the federal army and navy. Colonel William Birney, a scion of a well-known antislavery family, began organizing two African American regiments drawn from the free blacks and contrabands now residing in Washington. Henry Turner, the pastor of Israel A.M.E. Church in the District, helped Birney form the first black regiment, the First United States Colored Troops (USCT), which served as a model for the additional 137 USCT regiments that followed. Turner became the regiment's chaplain (Berlin 1982, 5, 184, 626–627).

Many joined the USCT and others joined the Fifty-fourth and Fifty-fifth Massachusetts; some found their way into the navy. All told, the District received credit for 3,269 African Americans who fought in the war. A few, like Moses G. Lucas, experienced the conflict from the perspective of both armies. Lucas, from Louisa County, Virginia, began the hostilities by marching along with the Confederate army in Virginia as a personal body servant to a rebel officer. He later escaped, made his way to the District, worked as a laborer in the contraband camps, and then joined the Union army. The District's USCT regiments fought mainly in the campaigns outside Richmond and Petersburg in 1864 and 1865. They played major roles in the 1864 Battle of the Crater and the Battle of Fort Harrison (Hutchinson 1977, 70).

This photo of Company E, Fourth United States Colored Troops, was taken at Fort Lincoln, part of the wartime defenses of Washington, D.C. (Library of Congress.)

The poet Walt Whitman, who came to D.C. to work in the hospitals, commented: "I am where I can see a good deal of them. . . . There are getting to be many black troops. . . . There is a good regiment here, black . . . they go around, have regular uniforms—they submit to no nonsense. . . . Others are constantly forming" (Lewis 1976, 57).

The African Americans in the Union army struggled to receive their due. Henry Peterson, a first sergeant, wrote that blacks received less than whites of the same rank. He, as a noncommissioned officer, was paid the same as a white private. In addition, most of the men within his unit had not received their enlistment bonuses. Chaplain Turner wrote to higher authorities requesting supplies for reading materials and spelling books. His charges wanted to become literate but Turner had had little success getting anything to work with through the regular army channels (Berlin 1982, 374–375, 626–627).

Alexander T. Augusta posed a different problem. Augusta, a surgeon, a major, and an African American, ranked the white officers with whom he served. These physicians claimed that Augusta's rank "compromised white self respect." His rank "blocked the promotion of deserving white officers." They continued that their original enlistment had been marred since "the original understanding was that all officers in USCT regiments should be white." The War Department left Dr. Augusta on detached service in the

District's contraband camps away from the gripping white officers but also away from the USCT troops. Eventually the administration promoted him to lieutenant colonel despite the protests of the white doctors and sent him to the refugee camps on the coast of South Carolina. Augusta held the highest rank that any African American attained during the Civil War (Berlin 1982, 355–357).

After the surrender of Robert E. Lee's Army of Northern Virginia at Appomattox Court House on April 9, 1865 to General Ulysses S. Grant, the Confederacy collapsed. What rights and opportunities would accrue to the burgeoning black population of the District? A special census carried out in 1867 showed that the African American population of Georgetown had doubled during the rebellion and that the entire federal jurisdiction held more than thirty-eight thousand blacks, about 44 percent of all denizens (Lewis 1976, 58).

The white population in Washington demonstrated an almost unanimous opposition to black suffrage. A referendum among white District residents counted only thirty-six who favored extending the right to vote to African Americans; 7,303 opposed this measure. Nevertheless, Republicans in both houses of Congress pushed legislation through to authorize black suffrage in Washington. In December 1866, Congress overrode President Andrew Johnson's veto as well as the stated wishes of its white citizens and passed an African American suffrage bill. Henceforth, all African American males, twenty-one and older, who had lived in the District for a year and in their electoral precinct for three months, could vote in any election (Bryan 1914, 549–553).

The Freedmen's Bureau stepped in and helped African Americans with education, health care, housing, and jobs. One-armed General Oliver Otis Howard, a veteran of many of the war's bloodiest battles, including Gettysburg, became the commissioner of the Bureau of Refugees, Freedmen, and Abandoned Lands (Freedmen's Bureau) on May 20, 1865. He consistently worked to improve the opportunities for the former slaves residing in the District (Hutchinson 1977, 76).

After the Emancipation Act of 1862, the Washington City government opened a public school for African Americans. The District's schools, however, remained segregated and blacks could not attend the ongoing white facilities. Other benefactors opened private schools for blacks and donated land that could be used to site educational facilities as soon as funding could be arranged. The Freedmen's Bureau allocated ten thousand dollars to convert empty army barracks into learning centers for former slaves and operated these as private schools run by the bureau. In addition, they took over and operated the Good Hope School in Anacostia. General Howard, through the bureau auspices, arranged for an endowment of fifty-two thousand dollars that could be used to provide for an institution of higher education. Chartered in 1866, Howard University, named for the general, opened in 1867 as an all black college with an enrollment of fifty students (Lewis 1976, 60, 81; Hutchinson 1977, 76–77).

Additionally, General Howard and the Freedmen's Bureau provided health care for District African Americans. The Bureau absorbed the Campbell Hospital on Capitol Hill within its jurisdiction and offered medical care to all blacks in Washington. Since many white doctors did not regularly treat blacks as part of their practice, the ones who did were overwhelmed with the increased numbers of African Americans needing medical attention. The Freedmen Bureau's Campbell Hospital partially filled this void (Bryan 1914, 539).

General Howard also became involved with providing individual families the opportunities for home ownership. He bought a 375-acre farm from the Barry family in Anacostia. Howard then hired freedmen at $1.25 a day to cut down the trees, clear the lots, and grade the streets. He sold the lots with the cut lumber to blacks for less than three hundred dollars. Many workers hired to clear the land ended up buying and building homes there (Hutchinson 1977, 81–82).

THE GOLDEN AGE

The 1860s and 1870s were generally remembered as a "golden age" for black participation in local politics. The newly enfranchised blacks comprised 45 percent of the District's registered voters from 1867 to 1870. African American politicians ran for office and received patronage political appointments. In these years, as many as seven blacks sat on the Washington City Council during the same sessions. Others held elective office as aldermen or in the District's House of Delegates. For example, Soloman Brown of Anacostia, a clerk employed by the Smithsonian, defeated white candidates for a seat in the District house in the late 1860s (Bryan 1914, 559–562, 592–593; Hutchinson 1977, 97).

Moreover, the Council and the District house gradually abolished the antebellum laws that had circumscribed free black liberties. Legislation enacted in March 1865 prohibited racial discrimination on streetcars. In 1874, Frederick Douglass sponsored a bill, which the District house enacted, that made it unlawful for proprietors to practice racial discrimination in venues offering public accommodations. Black and white politicians attended the same social functions without engendering opprobrium or stigma (Hutchinson 1977, 95; Lesko 1991, 20).

The efforts by Republicans in Congress, the opening of Howard University, and the strivings of General Howard and the Freedmen's Bureau all created a rather positive climate for the further development of African American activities. During these postwar years, the District became the home and the center for many exertions and expositions of America's black intelligentsia.

The well-known African American antislavery activist Frederick Douglass made his home in the District from 1872 to 1895. He resided first at 316 A Street, NE, and later moved to Anacostia where he lived out the remaining eighteen years of his life. He and his sons helped edit the *New National Era*, a Washington newspaper devoted to the "defense and enlightenment of the newly emancipated and enfranchised people" (Hutchinson 1977, 99–108).

In Georgetown, Father Patrick F. Healy, S. J., became the president of Georgetown University and served from 1873 until 1882. Healy was the son of a free black woman and a white Georgia planter. He had been sent north to be educated and was ordained as a Jesuit priest in 1864. When Father Healy took over at Georgetown University, he became the first African American to serve as president of a predominantly white university in the United States. Moreover, his brother, James Healy, was selected to be the first African American Catholic bishop (Lesko 1991, 37–39).

The postwar golden age petered out as the 1870s closed. In 1874, the U.S. Congress adjusted the form of the District's government, which resulted in more appointed officials. This lessened the impact of the high percentage of African American voters in Washington's electorate. Additionally, while the first ten years after the war saw restrictive laws for blacks eased, as well as legal racial discrimination abolished, the following decade reversed the trend. In 1883, the Supreme Court ruled that private acts of discrimination against individuals did not violate the Thirteenth, Fourteenth, or Fifteenth Amendments. This opened the door allowing the rollback of antidiscrimination laws. By the late 1880s, Jim Crow rules had again become commonplace in District establishments (Lewis 1976, 70).

As African American gains in employment, education, political position, and public visibility declined, the District, by the turn of the century, lost its primacy within the black community as the center of cultural and political activities for Americans of African lineage. The final riposte occurred when the administration of Woodrow Wilson implemented and enforced a completely segregated workplace in the federal government and for the District as well. The golden age of the late 1860s was only a memory (Lewis 1976, 72).

REFERENCES

Berlin, Ira, Joseph P. Reidy, and Leslie S. Rowland, eds. 1982. *Freedom's Soldiers: The Black Military Experience in the Civil War*. New York: Cambridge University Press.

Bryan, W.B. 1914. *A History of the National Capital*. 2 vols. New York: Macmillan.

Hutchinson, Louise D. 1977. *The Anacostia Story, 1608–1930*. Washington, D.C.: Smithsonian Institute Press.

Lesko, Kathleen M., Valerie Babb, and Carroll R. Gibbs. 1991. *Black Georgetown Remembered: A History of Its Black Community from the Founding of "The Town of George" in 1751 to the Present Day.* Washington, D.C.: Georgetown University Press.

Lewis, David L. 1976. *The District of Columbia.* New York: W.W. Norton.

Logan, Rayford W. 1969. *Howard University: The First Hundred Years, 1867–1967.* New York: New York University Press.

Powell, Mary G. 1928. *The History of Old Alexandria, Virginia: From July 13, 1749 to May 24, 1861.* Richmond: William Byrd Press.

Provine, Dorothy S. 1990. *Alexandria County, Virginia: Free Negro Registers, 1799–1861.* Bowie, Md.: Heritage Books.

Tremain, Mary. 1892. *Slavery in the District of Columbia: The Policy of Congress and the Struggle for Abolition.* New York: Putnam's Sons. Repr., New York: Negro University Press, 1969.

WEB SITES

The African American Civil War Memorial: http://www.afroamcivilwar.org

The African American Mosaic: http://lcweb.loc.gov/exhibits/African/intro

The Frederick Douglass National Historic Site: http://www.nps.gov/frdo/freddoug.html

The Underground Railroad: http://www.nps.gov/undergroundrr

Florida

TIMELINE

1526: Spanish explorers bring enslaved Africans to Florida

1565–1763: First period of Spanish colonial administration

1704: Spain opens Florida territory to fugitive slaves from the English colonies

1763–1784: Great Britain controls Florida territory

1784–1821: Second period of Spanish colonial administration

1821: Adams-Oniś Treaty is signed; Florida becomes a U.S. territory

1822: Territorial assembly enacts black codes that define and regulate slavery

1827: Free blacks are forbidden entry into the Florida territory

1832: Miscegenation is outlawed in the Florida territory

1842: Free blacks are required to have guardians and to register with authorities

1845, March 3: Florida enters the Union as a slave state

1861, January 10: Florida secedes from the Union and joins the Confederacy

1865, May: The Civil War and slavery end

1868, June 25: Florida is readmitted to the Union

Slave and Free Black Population

Census Year	Slave Population	Population Percentage	Free Black Population	Population Percentage
1830	34,730	45	844	2
1840	54,477	47	817	1.5
1850	87,445	45	932	1
1860	140,424	44	932	under 1

Net Slave Entries and Exits, by Decade
(Tadman 1989, 12)

1810–1819: + 1,000	1840–1849: + 5,657
1820–1829: + 2,627	1850–1859: + 11,850
1830–1839: + 5,833	

ORIGINS OF SLAVERY

Under Spanish control, the first enslaved Africans arrived in Florida in 1526 with the Lucas Vazquez de Ayllon expedition. Few slaves would make it to the region, however, until the seventeenth century when bondsmen began to arrive from Barbados, which was becoming overpopulated and overworked. Those that did arrive during the first period of Spanish control, 1565 to 1763, did so from a variety of regions in Africa, including the Congo, Mandinga, and Carabaldi nations. During Great Britain's brief control of the area from 1763 to 1784, thousands of slaves were sold to English planters for rice and indigo plantations. These slaves also arrived from a variety of regions including the Windward, Gold, and Guinea coasts of West Africa. Spain would again take control of the Florida region and rule the area from 1784 to 1821, reassuring the continual flow of slaves into the territory. Although the United States outlawed the slave trade in 1803, Spanish Florida continued to import slaves from Africa and from Cuba. Many bondsmen also came with their masters from Georgia and the Carolinas (Landers 1999, 157–160).

Between the 1830s and 1860s, the growth and expansion of slavery in Florida was similar to that of Texas. By the time Florida entered the Union in 1845, slavery was firmly cemented as part of the social, political, and economic foundation of society. While the number of slaves counted in the census was far less by comparison, only 39,310 slaves by 1850, the rapid rise and marked percentage of increase in slavery during the antebellum era was comparable to that of other Southern slave states. It was in middle Florida, that area closest to and bordering on Georgia, where the peculiar institution became a stronghold. In 1830, 60 percent of the slaves in Florida resided in a five county area, and by 1860, 70 percent of the slaves in the state lived in the middle region. The majority of slave owners in the middle region, however, owned fewer than ten slaves (Rivers 2000, 17–18).

ECONOMICS OF SLAVERY

The rise of the peculiar institution in Florida, as elsewhere, was due to the perceived economic necessity and the actual profitability of slave labor. Slaves were an expensive commodity affordable only for the economically stable and wealthy elite. Slaves were sold at open markets, with the human chattel going to the highest bidder. Edward Lycurgas, an ex-slave, recalled his experience at a slave auction where "They'd bring a slave out on the platform and open his mouth, pound his chest, make him harden his muscles so the buyer could see what he was getting. Young men was called 'bucks' and young women 'wenches.' The person that offered the best price was de buyer" (Rawick 1972, 17:206).

Not only did slavery prove profitable as a measure of wealth, with bondsmen often worth thousands of dollars, but also the institution provided profit for owners from the product of slave labor. Slave owners in Florida, especially on the larger plantations in the central region, experimented with sugar cane, tobacco, cotton, and other crops. In the end, King Cotton ruled the region and defined the economic output of the region. This was especially true of the larger plantations. The smaller farms in the central region also primarily concentrated on cotton. Nevertheless, they also had a more diversified output, growing potatoes, corn, watermelons, peas, and other vegetables.

On the smaller farms in east Florida, landowners produced cotton, sugar, indigo, rice, and various other crops with the help of slave labor. In west Florida, more industrial pursuits defined the economy, and owners profited from skilled slave laborers who worked at lumbering and brickmaking, served in the textile industry, and worked on federal construction projects.

Hiring slaves out, a third avenue of profitability, was a common practice among Florida slave owners. This was true not only among central Florida slaveholders, but also appeared prominent in the western counties where necessity of skilled labor dominated the economic environment. Although the legislature passed laws against the practice in 1822, 1824, 1831, 1855, and 1856, owners continued to hire out their bondsmen as an additional source of income and profit. A set arrangement for hiring out did not exist but rather was determined by the two parties. The common practice in Florida appears to be that owners hired out their slaves per task or by the month; some even leased slaves for an entire year. Those who hired slaves could expect to pay the owner twelve to fifteen dollars per month at the high end of the scale or, typically, they rented servants for one hundred dollars per year. By the 1850s, with the growth of the railroad, slave owners could expect a higher margin of profit by hiring their slaves out to railroad companies. Railroad companies offered to pay up to two hundred dollars per year per hand. In addition, they would feed, clothe, shelter, and provide medical care for the slaves (Rivers 2000, 31–32, 36, 83).

SLAVE LIFE

During the Spanish colonial period, landowners generally adopted the task system, as slavery characterized a paternalistic nature. As the number of slaves and the size of farms and plantations grew during the territorial and antebellum era, owners adopted the gang system, the task system, or a combination of both.

In east and west Florida, the task system was generally preferred due to the diversity of crop production. Since there were fewer slaves and more diversity of crop production and work, some historians believe that the slave's work life was harsher than that of the larger plantations in central Florida. Slaves woke well before sunrise to the blowing of a bugle or horn, generally ate a small breakfast, and spent the entire day in the fields, stopping only for a short lunch period and returning to their cabins for dinner. Gender in many cases did not determine a slave's duties; men and women worked the fields. Only on the largest plantations did a gender-based division of labor appear with women working as cooks, laundresses, seamstresses, household servants, midwives, and herb doctors. More often than not, women were expected to do the same tasks as men. Winston Davis, an ex-slave, remembered that "There was no difference in the treatment of men and women for work; my parents worked very hard and women did some jobs that we would think them crazy for trying now; why my mother helped build a railroad before she was married to my father." Children too did not escape the toil of the plantation. At a young age, children often were assigned specific tasks, such as hauling firewood, tending livestock, and running general errands. In addition, children were often trained and apprenticed for specific duties, ranging from the general field hand to carpenters and blacksmiths (Rivers 2000, 73; Rawick 1972, 17:86–87).

Slave work was a daily, exhausting grind, and bondsmen were afforded rest only on the weekends. Generous masters might allow their servants to stop work at noon on Saturday, giving slaves the opportunity to engage in their own activities for the rest of the day. Sunday, though, was commonly a day off for all slaves unless harvest season required extra labor. Many masters, however, woke their slaves early on the Sabbath and forced them to attend church, adding to the slaves' resentment of their masters. With their time off, though, slaves did have the opportunity to tend their own plots and care for their own small livestock. As a result, on the plantations in middle Florida, the small amount of personal autonomy resulted in a thriving internal economy. Slaves often were allowed to sell their goods at open market or contract out with their owners for the sale of their produce. Slaves might also hire themselves out. Although the law forbade this, many owners overlooked the practice. Furthermore, the work environment for urban slaves, especially in the eastern and western sections, also offered them a degree of autonomy over their work environment and lives, as they generally were hired out according to specific tasks. Nevertheless, if a slave refused to work or be hired out, he or she was summarily whipped (Rivers 2000, 29–31).

Although Florida developed a more relaxed attitude toward miscegenation (racial mixing) and provided slaves with a higher degree of autonomy, harsh punishment was still used to keep bondsmen in line. Owners used a variety of methods to punish their slaves, including cropping their ears, branding them, and tying them up by their thumbs with their feet barely touching the ground to paddle or whip them. In comparison to other slave states, though, it appears that the institution of slavery as a whole was not as harsh in terms of treatment and punishment. As elsewhere, however, such cases depended on the character of the owner, the slave's willingness to submit to forced labor, and the general work environment. Ex-slave Mama Duck remembered that not all slaves were treated poorly or whipped. Nevertheless, she recalled, "But dey be some niggahs he whip good an' hard. If dey sass back, er try t' run away, he mek 'em cross dey han's lak dis; den he pull 'em up, do dey toes jes' tetch de ground'; den he smack 'em crost de back an' rump wid a big wood paddle, fixed full o' holes. Know what dem holes for? Ev'y hole mek a blister. Den he mek 'em lay down on de groun', whilst he bus' all dem blisters wid a rawhide whip" (Rawick 1972, 17:118).

As elsewhere, the slave family provided bondsmen with a sense of belonging, a measure of hope and peace, an avenue to transmit their culture, and an escape from the confines of the peculiar institution. It is impossible to know exactly how many slaves actually married, but evidence suggests that slave families, both from the same plantations and cross-plantations were quite numerous. Oftentimes, masters encouraged slave unions. Owners understood the importance of the family unit for the slave and allowing them the opportunity to create families lent to a more controllable labor force. For owners, more importantly, the economic factor weighed on their decision to allow slave marriages, understanding that the union would produce offspring, a profit for the owner. Some owners even went so far as to force slave unions for breeding purposes. Louisa Everett, an ex-slave, remembered that "Marsa Jim called me and Sam ter him and ordered Sam to pull off his shirt—that was all the McClain niggers wore—and he said to me: Nor, 'do you think you can stand this big nigger?' He had that old bull whip flung acrost his shoulder, and Lawd, that man could hit so hard! So I jes said 'yassur, I guess so,' and tried to hide my face so I wouldn't see Sam's nakedness, but he made me look at him anyhow. Well, he told us what we must git busy and do in his presence, and we had to do it. After that we were considered man and wife. Me and Sam was a healthy pair and had fine, big babies, so I never had another man forced on me, thank God. Sam was kind to me and I learnt to love him." Regardless of the owner's intentions, marriage was an integral part of slave life taken seriously by the bondsmen. As elsewhere, couples who joined together often wished to express their union publicly by performing the broom-jumping ceremony. In other cases, couples chose the traditional Christian ceremony and were wed by either a white or a black minister. Evidence suggests that slaves who married did so at a very young age, generally by the time of fourteen or fifteen, and produced a child by the age of sixteen. The fact that Louisa and Sam were still together, at the ages of ninety and eighty-six, respectively, when interviewed in 1936, is testimony to the sacredness that many bondsmen held of their union regardless of the age or circumstances in which they were joined (Rawick 1972, 17:128; Rivers 2000, 93).

Despite the significance of slave marriages to the slaves themselves or the owners, families often were torn apart. In some cases, the master had no choice; he had to sell a slave to pay off debts. Cruel masters often separated families simply for the financial gain. Furthermore, it was often the custom for owners to give bondsmen to their children as gifts, especially in cases of marriage. Finally, many slave families were torn apart upon their master's death, sold apart to settle estate costs or as a part of the property-dividing process. If not torn apart, slave families were also subject to the whims of the master and his sexual intrusions. Male slaves could do little to stop this. Furthermore, family members often stood by helpless as they watched the lash being taken to a family member. While the family might have been assaulted in such a manner, such cruelty might also account for the strengthening of the kinship networks as the family provided love, care, and a sense of belonging against the harshness of forced bondage.

Religion too played a vital role in the lives of slaves. The Baptist, Methodist, Presbyterian, and Catholic denominations all attempted to bring Christianity to the slaves, and some churches even allowed bondsmen to worship in the same church. Their motive though was not the care of the soul but an attempt to create a docile labor force by teaching the slaves that God required obedience to their masters. Ex-slave Clayborn Cantling recalled that "Before freedom we always went to white churches on Sundays with passes but they never mentioned God; they always told us to be 'good niggers and mind our missus and masters.'" Some masters even allowed slaves to build their own churches and allowed black preachers, supervised by whites, to preach the gospel. What actually was preached and what was heard and internalized by the slaves were often two very different things. The slaves came to believe they were just as important in God's eyes as their owners were. Some even believed they were superior, for they were not hypocrites like their masters. Either way, Christianity reassured slaves of their humanity (Rawick 1972, 17:141).

More importantly for the slaves, they were able to take from Christianity what they wished and blend it with their own African rituals to create a vibrant faith that gave meaning to their lives. Often, slaves would wander into the woods at night and hold their own secret religious meetings with prayers, singing, drum playing, and dancing. Whether within the confines of the church and white Christianity or in the wood with their unique brand of worship, religion afforded slaves an outlet from their daily existence and in that they secured their bond between their God, family members, and the community (Rivers 2000, 106–111).

Despite whatever outlet religion might have afforded slaves, many bondsmen did seek to escape the confines of the peculiar institution by fleeing. The most important reason a slave chose to flee, though risking a severe beating, was to be near family and kin who often were torn apart during slave sales. Often, slaves simply sought to rebel against unjust masters or the system in general. Ambrose Douglass, an ex-slave, recalled, "I was a young man and didn't see why I should be anybody's slave. I'd run away every chance I get. Sometimes they near killed me, but mostly they just sold me. I guess I was pretty husky, at that. They never did get their money's worth out of me, though. I worked as long as they stood over me, then I ran around with the gals or sneaked off to the woods. Sometimes they used to put dogs on me to get me back" (Brown 1995, 297; Rawick 1972, 17:101–102).

Short of flight, slaves often rebelled against their masters on a daily basis in small and sometime unnoticeable ways, such as slowing down the pace of work or doing their tasks poorly. While these actions might have earned slaves a whipping, it was their way of signaling to the master their unhappiness with their present condition or a specific circumstance. A less detectable way to rebel was through feigning illness or injury. Such minor forms of resistance were normally a protest to overwork, inadequate diet, or restrictions from seeing loved ones. Only when such methods failed to yield the desired results did slaves turn to more violent acts of rebellion. Usually, more violent acts, which resulted in the harming of an overseer or owner, were a result of prolonged abuse. John Henry Kemp, an ex-slave, remembered one incident: "One day when an old woman was plowing in the field, an overseer came by and reprimanded her for being so slow— she gave him some backtalk, he took out a long closely woven whip and lashed her severely. The woman became sore and took her hoe and chopped him right across the head, and child you should have seen how she chopped this man to a bloody death" (Rivers 2000, 210–218; Rawick 1972, 17:185).

FREE BLACKS

Free and enslaved blacks had a long history of armed conflict in Florida. In 1683, for example, black Floridians formed a militia company to aid Spanish authorities in their struggle against European powers. In return, blacks received certain liberties including the continued right of miscegenation and the promise of freedom for runaways from the English colonies upon their conversion to Catholicism. Conversion to Catholicism was a prerequisite for freedom in Florida, a small price for runaway enslaved Africans. In 1704, the Spanish governor opened the territory to fugitive slaves, and Florida proved a haven for bondsmen fleeing from Georgia and the Carolina regions throughout the seventeenth and eighteenth centuries. Fugitive slaves established Cracia Real de Santa Teresa de Mose, the first free black settlement in North America. Many free blacks also congregated in southern Florida where the plantation economy had not taken hold. Instead, that region of the state was continually embroiled in Indian conflicts and thus many free blacks found an opportunity to prosper in Key West. There they worked as semiskilled laborers and were able to economically advance to a degree (Rivers 2000, 4–5; Landers 1999, 29–30; Garvin 1967, 1; Solomon and Erhart 1999, 322–323).

Although the census indicates that no more than 932 free blacks ever resided in Florida, that number is far from correct. Many blacks and fugitive slaves fled and joined Indian communities. While some Indians did own slaves, the vast majority of blacks lived among or simply nearby the Indian tribes. The two groups formed an amenable relationship. They worked together, intermarried, and fought together. Blacks served as allies to the Indians and played a significant role in the Seminole wars. Census takers, however, ignored these blacks, and, thus, the real number of free blacks living in Florida is unknown (Garvin 1967, 7).

BLACK CODES

Under the first period of Spanish control, the black population was quite small and therefore authorities did not institute severe slave codes. In 1821, the U.S. Senate ratified the Adams-Onís treaty that relinquished Florida to the United States. Although the treaty guaranteed free blacks the right to United States citizenship, the Jackson administration flagrantly ignored this. Instead, black codes quickly emerged to define the institution of slavery and the relationship between the races.

The Black Codes that emerged in 1822 established the death penalty for seven specific offenses. Any slave found guilty of arson, burglary, manslaughter, poisoning, murder, rebellion, or rape was sentenced to death. Furthermore, due to the number of free blacks already residing in Florida, and in an effort to maintain control over the institution of slavery, officials in 1827 ruled that free blacks could no longer enter the territory. This law was amended in 1832 to allow for the enslaving for ninety-nine years of any free black that entered the territory. The 1832 law was repealed, though, and officials realized that anti-immigration legislation could not successfully keep free blacks from moving into Florida (Garvin 1967, 11).

As the institution of slavery matured in Florida, and whites grew wary of an ever-increasing black population, free and slave, authorities sought to exert a tighter grip on white superiority by banning manumissions and the long-standing practice of miscegenation in 1832. Furthermore, it was illegal for a white person to be found at an illegal meeting of blacks. Those who were caught faced the possibility of themselves being whipped (Brown 1995, 301).

As the threat to slavery increased throughout the South, officials passed further legislation to control free and enslaved blacks, but due more to the fear of slave uprisings. In 1831, it became illegal for blacks, free or slave, to own or have a firearm unless under the supervision of whites. Due to the increasing fear of a free black population and its relationship with the Indian tribes in Florida, even more restrictions were placed upon free blacks in the late antebellum period. Legislation was handed down in 1842, 1848, and 1856 requiring all free blacks to have an authorized white guardian and register with authorities. The 1856 law imposed a fine of ten dollars for those who violated the law. Finally, in 1859, in an attempt to keep poor free blacks from being wards of the state and to further tighten the control over the black population, politicians declared that free black persons over the age of fourteen could choose their own master and enter slavery (Garvin 1967, 13–14, 16–17).

THE CIVIL WAR

Though Florida and Texas might have had many similarities regarding the rise of the peculiar institution, when it came to the Civil War, the situation was quite different. Florida fell easy and quickly to Union control as a result of its blockaded coast and land invasion. Many owners attempted to move their slave property inland, and the chaos of the conflict allowed many slaves to flee and simply free themselves from the shackles of bondage.

Slaves also found service in the Confederate army, generally conscripted into service to perform manual labor, such as digging ditches, building fortifications, and hauling wood, food, and ammunition. As elsewhere,

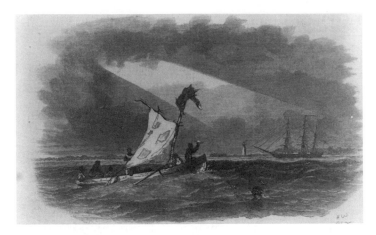

Slaves who ran away or otherwise came into the possession
of the Union army were known as "contrabands" because
they were considered property seized from the enemy.
Reaching Union lines thus became a way for slaves to obtain their freedom. In this drawing, escaped slaves off the
coast of Florida use a raft to reach the U.S. bark *Kingfisher*.
(Library of Congress.)

many owners fought against the impressment of their slave property for
fear of lost profits due to injury or death of their bondsmen.

During the Civil War, many free and enslaved blacks sought refuge behind Union lines. The first Confiscation Act, passed on August 6, 1861,
authorized Union seizure of rebel property, and it stated that all slaves who
fought with or worked for the Confederate military services were freed of
further obligations to their masters. During the beginning stages of war,
the Union even paid blacks for their labor. Many blacks also took up arms
to aid the Union cause, playing a significant role in raiding and defeating
Confederate forces, especially in southern Florida (Solomon and Erhart
1999, 324, 336–339).

The second Confiscation Act passed in 1862, which allowed Union forces
to free slaves and impress them into service, drastically altered the situation for many blacks. Union raiding parties made their way into the interior of Florida and seized wagons, livestock, food, and slaves. The newly
freed slaves, however, often found their immediate condition under Union
control far worse that what it was under slavery. More often than not, there
existed inadequate shelter, clothing, and food. Those bondsmen who did
fare well were those who served the Union cause in some capacity, such
as spies, guides, and river pilots. Other bondsmen were forced to work and,
depending on the character of the Union officer in charge, might find them-

selves under the lash once again. Those who actually served in a fighting capacity ran a dual risk of danger, by being killed in action or possibly captured by Confederate authorities, which would result in sure torture and death for the black Union soldier. In short, there is no general way to characterize the role and experience of slaves and free blacks in Florida during the Civil War crisis. Blacks took advantage of the crisis to free themselves, and they contributed in a significant manner to both sides in the sectional conflict.

RECONSTRUCTION

With the end of the Civil War and the emancipation of slaves from the chains of forced labor, many ex-slaves rejoiced over their new freedom. Harriett Gresham remembers that the slaves where she lived began to rejoice and sing spirituals. The one she remembered them singing went as follows:

> T'ank ye Marster Jesus, t'ank ye,
> T'ank ye Marster Jesus, t'ank ye,
> T'ank ye Marster Jesus, t'ank ye
> De Heben gwinter be my home.
> No slav'ry chains to tie me down,
> And no mo' driver's ho'n to blow fer me
> No mo' stocks to fasten me down
> Jesus break slav'ry chain, Lord
> Break slav'ry chain Lord,
> Break slav'ry chain Lord,
> De Heben gwinter be my home.
> (Rawick 1972, 17:160–161)

When freedom came to the slaves, though, many had no idea what to do. Some freedmen stayed on the farm or plantation where they had worked. As elsewhere, many freedmen set off to the more urban areas of the state to find employment and join other free blacks. In the urban environment, however, blacks found that carpetbaggers took most jobs, and many African Americans had no skills to work in the urban environment. In addition, those free blacks who had their own businesses prior to Reconstruction were not in the financial position to hire additional labor and help newly freed blacks. Still others went in search of family members sold during bondage.

As elsewhere, Florida was forced to deal with radical changes that took place as a result of the conflict, and the Civil War decimated the cotton economy in Florida. Nevertheless, planters continued to turn their attention to cotton growing. In its attempt to aid freedmen in their economic plight, the Freedmen's Bureau appeared somewhat more successful in

Florida than in other states, issuing more than three thousand homesteads to freedmen. Nevertheless, on the whole, the plan for land distribution was not widely successful due to white opposition, and freedmen were forced into tenant farming and sharecropping. The lack of capital and an end to slavery, though, placed the relationship between black laborer and white landowner in a precarious position. Many landowners employed the labor of new freedmen. Often they were given contracts and worked for a share of the crop or for low wages. Nevertheless, the former landowners continued to work black laborers in the same manner as during slavery, employing the gang system of labor, complete with whippings. Although the freedmen were theoretically in a better bargaining position, their need for work often left them at the mercy of landowners. Likewise, the need for labor might have forced landowners to bend to the demands of the black laborers. There is no easy way to characterize the postwar work environment for blacks. In some cases, freedmen fared better, and in other cases, they fared worse than during slavery. Mama Duck, an ex-slave, recalled, "I reckon I a heap bettah off dem days as I is now. Allus had sumpin t' eat an' a place t' stay. No sech thing ez gittin' on a black list dem days. Mighty hard on a pusson ol' az me not t' git no rashuns an' not have no reg'lar job" (Ouzts 1996, 3–4; Rawick 1972, 17:119).

REFERENCES

Brown, Cantor, Jr. 1995. "Race Relations in Territorial Florida, 1821–1845." *Florida Historical Quarterly* 73 (January): 287–307.

Garvin, Russell. 1967. "The Free Negro in Florida Before the Civil War." *Florida Historical Quarterly* 46 (July): 1–18.

Landers, Jane. 1999. *Black Society in Spanish Florida*. Chicago: University of Illinois Press.

Ouzts, Clay. 1996. "Landlords and Tenants: Sharecropping and the Cotton Culture in Leon County, Florida, 1865–1885." *Florida Historical Quarterly* 75 (Summer): 1–23.

Rawick, George P., ed. 1972. *The American Slave: A Composite Autobiography*. Westport, Conn.: Greenwood Publishing Company.

Riordan, Patrick. 1996. "Finding Freedom in Florida: Native Peoples, African Americans, and Colonists, 1670–1816." *Florida Historical Quarterly* 75 (Summer): 24–43.

Rivers, Larry Eugene. 2000. *Slavery in Florida: Territorial Days to Emancipation*. Gainesville: University Press of Florida.

Solomon, Irvin D., and Grace Erhart. 1999. "Race and Civil War in South Florida." *Florida Historical Quarterly* 77 (Winter): 320–341.

WEB SITES

Florida 1821–1845: http://www.floridahistory.org/floridians/territo.htm

Florida 1845–1865: http://fcit.usf.edu/florida/websites/links004.htm#slavery

Harper's Weekly Reports: http://blackhistory.harpweek.com/3CivilWar/
    CivilWarLevelOne.htm
Slavery and West Florida: http://www.geocities.com/Heartland/Bluffs/3010/
    slavery.htm
Slavery Timeline: http://www.africanaonline.com/slavery_timeline.htm

Georgia

TIMELINE

1732: Georgia is established as a royal colony by King George II of England

1733: First settlers arrive in Georgia

1750: Slavery emerges in the region

1755: First official black codes are established in Georgia

1770: Black codes establish a $25 fine for teaching slaves to read

1773: Georgia's slave population is estimated at 15,000

1788, January 2: Georgia enters the Union

1829: Fine for teaching slaves to read is increased to $500

1850: Georgia House of Representatives votes to repeal the 1829 law regarding the teaching of slaves, but the measure fails in the state Senate

1852: Georgia legislature increases the penalty for racial mixing

1858: 409 slaves from Africa arrive in Georgia

1861, January 19: Georgia secedes from the Union and joins the Confederacy

1862: Union forces seize control of coastal Georgia

1863: Blacks are permitted to enlist in the Union army

1865: Congress establishes the Bureau of Refugees, Freedmen, and Abandoned Lands

1870, July 15: Georgia is readmitted to the Union; Georgia begins tax supported school system for freedmen

Slave and Free Black Population

Census Year	Slave Population	Population Percentage	Free Black Population	Population Percentage
1790	29,264	35	398	under 1
1800	59,406	37	1,019	under 1
1810	105,218	42	1,801	under 1
1820	149,656	44	1,763	under 1
1830	217,531	42	2,468	under 1
1840	280,944	41	2,753	under 1
1850	381,682	42	2,931	under 1
1860	452,198	43	3,500	under 1

**Net Slave Entries and Exits, by Decade
(Tadman 1989, 12)**

1790–1799: + 6,095	1830–1839: + 10,403
1800–1809: + 11,231	1840–1849: + 19,873
1810–1819: + 10,731	1850–1859: – 7,876
1820–1829: + 18,324	

ORIGINS OF SLAVERY

General James Oglethorpe and several fellow Englishmen obtained a royal charter for the colony in 1732, and in 1733 the first Europeans settled in the region. Originally, the proprietary colony was intended as a utopian settlement of small farmers, each owning no more than five hundred acres of land. Slavery was initially outlawed because the region served as a buffer zone against the Spanish in Florida and because of the fear that slavery would cause whites to become lazy. The perceived necessity of slavery for economic survival, however, soon outweighed all concerns and, beginning in 1750, the peculiar institution began to take hold in the colony. By 1773, the slave population in Georgia had risen to fifteen thousand. While some slaves arrived from the West Indies, most were taken directly from Africa to either Savannah or to Sunbury and sold at auctions. Those slaves fresh off the boats, though, sold for less than slaves actually born in Georgia or on the American mainland. Planters and slave owners had determined through experience that domestic-born slaves were easier to assimilate into forced bondage and caused fewer disturbances. Human chattel brought directly from Africa often had to go through a "breaking-in" period to learn work discipline and the proper subservient behavior.

The increase in the number of bondsmen not only resulted from natural increase, but also from slave smuggling. Although the slave trade officially ended in 1808, slave trafficking continued, and an estimated fifty thousand slaves entered the Southern states after 1808. In one case in 1858, smugglers imported 409 slaves to Georgia from the Congo and Angola regions of Africa. The dramatic increase in the slave population each decade speaks to the significance that Georgians placed on the institution for economic growth and security. Moreover, it is estimated that slave owners transported approximately fifty thousand bonded African Americans from other slaveholding jurisdictions to Georgia during the antebellum era (1820 to 1860). Slavery stood at the center of Georgia's prosperous economy (Otto 1984, 82; Tadman 1989, 12).

ECONOMICS OF SLAVERY

In Georgia, as elsewhere in the deep South, slavery proved a profitable venture and it provided a level of security from the uncertainty of the market economy. Slaveholding became a way to measure an individual's wealth or net worth. Research in Georgia indicates that 60 percent of whites who owned only one slave owned a female under the age of forty-five. They did so for the potential of childbearing, which would increase their wealth and eventual labor supply with little out-of-pocket cost. Whether used for labor or not, society deemed slaves as property, often worth thousands of dollars. Increased slaveholding meant, in simple terms, more wealth for an owner. In down times, slaves could be used to liquidate debts as well as to gain credit.

From an income standpoint, though, slavery as an economic system proved most profitable from the sale of agricultural products grown through the use of forced labor. Georgians used their bonded workforce primarily to grow cotton. Originally, masters used the task system to organize and manage their enslaved workers. Gradually, however, they moved to a combination of the task system and gang labor and by the 1840s they wholly adopted the gang labor approach as a means to control their labor force and to ensure a good level of productivity. With a controlled labor force, cotton would emerge as the key to a Georgian's success. In 1801, the state produced an estimated twenty thousand bales of cotton. This increased to 326,000 bales by 1840. Without slave labor, however, this dramatic increase would not have occurred. In Houston County, for example, between 1850 and 1860, the number of slaves increased by 8 percent and the improved farm acreage increased by 27 percent. Cotton production, though, increased an amazing 49 percent. The increase in the number of slaves, the move toward gang labor, and the reliance upon overseers to manage a labor force that was increasingly becoming concentrated in the hands of the few account for this increase. Without slave labor, Georgians would not have achieved the same level of profitability from cotton production during the antebellum era.

Many slave owners also earned several hundred dollars a year from hiring out their bondsmen. Sometimes owners made private arrangements between themselves. Other times, slaves were hired out during auctions conducted in the winter, usually in January or December, with contracts for the entire calendar year (Reidy 1992, 84; Rawick 1972, 13:3:104).

SLAVE LIFE

During the eighteenth century, masters used slave labor to harvest rice along the Georgia coastal region. For bondsmen, this meant spending upward of sixteen hours each day in knee-deep water. In the nineteenth century, though, most owners devoted their attention to "King Cotton" or "White Gold." Cotton production was a yearlong process. In many areas of Georgia, especially in the tidewater region, the task system of labor generally prevailed as a means to maximize production and its eventual profits. This meant that slaves toiled for several hours to finish their assigned tasks in the fields. On some farms and plantations, once bondsmen completed their task, they were free to spend the rest of the day as they pleased. As the system of gang labor became more predominant, slaves were forced to work from before sunrise to sundown, witnessing the disappearance of what little free time they might have enjoyed. It was not uncommon, especially during harvest season, for field hands to labor fourteen to sixteen hours each day. If slaves became sick and could not work, owners generally gave them salts or castor oil. If they refused, they received the lash. More serious cases were handled by the doctor (Otto 1984, 34–35; Rawick 1972, 13:3:73).

As the commercial economy in Georgia expanded, leading to the rise of towns, slavery emerged in the urban areas. Urban slaves worked as domestic servants, carpenters, masons, and construction laborers and hauled cotton around town and served to maintain the streets. As noted in the opening summary, free blacks never comprised a major category of Georgia's population (Reidy 1992, 73).

Despite the harshness of the labor system, some slaves did maintain a level of control over their work environment and life. Except during harvest season, many masters did not force their servants to work on the Sabbath. This enabled some slaves, owners permitting, to hire themselves out, often earning from fifty cents to one dollar and fifty cents per day. During the harvest season, when the need for labor increased, slaves could often hire themselves out for more than this amount. Though these wages were paltry, it allowed them to purchase necessities, such as salt, sugar, coffee, tobacco, and blankets. On the larger plantations, this also allowed the slaves to establish a trade network where they bartered and exchanged goods among themselves. Thus, the practice of hiring themselves out along with the ability to purchase and barter goods did give slaves some measure of control over their work environment and life. Of course, there existed numerous instances when slaves rebelled against their work environment. This generally led to punishment, and, here, the lash held no respect for gender. Nancy Boudry, an ex-slave, recalled, "I had to work hard, plow and go and spit wood jus' like a man. Sometimes dey whup me. Dey whup me bad, pull de close off down to de wais'— my master did it, our folks didn' have overseer" (Reidy 1992, 61; Rawick 1972, 12:1:113–114).

Housing for slaves generally consisted of one-room cabins, twelve feet by twelve feet in dimension. On the larger and wealthier plantations, slave cabins might have fireplaces for cooking and heating, glass-paned windows, and doors that locked. More often than not, masters provided slaves with just the cabin. Other masters might provide a bed, table, or bench. Most bondsmen therefore simply ate and slept on the dirt floor of their cabin. James Bolton, an ex-slave, recalled, "We stayed in a one room cabin with a dirt floor. A frame made outen pine poles was fastened to the wall to hold up the mattresses. Our mattresses was made outen cotton bagging stuffed with wheat straw. Our kivers was quilts made outen old clothes. Slave 'omens too old to work in the fields made the quilts" (Otto 1984, 42–43; Rawick 1972, 12:1:92–93).

Masters also provided their slaves with the bare minimum of food. Slaves often received rations of corn, Indian beans, potatoes, and cracked rice unfit for exportation. Slaves in Georgia, as was customary throughout the South, received three pounds of bacon per week, salt, molasses, and vegetables in season. Masters often allowed their slaves to substitute rice or a bushel of sweet potatoes for corn. Slaves over the age of fourteen received nine quarts of corn per week. This, however, existed on the larger plantations, and slaves elsewhere most likely received lesser rations. Generous masters allowed their slaves to eat meat, have a small garden for vegetables, or allowed servants to supplement their diet by fishing or hunting small game (Davis 1976, 134; Otto 1984, 56).

Clothing too was extremely rudimentary. In the winter, slaves received a wool jacket, one pair of long pants, shoes, a woolen cap, and a blanket. During the summer, male and female slaves went naked or covered themselves with a loincloth. Children generally went naked or wore a long shirt. On the Cannon's Point Plantation, during the winter, men received seven yards of cloth, a cap, and a pair of brogans. Women received six yards of cloth, a kerchief, and a pair of brogans. Every second year, adult slaves received one blanket, and a blanket was handed out for every two children. During the summer, slaves received osnaburg cotton cloth, generally enough to afford male slaves two pairs of pants, two shirts, and two pairs of underwear; female slaves generally received two dresses, two pairs of drawers; and children, two long shirts. The Cannon's Point Plantation appears to be the exception and, most likely, the majority of Georgia slaves received less clothing. On this plantation, though, as in most areas, the slave women were responsible for sewing and making the clothes themselves, often working well into the night after long hours in the field (Davis 1976, 134; Otto 1984, 71).

Family and religion, however, offered slaves an escape from the confines of their strict environment. As elsewhere, slave families emerged, especially on the larger plantations. A considerable number of slave marriages took place between slaves from different plantations. This is especially true considering that 70 percent of all slaves lived on farms or plantations with fewer than fifty slaves. Given the fact that neighbors traded and borrowed slaves throughout the year as need dictated, and hiring out was an established practice, slaves had the opportunity to meet fellow bondsmen from other areas, establish relations, and marry. Nevertheless, the unity of the slave family remained subject to the whims and financial considerations of the owner. Although most masters verbally upheld the sanctity of the slave family, they actually held little regard for maintaining it. Financial concerns superceded the personal consideration of slaves; bondsmen were often sold to liquidate debts, and the older slaves were often sold when they neared their potential value in the market. In addition, owners often offered slaves as gifts to their children and other family members, especially when a child of the master's family married. This typically led to the separation of slave families. The high mortality rate among slaves also undermined the family unit. In some areas, the life expectancy rate was quite low. Susan McIntosh, an ex-slave, recalled that she had twelve siblings, "Seven died, soon after they were born, and none of 'em lived to git grown 'cept me." Nevertheless, the family served to provide care, a sense of belonging, and offered a measure of security in an uncertain and harsh society (Harris 1985, 44; Rawick 1972, 13:3:79).

Religion also played a vital role for slaves. In Georgia, several denominations reached out to the slave community. Twenty-eight independent black churches existed across the state in the antebellum era and by 1860, the Baptists claimed twenty-six thousand members, and the Methodists counted twenty-two thousand among their ranks. Religion served as the stimulus for humanizing the institution of slavery, which possibly explains the early efforts of many to educate and care for the social welfare of their bondsmen. Preachers also stressed the need for slaves to maintain loyalty and obedience to their masters, thus attempting to encourage a stable if not docile labor force. Slaves, though, did experience spiritual release beyond the confines of the church walls and separate from whites during camp meetings. Camp meetings provided a break from the arduous fieldwork and offered slaves a semblance of control over their free time and religious experience. They listened to the gospel preachers, had their own conversion experience, and spent time socializing with other blacks. The religious and social function of the camp meetings offered slaves a moment of egalitarianism.

A strong belief in superstition also played a role in the slaves' worldview that gave meaning to their lives. When asked if he believed in superstitions, ex-slave Charlie King replied, "I sho does for dis reason, once jest befo my baby brother died, ole screech owl, he done come and get up in the big oak tree right at the doah by de bed and fo' the next twelve hours passed, my brother was dead. Screech owls allus holler 'round the house before death." Aunt Harriet Miller, an ex-slave, recalled, "I'd be 'feared to say dere ain't nothing in voo-doo. Some puts a dime in de shoe to keep de voo-doo away, and some carries a buckeye in de pocket to keep off cramp and colic. Dey say a bone dey finds in de jawbone of a hog will make chillum teethe easy" (Rawick 1972, 3, 13:3:18, 129).

These outlets though did not make up for the confines of bondage. Even from the beginning stages of slavery, bondsmen rebelled against the institution of forced labor. Often groups of slaves fled to the swamps, returning to steal, destroy property, and in some cases commit murder. Slaves ran away for a variety of reasons, such as the desire to be near family who had been sold away, the fear of being sold themselves, a desire to return to a previous owner, or a period of bad treatment. Some were simply lured or encouraged to escape. For many, Florida proved to be the most appropriate destination. Escape, though, was not always a permanent venture. Sometimes slaves ran away for only short periods to visit relatives, to avoid immediate punishment, to protest against perceived unjust actions, or to carry out personal grudges against the owner. The constant reality of slave flight and the threat of slave revolt reveals that Americans of African lineage often did not accept servitude and raged against the society that enslaved them.

FREE BLACKS

Bondsmen could gain freedom by purchasing themselves or by earning it through good works. Very few slaves, however, earned their freedom in Georgia, and the population of free blacks in the state remained quite small. Comparatively speaking, the percentage of free blacks in Georgia was much lower than in other states. Those who did gain their freedom eked out an existence through a variety of means. Free black women generally earned a living as domestic servants or by ironing and taking in laundry. Free black men generally worked in the building trades. Only in rare instances did free blacks attain financial comfort; most barely scraped out a living. In addition, law required free blacks to post a bond testifying to their good behavior. This required free blacks to obtain a white guardian who would testify on their behalf. Failure to do so often resulted in a fine. Failure to pay fines resulted in the potential sale of the free black back into the bondage of slavery (Reidy 1992, 78).

BLACK CODES

The first black codes in Georgia appeared in 1750. Masters were permitted to punish their slaves, but could not physically maim them or endanger their life. Slaves found guilty of murdering whites were summarily hanged. In addition, law forbade sexual relations or marriage between the races. Laws in the beginning stages of slavery, however, only operated in theory. In reality, the laws were not enforced. Few slaves were actually executed, and those who were, were burned to death instead of hanged by the noose. These were unofficial black codes, and the first official codes appeared on the books in 1755. The 1755 codes written by Georgians were taken from the South Carolina black codes yet were more comprehensive in regulating the actions of blacks and whites. Free or slave, blacks received the death penalty for killing a white person, destroying agricultural products such as corn or rice, stealing another slave, setting fires, and poisoning another person. If a slave received the death penalty, the master received financial restitution for the value of the slave. For all lesser crimes, bondsmen were whipped or received prison terms. Furthermore, blacks could not travel without a pass; gather in groups unless supervised; or play drums, horns, or other musical instruments for fear of fomenting a rebellion. Laws also regulated the actions of whites. Theoretically, masters could not work their slaves on Sundays and no more than sixteen hours per day. Owners too had the responsibility, by law, for feeding and clothing their slaves, or they faced a fine (Davis 1976, 126–130).

As time passed, black codes were refined and reflected the changing and increasing fear of blacks. In 1770, a twenty-dollar fine was levied for teaching a slave to read. By 1829, this same offense carried a five-hundred-dollar penalty. If blacks were found guilty of teaching others, they received thirty-nine lashes. Nevertheless, there did occur a small movement in the 1850s to educate slaves. In fact, the Georgia House of Representatives voted and passed a measure to repeal the 1829 law. The Senate, however, refused to pass the measure. Most likely, the move to educate slaves emerged out of the need to defend slavery and not from a genuine concern for the welfare of slaves themselves. Some also viewed education as a way to foster loyalty to masters. The very fact that the House passed the measure reveals that the 1829 law most often was overlooked, and in some places slaves did receive a rudimentary education.

In 1852, the Georgia legislature increased the penalty for racial mixing, specifically for white men who lived with black women. Such legislation reflected the growing concern regarding an increasing free black population and the need to keep a tight rein on white supremacy. Thus, in Georgia, the black codes reveal the internal struggle within white society regarding the institution of slavery. Slowly whites came to recognize the humanity of slaves, but at the same time were forced to increase the restrictions on blacks and whites due to the perceived economic necessity of the institution and the desire to maintain a racial hierarchy.

THE CIVIL WAR

The capture of Port Royal, South Carolina, by Union forces in 1861 scared white Georgians. The proximity of Port Royal, where cannon shots could be heard, caused many coastal slave owners and whites to flee the area. By 1862, Union forces took control of Tybee and Wassah Islands, and the rest of coastal Georgia fell quickly. Thus, blacks began to take advantage of the chaos and many either destroyed property or fled under their own initiative once the violence erupted. Some waited and left during Union invasion. Initially, though, flight was a disastrous undertaking. Once Union forces arrived on the coast, blacks were able to escape to safety aboard Union ships. Some blacks enlisted in the Union ranks. They did so out of hatred for the slave owners and a desire for revenge. Others viewed it as an avenue to aid in the freedom of their family members and friends. The federal government began allowing blacks to enlist in the Union army in 1863 and agents openly sought black recruits. By 1865, Union forces had gained the service of approximately three thousand five hundred blacks from Georgia. Regardless of the reasoning, blacks quickly found they were expected to work, build fortifications, and oftentimes pick cotton from the fields deserted by slave owners. Union officers sometimes withheld food rations as a sure way to force blacks into labor, and many found themselves in virtually the same condition and position they had fled from (Mohr 1986, 69–70, 77, 80; Berlin 1982, 12).

Georgia slaves who did not or could not flee and join the Union ranks traveled inland with their masters. Thus, the vast majority of military-age black men from Georgia did not enter the Union army. Many slaves found themselves pulled from the cotton fields and placed in the war effort. They served in numerous military departments and "formed the backbone of Georgia's military labor force." Bondsmen also labored in industrial areas for the war effort. They worked in ordnance, gunpowder factories, and other military manufacturing to help produce the necessities of war. Approximately twenty-four thousand slaves and free blacks engaged in industrializing efforts at some point before war's end. Slaves also built fortifications, worked in railway construction (especially for the South-Western and the Augusta and Macon lines), and served in hospitals acting as cooks, nurses, and laundresses (Mohr 1986, 121; Berlin 1982, 15).

Flight and the use of bondsmen for the war effort served to undermine the institution of agricultural slavery. The climate and demands of continual war uprooted the daily routine of servitude, and slaves witnessed the fear of their owners, which in turn eroded the authoritative role of the masters. Furthermore, flight disrupted black families, as owners considered their own economic needs over the concern of slaves, thus often selling servants to recoup existing and potential financial losses.

EMANCIPATION

The sudden emergence of freedom left many former slaves perplexed and confused. Some stayed with their masters, others fled to the major urban areas such as Savannah, and most found their material condition immediately after the war worse than during slavery. Research reveals that many freedmen, kicked off their farms or plantations by cruel ex-masters who gave them no food or clothing, suffered severe deprivations, and some even died of starvation in the months following the conclusion of hostilities. The federal government, however, did attempt to aid the plight of the newly freed slaves. In March 1865, Congress established the Bureau of Refugees, Freedmen, and Abandoned Lands, generally known as the Freedmen's Bureau. This body, until 1870, had the responsibility of over-seeing employment contracts between former masters and ex-slaves to try to help the former chattel get a fair shake. Additionally, the bureau distrib-uted a few forty-acre parcels of abandoned lands to some blacks but by no means did all the new freedmen acquire farmland. Northern men and Union officers controlled the Freedman's Bureau. A white population, un-

Former African American slaves carry their wares to market near Savannah, Georgia. (Library of Congress.)

willing to be reconstructed and acting somewhat surly in defeat, consistently hampered bureau agents in carrying out their jobs and thwarted these officials in their ability to affect real change in Georgia. Thus, the bureau had very little lasting influence among Georgia whites, who despised the organization and its efforts.

African Americans viewed landownership as a right that should accompany their freedom. Freedmen who could afford to pay rent on government land parcels would have the right to hold the property for three years with an option for purchase. The vast majority of blacks nevertheless entered into sharecropping contracts instead of the ranks of landowner. Initially the Freedman's Bureau sought to secure equitable labor contracts with farmers and planters. The need for labor compounded with the lack of respect for the bureau, however, led many white farmers and planters to bypass the bureau and enter into individual contracts with African Americans. In countless cases, though, this was merely a disguise for a slavery-like relationship complete with harsh punishment. Often, at the end of the harvest season, whites would renege on the contracts leaving black laborers without a penny or a share of the crop. Furthermore, during the contract period, few whites felt responsible for the daily maintenance of their laborers, and many freedmen found their condition deteriorating and often worse than during slavery. The bureau simply did not have the manpower or the influence to safeguard the working environment of most freedmen. Abuse, fraud, neglect, and influence from the old planter elite hampered the Freedman's Bureau. In addition, an overbearing workload from the volume of cases presented by freedmen ensured that the bureau would not make a significant impact on economically reconstructing Georgia (Cimbala 1986, 74, 86; Cimbala 1997, 62–64).

After the war, race relations constantly verged on violent eruptions. Whites were unwilling to accept blacks unless they outwardly appeared to accept the role of inferiority. Few white Georgians tolerated anything that slightly attempted to undermine white supremacy. Black leaders, who often urged freedmen to fight for their rights regardless of the consequences, also caused heightened racial tensions. After the war, this rise in the temperature of racial relationships in all areas of the state prompted urban blacks to segregate themselves from whites. This was most apparent in the realm of religion, where blacks withdrew from white congregations and, if they attended services at all, established independent and separate black churches. In Savannah, the leaders and ministers of these churches emerged to play a role in the state's Reconstruction government. Although black politicians generally sided with white Republicans at the state level and attempted to push for legislation aiding freedmen—such as abolishing racial segregation in transportation and city areas—little was accomplished due to the white Democrats' refusal to accept racial equality. Furthermore, scores of blacks were turned away from polling areas during voting, thwarted by outright violence from mobs of angry whites and the Ku Klux Klan (Perdue 1973, 45).

During slavery and the beginning stages of Reconstruction, many slaves had some rudimentary education. Many churches opened schools and taught the basics of reading, writing, spelling, and arithmetic. Furthermore, many blacks began to establish their own schools wherever possible. A vast majority of the new teachers were prominent ministers and members of the black community. Working through the American Missionary Association and local churches, freedmen established fifty-four schools across the state and educated at a rudimentary level over four thousand students by 1866. Freedmen were wholly committed to the education process as an avenue for improvement. This dedication involved financial sacrifice on the part of the black community in Georgia. Despite the difficult economic burdens that blacks faced, by mid-1870, freedmen wholly supported thirty-five schools and contributed to the financial maintenance of an additional one hundred thirty-four schools. It would not be until 1870, however, that Georgia would begin a system of tax-supported schools. Even at that point, though, blacks received the majority of their education through religious and church avenues or from sympathetic whites. Nevertheless, many Georgians, though opposed to the efforts of the bureau and the black community, voted to extend education to freedmen. On many occasions, opponents resorted to outright hostility by interrupting classes, physically assaulting students and teachers, and firing upon schools (Perdue 1973, 71–73; Brown 1996, 59; Cimbala 1997, 110–113).

The black community moreover did have its problems. In the urban areas, social harmony did not always exist. In some areas, class distinctions rooted in skin color emerged. Lighter skinned blacks generally worked as teachers, doctors, ministers, and businessmen, serving in general positions of leadership. Mulatto blacks often separated themselves from darker skinned African Americans and, in some cases, opposed political equality for new freedmen due to their lack of education and distinction (Perdue 1973, 91–92).

In all areas, violence existed as whites fought to maintain a measure of racial supremacy. In many areas, the Ku Klux Klan sought to impose fear among blacks. James Bolton, an ex-slave, recalled, "'Course, they did have to straighten out some of them brash young nigger bucks on some of the other farms round about. Mos' of the niggers the Ku Kluxers got atter was'n on no farm, but was jus' roamin' 'round talking too much and makin' trouble. They had to take 'em in hand two or three times befo' some of them fool free niggers could be larned to behave theyselfs! But them Ku Kluxers kept on atter 'em twels't they lerned they jus got to be good effen they 'spect to stay round here." To counter assault and protect themselves, freedmen obtained firearms, keeping them in their homes and carrying them to the fields for protection against white adversaries. While in some circumstances this might have escalated the violence, blacks insisted on the right to maintain arms and to congregate where they pleased, rights denied them during slavery (Rawick 1972, 12:1:102–103).

Economic, political, and social freedom for Georgia's ex-slaves was hampered by outright violence and the inability of the Freedman's Bureau and benevolent organizations to make more than a superficial impact. Reconstruction in Georgia moved at a much slower pace than in other states.

RECONSTRUCTION

The frustrations the Freedmen's Bureau experienced in trying to help the former slaves, as well as the recalcitrance Southern whites exhibited in Georgia and elsewhere in accepting freedmen into the political and economic system, prompted Congress to step in. From 1867 until 1870, Georgia was administered as part of Military District Three, which Major General John Pope, a veteran of the victorious Union army, commanded. The primary purpose of the occupation was to ensure that freedmen could register to vote without threats of violence. Next the military would hold free elections for constitutional conventions to rewrite state charters that allowed black participation. The final step would be elections of a new state legislature that would then approve the Fourteenth and Fifteenth Amendments. States could then petition Congress to end the Military Occupation (Foner 1988, 271–412; Duncan 1986, 42–75).

Georgia completed this process in 1870 and was duly allowed to be readmitted into the Union. Black delegates participated in the legislative process and in the new assemblies drawn by the Reconstruction Constitution, though the apportionment districts allowed whites to maintain the balance of political power in the state. As soon as the Union military left, the Democrats began a policy of "redemption" and gradually recaptured control of the state political machinery (Foner 1988, 423–424; Duncan 1986, 76–110).

Although blacks continued to win a few elections in heavily majority black districts through the 1870s and 1880s, the Democrats reestablished control over the state only a year after the military left. They employed a strategy of using poll taxes and registration requirements to limit the black vote. By the 1880s, the assembly began passing Jim Crow laws and blacks in Georgia would be relegated to the second-class citizenship they endured until the civil rights era after World War II (Duncan 1986, 112–117).

REFERENCES

Berlin, Ira, Joseph P. Reidy, and Leslie S. Rowland. 1982. *Freedom: A Documentary History of Emancipation*, Series II, *The Black Military Experience*. New York: Cambridge University Press.

Brown, Titus. 1996. "Origins of African American Education in Macon, Georgia, 1865–1866." *Journal of Southwest Georgia History* 11 (Fall): 43–59.

Cimbala, Paul A. 1986. "A Black Colony in Dougherty County: The Freedmen's Bureau and the Failure of Reconstruction in Southwest Georgia." *Journal of Southwest Georgia History* 4 (Fall): 72–89.

———. 1997. *Under the Guardianship of the Nation: The Freedmen's Bureau and the Reconstruction of Georgia, 1865–1870.* Athens: University of Georgia Press.

Davis, Harold E. 1976. *The Fledgling Province: Social and Cultural Life in Colonial Georgia, 1733–1776.* Chapel Hill: University of North Carolina Press.

Drago, Edmund L. 1982. *Black Politicians and Reconstruction Georgia: A Splendid Failure.* Baton Rouge: Louisiana State University Press.

Duncan, Russell. 1986. *Freedom's Shore: Tunis Campbell and the Georgia Freedmen.* Athens: University of Georgia Press.

Flynn, Charles L., Jr. 1983. *White Land, Black Labor Caste and Class in Late Nineteenth-Century Georgia.* Baton Rouge: Louisiana State University Press.

Foner, Eric. 1988. *Reconstruction: America's Unfinished Revolution, 1863–1877.* New York: Harper & Row.

Harris, J. William. 1985. *Plan Folk and Gentry in a Slave Society: White Liberty and Black Slavery in Augusta's Hinterlands.* Middletown, Conn.: Wesleyan University Press.

Jones, Jacqueline. 1980. *Soldiers of Light and Love: Northern Teachers and Georgia Blacks, 1865–1873.* Chapel Hill: University of North Carolina Press.

Meyers, Christopher C. 1997. "'The Wretch Vickery' and the Brooks County Civil War Slave Conspiracy." *Journal of Southwest Georgia History* 12 (Fall): 27–38.

Mohr, Clarence L. 1986. *On the Threshold of Freedom: Masters and Slaves in Civil War Georgia.* Athens: University of Georgia Press.

Otto, John Solomon. 1984. *Cannon's Point Plantation, 1794–1860: Living Conditions and Status Patterns in the Old South.* Orlando, Fla.: Academic Press, Inc.

Perdue, Robert E. 1973. *The Negro in Savannah, 1865–1900.* New York: Exposition Press.

Rawick, George P., ed. 1972. *The American Slave: A Composite Autobiography.* Westport, Conn.: Greenwood Publishing Company.

Reidy, Joseph P. 1992. *From Slavery to Agrarian Capitalism in the Cotton Plantation South, Central Georgia, 1800–1880.* Chapel Hill: University of North Carolina Press.

Tadman, Michael. 1989. *Speculators and Slaves: Masters, Traders, and Slaves in the Old South.* Madison: University of Wisconsin Press.

WEB SITES

Antebellum Slavery in Georgia—Fanny Kemble: http://www.pbs.org/wgbh/aia/part4/4narr1.html

Federal Writers Project—Narratives of Former Slaves—Georgia, 4 parts: http://memory.loc.gov/ammem/wpaintro/wpahome.html

Georgia Slave Workplaces: http://www.rootsweb.com/~afamerpl/plantations_usa/GA/GA_plantations.html

Georgia's African American History: http://www.gavoyager.com/GLfiles/
    blackhistl.html
Harrison Berry Georgia Slave Narrative: docsouth.unc.edu/imls/berry/menu.
    html
Slavery in North Georgia: http://www.ngeorgia.com/history/antebel.html
Slavery in Savannah: http://www.kingtisdell.org/Slavery.htm

Kentucky

1828: Jim Crow performs for Thomas Rice who develops the "minstrel" show

1845: Cassius M. Clay publishes the antislavery tract *The True American*

1845–1848: Cassius Clay fights duels with pro-slavery advocates

1848: Seventy-five slaves from Fayette County make an unsuccessful escape attempt

1852–1853: Writer Harriet Beecher Stowe's serial *Uncle Tom's Cabin* is published as a book and sells over 300,000 copies

1858: Antislavery supporters found Berea College to educate black men and women

1861: Kentucky remains in the Union but continues to be staunchly pro-slavery

1864–1865: Over 23,000 African Americans from Kentucky enlist in the Union army

1865, December 18: Ratification of the Thirteenth Amendment ends slavery in Kentucky and throughout the United States

1904: Berea College stops admitting blacks to conform with Kentucky's "Jim Crow" laws

Slave and Free Black Population

Census Year	Slave Population	Population Percentage	Free Black Population	Population Percentage
1790	12,430	17	114	under 1
1800	40,343	18	739	under 1
1810	80,561	19	1,713	under 1
1820	126,732	23	2,759	under 1
1830	165,213	24	4,917	under 1
1840	182,258	23	7,317	1
1850	210,981	21	10,011	1
1860	225,483	19	10,684	under 1

Net Slave Entries and Exits, by Decade (Tadman 1989, 12)

1790–1799: + 21,636	1830–1839: − 19,907
1800–1809: + 25,837	1840–1849: − 19,266
1810–1819: + 18,742	1850–1859: − 31,215
1820–1829: − 916	

Slaveholders and Size of Slaveholding, 1860

Size of Slaveholding	Number of Slaveholders	Percentage of Slaveholders
1–4	22,026	57
5–9	9,793	25
10–19	5,271	14
20–99	1,548	4
100 +	7	under 1

ORIGINS OF SLAVERY

American colonial interest in the lands west of the Allegheny Mountains along the Ohio River began shortly before the French and Indian War of the 1750s. Newcomers had already flooded the western piedmont areas of Maryland and had extended their settlements through the verdant Shenandoah valley of Virginia in the years preceding the last war with the French. Tidewater Virginia grandees as well as their more modest neighbors during these same years had laid claim to most of the vast southside piedmont area of Virginia, which lay south of the James River all the way to the Carolina border. Real estate speculators and land hungry settlers began casting envious eyes to the extensive open space in the mountain valleys farther west.

In 1751, a group of well-to-do, politically connected colonials hired Christopher Gist, a noted frontiersman, to travel across the mountains and to bring back observations of the Ohio region. Gist took along his favorite frontier partner, an enslaved African American, as his only companion. Gist and his black colleague explored along the river as far as the Great Falls of the Ohio, the present site of Louisville. Thus, Gist's bondsman became the first recorded African American to enter what would become the Commonwealth of Kentucky (Dunnigan 1982, 3).

Other backwoodsmen, often called "long hunters" for their lengthy Pennsylvania-manufactured weapons, followed the route explored by Dr. Thomas Walker of Virginia a few years before Gist's expedition. Walker accessed the lands along the Kentucky River by crossing the mountains through the Cumberland Gap. The French and Indian War as well as the presence of many Native American hunting parties limited the number of whites who would risk their lives or their human chattel in the Kentucky wilderness until the eve of the American Revolution.

In October 1774, Virginia militia defeated a Native American army led by the Shawnee chief Cornstalk at Point Pleasant, where the Kanawha River enters the Ohio River. Cornstalk agreed to the Treaty of Camp Charlotte that required the Shawnee and their allies to withdraw from all lands south of the Ohio River. In addition, the Native Americans had to turn over all captives that they had accumulated during the frontier raids of the past half-dozen years. These prisoners included a number of African Americans who had been dragged away from homesteads by the Indians along with their white owners, as well as some individual blacks who had escaped slavery by fleeing into the wilderness. The defeat of Cornstalk opened up Kentucky for continued white settlement, though the Indians contested these incursions until 1782 (Harrison and Klotter 1997, 20).

During the American Revolutionary War years of the mid-1770s, a trickle of settlers, led by Daniel Boone, the well-known explorer and hunter, and James Harrod, built fortified encampments at Boonesboro and at Harrodsburg. These newcomers included numerous Virginians, especially in Boone's party, who owned a few slaves and who transported this human property to Kentucky as well. Captain John Cowan noted that, in 1777, the settlers in Kentucky numbered 198; this total included nineteen African American slaves, seven of whom were children under ten. Boone also owned a few slaves. One of his bondsmen was killed in the first Indian attack on the new settlement at Boonesboro (Dunnigan 1982, 3).

These blacks, involuntarily transported to the frontier, worked alongside the white settlers to clear land, to build stockades, to erect log cabins, and to plant small plots of corn and tobacco. They suffered through all the dangers, trials, and tribulations of opening up a wilderness region far distant from any other Americans. Their lives were as much at risk as their white owners during the harassing Indian attacks.

After the conclusion of the Revolutionary War, the trickle of humanity into Kentucky became a flood. Most of these new settlers started their trek to the "Blue Grass" state from locales in the slaveholding states of Maryland, Virginia, and North Carolina. They carried their slaves with them and brought along as well their ideas about how society should be organized, which included the right of whites to own African Americans as human chattel. In the six months from the autumn of 1783 to the spring of 1784, the population in the Kentucky region jumped from twelve thousand to twenty thousand. By 1790, the Commonwealth of Virginia had organized three counties for the territory west of the Appalachians and south of the Ohio River. This area now included more than twelve thousand enslaved African Americans among a population approaching seventy-five thousand (Coleman 1940, 14).

SLAVERY AND A PIONEER SOCIETY

The stresses and struggles as well as the constant dangers involved in opening up Kentucky in its first twenty years of American settlement left a remembrance of an idyllic era for race relations. Enslaved blacks and white settlers fought Indians side by side and labored together to hack out fields and to erect cabins in the aboriginal wilderness. Whites and blacks, working in tandem, overcame the challenges of surviving the pioneer Kentucky years. This memory colored the way whites perceived and understood slavery for the remainder of the antebellum era. Pro-slavery Kentucky whites continually argued that the peculiar institution in the Blue Grass state was of the mildest form known in the United States. They repeated oft-told anecdotal stories drawn from this frontier period to uphold and support this vision (Coleman 1940, 7).

The most famous frontier story involved Monk, a slave owned by Captain James Estill of Estill's Station. One March morning in 1782, a roving band of Wyandotte Indians surrounded the stockade, tomahawked the daughter of a settler who was outside milking a cow, and captured the slave Monk. He convinced the Indians that the fort was too strong for them to attack. They gave up their raid but dragged off Monk, carrying him along with their band. Captain Estill formed a rescue party and took off after the Wyandotte raiding party. Two days later, Estill's posse overtook the Indians and a battle ensued. Monk yelled out that the Wyandotte had only a dozen warriors and could be defeated. Estill pushed his attack, lost his life, but also created enough turmoil to allow Monk to get away. Estill's slave picked up a wounded member of the rescue party and carried him home on his back, a distance of twenty-five miles. Monk became a local hero and a celebrity. He later further aided the settlement by making gunpowder from saltpeter deposits found in the local caves, giving the newcomers sufficient munitions to hunt game and to ward off the Indians. He married three times successively and fathered thirty children, including the first African American baby born at Boonesboro (Coleman 1940, 8).

In another oft-told remembrance, Black Sam, a chattel of the Virginia-born Edward Cabell, saved the youngest member of his master's family, Augusta, after Indians attacked the homestead and torched their cabin. Cabell's wife and other children perished in the flames. Sam rescued the young girl and carried her to safety to the nearest fort. He hid during the day, gathering berries for sustenance, and after three nights was able to reach help. There he met his master who had just returned from Virginia bringing along with him other Cabell slaves, including Black Sam's father, mother, and wife (Coleman 1940, 10).

The final famous vignette about slave life in frontier Kentucky involved the fiddle player Cato, whose master settled at the site of present-day Louisville. During Christmas 1778, a party of French trappers stopped at the Falls of the Ohio (Louisville). One of their party was a skilled violinist, though he could render only French minuets and fashionable music. The settlement organized a dance, but the Americans were unfamiliar with the Frenchman's tunes. Cato saved the day. He traded three hides to the Frenchman for new strings for his worn fiddle and showed his musical counterpart the rhythms of the Virginia Reel to which the settlers could dance. Cato became the talk of the settlement and the most famous fiddle player in Kentucky (Coleman 1940, 12–13).

The white community remembered and repeated these stories. To them, these frontier tales exemplified the strong bonds between whites and blacks that frontier living created and also upheld the picture of benignity that characterized slavery in Kentucky, at least for its proponents. The stories also suggested that Virginia slaveholders moving west were the principal agents in establishing slavery in the Kentucky region. The laws and cultural assumptions regarding slavery in Kentucky drew directly from the experiences in the older commonwealth out of which the Blue Grass state emerged.

By the time Kentucky entered the Union in 1792, hostile Indian raids had become only a memory. Likewise, in a very few years, the Kentucky settlements moved quickly past the pioneering, frontier stage. Although the feel-good tales of whites and blacks working together to survive and conquer the wilderness remained a part of Kentucky's remembered past, by the early years of the new century, slavery in Kentucky had become more like that of the commonwealth's ancestor, Virginia, than many white Kentuckians cared to admit.

STATEHOOD AND SLAVE LAWS

The first settlers of European descent in what would become Kentucky processed their land claims through the county court system of colonial Virginia, which held legal title to all territory directly west of Virginia. The newly proclaimed revolutionary era Commonwealth of Virginia (1775) likewise extended its jurisdiction west of the Allegheny Mountains along the Ohio River valley. After James Harrod at Harrodsburg and Daniel Boone at Boonesboro established settlements in 1774 and 1775, the Virginia assembly set up a new county, Kentucky, encompassing everything west of the mountains and south of the Ohio River; this took effect in December 1776. All the laws regarding slavery, slaves, and free blacks that had jurisdiction in Virginia likewise applied to the new county.

In 1779, the Virginia legislature passed the Occupancy Claimant Law that allowed anyone holding a Virginia real estate warrant for unoccupied land to locate his claim on any vacant plot as long as the claimant paid for his own survey. This law applied to the newly recognized Kentucky County as well and led to a flood of newcomers seeking to site their claims on virgin lands west of the mountains. The resulting squabble over rival filings and inaccurate surveys gainfully employed an entire cohort of frontier attorneys for a generation. This law also prompted many Virginians to move west and to take their slaves to these unclaimed lands. By the end of 1780, the population had grown so rapidly that the legislature in Richmond trisected the

Kentucky territory into three counties, each of which held regular court sessions. Nevertheless, any appeals had to be carried back hundreds of miles to central Virginia across two mountain ranges (Allen 1872, 24–26).

As early as 1784, while the post–Revolutionary War land rush still descended on the Kentucky region, groups of settlers began to speak out in favor of statehood. Nine conventions followed, but all failed to adopt a resolution demanding a new state or to adopt a resolution that Virginia would sanction. In the spring of 1792, those delegates meeting to discuss a proposed new state tendered an agreement acceptable to the Commonwealth of Virginia. The house and senate of Virginia demanded that the new state instrument include clauses that clearly confirmed the legality of slavery and offered constitutional protections as well. Thus, the institution of chattel slavery became an inherent part of the legal framework of Kentucky from its inception as a state (Works Progress Administration 1939, 40).

As part of its new state constitution, the Commonwealth of Kentucky adopted the Virginia slave laws and codes. In 1798, the Kentucky assembly condensed these rules into one slave statute that included forty-three articles that were virtually identical to those provisions governing enslaved African Americans in Virginia. These laws defined slavery as applying to only those of African descent and did not allow baptism to alter the legal status or rights of any human chattel. While delegates included clauses to prevent physical abuses, as in Virginia, blacks were proscribed from testifying against whites; this provision effectively gainsaid the abuse statutes. Masters, owners, or hirers largely determined what would be acceptable treatment with little interference from the Kentucky courts. These laws held jurisdiction in the new commonwealth throughout the antebellum years (Coleman 1940, 17).

Embedding slavery within the legal framework of the first state west of the Appalachians did not pass without contention, however. Reverend David Rice, Presbyterian minister and founder of Transylvania Seminary, argued against the legalization of slavery in the new commonwealth. Although a native Virginian, Rice opined that slavery was inconsistent with justice and not good policy. He listed ten cogent points against the institution, including the infringement of the personal rights of the enslaved and the legality of enforced separation of families. His pleas and those of other free labor advocates made little headway since the majority of the delegates elected for the statehood convention owned slaves and most had more than five. Pro-slavery attitudes characterized the dominant opinion of this majority. Thus, slavery in the Commonwealth of Kentucky would be legal and protected until December 1865. The weight of public opinion offered by white Kentuckians supported this stance (Harrison and Klotter 1997, 62; Dunnigan 1982, 4–5; Thompson 1963, 115, 248).

THE SLAVE POPULATION

The slave population in the new commonwealth grew rapidly after state-hood. As the opening summary on slavery indicates, Kentucky residents owned more than eighty thousand enslaved African Americans in 1810. Slave owners, especially the incoming Virginians, brought significant numbers of bondsmen with their other possessions when they moved into Kentucky. The summary of slave entries and exits into Kentucky notes that newcomers carried more than sixty thousand enslaved African Americans into the state between 1790 and 1819. For example, Robert Carter Harrison, of impeccable Virginia lineage, settled with more than one hundred slaves on two thousand acres in the Blue Grass state outside of Lexington (Coleman 1940, 19; Tadman 1989, 12).

From 1790 until 1833, the number of slaves in Kentucky grew from 17 percent to 24 percent of the total population. When the slave totals in 1833 passed a quarter of the commonwealth's populace, the Kentucky assembly enacted legislation that banned further importation of bonded African Americans. Additionally, as noted, Kentuckians sold or carried more than seventy thousand slaves out of the commonwealth in the last three decades of the antebellum years. The Kentucky Blue Grass region ranked as a major slave-exporting area while Lexington stood as the state's chief slave auction market. The ban on importation and the large-scale sale of slaves south led to a gradual decrease in the slave population percentage. The absolute number of slaves in Kentucky grew, however, from 165,000 in 1830 to slightly more than 225,000 in 1860, but the population percentage attributable to bondsmen declined to just under 20 percent in the year before the Civil War's onset. Free blacks always represented an insignificant percentage of Kentucky's denizens (Tadman 1989, 12; Works Progress Administration 1939, 72).

Even though some Virginia grandees carried sizable numbers of slaves to their new lands in Kentucky, the more modest slaveholders dominated and characterized the commonwealth's slave owners. As the last opening summary chart notes, Kentucky's residents in 1860 included more than thirty-eight thousand slaveholders, the third highest total for any Southern state. The number of plantation-sized units that included twenty or more slaves, however, comprised only a small part of the total. Fifty-seven percent or more than 22,000 of Kentucky's slaveholders owned four or fewer slaves, while only 1,555 held twenty or more human chattel. The smaller and more modest slaveholder clearly typified the Kentucky slave owner.

Although a few slave manumissions made news in Kentucky, free blacks always formed a very small segment of the commonwealth's African American population, usually comprising less than 1 percent of the total populace. For example, Polly Ficklin of Fayette County emancipated all her slaves by will. She bequeathed to them the village of Kirkland to be held by all in common. In this manner, she attempted to provide for the aged and infirm. Although the well-publicized nature of these manumissions reinforced the idea of the benignity of Kentucky slavery, these anecdotal accounts belied the reality of slave manumissions, which were relatively rare and which did not affect very many African Americans in the commonwealth. Kentucky included fewer free blacks than other Upper South areas like Maryland or parts of Virginia, where manumissions were much more commonplace (Coleman 1940, 33).

Furthermore, the free blacks of Kentucky had to be wary at all times to avoid slavenappers who wished to drag them away and sell them back into slavery. They had to be sure to carry identification and proof of their status on their person. As in Virginia, the law in Kentucky assumed that an undocumented black was a runaway or escaped slave and liable to be arrested and incarcerated. Many of the African Americans in Kentucky who negotiated freedom, either through manumission by owners or by saving up enough for self-purchase fled the state for Canada. Small communities of free blacks from Kentucky, joined by escaped slaves, flourished in the villages of Ontario east of Windsor. John Davis observed, "I came here [Canada] in 1837, poor as any other man need to go to any country. I had only one shirt, and not a second suit of clothes to my back. . . . I came from Kentucky. . . . I believe the colored people here in Canada, within twenty miles around us, are doing as well as any people in the world" (Coleman 1940, 105; Blassingame 1977, 430–444).

Approximately 15 percent of Kentucky's free blacks lived and worked in Louisville. They toiled as barbers, dressmakers, domestics, factory hands, and also worked on the riverboats. Isaac Throgmorton stated that he was born in Kentucky and lived in the country until he was twenty-two: "Then I came to Louisville where I was put at the barber's trade." George Ramsey remembered, "I was not born free. . . . I worked very little on the plantation though. . . . I learnt the blacksmith's trade." Nevertheless, the most typical African American in Kentucky during the antebellum years lived on a farm and either worked in the fields or labored on domestic tasks around the "big house" (Blassingame 1977, 432–440).

AGRICULTURE AND SLAVES

Although non-slave-owners and small slaveholders far outnumbered the larger farmers with ten or more slaves, these bigger agricultural units led Kentucky in agricultural production. Only 2 percent of all Kentucky farm operators held ten or more slaves, yet these farms produced more than 50 percent of all the corn and tobacco, two-thirds of all the wheat, and 95 percent of the hemp, the quintessential slave crop of the Blue Grass state. Hemp fibers were used in antebellum America to make ropes, canvas, sails, grain and storage bags, and coarse cloth. The Kentucky Blue Grass region grew and processed much of America's hemp output.

Cotton planters in the Gulf states bought most of this woven hemp of rough rope and bagging, which was used to cover and tie together cotton bales. As cotton production increased, so too did demand for inexpensive "cotton bagging" and "bale ropes." Demand for hemp products varied directly with the price of cotton. Slaves worked at growing the crop and also labored in the small mills in Lexington, Frankfurt, and Louisville, where the hemp fibers for ropes and bags were drawn from the harvested plant (Channing 1977, 50; Coleman 1940, 44–45, 82–84).

Kentucky slave owners also grew and marketed substantial quantities of tobacco, and Louisville, in the decades before the war, emerged as a major tobacco sales mart and as a center for tobacco processing and manufacture. Additionally, the western counties of the commonwealth also grew large tobacco crops. In the antebellum years, Kentucky rivaled the older commonwealth, Virginia, for supremacy in tobacco production.

Tobacco was, however, less of a slave crop in Kentucky. In the Blue Grass state, tobacco was among a number of agricultural products. Many planters combined hemp and tobacco production, effectively managing their slave workforce to generate greater efficiency and profits. In the western counties, tobacco was grown by non-slaveholders as well as by slave owners, whereas in the 1840s and 1850s it had become the primary cash crop. Moreover, non-slaveholders grew more of Kentucky's leaf than was grown in the eastern tobacco region of Virginia and Maryland.

For enslaved African Americans, tobacco was more of a tedious crop than an onerous one. The plant required a great deal of care and know-how, but only the preparatory plowing entailed strenuous physical labor. Many of the tasks, such as pulling off the green tobacco worms or the offshoots from the main stalk called suckers, could be completed by women or by children as young as ten. Virginians and Marylanders brought their knowledge of harvesting and curing the plant with them when they moved to Kentucky, and their slaves often had extensive experience with the leaf crops as well. Virginia had, as early as 1787, established tobacco inspection warehouses in the Blue Grass region before Kentucky statehood. Hence, tobacco cultivation flourished in most parts of the commonwealth (Harrison and Klotter 1997, 135, 207, 292–293).

Enslaved African Americans likewise took care of the large herds of livestock grazing on Kentucky's pasturelands. In the early years of the commonwealth's settlement, Kentuckians drove large hog and cattle herds along the roadways to eastern markets, often crowding out traffic moving west. Francis Fedric, a Virginia slave from Fauquier County, remembered that on his way west to Kentucky with his master and other slaves, the party was interrupted and waylaid by droves of hogs, seven hundred or more at a time, headed for Maryland or Virginia markets. After the pioneer years, Cincinnati, just across the Ohio River, emerged as the leading pork packer in the country. Slaves also maintained Kentucky's valuable horseflesh, the ancestors of today's thoroughbreds. Most jockeys and train-ers at this time were either enslaved African Americans or free blacks (Harrison and Klotter 1997, 136–137; Coleman 1940, 20).

SLAVE LIFE

Kentucky slave families typically lived in huts or cabins that were usu-ally grouped together and called the "quarters." Often these quarters were sited near the other outbuildings common to all farms of the era—corncrib, woodshed, smokehouse—and the combined image projected that of a tiny village. These rustic shelters were erected a foot or so off the ground and generally consisted of one or two rooms with a fireplace. The hut build-ers, generally the slaves themselves, constructed bed frames built into the walls and filled the forms with mattresses stuffed with straw or corn shucks. A homemade or plantation-made table or chair completed the fur-niture accoutrements.

Most enslaved African Americans received clothes twice a year, in the spring and in the autumn. The winter clothes generally were made of lindsey-woolsey cloth, while their summer attire was typically sewn from inexpensive cotton goods. Some planters and farmers wove and sewed their own slave clothing; others bought already-woven cloth or already-made cheap slave clothes for their human chattel. Most masters provided one full suit of clothes for both men and women twice each year. Never-theless, many of the summer bonnets were handwoven straw hats made by the slaves themselves. Masters often had old flour sacks cut up and re-sewn for attire for slave children. Some households in Kentucky used sassafras bark and berry juice as dye to add color to slave garments.

The general food ration for Kentucky slaves amounted to from three to five pounds of pork and a peck of cornmeal a week. Normally this por-tion was augmented with a ration of sweet potatoes, molasses, and but-termilk. Children received a lesser amount. In Kentucky, most slaves had vegetable gardens and some kept poultry. Food in Kentucky for enslaved African Americans typically was plentiful.

The standard work schedule in Kentucky followed the accepted prac-tice in the Upper South. Most slaves worked a five-and-a-half-day week, having Saturday afternoon off to tend vegetable gardens. The day-and-a-half also allowed slave husbands, whose wives resided on other farms, to visit. They had to be careful to get a pass and carry it at all times to thwart the roving white slave patterollers. Since Kentucky slavery included so many small slaveholders, as previously noted, the number of broad hus-bands or broad wives in the Blue Grass state was substantial. A "broad" wife or husband referred to a consort who did not reside on the same place as his or her marriage partner.

The sun determined the length of the workday, which in the summer could be quite long. Older slaves, typically sixty and above, and the younger children tended the plantation vegetable gardens, fed the chickens, and managed the livestock. Even the smaller farms generally had a female slave "domestic" to perform at least part of the cooking and to take care of household chores.

The favorite times of the year for enslaved blacks in Kentucky were the occasions highlighted by music and merriment. Generally, slave owners held large corn shuckings that accomplished needed tasks but also allowed the slaves to get together with blacks from neighboring farms. Hog-killing time also included a social component. The week between Christmas and New Year's Day, however, was the chief time for rest and parties. Traditionally, slaves did no work that week and spent their time at dances, parties, socials, and church services. Most of the socializing among blacks from separate farms and plantations had to take place during these events, which comprised the primary locales for meeting potential marriage partners.

Most slave owners in Kentucky allowed their minions to celebrate weddings as well. These events were joyous occasions marked by music, singing, and refreshments often provided by the master. The ceremony was highlighted by the newlyweds "jumping over the broomstick" symbolizing the marriage union, which was recognized but not legalized in Kentucky. Most slave owners also gave their bondsmen a day off for funerals. In Kentucky, these lasted all day if possible and almost always were conducted out-of-doors (Coleman 1940, 14–16).

PATTEROLLERS AND SLAVE DISCIPLINE

As in most Southern areas, the Kentuckians adopted a system of white slave patrols to prevent blacks from fomenting insurrection and rebellion. These slave patrols, called "patterollers" by the bondsmen, made life difficult for many enslaved African Americans. Each county district and most towns had their own appointed slave patterollers. They were responsible for checking passes and keeping order. Additionally they could mete out up to thirty-nine lashes on would-be code breakers without legal interference (Coleman 1940, 96).

Free blacks likewise had to have their papers on their person at all times to prevent harassment by the patterollers. These documents identified the individual by name, by age, and by distinguishing physical characteristics. Any black without documents was assumed to be a runaway or an escaped slave and subject to arrest, incarceration, and possible sale. Slaves overstaying the time allowed by signed passes away from their home place were subject to whippings before being run back to their owner. This rule made life especially difficult for men with broad wives and with families on farms where they did not reside (Coleman 1940, 105).

In towns, the patterollers usually were called the "town watch," but functioned in the same manner as in the countryside. In Louisville, the large bell of the Presbyterian church tolled at 10:00 P.M. Any slave out in the street, unless with a signed pass, could be lashed up to fifteen times and held in jail until the following morning. In Lexington, the evening curfew fell at 7:00 P.M. and the penalty for violation could entail up to thirty-five lashes (Coleman 1940, 104).

When incendiary incidents in neighboring Virginia erupted, especially the Nat Turner insurrection and John Brown's incursion at Harper's Ferry, the patterollers clamped down even more conspicuously and further raised tensions between blacks and whites. Additionally, Kentucky experienced some minor incidents of its own. In August 1848, seventy-five slaves from Fayette County escaped. The organizer, Patrick Doyle, was a student at Centre College. The commonwealth posted a reward of five thousand dollars for all the escapees. A few days later, Doyle and the runaways were surrounded and captured in a hemp field. Three of the blacks were hanged, the remainder were whipped and returned to their home place. Doyle was sentenced to prison for twenty years (Coleman 1940, 87–91).

Regular treatment on the Kentucky farms and plantations varied, however, according to the whims of the master. Testimony from some former slaves suggested that violent whippings did not regularly occur. Isaac Throgmorton remembered, "I never suffered from any severe treatment." George Dunn related, "I was born in Virginia, I believe, but was reared in Frankfort, Kentucky. Our folks weren't treated so awful bad. . . . I don't believe I ever had but one whipping in my life, but still, I had to work rather hard." George Ramsey said, "I can't say that I experienced any hard treatment . . . but I worked hard, and got nothing for it." John Davis noted, "I can't say that I suffered anything particular down south" (Blassingame 1977, 432–444).

Yet others related incidents of severe arbitrary whippings. Henry Bibb, who later escaped to freedom in Canada and edited an antislavery newsletter there, remembered, "to be compelled to stand by and see you [his master] whip and lash my wife without mercy when I could afford her no protection . . . was more than I felt it to be the duty of a slave husband to endure while the way to Canada was open. . . . My infant child was frequently flogged . . . until its skin was bruised and literally purple. This kind of treatment drove me from home and family to seek a better home for them" (Channing 1977, 101).

Novelist Harriet Beecher Stowe used the stories related by slaves escaping via the Underground Railroad through Cincinnati to provide the background for the lifelike characters she so vividly created in *Uncle Tom's Cabin*. This book, which sold hundreds of thousands of copies in the mid-1850s, changed the way many Northern voters viewed the slavery issue and thus made an important contribution to American popular culture, which then influenced the political events leading up to the onset of the Civil War. Stowe's background stories dealt almost entirely with incidents drawn from Kentucky and from Kentucky slavery (Coleman 1940, 318).

MUSIC, MINSTRELS, AND JIM CROW

From the time the fiddler Cato outshone the French at the Falls of the Ohio in 1778, Kentucky slaves had well-known reputations far and wide as wonderful musicians and performers. Musical entertainment provided a needed relief and buffer from the continuous unchanging agricultural chores around the farms and plantations. Slaves played instruments and music in the "quarters" and also performed at parties in the "big house." Many masters bragged about the skill of their musical minions and showed off the plantation orchestra to visitors (Davenport 1943, 14).

Jim Crow was a Louisville, Kentucky, slave whose impromptu performances inspired white performer Thomas Rice to create the minstrel show. Pictured here is the title page to a series of African American songs and melodies published for minstrel show performers as the "Jim Crow Jubilee." (Library of Congress.)

A number of these blacks would pass on into history. The most famous was Jim Crow, a Louisville livery stable worker. To amuse the customers, Jim performed a little dance accompanied by a doggerel ditty upon request:

> Once upon the heel tap
> And then upon the toe
> An' ev'ry time I turn around
> I jump Jim Crow
> Wheel about, turn about
> Do just so
> And every time I wheel about
> I jump Jim Crow

Jim became the best-known resident of Louisville for a generation and attracted a great deal of business for his owner.

In 1828, Thomas Rice, a white performer and actor, observed Jim's song and dance while in Louisville for a playhouse engagement. He borrowed some old clothes, blackened his face, and, on stage, danced like Jim while singing the nonsensical ditty. This part of his act became a great hit not only in the Upper South towns, such as Louisville and Lexington, but also in the eastern cities of Philadelphia and New York. Rice's blackface "Jim Crow" evolved into a whole separate genre of performance entertainment, the minstrel show, which drew American audiences for a hundred years. Later, the name Jim Crow was attached to the segregation laws adopted by the former slave states in the 1880s and 1890s that relegated African Americans to a second-class status: economically, socially, and politically (Dunnigan 1982, 9).

In another instance, a trio of black musicians used their talents to help their escape from Kentucky slavery. In the antebellum era, Graham's Springs in Harrodsburg ranked as the most prestigious resort in Kentucky. Dr. Graham owned a famous slave band that comprised the house orchestra. The three enslaved blacks, Rueben, Henry, and George, were well known throughout the Upper South and played at Dr. Graham's during the summer season. In addition, for very good fees, Dr. Graham hired out the trio to play at plantations parties and at balls in Louisville and Lexington during the winter. In the late autumn of 1840, the band had been performing in Louisville, but were called to Lexington to be part of the festivities celebrating the great Whig political victory of that year. After the reception, they realized that their white patron was no longer carefully overseeing their activities. They had passes back to Louisville and took off; once they arrived at the river city, they were able to get across the Ohio River and make their way to Canada. All attempts by Graham to bring back his famous performers were thwarted by other former Kentucky slaves now living across the border (Clark 1942, 234–235).

Religion provided another essential outlet for cultural expression and for obtaining life experiences that helped buffer the harsh edges of slavery and enrich monotonous, dreary lives. Kentucky masters usually took their chattel to church with the white family and often provided passes as well so that slaves could attend their own services. The black preacher and slave exhorter were regular features of Methodist camp meetings. Additionally, both the Baptists and Methodists regularly sanctioned slaves and free blacks to conduct services for African Americans. For example, George Dupuy, a slave, ministered to the African American congregation at Pleasant Green Baptist church. He later became liable for sale to cover the debts of his owner. His angry congregation of African Americans worked out an arrangement with the white Baptist preacher, William Platt, who bought George. They made a weekly payment to Platt from the Sunday collection to pay him back for Dupuy's purchase price. In another example, Josiah Henson, a slave from Davies County, preached widely in Kentucky. After he escaped to Canada, he continued his ministry and spoke in the northern United States and in England. Louisville African Americans opened the first black church there, the Methodist Episcopal Zion church, in 1817. African American ministers were generally well thought of and were leaders within the black community. Some masters worried that these preachers would instigate rebellion and insurrection similar to Nat Turner in Virginia; however, most went only so far as to aid runaways on their road to Canada (Davenport 1943, 74–75; Coleman 1940, 138).

SLAVE TRADERS

Slave trading and selling enslaved African Americans south to plantations in the Gulf states formed the dark underbelly of Kentucky slavery. The volume of the trade in the last three antebellum decades, as well as its persistence into 1864, belied the benign paternalism argument many white Kentuckians ritualistically spouted to defend their support of the peculiar institution in the Blue Grass state. The only impact public opposition to slave trading effected was to cause some well-known Kentuckians to do away with their redundant slaves by private sale rather than at public auction. Sales produced the same results—split families for the slaves and large monetary proceeds for the masters. As noted in the opening summary, Kentuckians sent away more than seventy thousands bondsmen in the last three antebellum decades; most were sold to work on cotton plantations in the Gulf states. A typical slave sale ad would read as follows:

> I wish to sell a Negro woman and four children,
> a good cook and washer. The children are very
> likely from 6 years to 11/2.
> I will sell them together or separately.
>   (Coleman 1940, 119)

Approximately 15 percent of the entire slave population of Kentucky was sold away during the 1850s (Tadman 1989, 12; Channing 1977, 103; Coleman 1940, 118).

The slave marts at Lexington handled the greatest volume of traffic in human chattel. Even though Louisville ranked as a larger metropolis, its location just across the Ohio River from freedom made its slave jails more precarious and its slave denizens more likely to attempt escape and more likely to succeed. Lexington also lay in the heart of the Blue Grass state whose farms and plantations held large numbers of enslaved African Americans. Over time, Kentucky masters found that some of their minions were redundant and sought to capitalize on their sale to obtain substantial monetary payments. In the 1850s, the typical adult slave brought a thousand dollars or more at auction.

Additionally, virtually every county courthouse held slave sales in the late autumn. Throughout Kentucky in November and December, residents across the commonwealth heard: "Step up Gentlemen! What'll you offer for this sprightly wench—she'll make you a good cook, washer, or ironer. Come Gentlemen, bid up on this likely gal. What do I hear?" Female slaves often had to bear the indignity of being disrobed in public to display their physical attributes for prospective buyers. One auctioneer, after the price for a black woman had been bid up to $1,450, ripped open her dress and shouted, "Look here, Gentlemen! Who is going to lose such a chance as this? Here is a girl fit to be the mistress of a king!" The bidding continued (Coleman 1940, 115, 132).

Coffles of sold slaves shuffling south became a frequent sight on Kentucky's roads as the antebellum years passed, though some traders used riverboats to convey their human cargo down the Ohio and Mississippi rivers. One observer visiting in Lexington noted, "There were about forty black men all chained together; each of them hand cuffed and they were arranged in rank and file. A chain, perhaps forty feet long, was stretched between the two ranks, to which short chains were joined, which connected with the handcuffs. Behind them were, I suppose, about thirty women, in double rank, the couples tied hand to hand" (Coleman 1938, 8).

Slave traders could make excellent money if they kept down expenses and handled the markets correctly. In 1840, one trader bought thirteen slaves in Kentucky for $5,292. He later sold the thirteen in Natchez, Mississippi, for a total of $8,695. His expenses for transport, food, and shelter for his human "inventory" amounted to three hundred dollars. Thus, he cleared around three thousand dollars for his winter's work, a tidy sum in those days. Even if he had to borrow the money to create capital for his purchases, he still had a good business margin, returning more than 50 percent on his invested capital (Coleman 1938, 4).

William Brown, himself a slave at the time, remembered that he worked to help "groom" some of the older bondsmen. "I had to prepare the old slaves for market. . . . I shaved old men's whiskers . . . I blackened gray hairs . . . they looked ten years younger." Since every slave brought a different price based on age, gender, and appearance, this grooming could substantially improve a slave trader's potential returns (Coleman 1938, 7).

Lewis C. Robards ranked as one of Kentucky's most notorious slave traders. He looked out for comely females who had an interracial heritage and light complexions. Then he regularly paid high prices for those African American women meeting these descriptions. He dressed them up and transported them to New Orleans where he hawked his human wares to fancy bordellos. A number of former Kentucky female slaves ended up as some of the Crescent City's most famous courtesans (Coleman 1938, 11–13).

Furthermore, he later became the most talked about slave catcher, after the Fugitive Slave Act of 1850 allowed agents to pursue runaways into the free states. Robards and his employees regularly visited Cincinnati and other Ohio towns attempting to capture and return escapees. He was accused of also taking along unwary free blacks who could not immediately provide proof of their status (Coleman 1940, 210–211).

The famous theme song of Kentucky, "My Old Kentucky Home," also drew on the aftereffects of the slave trade. Stephen Foster attempted to catch in words and melody the sadness Kentucky slaves felt after they had been sold south and were remembering their original home and families (Coleman 1938, 18).

THE UNDERGROUND RAILROAD

Kentucky's extensive river border with the free-labor Great Lakes states, Illinois, Indiana, and Ohio, offered the most propitious escape route from any large slave state. Many slaves as well as numerous free blacks fled to Canada during the antebellum years by passing through Ohio to Cleveland or Buffalo or Detroit. Many of the little farm villages and towns in the Ontario countryside between Windsor and Buffalo had small free black and runaway communities. Other blacks worked in the larger cities of Windsor, London, and Toronto. If an African American could make it to Canada, help awaited. As in the east, the road to freedom was described as the Underground Railroad, a group of safe houses and hideaways escaping slaves could use on their journey north. From 1818 onward, runaways and escapees began making their way to freedom from Kentucky across the Ohio River. By 1830, the Underground Railroad had been fully organized and for thirty years operated at full bore (Coleman 1940, 225–226).

A number of stops became famous among their patrons. The Rothier House in Covington had a secret tunnel from the cellar to the river that provided hiding places, a supply cache, and a propinquitous exit allowing the water border to be discreetly crossed in the still of night. Another of the main routes began just below Maysville at Ripley and made use of the Rankin House, home of Reverend John Rankin, an outspoken abolitionist and industrious provider for the hidden railroad (Coleman 1940, 223).

For example, Francis Fedric made his desires of escape known to individuals who had contacts to Underground Railroad agents. They arranged for his flight. They first helped him reach Maysville in the back of a wagon hidden under a cargo of rugs. Here Fedric was concealed in an attic garret until midnight when a group of armed men rowed him across the Ohio River and deposited him safely at the first station. He then was spirited surreptitiously across Ohio from secret station to secret station. He noted that everywhere he stayed, he was lodged as if he were a chosen guest (Coleman 1940, 230–231).

Henry Bibb, who had earlier escaped to Canada, published a newspaper called *The Voice of the Fugitive* from Windsor and Sandwich, Ontario, that regularly reported on the successful escape attempts from Kentucky. On June 16, 1853, he addressed Robert Todd (one of Abraham Lincoln's in-laws) in a report, "To Robert Todd et al., ten slaves made their escape from Newport, Kentucky, . . . came by the Underground Railroad. They are all well. . . . They only regret that they might have been in Canada long ago." He closed this communication with this ditty:

Farewell, old Master,
Don't come after me,
I'm on my way to Canada,
Where colored men are free.
      (Coleman 1940, 244)

Kentucky slaveholders in the counties that bordered the Ohio River organized larger and more extensive slave patrols in the 1830s and 1840s yet never succeeded in interrupting the pipeline to freedom. Some of the white patrons of the railroad were eventually found out, arrested, and imprisoned or expelled from Kentucky; nevertheless, the escape routes remained open. All the while, Henry Bibb in Sandwich continued to report the monthly new arrivals to freedom in Canada (Coleman 1940, 242).

KENTUCKY ANTISLAVERY ACTIVITY

Although the majority white public opinion in Kentucky remained distinctly pro-slavery until its demise in December 1865, a vocal minority always protested against the peculiar institution in the Blue Grass state. As noted, Reverend David Rice spoke out eloquently opposing slavery in the 1792 constitutional convention. Later, his remarks were published in pamphlet form: *Slavery, Inconsistent with Justice and Good Policy*. This summary not only became the first antislavery tract published in the Blue Grass state, but also became an important resource for all future native-grown Kentucky antislavery spokesmen (Coleman 1940, 290).

Some Presbyterians, agreeing with Reverend Rice, attempted to apply the doctrine of antislavery to their congregations but were consistently foiled by higher authorities. In 1802, two Presbyterian churches in the West Lexington presbytery sought to exclude slave owners from communion. The presbytery overruled the decision. Likewise, Concord Church attempted to exclude a member, John Moore, from church privileges because he sold enslaved African Americans on the auction block. The various presbyteries in Kentucky recommended that communicants use private sales rather than public auctions but, nevertheless, refused to sanction violators. Additionally, Presbyterian ministers continually spoke to their charges about the necessity of providing Christian education for their enslaved minions (Thompson 1963, 324–328).

The "emancipating" Baptists in 1808 formed the first abolition organization in Kentucky, the Kentucky Abolition Society. This group lasted until 1827. The colonization movement also received a great deal of support in Kentucky, but the Liberia experiment failed to bare significant fruit. Nancy Bell, whose Kentucky owner freed her family and sent them to Liberia, remembered that "the President of Liberia when I was there was a man from Lexington, Kentucky, by the name of Joseph Roberts. He was a very agreeable man. . . . The fruits, animals, vegetables and trees are not like we have here. The sheep have long hair . . . the rice and coffee are the best I ever tasted. . . . They wear fewer clothes there." She returned after the Civil War to rejoin a husband who had been a hero in the Civil War with the United States Colored Troops (Blassingame 1977, 556–558).

Supporters of Kentucky antislavery interests also founded Berea College in 1858 for the specific purpose of educating African Americans of both genders. Slave owners and pro-slavery supporters spoke out vehemently against this purported affront, opposing any type of educational institutions for blacks from inception. Pro-slavery opponents of Berea College, of antislavery interests, and of Underground Railroad operators drove out from Kentucky at least forty antislavery spokesmen during the late 1850s (Coleman 1940, 321–323; Filler 1960, 222).

Cassius M. Clay ranked as the most famous native Kentuckian of antislavery bent during the final antebellum years. Although from a wealthy slaveholding family, Clay grew up, nevertheless, supporting the national policies of his Whig kinsman, Henry Clay, also the political light of another native of Kentucky, Abraham Lincoln. At Yale University, Cassius Clay met abolitionist William Lloyd Garrison, who would soon launch the most aggressive antislavery publication in antebellum America, *The Liberator*. While at New Haven, Clay likewise became acquainted with John Andrew, the future antislavery governor of Civil War Massachusetts, and with John G. Whittier, the abolitionist poet, as well as with other members of the New

England Transcendentalists. Cassius Clay returned to Kentucky as a staunch antislavery advocate. He argued that the institution of slavery stood out as a most flagrant violation of human rights as well as a great moral and religious wrong. He supported a constitutional approach to ending slavery in Kentucky through a system of gradual emancipation that had worked well in states like New York and New Jersey after the American Revolution. Other Kentuckians opposed this position, treating him with scorn and epithets. No shrinking violet, Clay protected his newspaper, *The True American*, with a brace of cannon. On other occasions he fought duels with opponents and, in one noteworthy instance, defended his right to address a political gathering by whipping out a bowie knife and meeting pro-slavery roustabouts, blow for blow, on the speaker's podium itself. Clay, though Northern antislavery audiences applauded his courage in standing up to pro-slavery mobs, nevertheless effected little change in most white Kentuckian's attitudes toward blacks and slavery. He and other prominent Kentucky antislavery advocates attempted to address the slavery issue when delegates met in October 1849 to discuss writing a new constitution for the commonwealth: They failed miserably in trying to get gradual emancipation on the agenda (Coleman 1940, 301–314; Filler 1960, 221–222).

THE CIVIL WAR AND UNITED STATES COLORED TROOPS

Kentucky politicians attempted to chart a neutral course after the secession of the deep South and the Gulf states led to the Fort Sumter (South Carolina) crisis that flared up leading to the onset of a shooting war. The majority of Kentucky whites at the Civil War's advent were both pro-slavery in outlook as well as unionist in intent. Kentucky ranked as the only state with more than two hundred thousand slaves that did not secede. President Abraham Lincoln in a famous comment noted that he felt that the Union could sustain the loss of Virginia to the Confederacy but must keep Kentucky within the fold to ultimately prevail. For the first two years of the war, Lincoln walked a tight rope in policy initiatives, trying to appease the antislavery wing of his party while still maintaining Kentucky pro-slavery unionists as allies. His attempt at retaining the loyalty of pro-slavery Kentucky led in part to the incomplete jurisdiction proffered by the Emancipation Proclamation, which specifically exempted slaves in regions or states that had not seceded (Donald 1996, 299–301, 316–317, 364, 379).

The Emancipation Proclamation and other 1863 legislation led to the enrolling of black troops in the ranks of the Union army as cavalrymen, as artillerymen, and as infantry by the middle of that year. Kentucky pro-slavery interests protested that these rules did not apply to Kentucky slaves and attempted to cordon off the state from provost marshals and enlistment agents. Contrarily, non-slaveholders in Kentucky welcomed black enrollment, which offset draft quotas. Nevertheless, by the end of 1863, Kentucky held out as the only area in the Upper South exempt from black enlistment (Berlin 1982, 183, 191).

For the next six months, Union generals, provost guards, enlistment agents, slave owners and pro-slavery politicians waged a political war over the right of blacks from Kentucky to enlist in the Union army. Eventually, agents received full freedom to enroll any Kentucky black. An African American's position as a soldier wearing the "blue suit" meant that his own legal standing as a slave had ended, and sometimes freedom also applied to his family as well. Moreover, Kentucky blacks, before being allowed to enroll in the army locally, flocked to enlistment agents across the border in Tennessee. At Clarksville, thousands of African Americans from Kentucky were mustered into the Union army (Berlin 1982, 191–193).

Some officers provided refugee camps for black families accompanying men enlisting into the army. Others drove the tagalongs away. Some Kentucky whites, since slavery still was legal there, gathered up these black dependents and resold them back into slavery within the state. A number of these women and children had accompanied their husbands and fathers from Tennessee or Missouri and should not have had to endure more personal travail with the peculiar institution but found no advocate among most white Kentuckians. Even after the war ended, former owners began instituting claims against employers who paid wages to freedmen who whites claimed still legally belonged to them. Slavery stubbornly hung on throughout the autumn of 1865. Black bondage did not completely end in the Blue Grass commonwealth until sufficient states ratified the Thirteenth Amendment; this enactment became effective on December 18, 1865. On that date, at least sixty thousand African Americans in Kentucky still toiled in bondage (Berlin 1982, 194–195).

According to the 1860 census, the commonwealth included almost forty-two thousand black men between the ages of eighteen and forty-five. Of these, more than twenty-three thousand were mustered into the Union army. This enrollment percentage for African American enlistment topped all the states with significant black populations. Kentucky blacks as members of United States colored regiments fought in Tennessee, Northern Alabama, and Southwest Virginia, and manned fortifications along the Mississippi River (Berlin 1982, 12).

EMANCIPATION, WHITE TERROR, AND SEGREGATION

Black soldiers coming home from the war became the leaders of African American communities of freedmen and freedwomen. They also became targets for white retribution and violence. They endured the most systematic episodes of terror provided by "night riders" and by the Ku

Klux Klan. Widespread violence in Kentucky continued for years (Berlin 1982, 767–768).

Because Kentucky had never seceded, the commonwealth did not have to be officially "reconstructed." The Freedmen's Bureau had offices there but primarily succeeded only in getting back wages paid to blacks who had been promised compensation but who had not been recompensed for work completed. The Kentucky legislature soon adopted black codes and segregation laws that eventually found acceptance before the United States Supreme Court. The white-dominated legislature provided very few tools to enable the black Kentuckians to lift themselves out of poverty. Only revenue raised from black taxpayers could be used for African American education and school buildings. No state-supported institution in Kentucky offered advanced or professional degrees. Even Berea College, which had been originally founded to provide an educational outlet for black Kentuckians, stopped admitting African Americans in 1904 to conform to segregation resolutions. Kentucky African Americans were free and no longer slaves; however, they lived in a racially bifurcated society that relegated them to a second-class citizenship: educationally, socially, economically, and politically (Works Progress Administration 1939, 74–75).

REFERENCES

Allen, William B. 1872. *A History of Kentucky*. Louisville: Bradley & Gilbert.

Berlin, Ira, Joseph P. Reidy, and Leslie S. Rowland, eds. 1982. *Freedom: A Documentary History of Emancipation*, Series II, *The Black Military Experience*. New York: Cambridge University Press.

Blassingame, John W., ed. 1977. *Slave Testimony: Two Centuries of Letters, Speeches, Interviews, and Autobiographies*. Baton Rouge: Louisiana State University Press.

Channing, Steven A. 1977. *Kentucky*. New York: W.W. Norton.

Clark, Thomas D. 1942. *The Kentucky*. New York: Farrar & Rinehart.

Coleman, J. Winston. 1938. "Lexington's Slave Dealers and Their Southern Trade." *Filson Club Historical Quarterly* 12 (January): 1–23.

———. 1940. *Slavery Times in Kentucky*. Chapel Hill: University of North Carolina Press.

Davenport, F. Gavin. 1943. *Antebellum Kentucky*. Oxford, Ohio: Mississippi Valley Press.

Donald, David Herbert. 1995. *Lincoln*. New York: Simon & Schuster.

Dunnigan, Alice Allison. 1982. *The Fascinating Story of Black Kentuckians: Their Heritage and Tradition*. Washington, D.C.: Associated Publishers.

Filler, Louis. 1960. *The Crusade Against Slavery: 1830–1860*. New York: Harper & Row.

Harrison, Lowell H., and James C. Klotter. 1997. *A New History of Kentucky*. Lexington: University Press of Kentucky.

Tadman, Michael. 1989. *Speculators and Slaves: Masters, Traders, and Slaves in the Old South*. Madison: University of Wisconsin Press.

Thompson, Ernest Trice. 1963. *Presbyterians in the South*, Vol. One: *1607–1861*. Richmond: John Knox Press.
Works Progress Administration. 1939. *Kentucky*. Lexington: University Press of Kentucky.

WEB SITES

Henry Bibb's Narrative: http://docsouth.unc.edu/neh/bibliography.html
Josiah Henson and the Canadian Underground Railroad: http://www.uncletomscabin.org
A Kentucky Slave Chronicle: http://docsouth.unc.edu/neh/Johnson/Johnson.html
Underground Railroad in Kentucky: http://www.ket.org/underground/history/questionof.htm

Louisiana

TIMELINE

1718: New Orleans is founded by the Company of the West headed by John Law

1724: French government passes the *Code Noir* (Black Code) governing slavery in Louisiana

1729: Natchez Indians revolt against the French

1731: Company of the Indies (formerly Company of the West) returns control of New Orleans to the French Crown

1748–1756: Louisiana cyprus industry flourishes

1763: Louis XV of France cedes Louisiana to Spain

1764: Organized slave patrols develop in Louisiana

1769: Spain announces the Laws of Castile and the Indies to govern slavery in Louisiana

1789: Charles IV of Spain orders large plantations to provide chaplains for slaves

1795: Pointe Coupee Conspiracy, consisting of creoles, slaves, and whites, unsuccessfully attempts to end slavery in Louisiana

1803: United States purchases the Louisiana territory from France

1806: Territory of Orleans adopts black codes

1807: Emancipation Act is passed

1811: Slaves revolt in St. John the Baptist parish

1812, April 30: Louisiana enters the Union as a slave state

1850s: Louisiana legislature strengthens state laws affecting runaway slaves

1861, January 26: Louisiana secedes from the Union and joins the Confederacy

1865, May: Confederate resistance and slavery end in Louisiana

1868, June 25: Louisiana is readmitted to the Union

Slave and Free Black Population, Colonial Era (Hall 1992, 282)

Year	Slaves	Free Blacks
1763	4,598	3,654
1766	5,873	5,930
1777	9,201	7,728
1788	20,673	18,737
1797	23,698	19,389
1800	24,264	19,852

Slave and Free Black Population

Census Year	Slave Population	Population Percentage	Free Black Population	Population Percentage
1810	34,660	45	7,585	10
1820	69,064	45	10,476	7
1830	109,588	51	16,710	8
1840	168,452	48	25,502	7
1850	244,809	47	17,462	4
1860	331,726	47	18,647	3

Net Slaves Entries and Exits, by Decade (Tadman 1989, 12)

1800–1809: + 1,159	1830–1839: + 29,296
1810–1819: + 20,679	1840–1849: + 29,924
1820–1829: + 16,415	1850–1859: + 26,528

ORIGINS OF SLAVERY

Early attempts in the late seventeenth century to settle Louisiana failed to establish a permanent colony or to introduce slavery into the region. The French explorers' search for gold and silver came up empty, contributing to the initial failures. In 1718, though, the Company of the West, a private French company headed by John Law and given a monopoly of Louisiana's trade for twenty-five years, founded New Orleans. Initially, Louisiana began as a penal colony for France. Prisoners were sent to the region for a period of three years of hard labor. Afterward, they received land that they had cleared and cultivated. Over the next couple of decades, thousands of Europeans, mostly French, arrived in the area. Realizing the need for labor, the Company of the West provided African slaves (Din 1999, 4; Hall 1992, 5).

Hardship plagued the beginning stages of slavery in Louisiana. In 1712, only ten black slaves lived in the region. By 1721, the number increased to 514. Sweltering heat, food shortages, and backbreaking work made it difficult for the institution to take hold in Louisiana. Indians also served as a threat to the French settlement. In 1729, for example, the Natchez Indians rose up against the new settlers, destroyed a significant amount of the tobacco production, and killed approximately one-tenth of the population. These factors contributed to the company's decision to return control of the colony to the French crown in 1731 (Din 1999, 5; Hall 1992, 8, 86, 177).

The French slave trade brought approximately 5,591 slaves to the territory. These slaves came directly from Africa, from the region of Senegambia between the Senegal and Gambia rivers, and they arrived within the span of a decade. During the initial stages of slavery, bondsmen primarily engaged in tobacco and indigo production, built levees, cleared fields, and built drainage ditches. Slaves brought to Louisiana were also skilled in growing rice and turned the swamps into rice paddies. Nevertheless, the slave population increased slowly during the early French colonial period prior to the 1760s. Hardship plagued the colony in New Orleans and the Seven Year's War retarded the growth of slavery as France focused on more pressing issues than settling the colony.

In the decade following 1763, slavery truly began to take hold in the region after King Louis XV ceded Louisiana to Spain. When Spain took over Louisiana, a census revealed that approximately 5,940 slaves resided there, comprising 51 percent of the population. Under the Spanish administrators, who encouraged increased slaveholdings, the number of slaves and slave owners quadrupled from the 1760s to the 1790s. By the time President Thomas Jefferson negotiated the Louisiana Purchase of 1803, slaves had become accepted as an integral and necessary part of the Louisiana economy and society (Hall 1992, 29, 58, 121–126; Din 1999, 39).

THE GROWTH AND ECONOMICS OF SLAVERY

As slavery increased in the United States, it too began to grow in the Louisiana region. The ending of the slave trade in the United States in 1808 did not end the importation of slaves from outside the United States. Although the new arrival of slaves after this date came primarily from the older southern states, smuggling operations were big business and many slaves were imported from Africa and the West Indies. Louisiana witnessed such an increase in slaves from the southern states after 1803 that the state legislature passed laws forbidding the entry of undesirable slaves, specifically those who had committed serious crimes. The initial law, passed in 1826 and strengthened in 1829, decreed that masters traveling with their slaves into the state must present two affidavits testifying to the character of the slave and forbid the entry of slaves under the age of ten unless accompanied by their mother (Taylor 1963, 35–40).

As in other states, slave owners in Louisiana profited economically from the product of slave labor. Evidence suggests too that the profitability of slave labor also increased throughout the antebellum period. For example, in 1802, the average sugar cane acreage cultivated per hand was approximately two acres. This amount increased to three-and-one-third acres by 1827 and to five acres per hand by 1850. Part of this productivity increase was attributed to a growth in the number of large slaveholdings. By the 1850s, the state witnessed a 7 percent increase in larger slaveholdings; an increase from 19.8 percent to 26.8 percent in terms of the total number of slaves held in groups of from one hundred to five hundred. Simultaneously, there occurred a drop in the percentage of small slaveholding by the 1850s. This does not mean, however, that the yeoman farmer with fewer slaves did not profit. Those with fewer slaves more likely engaged in subsistence farming, were market oriented, and operated at a profit (Taylor 1963, 95–96).

The upkeep of slaves did cost money. Owners spent approximately fifty dollars per year on food, clothing, shelter, medical care, and insurance for each slave. This miniscule amount hardly diminished their investment in slaves. Evidence suggests that slave owners who engaged in cotton production received approximately a 7.6 percent return on their investment, and sugar planters received at least a 9 percent return. These are the minimum estimates, and in seasons of good harvest or high prices, owners witnessed an even greater return on their investment in slavery (Taylor 1963, 105).

Slave owners not only profited from the product of slave labor, but also slaves themselves served as a measure of wealth. Throughout the antebellum period, the price of slaves in the state steadily increased. In the 1830s, male slaves sold for approximately seven hundred fifty dollars, and female slaves sold for six hundred fifty dollars. By the mid-1850s, field hands in the state sold for approximately twelve hundred fifty dollars, and by the end of the decade this amount increased to eighteen hundred dollars for male slaves and sixteen hundred fifty dollars for female slaves (Taylor 1963, 51–53).

SLAVE LIFE

In 1724, the French government passed the *Code Noir* (Black Code) that detailed the expected behavior of masters and slaves. The *Code Noir* required that owners provide their slaves with adequate food and clothing. The first territorial legislature in Louisiana declared that slaves should receive at least one barrel of corn, or its equivalent in other food, per month. Slaves also received two shirts and two pairs of pants per year: one for the summer season, one for the winter season. Most slaves, except young children, received shoes. Working slaves also received hats and all adult slaves received blankets for the cold weather. At Christmas time, generous masters often supplemented this with gifts of additional clothing.

Although slave quarters varied from place to place and over time, by the 1850s planters made specific recommendations regarding slave quarters. Some owners suggested that each slave family receive its own house. In such cases, these houses were generally sixteen by eighteen feet with a wood plank floor and a shingled roof. The nicer quarters contained a brick chimney. Most slave houses had hooks for clothing, a bed with a cotton mattress, and sufficient bedclothes. These accommodations, however, were more likely found on the larger and wealthier plantations. Owners with fewer slaves at least provided some rudimentary shelter for their slaves. In this case, houses generally were quite small with a dirt floor, no windows, and only a bed and stool for furniture. If the owner held fewer than ten slaves, then generally one house suited all the slaves.

Owners too were deeply concerned about the health of their slaves, and this meant that owners supplied their labor force with adequate amounts of food. In the eighteenth century, slaves received one-and-one-half pounds of corn and one-half pound of lard daily. By the nineteenth century, their diet consisted mainly of one-half pound of pork and one quart of cornmeal per day. Some owners also allowed their slaves to cultivate a garden of an acre or two for their own food. In most places, slaves supplemented their diet with fish and small game, such as birds, raccoons, and possum (Hall 1992, 128).

The poor living conditions, however, often caused slaves to fall ill. Slaves suffered from respiratory diseases, malaria, yellow fever, scarlet fever, dengue fever, typhoid, and cholera. For children, the most frequent cause of illness was intestinal worms. Some plantations did have their own medical facilities. On the lager plantations, the owner or overseer often administered medical care. In some instances, owners designated a slave woman to serve as a sick nurse, a prestigious position on the plantation. In critical cases, though, owners did not hesitate to call for more professional medical care (Taylor 1963, 113–122).

Louisiana was not an exception during the antebellum period: Cotton was king in the state. Sugar cultivation also remained crucial to the state's economy. The majority of the slaves in Louisiana cultivated cotton on large plantations. Historians estimate that approximately 75 percent of the slaves worked on plantations that held more than fifty slaves. Furthermore, only 5 percent of all slaves lived and worked on farms that held five or fewer slaves. The routine of slave work in the cotton fields followed the general pattern of other slave states. Slaves rose an hour before daybreak, prepared their breakfast, and headed out to the fields. Slaves caught in their cabins after daybreak were summarily whipped. Slaves worked all through the day, possibly taking a break for lunch on some plantations, and continued to work well into the evening. The cultivation and grinding routine for sugar, however, was even more arduous. On most sugar plantations, owners divided slaves into groups for shift work. Each shift lasted approximately eight hours, and each slave was assigned two watches. Groups of slaves were assigned to perform specific tasks, such as cutting the sugar cane, hauling firewood for the grinder, manning the kettles, manning the grinder, and serving as firemen in case of mishap. The process of sugar cultivation and processing almost had an industrial appearance to it due to the numerous tasks involved and the organized manner in which the process had to be carried out (Taylor 1963, 61, 73–75).

Slavery in Louisiana existed not only on the smaller farms and plantations, but also in the cities. Many cities in Louisiana witnessed an abundance of skilled slave labor. Slaves worked as carpenters, bricklayers, blacksmiths, and artisans. Slaves also worked on steamboats, in hotels, and as drivers and sellers in the market areas.

As in other states, owners did hire out their slaves. In the early periods, however, this practice was not as common as in other states due to the low population of slaves. Unlike Texas, arrangements for hiring slaves were conducted solely with the master. Of course, hiring out was not always a matter of choice for the owner. In Louisiana, as in other parts of the South, the state often required owners to furnish slaves for public works projects, such as the building and maintaining of roads and levees and the building of railways. While the state itself did own slaves through the Board of Public Works, it still required owners to contribute their labor force to finish its projects (Taylor 1963, 32, 87–88).

In Louisiana, several intermingling factors worked to ensure the development of a rich and vibrant slave culture. A minority of the whites owned slaves, which led to the tendency for larger slaveholding among the Anglo elite. In addition, a majority of the slaves came from the same region of Africa. Furthermore, owners generally bought and sold slaves as family units, thus reinforcing slave culture and the importance of family in slave society. In Louisiana, the existence of slave families was the norm. The *Code Noir* forbade the breaking up of families, and in later years, owners could not separate children under the age of ten from their mothers. It also appears that owners were more willing officially to acknowledge marital relations. This involved the customary "broomstick" ceremony and, in many cases, an official religious marriage. In addition, many owners did not object to slave preachers marrying two slaves. It was not uncommon for a Catholic master to allow the local priest to perform the marriage ceremony for his slaves. Slave families also contained grandparents, highly revered in slave society. Due to these numerous factors, slave culture in Louisiana appeared highly Africanized, more so than other places in the United States, thereby contributing to a rich slave culture (Hall 1992, 160–168; Taylor 1963, 123).

Although the system of slavery was indeed harsh, it did not prevent slaves from enjoying extracurricular activities. Slaves broke the monotony of their life by fishing and hunting, gambling, playing music, and dancing. On the larger plantations, slaves attended, as spectators, festivals and balls thrown by their masters. There is evidence too that some masters allowed slaves their own balls or parties during the holiday season. As the threat to slavery and the fear of slave revolts increased, however, legislation also increased that curtailed such activities for fear it would provide the slaves with a chance to plot an escape or rebellion (Taylor 1963, 125–130).

In the beginning stages of slavery, runaway bondsmen were often very well armed and difficult to pursue. They received their arms from French soldiers who also ran away from the colony. Due to the nature of society, flight for slaves "was often a family affair." Slaves escaped by sea, sometimes up the Mississippi River to Natchitoches, and often moved further west into Texas. The dominant reason a slave ran away was fear of or reaction to punishment. Other contributing causes included avoiding work and the desire to be closer to kinfolk sold to a nearby plantation. If a slave did flee, the *Code Noir* required masters to inform the local magistrate. The law allowed slave patrols to enter a person's property without permission to search for a runaway slave. The only prohibition was that the patrol could not enter an owner's house nor any place that might be under lock and key. The laws regarding runaways and slave patrols did not change much in the first decades of statehood. The legislature simply added to the existing laws, primarily creating depots where runaways would be transported. Legislation, though, was powerless to stop the problem of flight. By the 1850s, the number of runaways had become a serious problem in the state, and the legislature acted by increasing the penalties against those who assisted or harbored runaways. In 1855, the legislature decreed that anyone harboring a runaway would be liable to a fine up to four hundred

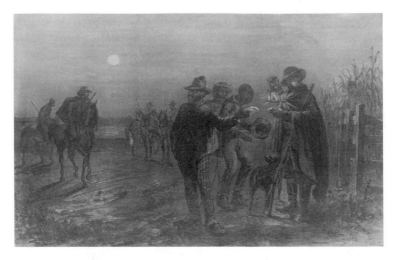

The patterollers, an institution peculiar to the antebellum
South, were a local guard raised and supported by planters to
control the movement of slaves and to hunt down escaped
slaves. In this drawing, the patteroller patrol checks the passes
of slaves moving along a levee road near New Orleans.
(Library of Congress.)

dollars. Those who furnished slaves with false papers faced a prison term
of up to fourteen years. Those who aided slaves in their plight faced a
potential twenty years in the state penitentiary (Taylor 1963, 169, 175, 183;
Hall 1992, 145–148; Ripley 1976, 7).

In Louisiana, more than any other area, organized Anglo religion
emerged as a significant aspect of slave life. Before 1800, Catholicism was
the official religion in Louisiana. Law required owners to teach their slaves
the rites and doctrines of the religion. The Jesuits and Capuchins, who
preached to the slaves and offered baptism and marriage rites, aided masters in this process. Unlike in the Protestant denominations, however, in
many Catholic churches slaves worshipped side by side with their masters. The Protestant denominations did not make inroads among slaves
until Louisiana became part of the United States; by then, however, owners were not required by law to give religious instruction to their chattel.
The Methodists, Presbyterians, and Episcopalians devoted some attention
to serving the religious care of slaves. The message that both Catholics and
Protestants preached to slaves generally emphasized loyal obedience to
one's master. Some churches in Louisiana allowed black ministers to lead
church services for slaves and free blacks; however, this was true only for
the Baptist and Methodist denominations. White ministers, however, constantly supervised black preachers. Although all the denominations lacked

sufficient missionaries to meet the slaves' needs on the plantations, many of the larger plantation owners did allow their slaves to receive religious instruction and to attend church services. The biggest obstacle to religious instruction, however, was the lack of qualified black and white ministers in the state. By the 1840s, a movement emerged to segregate the races for religious worship. This was due in part to the racial attitudes of whites, the prohibition against reading, and the emotional response of many black worshippers. The extent for which religious worship was made available to slaves, whether on the plantation or in a specific church, was always dependent upon the character and religious convictions of the owner. Some masters strongly encouraged slaves to worship in a Christian service, others flatly denied their slaves the opportunity to worship freely (Taylor 1963, 134–135, 145–148).

Despite any type of release that religion might have afforded slaves, it was not enough to keep slaves from rebelling against their situation. For example, the Pointe Coupee Conspiracy of 1795, consisting of Creoles, slaves, and whites, was aimed at ending the institution of slavery in Louisiana. Although it failed, it was significant because it revealed the organizational skills and the potential strength within the slave community. The conspiracy became therefore a turning point in terms of exacting control over slaves. In 1811, though, Louisiana witnessed another major slave revolt. Originating in St. John the Baptist parish, an estimated five hundred blacks, organized into companies with officers and armed with agricultural implements, marched toward New Orleans, destroying property and burning homes along the way. Their revolt eventually failed. Troops chased the rebels, swarmed upon them, and brutally killed approximately sixty-six individuals. Eleven blacks, accused of leading the revolt, were taken to New Orleans and promptly condemned to death. Their heads were then cut off and stuck on poles along the Mississippi River as a warning to other slaves. As a result of the 1811 revolt, politicians passed legislation requiring that for every thirty slaves, one white person should reside on the plantation proper. Slave revolts continued to worry fearful whites, and schemes did emerge occasionally, but, in general, whites successfully put down potential slave revolts by using confessions extracted through whipping and by the quick executions of suspected leaders (Hall 1992, 376; Taylor 1963, 213).

BLACK CODES

Rules affecting the lives of slaves and slave owners emerged from the very beginning of slavery. In 1724, the French government passed the *Code Noir*, which regulated the institution of slavery. Unlike others areas, masters in Louisiana were expected to give religious instruction to their slaves. In addition, they were restricted from punishing their slaves too severely.

Although they could whip their slaves, owners were prohibited from torturing or mutilating them. Violation of the law meant possible forfeiture of their slaves and prosecution. The exception to the rule, however, pertained to runaway slaves. In this case, law permitted owners to cut off the ears of the runaway slave and brand them on the shoulder with the fleur-de-lis (a flower design). Occurrence of a second offense meant a second branding, and a third offense was punishable by death by hanging. Those individuals found guilty of harboring runaway slaves received monetary fines. Whites were fined ten livres per day, and free blacks were fined thirty livres per day. Free blacks who could not pay the fine often were sold into slavery. The *Code Noir* did, however, provide slaves with an avenue of redress. If they were mistreated, they had the right to inform the attorney general of violations, who would begin proceedings against the master. Nevertheless, the slave could not testify against the owner. The *Code Noir* also prohibited masters from breaking up families through sale. Husbands and wives were to be kept together as well as children under the age of fourteen. Furthermore, slaves from age fourteen to age sixty could not be seized by authorities to pay for a master's debt unless the plantation itself too was seized. Thus, the common practice throughout much of Louisiana in both the French and Spanish period was to keep slave families intact. The *Code Noir* also permitted owners to manumit their slaves. Nevertheless, those slaves who received freedom received virtually no rights. Though this was the law, in reality its provisions were hardly enforced. Instead, masters took the law into their own hands, and slavery existed in a harsh and brutal atmosphere of complete restriction. During the French era, masters often brutalized and killed some slaves to keep the rest of the slave population in check. Although the *Code Noir* prohibited this, evidence suggests that no master was ever tried under the law (Din 1999, 8–10; Hall 1992, 154; Taylor 1963, 22).

When Spain took control of Louisiana in 1763, it continued to operate under the *Code Noir* for several years. In 1769, though, Spain announced that the laws of Castile and the Indies were in effect for Louisiana. Based upon the Justinian Code of the sixth century, Spanish law recognized the humanity of slaves and did not view them merely as chattel. Under Spanish rule, the law did not allow for the protection of slave families and parents could be separated from their children, as could wives from husbands. Slaves, however, did gain the right to complain to officials about their treatment and even demand that owners establish a slave's value so they might buy their own freedom or be sold. Nevertheless, Spanish officials had difficulty implementing these rules, for they faced dissension from the French colonial elite who owned the plantations in Louisiana. Although Spanish law provided many rights to slaves who converted to Christianity—the right of marriage, parenthood, fraternization, and avenues by which a slave could obtain his or her freedom—reality says that the planter elite retained much control over their slaves, regardless of the law (Din 1999, 42–46; Hall 1992, 304).

In 1806, the Territory of Orleans adopted numerous black codes covering the actions of owners and slaves. For example, slaves were prohibited from testifying against whites. In addition, masters were allowed to separate husbands and wives and sell children over the age of ten away from their mothers. Regarding the work routine, masters were required to give their slaves one hour for breakfast and a two-hour break at noon from May to November. By law, masters were permitted to whip their slaves or could have their slaves whipped by the local jailor. This practice was most notable in New Orleans. While whipping appeared the most common form of punishment, owners also resorted to other measures, for example, demoting a house servant to field labor. Slave patrols also were an effective means of keeping not only slaves, but also slave owners in their place. The parishes of Louisiana were divided into specific wards. Each ward was canvassed by a patrol that consisted of at least five men, generally between the ages of fifteen and fifty. Slave owners who refused the patrols access to their land and slave quarters received a fine between fifty and one hundred dollars (Taylor 1963, 196–199; Ripley 1976, 8).

During the Civil War, Louisiana strengthened its black codes. Slavery existed in such a tenuous position with the invasion of federal forces that the state government resorted to tightening its grip on the institution. Slaves during this crisis were not allowed to travel without a pass, were not allowed to assemble in groups outside of the plantation, were forbidden to gamble or even watch gambling, were forbidden to drink, and were forbidden to own a firearm, dog, or horse (Ripley 1976, 9).

FREE BLACKS

A free black population emerged in the early stages of slavery. Many avenues existed for slaves to obtain their freedom. Oftentimes, free black men would marry black slave women and pay for their freedom. Any children from this marriage were considered free as well. During the French era, black women often used sexual relations with white men to gain their freedom. Thus, the majority of free blacks in Louisiana, 81 percent, were mulatto. Additionally, some owners, out of belated kindness, freed their slaves after years of faithful service (Hall 1992, 129–130, 274; Taylor 1963, 162).

The emancipation of slaves persisted as a concern to the whites of Louisiana. Therefore, lawmakers passed the 1807 Emancipation Act that required owners to provide to a parish judge a statement of age and good behavior for their slave if they desired to emancipate him or her. Politicians made manumission procedures more difficult in 1827. The state legislature required that owners submit a statement of reasons why they were manumitting their slave. A police jury would review this statement whereupon approval had to be rendered by a three-fourths vote. This procedure applied specifically to slaves under the age of thirty. In addition, beginning in 1827, only those slaves who were natives of Louisiana could obtain their freedom. In 1830, though, legal codes made it more difficult for owners to free their slaves. Legislation required owners to post a one thousand dollar bond to insure that the freed slave would leave the state within a required thirty days. The exception to this rule was only if a slave was freed for a worthy reason and so deemed by a consensus of the local police jury. The law restricting manumissions in Louisiana, however, constantly changed, and there appeared to be no established pattern except of gradually restricting the practice. Furthermore, police juries had an increasing tendency to forgo the requirement of the slave leaving the state, adding to the increase in the number of free blacks in Louisiana (Taylor 1963, 155–157).

The immigration of free blacks into Louisiana also emerged as a considerable issue. Many of the free blacks came to Louisiana from Texas, especially after 1840 when Texas required that all free blacks leave the republic. Louisiana law, however, did attempt to keep the undesirables out of the state, and beginning in 1817, those free blacks who had a criminal record were forbidden entry. With the increase in the free black population, fearful whites moved to restrict the entry of free blacks in the 1840s. The immigration law of 1842 attempted to forbid all free black immigration into the state, but lawmakers over the next decade would amend the law several times to allow free blacks to remain. By 1850, the U.S. Census Bureau estimated the free black population at 17,462. This dramatic increase over the years worried many white residents who viewed the presence of a large free black community as a threat to the institution of slavery. This was especially true as abolitionist forces began to make their presence known in the state before the Civil War. In 1852, scared whites reacted and the governor declared that all newly freed slaves had to leave the state within one year of their emancipation. Furthermore, in 1852, the state legislature dealt a heavy blow to the practice of manumissions and the allowing of newly freed slaves to stay in the state. The assembly ruled that no slave could be set free unless he or she was sent out of the United States within one year. In addition, any owner who freed a slave was required to post one hundred fifty dollars to offset the slave's cost of return to Africa. Restrictions against manumissions increased in 1855 when the legislature passed a new act requiring owners to sue the state if they wished to free their slave. While slaves freed under the new act were not required to leave the state, owners were required to pay the cost of their suit, regardless of the outcome. The Louisiana Supreme Court, however, declared this act unconstitutional. The legislature, though, continued to press for restrictions on manumissions and in 1857 ruled slave emancipation illegal (Taylor 1963, 156–157).

Free blacks in Louisiana, as in other states, were not considered equals with whites, even in the legal sense. For example, an 1808 law required that all free black persons identify themselves as such on all business and legal documents. In addition, any free black who owned a gun was required to keep freedom papers in his possession. The law also restricted the social activities of free blacks by prohibiting them in many areas from socializing with slaves and gambling with whites. In some regions of Louisiana, free blacks were completely prohibited from moving from one place to another. Violations of these laws carried the penalty of whipping, fines, or jail time. Once slaves obtained their freedom, however, it was not uncommon for the free black males to hold their wives, children, and other family members in slavery. They did so with the intention of eventually setting them free. Some, however, did own family members and other blacks for personal economic gain.

Though legally and socially marginalized, free blacks were nevertheless protected by some legislation that protected their lives and limited liberties. For example, free blacks were allowed to sue white persons. Free blacks also were allowed to own land and slaves, and most lawsuits against whites involved cases of property damage or injury to slaves. Additionally, courts upheld the right of free blacks to enter into business contracts with whites and protected blacks from being kidnapped. Anyone found guilty of kidnapping a free black faced a one-thousand-dollar fine and a prison term of fourteen years.

Most free blacks who owned land eked out an existence as small farmers, and some who owned land appeared very successful. Many held estates valued in excess of ten thousand dollars. Such economic success for free blacks appeared extremely rare in the rest of the South. Free blacks also worked in a variety of skilled trades, such as coopers and blacksmiths. In the urban areas, free blacks generally held unskilled jobs, working as waiters, chimney sweeps, railroad hands, and laborers. Free black women generally served in some domestic capacity in the urban areas.

Whatever freedom or liberty they might have enjoyed, free blacks were expected to render their services to the community and state. They were required to accept duty on patrols as police and as firemen and were likewise liable for military service. Those who saw military duty, though, especially in the Battle of New Orleans, were held in high esteem in the black community.

THE CIVIL WAR

During the Civil War, Louisiana slaves found themselves impressed into Confederate service. Slaves were forced to build fortifications, to work on railroads, and to labor in salt works, coal mines, hospitals, and saw mills. Usually the government impressed no more than one-seventh to one-fifth of an owner's slaves, although law permitted the impressment of up to 50 percent. Service in the Confederate army generally was worse than on the plantation. Slaves had poor food and housing and often fell sick. In addition, they received beatings on a daily basis. Army overseers did not have a personal stake in this labor force and administered the lash at the least amount of provocation (Ripley 1976, 10).

Slave owners generally opposed the impressment of slaves. This practice by the Confederate government, and the early presence of Union troops, forced many slave owners to flee with their slaves. As the Union presence increased in 1862, many slave owners fled to Texas. Sometimes they left the women and children behind, taking only the strongest and most able workers. The act of fleeing was significant because it undermined the master-slave relationship. Slaves witnessed firsthand the fear and trepidation of their owners. This served to diminish the absolute power of the master over the slave. Not only did slaves leave with their masters, but slaves also took every opportunity of the crisis to flee themselves. This was especially true if they had knowledge of Union forces nearby, where they hoped to find freedom behind Union lines. Union forces did not help matters during the Civil War. Oftentimes troops would move through the parishes and free the slaves. In one of the most famous instances, the Teche expedition, federal troops crisscrossed through the parishes of Louisiana in the spring of 1863. They were often greeted by overjoyed slaves, who offered them food, supplies, and information. The Teche expedition liberated approximately eight thousand slaves. While this number accounts for only a fraction of the total slave population, it remains significant in terms of its impression, revealing the strength and the impact of federal forces in the area (Ripley 1976, 14–21).

A problem existed, however, with the number of free and runaway slaves. So many slaves made their way to Union lines, hoping for freedom, that they had to be turned away. Benjamin F. Butler, a prewar Massachusetts Democrat politician and lawyer, nicknamed "the Beast" for his strict rule, harshness, and verbal criticism of the South, held command of the federal forces occupying Louisiana. Due to the number of slaves, and the inability of federal troops to adequately feed and shelter them, Butler adopted the policy of refusing runaway slaves. Thus, those slaves not employed in some manner by the Union troops were turned away and subjected to the "laws of the community." Butler and his men did pad the work order sheets and falsified documents on the behalf of many slaves. Nevertheless, the numbers were too great, and the Union was limited in the number of runaways it could care for. Butler, however, changed his policy in 1863. After President Abraham Lincoln announced the Emancipation Proclamation, which freed the slaves in territory that the Union did not control, and with the arrival of more federal troops, Butler was forced to accept more runaway slaves and freedmen. Butler, however, took advantage of the situation. He used this labor force to harvest the sugar cane crops of abandoned plantations, a rich source of profit for the government. Black laborers, though, worked the plantations not as slaves, but as wage laborers (Ripley 1976, 26–29, 36–38).

In the spring of 1863, Federal officials began the widespread enlistment of Louisiana blacks into the Union army. Louisiana African Americans flocked to the Union banner. All told, a little more than twenty-four thousand blacks were mustered into the Union army before the end of the war. This comprised 31 percent of all eligible black males from the state, a percentage of black enlistment that was exceeded only by Tennessee among the seceded states (Berlin 1982, 12).

Three black Louisiana regiments, including the First and Third Louisiana Native Guards, joined the attack on the strongly fortified Rebel positions at Port Hudson in May 1863. These units even had a number of black company officers, which was very unusual for the Civil War. They received high praise for their valor from white troops and from their commander. In June, other black Louisiana troops met white Confederates with the same steadfast bravery at Milliken's Bend. These two engagements went a long way to reducing the skepticism many white Union soldiers had about African American troops when the first black regiments had appeared along the Mississippi River (Berlin 1982, 518).

EMANCIPATION AND RECONSTRUCTION

In 1865, Louisiana witnessed the birth of the Republican Party. Free blacks played an essential role in its formation and represented the most radical contingent, demanding an equal voice in the party. Unlike other states, a significant population of free blacks in New Orleans owned personal property, had skills, and held slaves of their own. Thus, entering Reconstruction, they had a solid economic foundation on which to stand to fight for further equality. In the 1867 Republican convention, for example, blacks held 50 percent of the delegate seats and research reveals that they played a more active role than whites did at the convention. As such, they wielded a strong voice in the writing of Louisiana's new state constitution in 1868. The new state constitution resembled that of most politically reconstructed southern states, yet it had it own unique and controversial features. For example, it included a bill of rights that asserted full social equality regardless of race. Blacks were theoretically able to enjoy the same rights and privileges as whites in areas of transportation, business, education, and voting (Tunnell 1984, 67, 111, 117–118).

Not only did the appearance of racial unity exist, but also during Reconstruction, the black community in many areas unified, erasing to a small extent the noticeable class divisions that existed between elite free blacks and plantation slaves. The appearance of unity, though, was based upon paternalism. The relationship was one of reciprocity; the newly freed slaves gained an elite leadership, the elite gained the masses, a necessary following. Because they held a productive role in society, elite blacks expected a level of deference from the newly freed slaves, and elite blacks appeared concerned that freedmen learn the importance of unity by embracing education, religion, and good moral values (Tunnell 1984, 88).

Although the Republican Party might have served as a unifying organ between the races somewhat and might have served to unify the black community on some level, Louisiana, like other states, was plagued by violence. As elsewhere, disgruntled whites found a home in organized secret societies, such as the Swamp Fox Rangers, the Hancock Guards, and the Seymour Knights. The most important group was the Knights of the White Camelia. These societies brought down a reign of terror in Louisiana, especially during the presidential election of 1868. They, through violence, kept blacks away from the ballot box, destroyed ballots, tampered with election returns, and rode in armed fashion during the day and night. Oftentimes their violence was of the most brutal nature: pulling blacks out of their homes, torturing them, shooting them, lynching them, and beheading them. In the months preceding the election, several hundred blacks, a conservative estimate, experienced brutal death. In many parts of Louisiana, full-scale race riots erupted, with free blacks generally on the losing side of the conflict (Tunnell 1984, 153–156).

In all, there is no simple pattern to Louisiana slavery and freedom. It appears to be an existence of extremes. In Louisiana, compared with other southern areas, free blacks enjoyed more right and privileges, slave families were more pervasive, the brutality and conditions of slavery were harsher, the racial mixing was more prevalent, and the racial tensions were more explosive and violent.

REFERENCES

Berlin, Ira, Joseph P. Reidy, and Leslie S. Rowland, eds. 1982. *Freedom: A Documentary History of Emancipation*, Series II, *The Black Military Experience*. New York: Cambridge University Press.

Din, Gilbert C. 1999. *Spaniards, Planters, and Slaves: The Spanish Regulation of Slavery in Louisiana, 1763–1803*. College Station: Texas A&M University Press.

Hall, Gwendolyn Midlo. 1992. *Africans in Colonial Louisiana: The Development of Afro-Creole Culture in the Eighteenth Century*. Baton Rouge: Louisiana State University Press.

King, Norma, ed. 1993. *A Northern Woman in the Plantation South: Letters of Tryphena Blanche Holder Fox, 1856–1876*. Columbia: University of South Carolina Press.

Macdonald, Robert R., John R. Kemp, and Edward F. Haas, eds. 1979. *Louisiana's Black Heritage*. New Orleans: Louisiana State Museum.

Ripley, C. Peter. 1976 *Slaves and Freemen in Civil War Louisiana*. Baton Rouge: Louisiana State University Press.

Rodrigue, John C. 2001. *Reconstruction in the Cane Fields: From Slavery to Free Labor in Louisiana's Sugar Parishes, 1862–1880.* Baton Rouge: Louisiana State University Press.

Taylor, Joe Gray. 1963. *Negro Slavery in Louisiana.* Baton Rouge: Louisiana Historical Society.

Tunnell, Ted. 1984. *Crucible of Reconstruction: War, Radicalism and Race in Louisiana, 1862–1867.* Baton Rouge: Louisiana State University Press.

WEB SITES

Louisiana Slavery: http://www.rootsweb.com/~afamerpl/plantations_usa/LA/LA_plantations.html

The Man Who Sold His Wife: http://docsouth.unc.edu/oneal/menu.html

Slave Narrative of James Robert: http://docsouth.unc.edu/neh/roberts/menu.html

Slavery in Early Louisiana: http://www.dickshovel.com/slavery.html

Slavery Petitions: http://history.uncg.edu/slaverypetitions/video/cowgill.html

Maryland

TIMELINE

1634–1635: Mathias de Souza and Francisco, mulatto servants of Father Andrew White, arrive in Maryland

1664: Slavery is legally defined—all blacks transported to Maryland are automatically considered slaves

1671: Statute is enacted declaring that baptism does not confer freedom on enslaved Africans

1698–1720s: Large numbers of Africans are imported into Maryland

1739–1740: Jack Ransom's slave conspiracy erupts in Prince George's County

1778: Maryland Quakers require members in good standing to sell their slaves

1780: Maryland enrolls slaves in its militia and Continental Line regiments

1783: Maryland bans the importation of slaves

1788, April 28: Maryland ratifies the U.S. Constitution and enters the Union

1790: Manumission statutes become legal and many Maryland slaves are legally freed as a result

1796: Free blacks are barred from voting and holding elective offices

1861, April 19: Riots break out in Baltimore, leading President Abraham Lincoln to suspend the writ of habeas corpus in the state and lock up numerous pro-Confederate spokesmen

1862, March: Military personnel are forbidden from returning runaways to slave owners

1864, November 1: New state constitution takes effect, ending slavery in Maryland

1864–1865, November–March: Major General Lew Wallace operates an unofficial Maryland "freedman's bureau" to protect newly freed former slaves

1865, September–November: Widespread burning of black churches occurs in Queen Anne's, Dorchester, and Kent Counties

Slave and Free Black Population

Census Year	Slave Population	Population Percentage	Free Black Population	Population Percentage
1790	103,036	32	8,043	2.5
1800	105,655	31	19,587	5
1810	111,502	29	33,927	9
1820	107,397	26	39,730	10
1830	102,994	23	52,938	12
1840	89,737	19	62,078	13
1850	90,368	15.5	74,723	13
1860	87,189	13	83,942	12

Colonial Maryland Slave Population Estimates

Year	Total, Slaves and Free Blacks	Population Percentage
1715	9,530	19
1734	36,000	28
1756	46,225	30

**Net Slave Entries and Exits, by Decade
(Tadman 1989, 12)**

1790–1799: – 22,221	1830–1839: – 33,753
1800–1809: – 19,960	1840–1849: – 21,348
1810–1819: – 33,070	1850–1859: – 21,777
1820–1829: – 32,795	

ORIGINS OF SLAVERY

In 1634, two ships, the *Ark* and the *Dove*, slid quietly out of the Thames River in London, England, carrying settlers bound for the new colony of Maryland. The adventurers stopped briefly at Isle of Wight off the southern coast of England, and surreptitiously brought aboard two Jesuit priests. One, Father Andrew White, carried along his personal body servant, Mathias de Souza, a mulatto of African ancestry. Mathias survived the trans-Atlantic crossing and became the first black to reside in Maryland. The following year, Father White sent for a second servant, Francisco, also a mulatto of African ancestry. Both Mathias and Francisco were probably indentured servants rather than slaves but, nevertheless, ranked as the first persons with an African lineage to live in Maryland (Andrews 1929, 63–64; Brugger 1988, 6).

As in Virginia, Maryland's Chesapeake Bay neighbor, few blacks resided in the colony before the 1670s. Their legal status in Maryland, likewise, remained a gray area until the Colonial Assembly passed an act in 1664: "that all negroes or other slaves already within the Province and all negroes and other slaves to be hereafter imported into the Province shall serve *durante vita* [during their life]. And all children born of any negro or other slave shall be slaves as their fathers were for the terms of their lives." Thus, Marylanders automatically considered any black entering the colony a slave with lifetime service (Andrews 1929, 192).

Before 1700, however, the Maryland colonial court granted freedom to a number of residents with African ancestry who provided proof that they indeed held papers of indenture. Maryland's judiciary freed these blacks with limited bonds who had been held past their agreed-upon years. Blacks, such as John Baptiste, had signed labor contracts and promised to serve a master in Maryland for a stated period. The master then went back on the contract and tried to turn an inexpensive servant into a lifetime bondsman, since an indentured servant cost about 50 percent less than a slave. The court freed Baptiste in 1653 and others in 1676, 1678, and 1693. Yet the court also presumed that any black without papers automatically ranked as a slave with a lifetime's service (Brugger 1988, 43).

Moreover, the Maryland Assembly declared in 1671 that baptism into Christianity did not confer freedom upon African slaves. They reiterated this statement in a 1692 resolution. In 1695, the Maryland representatives enacted rules that restrained the "frequent assembly" of blacks. Furthermore, a 1705 statute prohibited slaves from bearing arms without written permission from their owners. Thus, by the time large numbers of African slaves began appearing in the colony, the codes defining slavery and slave life along the upper Chesapeake Bay area had already been enacted and African American bondage-in-perpetuity had taken on its familiar form (Brugger 1988, 51; Andrews 1929, 203).

The number of slave imports into Maryland increased dramatically after 1695. Most were carried directly to the Chesapeake Bay region from West Africa. By 1710, slaves comprised a quarter of the population on the "Western Shore," as the locals then designated southern Maryland with its siting on the western side of the Chesapeake Bay. Moreover, Colonial officials encouraged the slave trade, as the provincial government received a head tax on all imported Africans. The Colonial Assembly distributed part of this revenue to trustees who set up St. John's College in Annapolis (Brugger 1988, 51; Andrews 1929, 203).

THE MIDDLE PASSAGE

Slave traders and ship's captains initially transported mostly enslaved blacks from the Caribbean to Maryland. Hence, many of the first Africans toiling in Maryland's tobacco fields already knew what was expected of slaves and most evidently knew at least some English. After 1698, however, traders shipped the overwhelming majority of imported blacks brought to Maryland directly from Africa. From 1700 to 1770, thousands of West Africans who survived the "Middle Passage" ended up in the Chesapeake Bay region (Kulikoff 1986, 40).

The process began along the West African coast. An English captain in charge of a "slaver," an oceangoing ship that specialized in carrying human cargo, traded for slaves at depots, called factories, sited along the coastline often near river mouths. Most Africans bound for the Chesapeake area originated from settlements near the west coast of Africa and were typically purchased from locations extending from the Gambia River in the north to the Congo River in the south. English ship captains bought the largest numbers for Atlantic transport from depots along the "slave coast" in Benin at the mouth of the Niger River delta. After acquiring a full load of human chattel, held in stinking cargo holds below decks, the captain would set out across the Atlantic Ocean. Deaths among the African cargo generally ranged from 2 to 20 percent during the crossing (Kulikoff 1986, 321–322).

Each transported individual, seldom clothed, was chained onto wooden planking directly up against his or her neighbor with no privacy, men and women interspersed. The holds quickly became pestilential pits overflowing with vomit and human waste. "Good" captains would occasionally bring everyone up onto the open deck where each captive would be subjected to a dousing from seawater and allowed to get back circulation in their limbs. Some captains also ran water through the lower holds periodically to at least cursorily clean out the mess. A daily inspection of the human cargo uncovered any dead who were summarily discarded over the side of the ship. On the open ocean, sailors in other vessels said that they could smell the "slavers" before they saw them. This horrendous experience of being chained into a stinking, filthy cargo hold for the Atlantic trip became known as the "Middle Passage."

Some captains laid over for a few weeks in the Caribbean to give time for the survivors to recover from the journey and to improve their potential sale price. Ships then made their way up the coast to the Chesapeake Bay where "slavers" called at Jamestown and Annapolis. They also put in at plantation wharves along the tidal estuaries. Captains then paraded their human cargo before potential buyers: neighboring planters as well as local slave traders who bought coffles of Africans that they carried into the interior for sale to landowners who lived farther away from the river highways. Most captains disposed of their human cargo within a month or two. Most slaves experienced being publicly displayed three or four times before a bargain was struck (Kulikoff 1986, 323; see Virginia chapter).

The captains and their financial backers could extract a great deal of profit from buying and selling humans as long as the mortality of their cargo remained manageable. The cost for slaves along the coast of Benin averaged from four to six pounds each. The price for slaves in the Chesapeake area averaged from twenty-five to thirty-five pounds per individual in the 1720s and forty pounds or more by the 1750s. Thus, the profit margins ran from seven to ten times the original purchase price. Two hundred slaves successfully transported across the Atlantic could generate two thousand to five thousand pounds of profit. Bristol, England, merchants in particularly greatly benefited from this trade in human commodities (Middleton 1953, 136–139).

COLONIAL SLAVE LIFE AND SLAVE POPULATION

When African-born chattel first arrived in Maryland, still in shock from the Middle Passage, completely new life circumstances immediately confronted them as they attempted to survive from day to day. Most of the experienced bondsmen who already lived on the local farms and plantations came from the Caribbean and spoke English; the African-born used any one of a dozen different West African dialects. The Caribbean-born or Caribbean-experienced slaves understood what type of behavior masters required; the African-born slaves did not. Most owners, therefore, felt that their new minions needed to be "broken-in." Some masters even distributed their new human chattel to "slave-breakers" who would be responsible for teaching the new slaves the correct behavior and instilling work discipline. Most slave-breakers used the lash and whippings to educate their charges (Kulikoff 1986, 6, 319, 324).

Many masters also stripped their new chattel of their last bit of individuality by changing or altering their African names to ones chosen by the slave owner. Blacks had to adjust to different food, to different weather (including harsh cold winters), and to a different lifestyle. They likewise confronted new germs and had to experience their own "seasoning" in acquiring immunity to local viruses. Approximately one in four newly imported African-born slaves failed to survive their first year in the Chesapeake area (Kulikoff 1986, 324–326).

As greater numbers of newly imported Africans arrived through the years, newcomers more easily found other native-Africans who could help them adjust and sometimes others who spoke their language. By the 1720s, family life became possible as the numbers of women rose. By the 1740s, most black men on the Eastern Shore and southern Maryland (Western Shore) could generally find marriage partners. Large plantations offered the best locations for family life, as often husband and wives could live on the same home place. Others had to be content with broad husbands and wives. A broad husband or wife referred to a marriage partner who did not reside on the same site (Kulikoff 1986, 335–337).

Furthermore, even large slaveholders like Captain Charles Calvert, who owned fifty-five human chattel, split up his African American population among four different venues. Thus, broad husbands were common and many had to travel to visit and spend time with their families. Children almost always lived with the mother. Most husbands joined their wives and children on Saturday night and stayed through Sunday, returning to their home place on Sunday night. Each had to be careful to get back home on time to avoid punishment for surpassing their allotted permissible time away from their own masters (Kulikoff 1986, 371–372; Yentsch 1994, 172–173).

Slaves lived in two types of houses: log cabins and duplexes that had doors at opposite ends and a shared main wall separating the living spaces. Masters grouped most housing for slaves in one area, called the "quarters." Larger slave owners, like Calvert, had four separate quarters on his acreage. Once Africans developed family lives, the slave experience became more tolerable. The family and the quarters became the center of love, life, and enjoyment. Africans gathered to play the banjo and balafo, a xylophone-type instrument, and to tell folk stories. In Annapolis, with its more concentrated population, blacks gathered on Saturday evening or Sunday afternoon for "tumultuous meetings." Here the men and women dressed up in their best before going out. At the meetings they played music, danced, shouted, and sang (Kulikoff 1986, 348, 368; Yentsch 1994, 178).

Runaways and blacks without papers were also relatively frequent at this time. Furthermore, the proximity of the frontier and the wilderness provided a potential destination for blacks on the lam. In 1728, escaped slaves attempted to organize a small maroon community west of Prince George's County with the help of local Native Americans. (Maroon communities were settlements of some duration organized by runaway slaves.) Many runaways, however, were simply men who were trying to visit family and friends without written passes. Some tried to visit family members who had been moved by masters to distant quarters or who had been sold away from the home place. Roughly a third of all runaways were men attempting unauthorized visits (Land 1977, 190; Kulikoff 1986, 328).

Colonial Maryland also experienced one well-documented slave conspiracy. Jack Ransom organized a group of mostly recently imported Africans in an attempt to overthrow their white masters. Ransom evidently planned the attempt for many weeks and involved numerous slaves in the St. Paul's parish area of Prince George's County. The conspirators hoped to forestall discovery by communicating with other plotters by speaking only in African dialects. After eight months of delays, the plans for the attempted uprising finally leaked out. Local authorities arrested Ransom; he was later tried and executed. The town of Annapolis then set up a military "troop" of cavalry and infantry to guard against further insurrections and to more assiduously check wandering blacks for passes (Land 1981, 166; Kulikoff 1986, 329–330).

The great increase in African slave imports, moreover, altered the relationship between white indentured servants and slaves. In Talbot County, for example, in the 1680s, the population included about eight hundred white indentured servants and only two hundred slaves. By the 1730s, this ratio reversed. The Talbot County population in 1733 included about seven hundred fifty slaves and only one hundred thirty servants (Land 1977, 161–165).

As the summary chart notes, the slave population in Maryland increased rapidly in years from 1700 to 1760. By 1715, more than nine thousand slaves resided in Maryland, comprising 19 percent of the total population. By the 1750s, the African American population had jumped to more than forty-six thousand or about 30 percent of the entire populace. By 1760, almost half the planters owned slaves (Land 1981, 166; Greene 1932, 123–142).

THE ERA OF THE AMERICAN REVOLUTION

The era of the American Revolution (1770–1790) provided a watershed for Maryland slavery. In the years immediately preceding the Revolution, slavery was still on the incline. Ship captains, with slaves for sale, continued to visit the Chesapeake area up through the early 1770s. By the end of the revolutionary era, however, slave importations had been banned and the tendency toward increased manumissions had led to a decided jump in the free black population. Only the tobacco-growing slave owners in the southern Maryland counties continued to find bonded labor profitable in agricultural pursuits. This long-term trend extended throughout the Early National period (1790–1820) and the antebellum era (1820–1861). This result was characterized by the large-scale sale or transportation of enslaved African Americans to areas farther south, by the increase in the number of free blacks, and by the decline in the number of Maryland slaves. Four general factors contributed to the change in the long-term outlook for slavery: the widespread use of human rights language and rhetoric by revolutionary era politicians, the antislavery convictions of some religious denominations, the declining economics of agricultural slavery—particularly on the Eastern Shore, and the actions of the British (Kulikoff 1986, 418–422).

At the onset of the revolt against British rule, Maryland slaveholders became terrified at the events transpiring in neighboring Virginia. Lord Dunmore, the exiled Royal Governor of Virginia, had declared that he would free the slaves of Patriots if their bondsmen could reach his military forces or ships. Maryland slave owners had already taken steps to better arm the local militia and had wheedled four hundred stands of arms out of Governor Robert Eden to help four southern counties guard against any attempted slave uprising. When Dunmore made his proclamation, the Maryland Council of Safety ordered a militia military force to St. Mary's County to "guard the shores from thence to the river Powtowmack [Potomac] to prevent any servants, negroes, or others from going on board [Dunmore's] ship of war" (Quarles 1961, 14–24).

As the war progressed, Maryland legislators became more amenable to using slaves for military purposes. From the early days of the Revolution, African American watermen, slaves, and free blacks had proved invaluable in negotiating the bays and rivers along the Chesapeake as pilots. When a manpower crisis approached in 1780, the Maryland Assembly authorized slave enlistments. The October 1780 Act stated, "any able-bodied slave between 16 and 40 years of age, who voluntarily enters into service, and is passed by the Lieutenant, in the presence and with the consent and agreement of his master, may be accepted as a recruit." Moreover, prior to 1780, a number of Maryland slaves had served in the army as substitutes for their owners. Major Edward Giles of Harford County noted, "I am of the opinion that the Blacks will make excellent soldiers—indeed experience has proven it." The success of blacks positively contributing to the fight for American independence persuaded a number of Maryland leaders to rethink the idea of African slavery. The freedom rhetoric emanating from politicians like Luther Martin demonstrated the hypocrisy of slaveholding in a republic where "all men are created equal." Martin strongly supported ending the slave trade (Quarles 1961, 56–59, 84–87).

Furthermore, whenever the British navy sailed close to Maryland wharves, African Americans attempted to reach freedom via escape to the English ships. Substantial numbers made away in 1777–1778 and again in 1780–1781. One resident of St. Mary's County wrote Governor Thomas Sim Lee, "I am convinced all our most valuable Negroes will run away." Thus, the war with the British interfered with masters maintaining total control over their human chattel (Quarles 1961, 116–117).

Quakers and some Methodist congregations also joined in the movement toward increased manumissions. The Quakers of Maryland agreed in 1778 to call on individual members to free any human chattel and to abjure from slaveholding. Some of the Methodist churches on the Eastern Shore as well as a number in counties bordering Pennsylvania that had been deeply influenced by the great Methodist leader Francis Asbury likewise called for members to get rid of slaves and to abstain from the practice. In 1780 a Methodist conference, meeting in Baltimore required all traveling Methodist preachers under its sway to free their slaves (Land 1981, 166; Quarles 1961, 192–193).

Additionally, the Annapolis Assembly took action to circumscribe slavery. In 1783, Maryland banned slave importations "by land or water." This act effectively ended the foreign slave trade. Nevertheless, individual Marylanders could apply for exemptions and some slave owners continued to bring in slaves from nearby Delaware or Virginia. The domestic export trade to other states, however, was not interrupted. Importantly, in 1790, the assembly eased the rules for manumission. Many slaveholders immediately filed papers and the number of free black Marylanders increased substantially almost overnight (Whitman 1997, 10–11; Kulikoff 1986, 432).

The economics of tobacco growing likewise contributed to the trend. The plant had quickly destroyed the fertility of the sandy soils of the Eastern Shore and largely had disappeared as a crop choice in these counties. By the Early National era, only the farmers and planters in the southern Maryland counties continued to grow large tobacco crops. Here the institution of slavery would remain entrenched until the Civil War.

THE ANTEBELLUM SLAVE POPULATION

The trends begun in the revolutionary era continued throughout the years between the establishment of a permanent federal government and the onset of the Civil War (1789–1861). Manumissions continued to be a common occurrence. A number of indigenous religious groups and congregations continued to oppose slavery and seek solutions as to what should be done with the increasing numbers of free blacks. More and more bonded African Americans worked as hired-out slaves in urban settings and in the Baltimore factories and on the wharves. Increasingly, these slaves became self-emancipators as they were able to accumulate enough money to buy their own freedom and that of family members. Maryland slave owners, particularly those from the Eastern Shore and southern Maryland, sold or transported thousands of African Americans, who had been born into bondage within the state, to the Gulf states and deep South where they would soon be found toiling in the expanding cotton fields.

The slave population details in the opening summary chart indicate that Maryland's slave population experienced significant declines from the 1790s to the 1860s. In 1790, Maryland's population included over one hundred thousand slaves, a third of the total population. In 1830,

Maryland's slave population still topped one hundred thousand but had not expanded or kept pace with the state's general demographic trend. The number of slaves had decreased to slightly less than a quarter of the total population. Even in 1830, though, Maryland still counted more human chattel in its populace than Mississippi, which in the years prior to the Civil War became, in many ways, the quintessential Southern slave state. From 1830 to 1860, Mississippi's slave population grew from sixty-five thousand to over four hundred thousand. Maryland's slave totals declined in the same thirty years to fewer than ninety thousand.

At the same time, the continuing trend of manumissions as well as of slave self-emancipation propelled a jump in the numbers of free blacks. Maryland's free black population in 1860 approached the total for the number of slaves living in the state. African Americans still comprised 25 percent of the total population; however, this figure was split almost equally among free blacks and chattel.

Not all of the African Americans who left Maryland's slave ranks joined those who inhabited the twilight world of free blacks with their circumscribed liberties. It is calculated that Marylanders transported or sold south more than one hundred eighty thousand bondsmen during the years from 1790 until the opening of the Civil War. The domestic slave trade ranked as an important business in both Baltimore and Annapolis throughout the antebellum years. Many Maryland slaves also became acquainted with the auction blocks in nearby Virginia or in the District of Columbia. Alexandria, part of the Federal District from 1800 to 1846, served as a primary slave-sale auction site for the southern Maryland counties. A great fear among Maryland slaves was to be sold south and to be separated from family and friends. George Ross, who escaped to Canada from Maryland, noted, "I came away because I was standing in fear of being separated from my wife and children. . . . That was one of the principal reasons of my coming way" (see District of Columbia chapter; Tadman 1989, 12; Blassingame 1977, 405).

ANTEBELLUM SLAVE LIFE

The majority of the slaves remaining in the state during the antebellum decades (1820–1861) continued to labor in the tobacco fields of southern Maryland. Although tobacco planting had ceased to be a viable option for most Maryland farmers, those in the six southernmost counties continued to harvest substantial leaf crops throughout the years before the Civil War's onset. These jurisdictions included the counties of Montgomery, Anne Arundel, Calvert, St. Mary's, Charles, and Prince George's (Fields 1985, 12–13).

Slaves laboring in agriculture worked from sunup to sundown except on Saturdays. Most Maryland farmers gave their minions this afternoon and Sundays off. Broad husbands left with written passes to visit wives and family on other home places. In the colonial days, slaves used only hoes in tobacco cultivation. In the antebellum days, farmers employed plows and more farm tools. They typically combined tobacco planting with grains and livestock production (Kulikoff 1986, 408–409).

Tobacco continued to be a tedious crop that required experience and know-how. In February and March, slave workers cleared a small plant bed in which they sowed the miniscule tobacco seeds. They then covered the ground with brush and branches to ward off frost. Heavy plowing to prepare fields began in April. By late May, the tobacco seedlings had matured enough to be transplanted. Most tobacco growers in this era used a team of workers for tobacco planting. One slave would make a hole in the plowed row with a wooden peg, a second would put in a plant, and a third would spread the dirt smoothly around the transplant. Women and children could and often did take part in planting tasks.

In June and July, slave gangs moved through the tobacco field hoeing the weeds out of the fields and forming individual dirt hills around the growing plant. As the tobacco plant matured, horned worms had to be picked off the leaves to prevent plant destruction. Also at this time, men, women, and children walked down the rows and removed new shoots off the main stem. These growths, called suckers, would draw nutrition away from the larger and more valuable leaves. Lastly, in late July or in early August, the plant's large scented bloom was broken off. This furthered the broadening of the valuable lower leaves. In September, after ripening in the field, the plant was cut off next to the ground and attached to a stick. These sticks draped with plants were first hung on scaffolds by the fields to allow the leaves to wilt and later were moved to barns for drying. Most growers occasionally applied some heat from wood or charcoal fires dug into a pit in the center of the barn's dirt floor. Sometime during the winter months, the plant's leaves were stripped from the plant stem, separated by grade, and bundled. These bundles were later prized into a wooden hogshead holding from twelve hundred to fourteen hundred pounds of tobacco. The entire time for this process, from seeding to market, required fourteen or fifteen months. Many of the required jobs were tedious rather than onerous, and most slave owners utilized slave women and slave children for a number of these tasks. While taking care of the tobacco crop, most slave owning farmers also had their laborers grow and harvest acres of corn and wheat (Kulikoff 1986, 405–414).

Although individual experiences varied, many former Maryland slaves generally did not feel that they had been cruelly treated. Joseph Smith recalled, "I can't say that I had a very tough time in slavery." His wife noted, "I was born and brought up on the Eastern Shore of Maryland. I didn't have a hard time, but a pretty easy one." Tabb Gross noted that he had a "smooth" back, one never furrowed by a lash. William Cornish remembered, "I was born on the Eastern Shore of Maryland. . . . I had a very good time down in Maryland, considering I was a slave. . . . I didn't come here because I was abused" (Blassingame 1977, 346, 410–411, 423).

Some, however, remembered harsher treatment. John Boggs recalled, "I lived with old William Merrick, as bad a man as ever lived in the world. I was born on the Eastern Shore of Maryland. . . . Old Merrick would cut and slash his slaves." Regardless of their experience, freedom was a universal desire (Blassingame 1977, 421–422).

BENJAMIN BANNEKER, HARRIET TUBMAN, AND FREDERICK DOUGLASS

Maryland was the birthplace of three of the most famous African Americans in antebellum America: Benjamin Banneker, Harriet Tubman, and Frederick Douglass. All three played major though different roles in the quest of blacks to be recognized as capable, productive residents who could thereby enjoy the full fruits of American citizenship.

Benjamin Banneker (1731–1806) became a nationally known surveyor, mathematician, and almanac publisher. Banneker was born and grew up in Ellicott City where the Ellicott family of Quakers recognized his intellectual gifts. They helped him obtain adequate schooling, and for years Banneker assisted Andrew Ellicott in large-scale surveying jobs. When Ellicott received the commission to survey the new Federal District (the District of Columbia), Banneker, as his assistant and head of a work party, completed most of the actual job (see District of Columbia chapter).

Banneker also made astronomical calculations for almanacs and successfully predicted the eclipse of 1789. He later wrote and sold his own annual almanac for farmers from 1792 to 1802; this endeavor stands as the first scientific book published by an African American. Additionally, he wrote a scientific article on his observations of bees and computed accurately the life cycle of the seventeen-year locust (Bedinia 1971).

Frederick Douglass (1818–1895) was the most famous black abolitionist in the antebellum years. Douglass was born a slave in Tuckahoe Creek on the Eastern Shore. He was moved to Baltimore when a boy and there became literate. Douglass regularly accompanied his master's son to school as the boy's personal servant and thereby became acquainted with reading and writing. He escaped from Maryland and from slavery in 1838 and became a leading speaker and writer for antislavery groups. His home and office in Rochester, New York, became a safe house for the eastern Underground Railroad. He tirelessly lobbied for the antislavery cause and continued during the Civil War era to champion programs to assist the newly liberated freedmen. After the war, he moved to the District of Columbia. He there became a leading representative of a group of African American intellectuals who for a decade created a golden age for the black intelligentsia of the nation in the District (see District of Columbia chapter; Foner 1964).

Harriet Tubman, a former slave from Dorchester County, Maryland, was one of the leading conductors on the eastern Underground Railroad. She made at least nineteen trips from tidewater Virginia and southern Maryland across the Chesapeake Bay, through the Eastern Shore counties, and into Delaware. Her final stop usually was at Thomas Garrett's home in Wilmington. He helped her spirit the escapees across the bridge into Pennsylvania and provided each black with a new pair of shoes. She reputedly brought more than three hundred former slaves to freedom in Canada. During the Civil War, she helped the Union army by spying on the Confederates while visiting some of her former haunts in tidewater Virginia. She received the sobriquet of the "Moses" of her people (Bradford 1869; see Delaware chapter).

FREE BLACKS

As the opening summary of slavery indicates, free blacks became an increasingly larger part of Maryland's population as the antebellum years passed. In the growing city of Baltimore, free blacks comprised 10 to 20 percent of the population during the decades from 1830 to 1860. The city of Baltimore's free blacks also typically numbered 20 percent or more of all the free blacks in the state (Fields 1985, 62).

Free blacks in Maryland lived in a world of circumscribed liberties; they could not fully participate in the political or legal systems. A 1796 law prohibited free blacks from voting and from holding elective political offices. Local ordinances further limited their employment options especially when they attempted to engage in trade. Sheriffs could force free blacks, whom they deemed as vagrants, to be bound out for a year at a time. Black orphans or children abandoned or not supported by parents could be contracted out as apprentices. For certain crimes, free blacks could be sold back into slavery. Free blacks had to carry, at all times, documentation of their free status on their person, as the law presumed that any African American was otherwise automatically a slave. Nevertheless, the size of the free black population worried many of Maryland's white slaveholders. A solution that appeased white concerns had yet to be found by the onset of the Civil War (Fields 1985, 63–89; Whitman 1997, 28–29, 151–152).

THE CIVIL WAR

When the Ft. Sumter, South Carolina, crisis erupted into a shooting war in April 1861, President Abraham Lincoln responded by calling on all the states loyal to the Union to provide troops to put down the armed rebellion.

This event precipitated Virginia's departure from the Union. Lincoln felt that he could not afford to chance Maryland's potential for secession, since this eventuality would leave the federal capital surrounded and beleaguered. Throughout the war, the president used the military to ensure that the supporters of the Union in Maryland always held the upper hand.

Furthermore, violence broke out in Baltimore on April 19, 1861, a week after the shelling of Ft. Sumter. Massachusetts' troops, on their way to guard the District, had to transfer trains within the city. As the New Englanders marched through the Baltimore streets, an angry crowd accosted the inexperienced blue-clad ranks. The ugly mob attacked and the soldiers opened fire. Four troopers and a dozen or more demonstrators perished while many more were wounded. The fracas in Maryland's chief city caused far more bloodshed than the Ft. Sumter bombardment that instigated hostilities (Fields 1985, 93).

President Lincoln benefited from Maryland's geography in his efforts to keep the state firmly in the Union. Southern Maryland ranked as the most pro-slavery, pro-Southern, and pro-Confederate section of the state. Luckily, for Lincoln, the wide Potomac River below Washington separated these counties from Confederate Virginia. North of the Federal District, where usable fords across the narrowing river were far more numerous, the Maryland population was much less enamored with the Rebel cause. Thus, the Confederates could not easily tap potential manpower offered by its Maryland supporters.

Nevertheless, a number of Maryland military units joined the Confederate army. The Maryland artillery companies were particularly well led, well served, and enjoyed an excellent reputation in Lee's Army of Northern Virginia. A number of Maryland-born officers also rose to high rank in Lee's army. Isaac Trimble, from Baltimore County, and Bradley T. Johnson, from Frederick, commanded infantry divisions. "Maryland" Steuart at times led both infantry and cavalry brigades. Nevertheless, more of Maryland's military manpower flowed to the Union than to the Confederate armies.

In the political arena throughout the war years, Lincoln's government brooked no challenges from pro-Confederate officials in Maryland. During the summer and autumn of 1861, the federal military took over command of the Baltimore police force. Additionally, Lincoln suspended the writ of habeas corpus within the state and, when challenged by the Supreme Court, simply continued to arrest Marylanders who appeared to be a threat, without specific charges, for indefinite periods of incarceration. The state, for all intents and purposes, fell under federal marshal law for the war's duration (Wagandt 1964, 21–31).

Slavery ended in Maryland as the result of this very questionable legal and political process. In the autumn of 1863 before the state elections of that year, the federal military in Maryland commanded by Major General

Lew Wallace, shipped out Southern supporters and locked up pro-Southern editors. These army detachments also prevented any Marylanders serving in the Confederacy or temporarily residing in Virginia from returning to participate at the polls. This election broke the pro-slavery political power in Annapolis. In 1864, a Constitutional Convention was selected using these identical arbitrary and highly questionable tactics. This convention then adopted a new state constitution that proscribed slavery; the institution officially ended on November 1, 1864. Thus, Lincoln and his government achieved their primary aims: the maintaining of Maryland within the Union and the ending of slavery within the state. That the rules had to be bent, broken, and dismantled was all part of the war effort (Wagandt 1964, 184–265).

MARYLAND'S BLACK UNION TROOPS

Slaves in Maryland during the Civil War attempted to take full advantage of all avenues to secure freedom for themselves and for their families.

Like this African American cavalryman, many blacks in Maryland, both slave and free, joined the Union army as part of a unit of United States Colored Troops. (Library of Congress.)

That Maryland had not seceded posed numerous problems to politicians and to slaveholders alike. Initially, President Lincoln did not wish to alienate loyal slave owners who he hoped would eventually adopt his road to compensated emancipation. When Maryland slaves escaped to the District or to federal army units, a thorny issue arose. These slaves could not be held as "contraband of war" as was the case in Virginia. When irate Maryland slave owners accosted Union officers about their chattel, no good solution could be instituted. Many politicians as well as all antislavery proponents and abolitionists thought that returning runaway blacks back to Maryland slaveholders was beneath contempt. Yet this, the law required. Some officers complied; others protected the runaways. Additionally, numerous Maryland runaways lived in District refugee camps and labored on the military fortifications erected to surround and to protect the U.S. capital. Furthermore, some Maryland slave owners even had their human chattel jailed to prevent their escape (Berlin 1982, 183–184; see District of Columbia chapter).

In March 1862, the Congress overrode President Lincoln's appeasement of loyal Maryland slaveholders by forbidding military personnel from returning runaway slaves held in their custody. This act, properly enforced and implemented, would have been a potential death knell to Maryland slavery. The more famous Emancipation Proclamation of January 1, 1863, however, did not apply to Maryland because the state was not party to the rebellion (Fields 1985, 109–110).

Enlisting in the Union army provided one avenue that Maryland's African American slaves could use to obtain freedom. Colonel William Birney, son of antislavery politician James G. Birney, opened a recruitment office in Baltimore in July 1863. He cleaned out the jails of slaves held under house arrest to keep them from running off, enlisted hired-out slaves laboring to repair Baltimore's fortifications, and otherwise raised the ire of slaveholders. Although one of his officers was arrested for enrolling slaves into the Union army, eventually Birney was given a free hand. By December 1863, Birney had gained the authority to recruit any slave who wished to join and could offer the promise of freedom to enlisting blacks at the end of their military service. He filled up the Fourth United States Colored Infantry Regiment almost immediately. All told, over eight thousand black men of military age from Maryland joined the Union army (Berlin 1982, 184–186, 203–206).

EMANCIPATION

The new state constitution that came into effect on November 1, 1864, ended slavery forever in the state. Major General Lew Wallace, whose military intervention in the elections of 1863 and 1864 played such an important role in the victory over pro-slavery politicians, anticipated the Federal

Freedmen's Bureau by operating an unofficial version in Maryland before the nationwide program took effect. From November 1864 through the summer of 1865, Wallace's subordinate military officers attempted to intervene on behalf of the newly freed blacks. They particularly worked to undermine the efforts of former slave owners who attempted to continue to bind blacks in work contracts using an apprenticeship system (Fields 1985, 148; Fuke 1999, 290).

The Maryland Freedmen's Bureau also tore down old army barracks and used the lumber to aid blacks in constructing schools. Using these newly built structures and meeting spaces in historic black church buildings, the African Americans in Maryland were able to enroll more than five thousand students by the autumn of 1865. In some areas, white reactions to these attempts was severe. White crowds burned and destroyed black churches used as schools in the counties of Queen Anne's, Dorchester, and Kent. Nevertheless, African Americans persevered, rebuilt, and continued with life (Fuke 1999, 290–295; Fields 1985, 144–145).

The new constitution of 1864 did not grant full citizenship to African Americans. Free blacks still could not vote, hold elective office, or testify against whites in court. Black groups, conventions, and political gatherings protested these circumscribed rights in 1864, 1865, 1867, 1868, and 1869. The ratification of the Fourteenth and Fifteenth Amendments removed these restrictions by 1870, even though the Maryland Assembly voted against both amendments. For the next hundred years, African Americans in Maryland would labor to achieve full citizenship within the American nation (Fields 1985, 132–134).

REFERENCES

Andrews, Matthew Page. 1929. *History of Maryland: Province and State*. New York: Doubleday.

Bedinia, Silvio A. 1971. *The Life of Benjamin Banneker*. New York: Scribner.

Berlin, Ira, Joseph P. Reidy, and Leslie S. Rowland, eds. 1982. *Freedom: A Documentary History of Emancipation, 1861–1867*, Series II, *The Back Military Experience*. Cambridge, Mass.: Cambridge University Press.

Blassingame, John W., ed. 1977. *Slave Testimony: Two Centuries of Letters, Speeches, Interviews, and Autobiographies*. Baton Rouge: Louisiana State University Press.

Bradford, Sarah H. 1869. *Harriet Tubman: The Moses of Her People*. Reprint, Secaucus, N.J.: The Citadel Press, 1974.

Brugger, Robert J. 1988. *Maryland: A Middle Temperament, 1634–1980*. Baltimore: Johns Hopkins University Press.

Fields, Barbara J. 1985. *Slavery and Freedom on the Middle Ground: Maryland During the Nineteenth Century*. New Haven: Yale University Press.

Foner, Philip. 1964. *Frederick Douglass, A Biography*. New York: Citadel Press.

Fuke, Richard P. 1999. "Land, Lumber, and Learning: The Freedmen's Bureau,

Education, and the Black Community in Post-Emancipation Maryland." In *The Freedmen's Bureau and Reconstruction*, ed. Paul A. Cimbala and Randall M. Miller. New York: Fordham University Press.

Greene, Evarts B., and Virginia D. Harrington. 1932. *The American Population before the Federal Census of 1790*. New York: Columbia University Press.

Kulikoff, Allan. 1986. *Tobacco and Slaves: The Development of Southern Cultures in the Chesapeake, 1680–1800*. Chapel Hill: University of North Carolina Press.

Land, Aubrey C. 1981. *Colonial Maryland: A History*. Millwood, N.Y.: KTO Press.

Land, Aubrey C., Lois Green Carr, and Edward C. Papenfuse, eds. 1977. *Law, Society, and Politics in Early Maryland*. Baltimore: Johns Hopkins University Press.

Middleton, Arthur Pierce. 1953. *Tobacco Coast*. Richmond: Whittet & Shepperson.

Quarles, Benjamin. 1961. *The Negro in the American Revolution*. Chapel Hill: University of North Carolina Press.

Tadman, Michael. 1989. *Speculators and Slaves: Masters, Traders, and Slaves in the Old South*. Madison: University of Wisconsin Press.

Wagandt, Charles Lewis. 1964. *The Mighty Revolution: Negro Emancipation in Maryland, 1862–1864*. Baltimore: Johns Hopkins University Press.

Whitman, T. Stephen. 1997. *The Price of Freedom: Slavery and Manumission in Baltimore and Early National Maryland*. Lexington: University Press of Kentucky.

Yentsch, Anne Elizabeth. 1994. *A Chesapeake Family and Their Slaves*. New York: Cambridge University Press.

WEB SITES

Abolitionists, Free Blacks, and Runaway Slaves: http://www.udel.edu/BlackHistory/abolitionists.html

Autobiography of Frederick Douglass: http://odur.let.rug.nl/~usa/B/fdouglas/dougxx.htm

Frederick Douglass Papers: http://www.pbs.org/wgbh/aia/part4/4p1539.html

Freedmen and Southern Society: http://www.history.umd.edu/Freedmen/

Life of Benjamin Banneker: http://www.Princeton.edu/~mcbrown/display/banneker.html

Life of Harriet Tubman: http://www.nyhistory.com/harriettubman/life.htm

Mississippi

TIMELINE

1718: French officials establish rules to allow slave imports into the Biloxi area

1719: First slave shipments arrive; most early slaves are Caribbean Creoles

1724: Black Code is enacted and slavery is defined in the Mississippi territory

1763–1779: British administer Natchez and Biloxi as the Province of West Florida; British slave traders bring large numbers of Jamaican-born African Caribbeans to the Natchez region

1779–1798: Natchez region is governed by the Spanish, who encourage the slave trade by offering land grant bonuses to settlers who transport slaves

1795: Pinckney Treaty with Spain transfers the territory along the eastern bank of the Mississippi River to the United States

1795–1810: Cotton replaces tobacco as the main cash crop; demand for slave field workers grows substantially

1798: United States begins to administer the Natchez region; attempts to limit the slave trade are thwarted by white settlers

1801–1837: Various Indian land cessions lead to the removal of all Indians east of the Mississippi by 1837; opening of new lands resulting from each cession creates land rushes and increased demand for additional African American slaves

1817, December 10: Mississippi enters the Union as a slave state

1823: Mississippi Assembly enacts the Slave Code of 1823

1861, January 9: Mississippi secedes from the Union and joins the Confederate States of America; Mississippian Jefferson Davis becomes the Confederate president
   April: Davis orders bombardment of Ft. Sumter, South Carolina, which opens the American Civil War

1864, December: Third U.S. Colored Troops Cavalry attacks and burns the Big Black Railroad Bridge

1865, May: Confederate General Richard Taylor surrenders the last Confederate forces of Mississippi; the Civil War and slavery end in Mississippi
   November: Mississippi legislature enacts the Black Code of 1865

1867, March: Mississippi becomes part of Military District #4 commanded initially by General E.O.C. Ord

1870, February 23: Mississippi is readmitted to the Union; military Reconstruction ends in the state

1874: Voters elect 60 African Americans to the Mississippi Assembly

1875: Democrats use the "Mississippi Plan" to reestablish their statewide political hegemony; a gunfight erupts at a Clinton, Mississippi, political meeting

Slave and Free Black Population

Census Year	Slave Population	Population Percentage	Free Black Population	Population Percentage
1800	3,489	39	182	2
1810	17,088	42	240	under 1
1820	32,814	43	458	under 1
1830	65,659	48	519	under 1
1840	195,211	52	1,366	under 1
1850	309,878	51	930	under 1
1860	436,631	55	773	under 1

Net Slave Entries and Exits, by Decade
(Tadman 1989, 12)

1800–1809: + 2,152	1830–1839: + 101,810
1810–1819: + 9,123	1840–1849: + 53,028
1820–1829: + 19,556	1850–1859: + 48,560

ORIGINS OF SLAVERY

From 1699 until 1798, the pioneer enclaves around Biloxi and Natchez, which were later to become the original settlements of the state of Mississippi, were administered as parts of the overseas American provinces of three European powers: the French, the English, and the Spanish. The Biloxi area was first settled by the French and administered as a part of Louisiana in the last years of the seventeenth century. As early as 1706, French officials began discussing the benefits of bringing slaves to the Biloxi region. These French colonial officials subsequently set up rules and regulations for the trade in Biloxi during 1718, and, in the following year, the slave trade began in what would become Mississippi (McLemore 1973, 120–127; Claiborne 1880, 31–35).

The French enacted a "Black Code" in March of 1724 to regulate the slave trade and slavery in all parts of Louisiana. These resolutions defined the degree of authority slave owners possessed. Masters had complete control over a slave. Every individual bondsman needed permission to marry, to carry firearms, or to engage in a trade. The laws did, however, contain additional "humane" provisions: The rules forbade owners from splitting up husbands and wives by sale. Additionally, masters had to adequately clothe and feed their human chattel or be subject to fines. The levels of adequate apparel and provisioning, however, remained undefined. Owners could manumit any slave by letter, will, or deed, and any freed black would enjoy all the rights of any other free French colonist (McLemore 1973, 129).

The French hoped that the slave economy of Louisiana would expand and would produce tobacco that the French traders could use to compete with the Spanish leaf from Cuba and the British exports from the Chesapeake area. Thus, slaves in Mississippi's provincial period labored growing tobacco, general crops, and some cotton, although cotton did not become a major alternative until the 1790s. Moreover, the French leaf product never gained the market share or the acceptance accorded the Spanish tobacco, yet planters continued to import more slaves and to expand landholdings as well as tobacco crops. Many of the slaves brought to the Mississippi part of Louisiana at this time were from the Caribbean. Most were Creoles (blacks of African descent born on the Caribbean Islands) whose ancestors had been taken from Africa to work in sugar production on the islands of the West Indies (McLemore 1973, 128; Claiborne 1880, 37).

As part of the settlement of the Seven Years' War (The French and Indian War), the British received the eastern part of French Louisiana and administered this for sixteen years (1763–1779) as the Province of West Florida. While a part of this British provincial administration, the Natchez settlement grew and numerous would-be planters purchased many slaves from the British-held Caribbean Island, Jamaica. The Spanish seized the

Mississippi River settlements around Natchez from the British in 1779 when the Spanish joined the French in supporting the Americans against the London government of George III during the American Revolution (McLemore 1973, 134–157).

Moreover, the Spanish officials overseeing the Natchez region encouraged settlers, settlements, and slavery. They offered additional land grants to newcomers bringing in or importing slaves. By the 1790s, African slavery had become an accepted part of the agricultural and social fabric of local society. Spanish census reports indicated that the Natchez region's population in 1798 stood at four thousand five hundred whites and two thousand four hundred blacks, almost all of whom were enslaved. The Americans living under the rule of the Spanish officials remembered the benevolence of their administration as something of a "golden age" in Mississippi's provincial era (McLemore 1973, 168–169, 173).

In 1795, Spain ceded the lands along the eastern bank of the Mississippi River to the United States per the Pinckney Treaty of 1795. The Americans officially took over in 1798 and created the Territory of Mississippi on April 7, 1798. Initially, Congress banned slave imports; however, white settlers objected so vociferously to this law, which they felt limited their opportunities to exploit the agricultural lands for economic gain, that the Washington legislators recanted. Prominent citizens likewise had complained that they owned plantations on both sides of the Mississippi River and this rule did not allow them to transfer enslaved workers among their properties as farm conditions demanded (McLemore 1973, 189).

Planters and businessmen wrote to congressmen explaining that slave labor along the Mississippi River was considered very desirable in the production of cotton and tobacco. The traffic in humans was looked at as "not only proper but laudable." One Mississippi planter wrote in 1799, "We need more slaves." Rules barring the bringing of slaves to Mississippi from other parts of the United States quickly disappeared (Claiborne 1880, 144).

BLACK CODES

The Territory of Mississippi officially entered the Union as a slave state in 1817. In 1823, the Mississippi legislature enacted a comprehensive slave code that amplified the colonial rules covering slaves and free blacks. This enactment kept most of the old colonial laws and further circumscribed black mobility. Only a limited number of blacks, slave or free, could congregate without white supervision. Any gathering of five or more individuals of African ancestry would constitute an "unlawful assembly." Slaves also would henceforth need a written pass to travel off the home place for religious services and gatherings. Throughout the antebellum era, Mississippi additionally employed slave patrols whose members routinely checked passes of wandering slaves and who soon became the most visible instrument of implementing and enforcing white control over enslaved

African Americans (Claiborne 1880, 385; McLemore 1973, 330; Sydnor 1933, 78–79).

THE ANTEBELLUM SLAVE POPULATION

Although the lands within the new territory of Mississippi proved amenable to the growing of cotton using slave labor, the population of both whites and blacks remained relatively small until the late 1820s. The Choctaw and Chickasaw Indian tribes occupied most of the northern two-thirds of the territory and blocked new settlements. White Mississippians, clamoring for more land, benefited from the Indian campaigns of Andrew Jackson as well as from his policies of Indian removal when he obtained the presidency in 1828. From 1801 until 1837, the United States negotiated a number of Indian cessions that gradually removed all the Native Americans from lands east of the Mississippi River. Every new territorial cession in Mississippi led to a small land rush. Moreover, the new settlers invariably demanded slaves to help them exploit their new homesteads by planting cotton. In response, traders and slave owners continually transferred thousands of enslaved blacks from the Upper South and from the eastern slaveholding states to the newly opening plantations of Mississippi (McLemore 1973, 87–89).

As the introductory summary notes, the slave population of Mississippi always totaled a considerable percentage of its inhabitants, ranging from just under 40 percent in 1800 to 55 percent in 1860. Furthermore, free blacks never ranked as a significant group within Mississippi's antebellum population. The great expansion of the state's populace occurred after 1830 as a result of the complete removal of the Choctaws and Chickasaws. The new lands proved agriculturally rich and slaveholders poured in. From 1830 to 1860, the slave population of Mississippi rose from just over sixty-five thousand to more than four hundred thirty-five thousand, an almost seven-fold increase. It is estimated that slave traders and slave owners transferred, through outright sale by testamentary provisions or by transport, more than two hundred thousand enslaved African Americans to farms and plantations within Mississippi in the years from 1830 to 1860 (Tadman 1989, 12).

Not all Mississippi bondsmen arrived in the state through lawful means. Stephen Dickenson was a free black who worked as a sailor. He shipped over on a New York–based vessel that eventually found its way to New Orleans. There, he was shanghaied by a slave trader with the knowledge and help of the ship's captain. The slave trader carried him to Vicksburg along with a number of other slavenapped African American sailors and offered them for sale. After they had been routinely whipped, they were paraded through the streets of Vicksburg carrying a red flag and ringing a bell to indicate that they would be put up for auction. Eventually, after a number of years in slavery, Dickenson was able to legally regain his freedom (Blassingame 1977, 690–695).

So many slaves transported to Mississippi had had to endure the hardships of family separation that songs about the experience became popular in the fields and in the quarters. "The Coffle Song" captured the pain caused by unwanted separations:

> Oh! fare ye well, my bonny love,
> I'm gwine away to leave you.
> A long farewell forever love,
> Don't let our parting grieve you.
> I'll think of you in the cotton fields;
> I'll pray for you when resting;
> I'll look for you in every gang,
> Like the bird that's lost her nesting.
>   (Blassingame 1977, 705–706)

THE COTTON KINGDOM

The exploitation of cotton cultivation with slave labor dominated the economy of Mississippi during the entire antebellum era (1820–1860). By 1815, cotton had emerged as the primary agricultural option for Mississippians. Two factors eventually led to the production of very large cotton crops: the invention of the cotton gin and the use of hybrid varieties of the cotton plant. The cotton gin allowed the green seed type to become commercially viable. Green seed varieties grew better on piedmont and interior lands than the old Carolina sea island type; however, the shorter fibers of green seed cotton made extracting the tough seeds a time-consuming process. A usable gin, which mechanically removed the troublesome seeds, solved the problem.

Additionally, in Mississippi, planters crossed the Tennessee upland green seed variety with a Mexican type that produced large easy-to-pick bolls. The resulting hybrid was sturdy enough to withstand Mississippi diseases and offered a plant that produced large white bolls heavy with lint. As former Indian lands opened up, farmers and planters expanded their acreages while growing more and more cotton. In 1859, the state's agriculturalists harvested more than 1,200,000 bales (at four hundred pounds each) of cotton fiber. This was equal to half a billion pounds of cotton for a single year's harvest. By the 1850s, in counties along the Yazoo and Mississippi rivers, where planters harvested prodigious cotton crops, slaves comprised from 75 to 85 percent of the total population (Sydnor 1933, 182–185; McLemore 1973, 310–312, 321, 327).

The cultivation of cotton required much labor but less know-how than tobacco. Plantation managers and overseers formed gangs of slaves that moved together through the fields accomplishing the varied tasks involved in cotton cultivation. In February, March, and into April, slave gangs plowed the cotton fields. In late April, the task of planting began; usually three-man gangs divided the task. The first man cut a shallow furrow in a prepared row with a single-prong plow. A second sowed the seed. The third covered the seed with a hoe. Planting was usually completed by early June.

After planting, as the new shoots emerged from the soil, gangs of slaves walked through the field "chopping cotton" with a hoe. They removed excess shoots to leave one vigorous plant per hill and removed any unwanted weeds from the field. Cotton fields were generally chopped and scraped with hoes two or three times during the hot summer months. In August, the cotton was "laid by" and the slave laborers gathered in the other grain and fodder crops. Cotton picking began in September or October and ran through the remainder of the year. Most slave field workers slung a sack over their shoulders that they then filled with the lint from the bolls. Most masters required workers to pick from one hundred fifty to two hundred pounds of cotton a day. The pickers went through most fields three times to get the top, the middle, and the bottom bolls. The middling cotton brought the highest prices. Larger planters and farmers used overseers or farm managers for day-to-day supervision; however, most field gangs of enslaved blacks also had a slave driver who set the pace of work (Sydnor 1933, 16–18).

The bags of picked cotton were loaded onto wagons and carried to the gin mills either on the home place or in the neighborhood. The cleaned lint was then packed into bales of roughly four hundred pounds apiece and the bales were covered and tied with cheap hemp wrappings. Planters subsequently carried their baled Mississippi cotton to market using wagons, railroads, and riverboats, depending on the location of their farms and

Entitled *The Cotton Field*, this print by Horace Bradley depicts a typical scene on antebellum plantations in Mississippi and elsewhere in the Deep South. (Library of Congress.)

the nearest and most cost-effective transportation source available. Major cotton markets in the antebellum era included Memphis, Natchez, and New Orleans (McLemore 1973, 312–321).

SLAVE LIFE

Most Mississippi slaves lived in small log cabins or in duplexes that shared a common main wall and had doors at the opposite ends of the building. Masters clustered the cabins together into "quarters," which, when combined with other farm outbuildings, offered the image of a small village. Large plantations often had more than one set of village-like quarters. Slave life centered within these mini-villages, which became the primary areas for enjoying family, music, and conversation. Within the cabins, most bed frames were built into the walls, and mattresses generally were filled with straw and corn shucks. A homemade table or chair normally completed the furniture ensemble (McLemore 1973, 340; Sydnor 1933, 32).

Most masters allowed their enslaved minions three and a half to four pounds of pork a week plus a peck, eight quarts, of cornmeal. Many owners provided additional rations of sweet potatoes and molasses or sometimes grits and rice. Additionally, most slaves had individual vegetable gardens and could trap or fish in off-hours, usually Sundays. Masters generally provided clothes twice a year: two complete ensembles for summer; another two for winter (Sydnor 1933, 32; McLemore 1973, 340).

Music and religion as well as family life offered diversions from the oppressive daily grind of working in the cotton fields. Getting to church could prove difficult, however, as many masters did not approve of their chattel going to public church services. "They do not like to let slaves go to public church because there is danger of their misbehaving when they are away from home . . . each master has something particular in his regulations" (McLemore 1973, 406).

All bondsmen had to have written passes to go to church services off the home place. Some masters took their human chattel to their own church services; others encouraged blacks to use their own preachers. A number of Baptist and Methodist congregations in Mississippi had more black members than white members. About a third of all Baptists and a quarter of all Methodists during the antebellum years in Mississippi were African American slaves (McLemore 1973, 407).

Betsy Crissman remembered her struggles to build a church for her black community. Through hard work, she had saved enough money to purchase her own freedom. She later bought other family members as well, to keep the family together. In her neighborhood, blacks could worship separately but had no facility and carried boards and planks to the cemetery. They balanced the makeshift benches on the headstones and placed them on the ground to provide seating. Crissman eventually helped raise enough money, collected one dollar at a time, to build a small church (Blassingame 1977, 468–469).

Restrictions on slave movement from place to place remained severe throughout the antebellum years. All slaves traveling away from home places had to have written passes. Violators received punishment from slave patrols, the infamous "patterollers." Additionally, local justices of the peace handled most minor crimes committed by enslaved African Americans. Punishment usually entailed whippings of from ten to thirty-nine lashes (McLemore 1973, 329–330; Sydnor 1933, 78–79, 83–84).

The major annual holiday and vacation time fell during the week between Christmas and New Year. Most Mississippi bondsmen enjoyed a stretch of days with no chores other than seeing after the livestock. Masters provided food, whiskey, and allowed parties of blacks from other plantations to visit, offering the opportunities for large social gatherings. The Christmas break provided a refreshing interlude in an otherwise tedious year filled with long workdays. The one redeeming feature for Mississippi's slaves was family life. Many had already been sold or moved and separated from loved ones. Since most farmers and planters were constantly attempting to increase their workforces, once slaves arrived in Mississippi, they most often stayed there and hence did not have to experience the heartrending challenge of additional forced separations from family and friends. The size of the slaveholdings and the number of sizable plantations also meant that fewer men needed to find broad wives. (A broad husband or wife was a marriage partner who lived on another home place.) Husbands generally visited their broad families on Saturday night and Sunday (McLemore 1973, 340–341; Sydnor 1933, 21–22).

THE CIVIL WAR

The slaveholders of Mississippi met in a secession convention a few weeks after Abraham Lincoln had been elected president of the United States in 1860 as a candidate from a northern-only party, the Republicans. The previous party divisions in Mississippi splitting the Old Whig/Opposition from the Democrats fell away and a slaveholder's consensus was easily reached. These individual slave owners supporting this political consensus agreed to Mississippi's secession from the federal Union on January 9, 1861. Within a few weeks, the Mississippi legislature ratified the constitution of the nascent Confederate States of America, initially only a Gulf states and Deep South alliance. Jefferson Davis, one of Mississippi's U.S. senators, became the first and only president of the Confederacy as of February 18, 1861. Davis subsequently gave the orders to General P.G.T. Beauregard in Charleston Harbor to reduce the federal garrison in Ft. Sumter through an artillery cannonade. By April 12, 1861, a shooting war had begun. At its conclusion, American slavery would be forever destroyed (Rainwater 1969, 220–225).

From the beginning of the war's onset, a major or perhaps the major federal strategy involved opening up and controlling the Mississippi River, thereby dividing the new Confederacy and limiting the economic and demographic support that the rebels could draw from west of the great river. Future Union General John A. Logan of Illinois vociferously proclaimed, "the men of the Northwest will hew their way to the Gulf of Mexico with their swords." They did.

This overarching goal led to General Ulysses S. Grant's historic nine-month campaign to conquer Vicksburg, the Confederate bastion guarding the Mississippi River thoroughfare. When Grant successfully compelled the surrender of the Rebel forces manning the Vicksburg defenses, the western Confederacy was sundered from the east. The death knell had sounded for the Confederacy although the war would drag on for nearly two more years before Grant orchestrated the surrender of General Robert E. Lee at Appomattox Courthouse, Virginia, on April 9, 1865. The Civil War ended in the "Old Southwest" a few weeks later on May 4, 1865, when Confederate General Richard Taylor surrendered the remaining Confederate armed forces of Mississippi, Alabama, and Louisiana to Union General R.S. Canby. Slavery in Mississippi officially ended with Taylor's capitulation (McLemore 1973, 447–491).

UNITED STATES COLORED TROOPS (USCT)

By the summer of 1863, President Lincoln and the federal government had decided to begin to employ Southern blacks escaping to the Union army lines as regular soldiers. Prior to 1863, the federal forces had determined that they could protect the runaways from angry slaveholders by declaring that the escaped blacks were "contraband of war." Nevertheless, most African Americans entering Union lines along the Mississippi in 1862 ended up initially laboring as camp servants or working in transport and supply. The Union army Inspector General Lorenzo Thomas traveled to the Mississippi River Valley to oversee the organization of the black troops in the region during the latter months of 1863. Wherever the federal forces maintained control over the local denizens along the Mississippi River in former Confederate territory, African Americans flocked to the Union army recruiters. Joining the Union army and getting to wear the "blue suit" were visible, tangible symbols of freedom, a freedom that they as federal soldiers would help bring to the rest of the enslaved blacks in the South. By the end of the war, more than seventeen thousand African American men from Mississippi had joined the Union army (see Virginia chapter; Berlin 1982, 12, 15, 164).

In 1864, most of the regiments made up of Mississippi blacks provided occupation garrisons for the forts along the Mississippi River. Nothing expressed the changed circumstances for former slaves more than having black soldiers guarding the river fortifications in plain sight of seething Southern slaveholders. Black troops, who usually were commanded by white officers, nevertheless also fell short of full equality within the army itself. For most of the war, black troops received pay at a lower monthly rate (Glatthaar 1990, 169–176).

Mississippi Black Regiments

Original Unit Designation	1864–1865 Designation	December 1863 Enrollment
1st Mississippi Cavalry	3rd USCT Cavalry	425
1st Mississippi Heavy Artillery	5th USCT Heavy Artillery	644
2nd Mississippi Heavy Artillery	6th USCT Heavy Artillery	1,008
1st Mississippi Infantry	51st USCT Infantry	440
2nd Mississippi Infantry	52nd USCT Infantry	568
3rd Mississippi Infantry	53rd USCT Infantry	599
4th Mississippi Infantry	66th USCT Infantry	175
6th Mississippi Infantry	58th USCT Infantry	760

Furthermore, general military hospitals along the river were regularly segregated by race. Inspectors determined that the black wards were more likely to be unkempt and less sanitarily maintained. They noted that these differences apparently caused little concern for most white officers. As a result, mortality in black wards and hospitals was about double that of the experience in white units. While approximately 14 percent of whites died in the larger military hospitals, about 30 percent of the black patients perished. One inspector noted of an Arkansas hospital, "it was tolerably clean in the white hospital but no so in the negro ward." He added, "Of all the military hospitals in New Orleans, by far the worst one was the Corps d'Afrique Hospital" (Glatthaar 1990, 193).

The Fifty-first USCT Infantry also was set upon by Southern guerilla fighters. This regiment sent out a scouting detachment that was attacked and surrounded by Confederates. The rebels, after capturing the unit, executed the twenty-man black patrol as well as the white officer in command. Wherever black troops and Confederates clashed in battle, more deaths and fewer prisoners resulted. Black units in combat tended to have much higher ratios of killed to wounded soldiers than corresponding white Union regiments. The fight between blacks and "Johnny Rebs" was often bitter and to the death (Glatthaar 1990, 157).

The Third USCT Cavalry (formerly the First Mississippi Cavalry) gained wide acclaim for their 1864 campaign. They engaged in no fewer than eight sweeping forays through the heart of the slaveholder's kingdom in Mississippi and Louisiana. Although they regularly paid the price in casualties, they constantly added new troopers as they rode among the plantation slaves of Mississippi. On one raid in September 1864, they added 185 recruits and brought along 215 others who would then reside within the Union encampment. A month later, a wide sweep netted more than one hundred additional recruits.

In December 1864, the Third Cavalry delivered perhaps the most audacious successful assault by USCT forces in the war. The Union army was attempting to destroy the bridge over the Big Black River to deny that road to the Confederate supply trains that were attempting to victual John B. Hood's forlorn tattered army in its death-throw's foray into Tennessee in late 1864. The bridge was protected by swamps and by a well-manned formidable stockade. Troopers of the Third Cavalry waded through the chest-deep swamp and attacked from the side as other squads made a frontal assault on the stockade. After they had completed the conquest of one side of the archway, they charged across the bridge itself and drove out the Confederate defenders in a hand-to-hand contest. They then set the entire span on fire while still under heavy fire. The overall theater commander, Union General R.S. Canby, declared this attack "one of the most daring and heroic acts of the War" (Glatthaar 1990, 151–152).

EMANCIPATION

After the Confederate capitulation, black soldiers continued to garrison a number of Mississippi's towns. While many black soldiers delighted in their role as part of the army of occupation, most Mississippi whites were furious. To whites, the black troopers symbolized the destruction of slavery, the defeat of the Confederacy, and a world turned upside down. The Freedmen's Bureau attempted to help the newly freed blacks contract fairly for wages with employers, who were quite often their former masters. Mississippi whites felt that the authority given blacks and the fair bargains for wages overseen by the bureau created a social environment that belittled the former slave owners. On the other hand, the blacks simply wanted their freedom recognized (Berlin 1982, 734–735).

Former slave owners fought back politically and passed the stringent Mississippi Black Code of 1865. Its various sections set up vagrancy laws and sought to control social relations between the races. Black children would be bound out in apprenticeship programs to white masters. Freedmen could not lease or rent agricultural lands. Blacks had to have licenses if irregularly employed or written contracts if applicable. Anyone without papers could be jailed and fined. Blacks were forbidden to carry weapons without a similar license. Black soldiers felt that the fruits of their hard-won victory were being dissipated (Wharton 1949, 86–90).

Black soldiers in Mississippi soon began writing to the Freedmen's Bureau that the state of affairs for the freedmen was deteriorating. One white official noted, "The freedmen are much discouraged by these persecutions, and say they will soon be slaves again unless some check is placed on the actions of civil authorities." Calvin Holly, a black Union soldier, wrote in December 1865: "The Rebs are doing all they can to prevent free labor and reestablish a kind of secondary slavery. . . . Now believe me as a colored man that is a friend to law and order, I blive [*sic*] without the intervention of the General government in the protection of the (col.) popble [*sic*] that there will be trouble before spring" (Berlin 1982, 754–756, 821).

After Congress wrested control of the reconstruction process away from President Andrew Johnson, Mississippi fell under the purview of the military commanders who administered each district. In Mississippi's case, the first military administrator was General E.O.C. Ord, who had commanded an army under General Grant in the final Virginia campaign. This military reconstruction took effect in March 1867 (Wharton 1949, 138–139).

RECONSTRUCTION

Ord and his successors, especially Adelbert Ames, attempted to ensure that the freedmen would have the basic rights entitled by their citizenship within the nation. They set about registering black voters who soon became a majority of the electorate within the state. The new voters selected delegates for a constitutional convention that included a number of black representatives. This convention adopted a state structure that allowed blacks full participation in the political process. The first legislature elected under the new constitution included black members, ratified the Fourteenth and Fifteenth Amendments, and set up a public school system. The progress made in three short years allowed Congress to grant approval for Mississippi's military reconstruction to end in February 1870 (Garner 1901, 272–275).

The Ku Klux Klan began active operations in Mississippi during the 1868 elections, but the Union military still stationed within the state discouraged their tactics. When the final federal troops left Mississippi, the Klan and other vigilante-style bands took wholesale aim on black churches, teachers, and schools. Eventually, the federal government intervened again. Congress passed the Enforcement Act, which allowed perpetrators of Klan violence to be tried in federal rather than local courts. White juries had refused to render guilty verdicts against Klan members regardless of the evidence. After 1871, Klan outrages waned and Mississippi whites began a more subtle campaign to regain control of the state and local government (Garner 1901, 338–353).

The years from 1871 to 1874 marked the postbellum high point for black participation in the Mississippi political arena. Voters elected sixty black legislators to the 1874 state assembly. James Lynch, a noted African American, held statewide office and also was elected to serve three terms in the U.S. House of Representatives. Hiram Revels, a black minister, represented the state in the U.S. Senate to fill out an unexpired term. Yet the lily-white Democrats were determined to regain control of Mississippi's government, a process the white citizens of the state termed "redemption" (McLemore 1973, 569, 584; Garner 1901, 327–328).

REDEMPTION

Even though the Mississippi Democrats could no longer employ the KKK to terrify communities, they, nevertheless, set about to regain control over the state's government through a planned campaign of intimidation and fraud. Democratic committees asked employers and farm owners to speak to their black employees and African American sharecroppers about voting. They were to suggest that there would be financial repercussions if the blacks voted or if they voted Republican. Democrats took notepads to election precincts to write down which African Americans chose to vote and seated themselves so that they could tell which party the voter selected. Additionally, they planned to defraud illiterate blacks by switching Republican tickets for Democratic tickets. If all else failed, Republican votes were to be destroyed. This "bulldozing" of an election came to be known as the "Mississippi plan" (McLemore 1973, 586; Garner 1901, 372–389).

Additionally, attempts at intimidation broke out into violence in Clinton, Mississippi, in early September 1875 as the heated election season neared its conclusion. At a political meeting including both Democratic and Republican speakers, a gunfight erupted. Numerous casualties as well several deaths resulted. Consequently, Democrats attempted to inflame rural white voters by proclaiming that the blacks were on the verge of starting a race war. Republican officials and supporters of the freedmen asked for federal troops to oversee the autumn polls to try to validate the election process and to render intimidation ineffectual, as had been the case when Union troops nullified Klan tactics in the late 1860s. President U.S. Grant's advisors recommended against any intervention. They argued that the northern white base of the Republican Party had lost interest and had grown increasingly tired of these Southern shenanigans and were opposed to further confrontations. Hence, President Grant chose not to intervene, and the Democrats in Mississippi won control of the state government in an election replete with fraud and intimidation of voters. Yet this verdict stood. White Mississippi had been "redeemed" (McLemore 1973, 587–588; Garner 1901, 389–410).

The Democrats quickly impeached the sitting African American lieutenant governor and forced the former Union officer Adelbert Ames, who was
serving as governor, to resign and to leave the state. Although blacks in
Mississippi did not immediately disappear from the political scene, they
gradually decreased in political importance as the number of African
American voters declined. By the 1880s, only six blacks remained in the
state legislature. The Democrats had won the peace in Mississippi. Jim
Crow laws and legal segregation of public facilities followed (Garner 1901,
401–408).

REFERENCES

Berlin, Ira, Joseph P. Reidy, and Leslie S. Rowland, eds. 1982. *Freedom: A Documen-
    tary History of Emancipation, 1861–1867*, Series II, *The Black Military Experi-
    ence*. New York: Cambridge University Press.

Blassingame, John W., ed. 1977. *Slave Testimony: Two Centuries of Letters, Speeches,
    Interviews, and Autobiographies*. Baton Rouge: Louisiana State University
    Press.

Claiborne, J.F.H. 1880. *Mississippi, as a Province, Territory, and State*. Jackson: Pow-
    ers & Barksdale. Repr., Baton Rouge: Louisiana State University Press, 1964.

Garner, James Wilford. 1901. *Reconstruction in Mississippi*. New York: Macmillan.
    Repr., Gloucester, Mass.: Peter Smith, 1964.

Genovese, Eugene D. 1974. *Roll, Jordan, Roll: The World the Slaves Made*. New York:
    Pantheon Books.

Glatthaar, Joseph T. 1990. *Forged in Battle: The Civil War Alliance of Black Soldiers
    and White Officers*. New York: Free Press.

McLemore, Richard A., ed. 1973. *A History of Mississippi*. Jackson: University Press
    of Mississippi.

Rainwater, Percy Lee. 1969. *Mississippi: Storm Center of Secession, 1856–1861*. New
    York: Da Capo Press.

Rawick, George P., ed. 1972. *The American Slave: A Composite Autobiography*, Series
    I, vol. 7, *Oklahoma and Mississippi Narratives*. Westport, Conn.: Greenwood
    Press.

Sydnor, Charles S. 1933. *Slavery in Mississippi*. Repr., Gloucester, Mass.: P. Smith,
    1965.

Tadman, Michael. 1989. *Speculators and Slaves: Masters, Traders, and Slaves in the Old
    South*. Madison: University of Wisconsin Press.

Wharton, Vernon L. 1949. *The Negro in Mississippi, 1865–1890*. Chapel Hill: Uni-
    versity of North Carolina Press.

Willis, John C. 2000. *Forgotten Time: The Yazoo-Mississippi Delta after the Civil War*.
    Charlottesville: The University Press of Virginia.

WEB SITES

Charles Thompson's Slave Narrative: http://docsouth.unc.edu/neh/thompson/
    menu.html

Guide to the Microfilm Primary Source Material for African-Americans, Missis-
    sippi, and Southern History in the J.D. Williams Library at the University
    of Mississippi: http://docsouth.unc.edu/neh/bibliography.html
Mississippi Delta: http://xroads.virginia.edu/~UG99/brady/miss.html
Mississippi Plantation Life: http://www.blackokelleys.net/mississippi_
    history.htm
Natchez and Slavery: http://www.stlcc.cc.mo.us/fp/users/jangert/natchez/
    slavery.html
Nile of the New World: http://www.cr.nps.gov/delta/underground/slave.htm

Missouri

TIMELINE

1720: P.F. Renault imports slaves from Santo Domingo, Dominican Republic, in the Caribbean to work in lead mines along the Des Peres River

1720–1764: Missouri region is under French administration

1763: Peace of Paris transfers control of Missouri region to Spain

1803: United States purchases Louisiana Territory, including Missouri, from France

1804: Missouri becomes part of the District of Upper Louisiana
    Black codes are enacted by the territorial legislature

1820: Missouri Compromise—Maine enters Union as a free state to offset Missouri's entrance as a slave state; southern boundary of Missouri henceforth defines the dividing line between slave and free territory farther west

1821, August 10: Missouri enters the Union as a slave state

1833: Missouri Assembly enacts black codes that strengthened rules regulating social activities

1837: Missouri Assembly enacts additional black codes that further regulate religious activities

1854: Congress approves the Kansas-Nebraska Act, which invalidates the Missouri Compromise

1861: Missouri is split by the secession crisis—Governor Claiborne Jackson tries to carry Missouri into the Confederacy; Missouri is recognized with a star in the Confederate flag but, on March 22, the Missouri Convention votes to stay in the Union and the state never officially secedes

1862–1865: Missouri countryside is rent by a guerilla war between pro-Union and pro-Confederate armed gangs

1864: Missouri slave market collapses

1865, January 11: Slavery ends in Missouri by proclamation of Governor Thomas C. Fletcher

1868: Ku Klux Klan violence against freedmen and their white supporters escalates in Missouri

Slave and Free Black Population

Census Year	Slave Population	Population Percentage	Free Black Population	Population Percentage
1810	3,011	15	607	3
1820	10,272	15	347	under 1
1830	25,091	18	569	under 1
1840	58,240	15	1,574	under 1
1850	87,422	13	2,618	under 1
1860	114,931	10	3,572	under 1

Net Slave Entries and Exits, by Decade
(Tadman 1989, 12)

1810–1819: + 5,460	1840–1849: + 11,406
1820–1829: + 10,104	1850–1859: + 6,314
1830–1839: + 2,428	

ORIGINS OF SLAVERY

Before 1764, the region that eventually became Missouri was administered as part of the French colony of Louisiana. The Peace of Paris, ending the French and Indian War, which was signed in 1763, transferred the sovereignty of Louisiana to Spain, and settlers along the Mississippi and Missouri rivers suddenly found themselves under the rule of the Spanish. Local control and authority generally prevailed in the region until the 1790s. At that point, Spain opened the area to white settlers with the offer of generous land grants. They encouraged slaveholders by offering additional grants for each slave carried into the territory. In 1803, President Thomas

Jefferson purchased Louisiana from the French who had just received title back from Spain, and Missouri passed to the United States. By 1810, 19,783 whites lived in the region that was administered as part of Upper Louisiana. After the conclusion of the War of 1812, large numbers of Southerners moved into the area. A majority of the early immigrants to Missouri moved west from the Upper South slave states of Kentucky, Virginia, North Carolina, and Tennessee. These settlers brought along their Southern culture and slaves as well as knowledge of tobacco and hemp cultivation.

Missouri in 1821 entered the Union as a slave state after a famous political compromise. Contention already had grown up between the western and southern states, which were quickly being organized, and the older New England areas. For New England to not be overwhelmed politically by slave states, politicians offered to match the admittance of slave-state Missouri and free-labor Maine to maintain the North/South balance. Additionally, the southern border of Missouri would mark the northern limit of slavery's extension in the western territories. Thus, although owning slaves would be legal in Missouri, slavery would be limited to lands in the western, unorganized areas to lands south of Missouri's southern border. This geographical agreement dividing slave and free territory lasted until the passage of the Kansas-Nebraska Act of 1854 repudiated the boundary compromise.

After Missouri became a state in 1821, another wave of immigration occurred, and the population rose from 66,586 in 1820 to 140,455 by 1830. These new immigrants also primarily hailed from the Upper South and, like their predecessors, they brought along their human chattel. Thus, the tremendous rise in white immigration to Missouri was also matched by an expansion of the slave population that grew apace. Between 1810 and 1820, the number of slaves more than tripled to 10,222, and that total more than doubled to 25,091 by 1830 (Hurt 1992, 6, 51; Pool and Slawson 1986, 2–4; Atherton 1998, 3).

ECONOMICS OF SLAVERY

The dramatic increase in the number of slaves indicates a commitment to a system of labor that proved economically beneficial for these early Anglo immigrants. While most farmers did engage in grain crops and livestock, it was slavery and the product of slave labor that proved most profitable. As elsewhere, slaves were an expensive commodity. In 1823, a male slave cost as much as $350. This amount increased to $450 by the end of the decade. In the early 1830s, nine-year-old boys sold for $325, and boys, from twelve to fifteen years old, sold for $400. As the need for slave labor increased in the early antebellum era, so too did the price of slaves. By 1835, male bondsmen sold for $700, and by the mid-1850s, a good field hand cost $1,500. The price of slaves in Missouri primarily reflected the value each human chattel could command in the cotton states farther south. Many owners covered their minions with death and disability insurance, especially if they hired them out. Missouri insurance companies generally covered male slaves for a maximum of $700, and a female slave for a maximum of $500. Thus, if a slave owner lost a bondsman due to death, escape, or injury, only part of the market capital value could be recouped through insurance. The insurance market therefore tended to temper the very high market value of slaves in the late 1850s.

Missouri slave owners used their valuable labor in growing the cash crops of cotton, tobacco, and hemp. As elsewhere, owners spent the minimum amount necessary to ensure the basic level of existence of their slaves. In this manner, owners ably maximized their profits. Generally, slave owners in Missouri could expect a 10 percent return on their investment in slaves from the agricultural products grown by the slave laborers. Owners supplemented this profit through the practice of hiring out slaves for tobacco and hemp production, domestic service, and other agricultural needs, such as building fences, plowing fields, or clearing land. Female slaves were hired out as babysitters or for domestic service. Hired-out slaves cost 50 percent less than free white labor. Whites who hired bondsmen either did not want to be slave owners, did not have the capital to invest in slaves, needed laborers for short-term projects, or desired additional labor to exploit production in times of low prices. A set arrangement did not exist for the hiring of a slave. Agreements made between the two parties, and the length and terms of the contract depended on the owners themselves and the nature of the work involved. Generally, the agreement included provisions for the renter to furnish summer and winter clothing and prohibited the renter from taking the bondsman out of the county or from hiring the slave out to a third party. Slave owners could expect a 10 to 12 percent return on their investment from the hiring out of slaves. Finally, as the need for slave labor increased throughout much of the South in the 1850s, the selling of slaves for a profit to the Deep South ensured owners a higher rate of return on the initial investment. Research indicates that the talk of secession and a looming Civil War did little to quell the investment and excitement over slavery. Only in 1864, with the Confederacy sinking, did the slave market collapse in Missouri; bondsmen declined in market value to no more than $150 each (Hurt 1992, 223–225, 230, 237–241).

SLAVE LIFE

The work routine of slaves in Missouri resembled that of other Southern states. Slaves woke well before the sun rose and continued to toil until after dark. Both men and women worked the fields, and oftentimes masters had little regard for their well-being unless it appeared an absolute necessity. For example, Aunt Hannah Allen, an ex-slave, recalled a situation she witnessed in the field one day. "One of the darkies [slaves] had a baby out in de field about eleven o'clock one morning. De doctor come out there to her. She was sick a long time 'cause she got too hot before de chile was born." Such situations reveal that slaves worked in the harshest of conditions with little regard from their masters. Despite such circumstances, bondsmen did control to a certain extent their work environment through passive resistance. Feigning illness, working only the bare minimum to avoid punishment, and slowing down work when unsupervised all proved effective methods and illustrate to a degree the ability of bondsman to transcend their restrictions (Rawick 1972, 11:9).

Not only did slaves work under extreme conditions, but also their daily diet was often very poor. Slaves received only basic foods, such as cornmeal and pork, and some owners even fed their slaves in the most humiliating manner. For example, one ex-slave recalled, "To eat we had cornmeal and fried meat dat had been eaten by bugs. We had some gravy and all ate 'round de pans like pigs eating slop. And we had a tin cup of sour milk to drink. Sometimes we would have gingerbread. Dis was 'bout twice a year." Nevertheless, depending on the character of the owner and time of year, some slaves were permitted weekends off from the fields. In such circumstances, slaves might tend their own garden, rest, or spend time trapping and fishing to supplement their diet.

Housing too resembled that of the other Southern states. Slave cabins were generally rudimentary one-room buildings with no windows or floors. Cabins contained one bed and one table, and slaves provided any additional furniture they desired. Oftentimes, several families were cramped into one cabin. According to George Ballinger, an ex-slave, twenty slaves on his plantation lived in one big log cabin. Clothing too was a bare minimum. While many owners did provide their slaves with the basic necessities, such as one pair of pants and one shirt per year, on many plantations slaves made their own clothes (Rawick 1972, 11:40, 73).

Despite the harshness of the peculiar institution, avenues did exist for slaves to develop their own lives and culture. Marriage presented one such opportunity. Although not legally sanctioned, owners did support to some extent slave marriages. Many owners believed marriage would cause a slave to be less likely to instigate trouble or run away. Many owners also acknowledged the potential financial and economic benefit if the union produced a child. Nevertheless, slave owners in Missouri did not recognize the sanctity of slave marriage, and masters often destroyed the union by selling off one or both of the bondsmen. For example, in Boone County, Missouri, of the thirty-four slave marriages that occurred between 1830 and 1864, twenty-seven of those ended by forced sale. This is only an estimate and there is no certain way to account precisely for all slave marriages, even from that county. The general trend is that marriage might have been accepted by the owners, but not respected; economic concerns prevailed (Hurt 1992, 232, 263–264).

Religion also represented an avenue by which bondsmen could transcend their restrictive environment and, on occasion, experience a level of equality with their owners. The antebellum frontier was known for its emotional camp meetings, and Missouri whites and blacks often shared the same religious experience. Richard Bruner, an ex-slave, recalled his experience at a camp meeting where "de whites and de blacks, we all just fell down at de mourners' bench and got religion at de same place. Ole Marsa let us jine whichever church we wanted, either de Methodist or Baptist." At these religious revivals, slaves and owners often worshipped side by side and experienced the same emotional release and salvation that religion offered (Rawick 1972, 11:59).

While religious revivals offered an opportunity to escape temporarily from the fields and offered an emotional outlet for slaves, so too did the secret night meetings that slaves held. Oftentimes, slaves would steal away into the woods at night to practice their own religious worship or simply gather for their own festivities. As elsewhere, slave religion was a combination of Protestant Christianity and African rituals. The enslaved Africans took what they needed from both to create their own vital religious experience. Nightly escapes, however, did not always serve a religious function. Oftentimes, bondsmen simply stole into the night to sing and dance. While most masters did discourage and attempted to prevent such meetings, there did exist occasions where slaves escaped the wrath of their owners. For example, William Black, an ex-slave, recalled, "I 'member one day when de master was gone, us darkies thought we would have a party. I guess de master knowed we was going to have one, 'cause dat night, when we was all having a good time, my sister said to me, 'Bill, over dere is old master Sam.' He had dressed up to look like us and see what we was up to. Master Sam didn't do anything to us dat time 'cause he had too good a time hisself" (Rawick 1972, 11:33, 40).

Despite whatever release religion and secret gatherings might have offered slaves, their existence remained harsh. As such, bondsmen often resorted to flight. A slave's attempt to flee resulted from harsh treatment, the fear of being sold, the yearning to find family members, and simply from a desire for freedom. Slaves usually attempted an escape to Iowa or Illinois. Running away by simply crossing the Missouri River into Illinois proved more difficult than it might first appear. For while it was true that abolitionists waited on the other side to aid the fleeing slaves, so too waited many individuals who readily captured the bondsmen to obtain a reward. Runaway slaves captured and not claimed were sold at public auction. Any slave apprehended more than twenty miles from his or her residence without a pass was whipped and taken to the justice of the peace and considered a fugitive. Flight was a constant concern for whites in Missouri, and the fear of losing slaves increased through the years as abolitionists became more active in the state. Nevertheless, the actual rate of escape appeared no higher in Missouri than other slave states because the institution of slavery remained tightly controlled (Naglich 1993, 258; Hurt 1992, 255–256, 259).

BLACK CODES

Black codes regulating the lives of owners and slaves existed in the very beginning stages of slavery. Beginning in 1804, individuals were prohibited from transporting slaves on the Missouri River without the owner's permission. Those found guilty of violating the law faced a fine and potential lawsuit—an attempt to punish people for aiding a runaway slave. Politicians increased the penalty for aiding runaway slaves in the 1840s, and anyone convicted faced a five-year prison term.

Laws also existed regulating the treatment of slaves, and the state constitution prohibited owners from endangering the life of or maiming a slave. Furthermore, in 1835, the state legislature required any owner who manumitted slaves to care for the males until they reached the age of twenty-one and women until the age of eighteen. Owners also remained responsible for all manumitted slaves more than forty-five years old and those who were sick or mentally ill. These laws were designed to keep freedmen from being wards of the state.

The vast majority of laws, however, were designed to protect whites rather than slaves. As part of the District of Louisiana in 1804, Missouri had slave codes that regulated the actions of slaves. Slaves could not visit another plantation or travel in general without a pass from their owner. Those who did, and were caught, were whipped. Furthermore, any assault or attempted assault upon a master would earn the bondsman thirty lashes. A slave found guilty of conspiring to revolt generally received the death penalty.

When Missouri entered the Union, the slave codes were drafted from and resembled those of Virginia, since many of the early immigrants to the region had previously resided in that state. Many of the laws specifically addressed the political and social life of slaves and free blacks. For example, the Missouri constitution provided slaves with a trial by jury and specified that slaves were not to receive a harsher sentence than what might be imposed upon whites. The appearance of legal equality, however, was only a mirage, considering it is doubtful that slaves received a fair trial. For most transgressions, slaves were not to receive more than thirty-nine lashes at one time.

While in other states the practice of a slave hiring himself or herself out to other owners existed as common practice, the state of Missouri, by law, banned the practice. Oftentimes, a slave would ignore the law to earn spending money. Any owner found guilty of allowing this to occur, received a fine of up to a hundred dollars, and the slave faced arrest.

As slavery increased in the state, so too did laws regulating their social freedoms. For example, in 1833, the state legislature forbid slaves or free blacks from congregating or loitering at business establishments. The 1833 law also prohibited disorderly conduct. Slaves found guilty of violating the law were whipped publicly, receiving twenty lashes. The 1833 law represented a reaction to events in Virginia, specifically to Nat Turner's Rebellion in 1831, and reveals the fear that existed among slave owners. By 1837, the fear of slave insurrections caused the state to act further by prohibiting bondsmen from attending church services if the minister was black, unless law enforcement officers were present. During the 1850s, as abolitionist activity increased in Missouri, the greatest concern facing whites was that of individual acts of violence. As such, many counties and localities strengthened their patrol system. Slaves who were found away from their home place without a pass were immediately whipped on the spot. Mob law also existed, and often slaves merely suspected of crimes fell to the hands of vigilante justice.

The harshness of the slave system, the increased social management of free blacks, and the proximity of Missouri to free territory prohibited the formation of a large free black population in the state. By 1860, only 3,572 free blacks were counted in the population, comprising only 3 percent of all blacks living in Missouri (Hurt 1992, 239, 245–247, 251–252, 255, 257, 269).

A Missouri slave, Dred Scott, became the subject of the most famous antebellum legal case involving slavery. Scott's owner was an army surgeon who took Dred with him to posts in Wisconsin and Illinois where they lived for several years before returning to Missouri. Upon the surgeon's death, Scott sued for his freedom on the grounds of his long residence in the Wisconsin Territory where slavery had been proscribed by the Missouri Compromise. When the case reached the U.S. Supreme Court, it encountered a judicial makeup dominated by five justices from the slave states. President James Buchanan pressured a Pennsylvania justice to join with the Southern majority in finding against Scott. The ruling stated that Congress had no power to keep slaves out of the territories because slaves were property and the Constitution protects the rights of property. This rendered the Missouri Compromise, already violated by the Kansas-Nebraska Act, unconstitutional. Chief Justice Roger B. Taney, of the slave state of Maryland, added that Scott should not even have been able to be heard anyway because blacks were not citizens and had "no rights which a white man was bound to respect." This ruling handed down in 1857 created turmoil in the free states, confusion in the territories, and warned abolitionists that they truly faced an ideological battle with the "slave power" in the judicial as well as in the political realms. The Dred Scott decision added credence to

Republican Party positions about the dangers of the extension of slavery into the western territories, a plank that helped elect Abraham Lincoln in 1860. Thus, the Dred Scott case has been remembered as an important step on the road to Civil War (Fehrenbacher 1978).

THE CIVIL WAR

Missouri's proximity to the Union states presented a certain hazard to slavery during the Civil War. Scores of slaves left their farms and plantations, dealing a heavy blow to the state's agricultural system. Many slaves were forced to remain on their plantation, however. The continued need for a labor force during the time of crisis led many areas of Missouri to strengthen the patrol system. William Black, an ex-slave, recalled that "Durin' de war we could not leave de master's house to go to de neighbors without a pass. If we didn't have a pass de paddyrollers would get us and kill us or take us away." Those bondsmen who remained also faced violence and oppression from Union forces moving through the area. Oftentimes, when Union soldiers arrived at farms and plantations, they forced slaves to gather food and cook for them. African Americans were likewise subject to acts of violence perpetrated by the prevalent guerilla bands, both pro-Confederate and pro-Union, that roamed the countryside. Furthermore, although reports are rare, physical abuse and rape did occur (Rawick 1972, 11:33, 75).

Although Missouri faced an unquestionable assault on the institution of slavery like most states, a unique occurrence did exist there during the war. Due to the heavy influence of Northern abolitionists in the state, there existed a concerted effort to extend education to black children, especially in St. Louis. Although some black schools in St. Louis existed before the war, the American Missionary Association, the Western Sanitary Commission, the African American community, and other organizations worked together to further free education. The effort to organize these schools was a joint effort of blacks and whites, and ministers superintended many of the schools. Although free education for African Americans faced severe criticism from whites, and the shortage of money limited teacher pay as well as the funds available for buying books and supplies, many black youth did receive a rudimentary education during the Civil War (Christensen 2001, 306–307, 314).

Because Missouri never seceded, the Emancipation Proclamation, which took effect in January 1863, did not have jurisdiction over slavery within the state. By the autumn of 1863, however, federal agents had begun actively enrolling blacks from the border states in the Union army even in the face of concerted opposition by slaveholders. These bondsmen used entry into the Union army as an avenue to further strengthen their bid for freedom. In Missouri, 8,344 African American men joined federal regiments, approximately 40 percent of all eligible black males within the state. Additional Missouri blacks served in units organized in Kansas (Berlin 1982, 12–15).

African Americans from Missouri served in the Sixty-second, Sixty-fifth, and Sixty-seventh USCT (United States Colored Troops) regiments, which manned fortification along the Mississippi River south of Missouri. These units suffered significantly high casualties caused by disease in the summer and fall of 1864, as many blacks from the Missouri interior evidently had no immunity to the fevers common to the river lowlands (Berlin 1982, 487).

The state government in Missouri finally took steps to end the peculiar institution early in 1865. Missouri governor Thomas C. Fletcher issued an executive proclamation that finally ended slavery in the state on January 11, 1865.

EMANCIPATION

Similar to Kentucky, which also had not seceded, Missouri did not have to endure political or military reconstruction, or the intrastate turmoil this effected. Nevertheless, African Americans and whites had to work out new economic and social relationships. The assumptions on which society had previously been constructed were now forever changed.

Log cabins like this one belonging to a black freedman were a common form of housing in both antebellum and postwar Missouri. (Library of Congress.)

After the Civil War, freedom presented blacks with an awkward and uncertain situation. William Black, an ex-slave, recalled that when the slaves were set free, his master gave the freedmen five dollars and told them they could leave or stay if they desired. Many slaves chose to stay on the farms that they knew as home, believing their current residence a preferable place. This was especially true in the cases where slaves had kindly masters. Other freedmen sought out kinsmen who had been sold during slavery, and still others moved to the North where larger black communities existed. Now, however, the former slaves worked for wages and made their own contracts and living arrangements. Black agricultural laborers provided a cheap source of labor, and earned between fifty cents and two dollars per day, a little less than white laborers (Rawick 1972, 11:33, 76).

The freedom of slaves caused racial tensions to rise in Missouri. By 1868, the Ku Klux Klan had become active in terrorizing blacks as organized attempts to maintain white supremacy. The Klan brutalized and humiliated freedmen without regard to age or gender. Lula Chambers, an ex-slave, recalled, "I never will forget, I saw a real old darkey woman slave down on her knees praying to God for his help. She had a bible in front of her. Course she couldn't read it, but she knew what it was, and she was prayin' out of her very heart, until she drawed the attention of them old Ku Klux and one of 'em just walked in her cabin and lashed her unmerciful. He made her get up off her knees and dance, old as she was. Of course de old soul couldn't dance but he just made her hop around anyhow" (Hurt 1992, 302; Rawick 1972, 11:80–81).

Compared overall to other slave states, the peculiar institution in Missouri appeared more restrictive. The proximity of Missouri to the North, and the abolitionist infusion into the state, forced owners to maintain a tight grip on slavery from its earliest stage. This, in part, explains the lack of a large free black population in the state, which only reached 3,572 by 1860. Missouri was similar to other states in that after the Civil War crisis, the effort to maintain white supremacy spawned racial segregation and widespread violence against blacks.

REFERENCES

Atherton, Lewis E. 1998. "Missouri's Society and Economy in 1821." *Missouri Historical Review* 93 (October): 2–25.

Berlin, Ira, Joseph P. Reidy, and Leslie S. Rowland, eds. 1982. *Freedom: A Documentary History of Emancipation, 1861–1867*, Series II, *The Black Military Experience*. New York: Cambridge University Press.

Christensen, Lawrence O. 2001. "Black Education in Civil War St. Louis." *Missouri Historical Review* 95 (April): 302–316.

Fehrenbacher, Don E. 1978. *The Dred Scott Case; Its Significance in American Law and Politics*. New York: Oxford University Press.

Harvey, Charles M. 1998. "Missouri from 1849 to 1861." *Missouri Historical Review* 92 (January): 119–134.

Hurt, R. Douglas. 1992. *Agriculture and Slavery in Missouri's Little Dixie*. Columbia: University of Missouri Press.

Naglich, Dennis. 1993. "The Slave System and the Civil War in Rural Prairieville." *Missouri Historical Review* 87 (April): 253–273.

Poole, Stafford, and Douglas J. Slawson. 1986. *Church and State in Perry County, Missouri*. Lewiston, N.Y.: The Edwin Mellen Press.

Rawick, George P., ed. 1972. *The American Slave: A Composite Autobiography*. Westport, Conn.: Greenwood Publishing Company.

Tadman, Michael. 1989. *Speculators and Slaves: Masters, Traders, and Slaves in the Old South*. Madison: University of Wisconsin Press.

WEB SITES

Dred Scott Case: http://www.pbs.org/wgbh/aia/part4/4h2933.html

Geographical Distribution of Slavery in Missouri: http://www.missouri-history.itgo.com/slave.html

Role of the Negro in Missouri History: http://www.umsl.edu/~libweb/blackstudies/

Slavery in Missouri and Little Dixie: http:// http://www.rootsweb.com/~mocallaw

Timeline of the Lincolns: http://www.pbs.org/wgbh/amex/lincolns/politics/es_shift.html

North Carolina

TIMELINE

1586: English explorer Sir Frances Drake drops off captured African-Caribbean slaves on Roanoke Island

1669: Colonial Carolina Fundamental Constitution defines and legalizes slavery

1669–1715, 1737–1776: Years of limited suffrage for free black males

1765: Wilmington Slave Ordinance is enacted

1775: Merrick's Slave Insurrection—an unsuccessful attempt by a slave named Merrick to instigate a slave revolt frightens North Carolina slaveholders

1789, November 21: North Carolina ratifies the Constitution and joins the Union

1791–1793: North Carolina slave laws are codified

1831: Eruption of the Nat Turner slave insurrection in neighboring Virginia leads to the summary execution of more than a dozen North Carolina African Americans

1851: Adam Crooks and Jesse McBride, antislavery preachers, are run out of the state

1861, May 21: North Carolina secedes from the Union and joins the Confederacy

1865, March: United States Colored Troops march into Wilmington as an
army of liberation
    April: Confederate General Joseph E. Johnston surrenders to Union
General William T. Sherman at Durham Station; Confederate resistance
and slavery end in North Carolina

1866: North Carolina's "unreconstructed" assembly enacts the Black Code
of 1866

1868, June 25: North Carolina is readmitted to the Union

1868–1870: North Carolina becomes part of Military District #2 commanded
by Major General Daniel Sickles
    21 African Americans are elected to the state legislature

1870–1871: Ku Klux Klan terror disrupts state elections

1870–1876: White Democrats "redeem" the state, establishing their political control

1877: "Jim Crow" segregation laws are adopted by the state legislature

Slave and Free Black Population

Census Year	Slave Population	Population Percentage	Free Black Population	Population Percentage
1790	100,572	25	4,975	1.2
1800	135,296	28	7,034	1.5
1810	168,824	31	10,266	2
1820	205,017	32	14,612	2.2
1830	245,601	33	19,543	2.6
1840	245,817	33	22,732	3
1850	288,548	33	27,548	3.1
1860	331,059	33	30,463	3

Net Slave Entries and Exits, by Decade
(Tadman 1989, 12)

1790–1799: + 3,671	1830–1839: – 52,044
1800–1809: – 407	1840–1849: – 22,481
1810–1819: – 13,361	1850–1859: – 22,390
1820–1829: – 20,113	

THE ORIGINS OF SLAVERY

The first recorded mention of Africans in what would become North Carolina appeared in the chronicle of the Ralph Lane Colony. Lane headed an

expedition of 107 adventurers who attempted to make a lodgment on the coast of North America. A fleet commanded by Sir Richard Grenville transported the would-be settlers to the outer banks of what would become the North Carolina coast in the summer of 1585 and then returned to England leaving Lane's band on Roanoke Island for the winter of 1585–1586. In the meantime, English explorer Sir Francis Drake led a fleet to the Caribbean where he and his English crews looted Spanish vessels whenever the opportunity arose. In the summer of 1586, Drake began the sail back to England taking with him more than three hundred prisoners including a number of captured African-Caribbean slaves. He decided to stop by the nascent settlement at Roanoke and found Lane's adventurers in sad straits. Lane convinced Drake to take the ninety-seven survivors back to England. Drake then off-loaded most of the prisoners, including all the blacks, to create sufficient room and transported Lane's beleaguered company back to the motherland. No further mention of the fate of the stranded captured prisoners was made. Eighty years would pass before a new generation of settlers carried enslaved African Americans into the freshly established colony of North Carolina (Powell 1989, 42).

In 1663, King Charles II, recently restored to the English throne in 1660, rewarded eight gentlemen friends for their loyalty to him and for exertions in his behalf during the Cromwellian interregnum with the Carolina Charter of 1663. This grant formed the basis for the future colony of North Carolina. By the time these gentlemen organized their windfall, five hundred or so colonists from Virginia already had moved across the boundaries into the new jurisdiction along the Albemarle Sound. A few owned slaves and brought these bonded Africans with them (Powell 1989, 52–53).

During the first fifty years of the colony, relatively few Africans or persons of African ancestry lived in North Carolina. In 1715, historians estimated that fewer than three thousand enslaved Africans or African Americans resided there; individual settlers from neighboring Virginia or from South Carolina carried most of these bondsmen over the borders into the nascent colony. Moreover, the owners of lands along the northern border with Virginia participated in the Chesapeake tobacco economy while those along the lower Cape Fear River near Brunswick and Wilmington prospered by growing the South Carolina plantation crops of indigo (used to dye cotton) and rice. Most of the blacks in North Carolina lived in these two areas up until the 1720s (Powell 1989, 112; Merrens 1964, 78–79).

SLAVE CODES

The Colonial Carolina Fundamental Constitution of 1669 established the legality of African slavery. Baptism did not confer freedom to human chattel of African descent. Although most of the few African Americans in the colony lived as slaves, a tiny number of free blacks also resided in their midst. Until 1715, these individuals had the legal rights and privileges of any free person. Free black males could vote if they had sufficient property to qualify. The colony's statutes were changed in that year to prohibit anyone of African ancestry from participating in elections and likewise proscribed marrying between the races. From 1737 until 1776, free black males could vote under certain circumstances. Moreover, North Carolina's colonial era "black codes" began to resemble those of its larger Chesapeake neighbor to the north, Virginia's Old Dominion, as the slave population increased. In the late colonial era (1725–1775), white owners had to provide passes to blacks for travel off the home place. In addition, slaves were legally banned from using firearms even to hunt. Any violation resulted in twenty lashes as a punishment (Powell 1989, 112–116; Crow 1977, 22, 31).

Most slaves who ran afoul of the black codes were tried by a coterie of three local justices of the peace who could mete out whippings as punishments for minor offenses, such as curfew violations and petty thefts. More severe crimes resulted in execution. Slave owners could petition to be reimbursed for the value of any executed slave. When this provision became too expensive, the North Carolina assembly passed an enactment that allowed castration-in-lieu-of-execution for some crimes. During the 1750s, nineteen African American males received this punishment (Crow 1977, 25).

The Wilmington Slave Ordinance of 1765 installed curfews of 10:00 P.M. Any enslaved black out after ten o'clock had to have a pass from his or her master or be subject to a whipping. No gathering of four or more blacks could occur without a white being present (Crow 1977, 28).

During the latter half of the colonial era, North Carolina's human population jumped rapidly. Both the whites and the blacks showed increasing totals. By 1770, forty thousand slaves resided in the colony, and the first census of 1790, noted in the opening slave summary, counted more than one hundred thousand enslaved African Americans in the new state of North Carolina, two and a half times the totals of twenty years earlier. Moreover, slaves comprised 25 percent of the entire population in 1790. The eastern and central counties remained the primary domicile for most bonded African Americans at the turn of the nineteenth century (Powell 1989, 112).

COLONIAL ERA SLAVERY

Before the American Revolution, slaves labored primarily in three settings—tobacco fields, swamps, and rice paddies. Farmers and planters in the northern tier of the eastern and central counties grew tobacco as a cash crop. Here slaves engaged in the same chores as in the nearby Chesapeake areas of Maryland and Virginia. These slaveholding farmers' agrarian pursuits and their planting calendar strongly mirrored the activities of the Virginians where so many had originated. Tobacco required about 50 percent of a field hand's yearly time allocation, with the remainder spent growing corn and food crops. Most slaveholders in these years allotted two to three acres of tobacco per worker. For the bonded laborers, tobacco as a crop proved more tedious than arduous (Merrens 1964, 123).

Slaves also worked in naval stores production, a major business along the Cape Fear and Tar rivers as well as along the inlets flowing into the Albemarle Sound. A number of the bigger producers owned large numbers of enslaved African Americans whom they employed in making tar and pitch. These tasks involved substantial hours spent outside in swampy environs and large blocks of time spent rendering resins in large cauldrons over open fires to produce the tar and pitch that naval builders used to waterproof eighteenth-century wooden sailing ships. Additionally, slaves worked on the labor-intensive task of making wooden shingles (Merrens 1964, 79–80, 128).

The third setting for the slave economy was situated on the low tidewater lands and "sea islands" around Wilmington. Here, South Carolina planters, who already had the expertise, brought in slaves to work growing rice and indigo. The largest slave density in the colony and in the new state fell in the counties of Brunswick and New Hanover bordering the lower Cape Fear River in propinquity to Wilmington where slave owners harvested these cash crops. Indigo played a large role for a small number of planters in Brunswick County but quickly disappeared after the Revolution. Rice growing was more widespread and persisted around Wilmington throughout the antebellum era. Planters generally allocated one field hand for each five acres of rice. Beginning in December, slaves cleaned out the ditches and repaired the levees that provided the means for inundating the rice fields with water at the correct time of year. The entire acreage then had to be hoed by hand to prepare for planting that began in March and ran through the middle of June. The fields were then hand-hoed twice more during the summer months while inundated. Harvesting began at the end of the summer with a hand sickle. Thus, rice planting required a strenuous effort over extended periods in hot, humid weather. Much of the labor necessitated bending at the waist for hours on end. While tobacco was a tedious crop to grow, rice farming proved to be pure drudgery for enslaved African Americans (Cathey 1956, 142–143).

A few African Americans in the early years of the colony even joined the pirates operating out of Pamlico and Albemarle sounds. The infamous pirate Edward Teach, known as Blackbeard, included at least five African Americans among his crew (Crow 1977, 34).

As in Virginia and in South Carolina, land and slaves formed the chief categories of wealth during the provincial period. North Carolina gentry and colonial officials normally were slaveholders residing along the tidewater estuaries or in the eastern piedmont. A few even rivaled the tidewater "grandees" of colonial Virginia. Governor Gabriel Johnston owned more than one hundred slaves. Planter Cullen Pollock had one hundred fifty bondsmen, and the very wealthy Roger Moore counted more than two hundred fifty human chattel in his inventory (Powell 1989, 113).

On the other end of the scale, during the generation before the Revolution, many newcomers entering the American colonies through Baltimore and Philadelphia trekked down both sides of Virginian's Blue Ridge Mountains looking for suitable acres to site new settlements. Many of the Scots, Scots-Irish, and German groups who streamed into western and central North Carolina from the north during these years did not initially approve of slavery or become entangled in owning African American slaves. The Moravians, members of a Protestant denomination who had been persecuted in central Europe, who settled around Salem, particularly disapproved of the practice but did not speak out politically to object to the peculiar institution (Powell 1989, 116).

THE ERA OF THE AMERICAN REVOLUTION

At the onset of the American struggle with England, a slave insurrection scare helped along the growing alienation much of the tidewater region of North Carolina felt toward the British in the opening months of the Revolution. A slave named Merrick tried to instigate a slave uprising in July 1775. He wanted his followers to destroy their white owners and to run away to the backcountry. In subduing the attempted revolt, North Carolinian patterollers killed one African American and arrested forty more. Five of these were publicly whipped and subsequently had their ears cropped. For the following months, most North Carolina whites went armed and the patterollers searched everywhere to oppose any further insurrection and strictly enforced the nightly curfew, whipping any violators (Crow 1977, 58).

Furthermore, in November 1775, Lord Dunmore, the last colonial governor of Virginia, who earlier had been run out of that colony, attempted to instigate a slave insurrection to weaken the power of tidewater slaveholders. He proclaimed that any slave who joined his army to help put down the American rebels would be freed. Many North Carolina slaves in the northeastern part of the state attempted to reach Dunmore and to join his "Ethiopian Regiment." Free blacks in these border counties tried to help slaves reach Dunmore's troops to gain their freedom. For the most part, African Americans who made it to the British lines during the Revolution ended up serving as laborers. Moreover, Dunmore's Ethiopian Regiment was ravaged by disease and suffered from a deficiency of supplies. He appeared to be more interested in weakening the slaveholders than in providing a black military force to aid British troops (Crow 1977, 58–61).

The southern campaign of Lord Cornwallis from 1778 until 1781 played havoc with the institution of slavery wherever the British army neared. In North Carolina, escaped slaves poured into Cornwallis's lines during his maneuvers from Guilford Court House in the Carolina interior to Wilmington on the coast. According to a British officer serving under Cornwallis, his marching column contained almost as many blacks as troops. Ewald noted that "every soldier had his Negro who carried his provisions . . . every officer had three or four Negroes as well as one or two Negresses for cook and maid . . . every non-commissioned officer had two horses and one Negro" (Frey 1991, 163).

Cornwallis and his subordinate commander at Wilmington, Major James Craig, organized some of the African Americans into foraging parties of from five hundred to two thousand who plundered local white farms and plantations although they appeared to commit no additional outrages. Hardy Murfee, a local landowner of Murfee's Landing, North Carolina, noted at the time, "A great many Negroes goes to the enemy" (Quarles 1961, 116; Frey 1991, 164).

In addition, the passage of the armies as well as the constant guerilla warfare between Patriot and Loyalist bands loosened the bonds holding many African Americans in servitude. Many simply took this opportunity to escape rather than joining the British. Some of the runaways set up "maroon" communities as far away as the swamps on the Gulf Coast. African American runaways likewise organized a sizable maroon community within the nearly impenetrable Dismal Swamp, located on both sides of the North Carolina–Virginia border south of Norfolk. Here the refugees built cabins, planted gardens, and raised livestock. This group maintained their freedom for more than ten years (Frey 1991, 276).

The British attempted to protect the blacks fleeing to their forces with the Philipsburg Announcement of June 30, 1779. This gave the escaping refugees some security that they would not immediately be sold back into slavery by unscrupulous Loyalists. After the Yorktown surrender, Alexander Leslie's Commission also tried to protect those blacks who had fled to British lines in Charleston and Wilmington. On the other side, local Patriot politicians and military forces tried to prevent a mass exodus of blacks from the Southern states when the British departed; however, thousands of former slaves were taken to the Bahamas and Nova Scotia. Loyalist slave owners fleeing Patriot retribution additionally transported thousands more to the settled parts of Florida, which included the river bottoms and tidal lands around Mobile Bay (officially part of West Florida at this time). Moreover, these slave-owning refugees helped more firmly establish the peculiar institution within the social fabric of what eventually became Alabama and Florida (Quarles 1961, 113; Crow 1977, 79–81).

Although some North Carolina blacks joined the American army or fought as substitutes for their owners, evidently relatively few received freedom for their service. The rules were very sketchy with jurisdiction being held by the local justice of the peace courts. Even so, some of the white revolutionaries in North Carolina imbibed the drink of liberalism and freed their slaves at this time. In addition, some of the Moravian congregations, and especially the Quakers, kept demanding an end to the slave trade. A majority of the five thousand free blacks in the state in the first census of 1790 had benefited from the American Revolution and its rhetoric of inalienable human rights to achieve their freedom through emancipation or manumission during the twenty years from 1770 to 1790 (Crow 1977, 69, 83–85).

THE ANTEBELLUM SLAVE POPULATION

The opening summary shows that North Carolina included just over one hundred thousand enslaved African Americans in 1790. They represented a quarter of the population. By 1820, the slave population had doubled and in that census year, enslaved African Americans represented a third of North Carolina's populace. For the next forty years, the enslaved black population increased at the same pace as the total populationand maintained a steady one-third percentage of North Carolina's residents.

For almost twenty years after George Washington's government took office in 1789, African slaves continued to be carried into the state by slave ships legally trading under the compromise resolution that led to the adoption of the Constitution. Slaves could officially be imported into the slave states until 1807, and anecdotal evidence suggests that not until 1816 did Carolina authorities get around to enforcing the closing of the African trade (Johnson 1937, 472).

At the same time, North Carolina became a warehouse for slave sales to the newly opening southern lands further west and south. New landowners in the developing slave territories bought many Carolina bondsmen. Additionally, masters, who desired to exploit rich new acres, also migrated there from North Carolina carrying along their human chattel. The cotton boom, following the invention of the cotton gin in the 1790s, led to a large-scale movement of farmers and planters out of North Carolina onto these new lands. A land rush to Alabama captivated restless Carolinians in the late 1810s. There followed a rush to Mississippi in the 1820s and early 1830s and then a later one to Texas. From 1810 to 1860, North Carolina masters either sold out of state or transported more than one hundred forty thousand enslaved African Americans. Most ended up in these Gulf states (Tadman 1989, 12).

The aftermath of the Revolution as well as the liberal rhetoric of the day led to a rise in the number of North Carolina free blacks for the next twenty years, who increased from just over 1 percent of the population in 1790 to twice that figure by 1820. Additionally, before 1840, some masters in the eastern towns allowed slaves with trades or professions gradually to buy their freedom and that of family members. This trend slowed in the last two decades before the Civil War. Additionally, the number of slaveholders within the state jumped by more than 20 percent in the 1850s; this resulted from a boon economy during the decade caused by higher cotton and tobacco prices.

ANTEBELLUM SLAVE CODES

The application and better local enforcement of the colonial era black codes after the Revolution saw whites reestablishing control over slaves and free blacks. Generally, the Legislative Acts of 1791 and 1793 reconfirmed colonial era resolutions. Slaves could not testify against whites. Bonded African Americans could not be insolent, could not move about the countryside without a pass, could not raise or own livestock, could not trade or buy and sell without written permission, could not sell spirits, could not gamble, and could not bear firearms even to hunt. Violations of minor ordinances could be brought before one justice of the peace who could mete out a specific number of lashes as punishment (Johnson 1937, 498–499).

An 1830 statute noted, "whereas the teaching of slaves to read and write has a tendency to excite dissatisfaction to their minds and to produce insurrection and rebellion to the manifest injury of the citizens of this state," any whites teaching slaves were to be fined between one hundred and two hundred dollars. Any free black violating the enactment would be whipped with nine to twenty lashes. Nevertheless, many North Carolina slaves gained some literacy (Butler and Watson 1984, 209).

The 1793 act provided that slaves accused of capital crimes be tried before a jury of twelve slaveholders. The court appointed counsel if the slave's owner refused. In 1816, capital crimes were moved to the jurisdiction of a circuit court. Masters were to be reimbursed for any slaves executed because of a capital crime (Johnson 1937, 497).

A legislative enactment of 1791 purportedly protected slaves against violent physical abuse and malicious killing; however, since blacks could not render testimony against whites, this statute had little impact. Even public killings of blacks by whites remained unpunished. For example, one master, in a crowded locale outside Tarboro, lashed a slave more than three hundred times for supposed theft and caused his death. The slave owner was tried and acquitted. In another example, Jacob Pope of Halifax County beat an enslaved African American woman to death. He was fined two hundred dollars. In 1829, Thomas Ruffin of the supreme court of North Carolina declared, "the master is not liable to an indictment for a battery committed upon a slave. . . . The power of the master must be absolute to render submission of the slave perfect." Even a killing of a slave by a master could only be manslaughter and never murder. Any mitigating struggle or circumstance (and there always appeared to be one) could negate the crime entirely (Johnson 1937, 503).

Additionally, local patterollers occasionally used "vigilante" justice against black men accused of rapes of white women. The usual penalty was immediate hanging or possibly burning without a trial. These posses were never brought before the courts. At times when whites feared black conspiracies or plots, vigilante justice increased. The aftermath of slave Nat Turner's insurrection in Virginia led to a bloodbath in the neighboring counties across the border in North Carolina (Powell 1989, 237–238).

ANTEBELLUM SLAVE LIFE

Most African American slaves in North Carolina worked as farm laborers and followed an agricultural clock and calendar. Bondsmen generally worked from sunup to sundown for five and a half days a week; hence, summer workdays were longer. Moreover, most farmers and planters in the state converted to cotton production during the antebellum era. The agriculturalists in the northern piedmont border counties continued to grow tobacco, which increased in profitability during the 1850s. Some farmers and planters in counties such as Granville combined tobacco and cotton production. Thus, North Carolina enslaved African Americans typically worked growing corn, the primary food staple, as well as cotton and/or tobacco, the major cash crops. Women as well as men worked in fields. Clara Jones remembered, "I worked like a man . . . hours, sunup to dark . . . we had our tasks set out every day." Lila Nichols of Wake County said that her mother had been on a plow gang (Rawick 1941, 31, 149).

Children and older folks took care of the livestock and the vegetable gardens. Isaac Johnson remembered that when he was little, he fed the chickens. Emeline Moore also fed the chickens as a child. Lily Perry of Louisburg remembered that she had to "slop" the hogs. Lila Nichols had to go to the henhouse to collect the eggs and was whipped if she didn't do her chores correctly (Rawick 1941, 16, 125, 148, 163).

Most enslaved blacks in North Carolina lived in huts or log cabins. These typically had one or two rooms with a fireplace and were raised a foot or so off the ground. Slave owners generally designated the grouped-together huts as the "quarters," and when combined with the other farm outbuildings—corncribs, smokehouse, kitchen—offered the visual picture of a small village. Jane Lassiter of Chatham County remembered, "We lived in little ole log houses . . . had stick and dirt chimneys with one door and one window." Roberta Manson of Warren County recollected that her family lived in a log cabin with a dirt floor and a stick and mud chimney. The shelter had "one door and one window." Most bedsteads were frames built into the sides of the cabin. Slaves then put mattresses into the frames. Blacks typically filled their mattresses with corn shucks or straw but Charity McAllister of Harnett County remembered that her mattress had been filled with old flour and grain sacks (Rawick 1941, 39, 61, 103).

Most slaves received a food ration of from three to five pounds of smoked and salted pork per week along with a peck of cornmeal. Most masters also meted out additional portions of buttermilk, molasses, and sweet potatoes. Some former slaves remembered plentiful amounts of food; others recounted scant meals. Anna Mitchell of Granville remembered eating only two meals a day; however, three meals appeared the norm, at least in the summertime with its long hours. North Carolina slaves called one favorite cornmeal dish, kush. This was made from cornmeal, onions, and seasonings cooked with water in a frying pan coated with pork grease. Clara Littlejohn of Warren County remembered that her mistress gave them extra food including biscuits on most Saturdays and Sundays. Some slave families grew gardens; others did not. Isaac Johnson recollected that he augmented his family's victuals with birds and game from trapping. He often "went bird blinding . . . caught lots of birds." North Carolina slaves could not by law hunt with firearms; most counties enforced this regulation especially after the Nat Turner insurrection in 1831 just across the Virginia border in Southampton County (Rawick 1941, 16, 39, 55, 114, 139, 145, 208).

Owners provided most male and female slaves with two suits of clothes a year. Summer wear typically was sewed from inexpensive cotton cloth; winter clothes, from lindsey-woolsey cloth. Most goods were locally made. Jane Lassiter remembered, "clothes were home-made." Jacob Manson recollected that he was "badly treated, often whipped . . . had poor handmade clothes . . . mostly bareheaded and barefooted." Many owners parceled out clothes as part of Christmas. Charity McAllister received "one pair of shoes a year given out at Christmas." Children's clothes were often made of old flour sacks or gunnysacks that had been ripped apart and resewn. Most summer straw hats worn in the fields were of the local handmade variety (Rawick 1941, 39, 62, 96, 145).

The amount and availability of food, the quality and quantity of clothes, and the frequency of whippings normally determined the degree of comfort enslaved African Americans enjoyed. Some were distinctly uncomfortable most of the time; others got by much better. The vagaries of treatment varied substantially. Most bondsmen had a very good idea how well their owners provided for them and the general reputation the individual white slave owner had within the black community. Clara Jones of Wake County, who was owned by two different masters and lived and worked on two separate home places, remembered that the difference was in the amount of work, the amount of food, and the clothes. She "had some fun on the second plantation" but none on the first (Rawick 1941, 31–32).

The blacks also preferred owners who allowed them time for social activities during the year. These whites permitted their minions to get together with other slaves in the neighborhood for socials. These events included corn shuckings, candy pullings, and watermelon slicings. Some allowed their chattel to attend prayer meetings and religious services at other locations. These events provided the opportunities for picking out possible marriage partners. Slave children played games such as hop-scotch and jump rope. Older boys and men played "town ball" or "round town," an early form of baseball. Sometimes teams from one plantation faced off against a neighboring plantation. Plantation owners' sons would occasionally join in the competition (Rawick 1941, 17, 31, 58).

The chief vacation celebration occurred over Christmas. Most owners gave their chattel the whole week off between Christmas Day and New Year's Day when no work would be done. Many provided extra food and hosted religious services or parties. African Americans broke out their fiddles and banjoes forming makeshift plantation orchestras. On some home places, the Christmas break was the only time of the year that slaves could drink alcoholic beverages without incurring a whipping. Christmas week always topped the list as the most fun time of the year (Rawick 1941, 74, 139, 145).

Religion, family life, and music provided the most important buffers that mitigated the harsh edges of slavery and provided avenues through which enslaved African Americans could enjoy richer life experiences. Some owners allowed their slaves to go to worship services; others did not. Many blacks attended both white services as well as prayer meetings conducted by the African Americans themselves. Isaac Johnson of Harnett County noted that his family "went to church with the white folks." Jane Lassiter remembered that "we went to the white folk's church and sat in the back." Charity McAllister, also of Harnett County, recollected that the African Americans on her home place did not go to church with the white folks. She also stated that her master did not allow separate prayer meetings. Jacob Manson of Warren County also said that his master did not allow separate prayer meetings for blacks, but instead they "went to the white folk's church." Henrietta McCullers's mistress, however, permitted the enslaved blacks on her place to go to prayer meetings. She also threw them parties at weddings and at Christmas. Most masters allowed big wedding celebrations. Richard Moring of Apex remembered that his owner permitted slave couples to be married by the white preacher, "just like the white folks." At the wedding party the blacks played on banjoes and fiddles (Rawick 1941, 16, 40, 62, 73–74, 96–97,139–141).

The incidence of owners whipping slaves with a lash also varied greatly. Jane Lassiter remembered that she had a generally good master who gave "no whippings." Jane Lee recalled, "Marsh Henry whipped whoever needed it." Charity McAllister said, "they whipped us with horse hair whips." Jacob Manson of Warren County noted that he was "whipped often." Some masters refused to use the lash but permitted their overseers to use whips to enforce behavior, authority, and work discipline. Anna Mitchell remembered, "the overseer used the whip, not the master." Roberta Manson said that her master allowed the overseer to whip the slaves (Rawick 1941, 40, 52, 61, 96, 101, 114).

Slave patrols kept general order within county districts and towns. They were appointed and paid by local authorities, generally committees made up of the local justices of the peace. These white patterollers, could enforce curfews and whip offenders for minor violations. They also checked passes, making life particularly difficult for husbands with "broad" wives: A broad husband or wife lived on a different home place from his or her consort (Rawick 1941, 38).

Slaves in towns worked as artisans and craftsmen as well as domestics. Uncle Jackson remembered, "most all the fine work around Wilmington was done by slaves. They called them artisans. None of them could read, but give them a plan and they could follow it to the last line . . . education is one thing and fireside training is another. We had fireside training" (Rawick 1941, 2–3).

INSURRECTIONS AND ESCAPES

The slave insurrection that created the greatest impact in North Carolina occurred a few miles across the Virginia border in Southampton County. Nat Turner's rebellion of 1831 put fear in the heart of tidewater North Carolina slave owners. In many areas panic nearly ruled while unfounded rumors spread of more uprisings along the coastal areas. Slave patrols and armed bands of whites in the counties bordering Southampton rampaged through the black population whipping many just to restore authority. Over a dozen North Carolina African Americans were summarily executed. After the scare ebbed, conditions returned to normal except that rules, such as the ban on slaves using hunting weapons, began to be more rigorously enforced (Johnson 1937, 499–500, 519–521).

North Carolina also suffered from eruptions caused by conflicts between antislavery and pro-slavery groups. From the time of its initial settlement, the state, in its western counties, included numerous church congregations that opposed slavery, especially among the Moravians, the Quakers, and certain Methodists. In 1851, two Methodist preachers created a statewide uproar. Two young clerics had moved to North Carolina from Ohio in the late 1840s to preach the unvarnished "Wesleyan" Methodism (after John Wesley) to congregations in the Guilford and Stokes county areas. Many Methodists in this region did not approve of the splintering of the Methodist church into a northern and a southern branch. The two, Adam Crooks and Jesse McBride, were very successful at increasing church attendance and at converting other locals to their faith. They adhered to the original Wesleyan creed that included a mild antislavery outlook combined with a call for eventual emancipation of enslaved African Americans. They, however, focused more on temperance issues. Nevertheless, pro-slavery groups as well as churches that had lost members to the Wesleyan proselytizers campaigned to stop the two from preaching. Both suffered from harassment and from arrest on flimsy grounds. A pro-slavery mob even dragged Crooks from a pulpit while he tried to deliver a sermon. Eventually both opted to leave the state rather than run further risks of bodily harm (Johnson 1937, 575–577).

Although North Carolina, as an interior state, had no borders with free labor jurisdictions, some slaves nevertheless managed to elude their owners, the patterollers, and the hired slave catchers who often used dogs to track runaways through the swampy tidewater. The close-at-hand eastern Underground Railroad operated up the Chesapeake Bay and on through Delaware. Runaway slave Harriet Tubman led hundreds along this route to safety to Philadelphia by way of Wilmington, Delaware. Tidewater North Carolina slaves also made use of this path with its operators and safe houses (see Delaware chapter).

Harriet Jacobs's story provided a famous example of escape by this route. She was able to reach Philadelphia after help from a waterman Underground Railroad operator. Her story, however, included much more. She detailed the plight of a young female, fair-skinned African American slave and the difficulties a slave girl and woman faced in trying to keep her personal dignity. She later wrestled with the fear of losing her children. She finally ran away and hid out in a swamp, getting snake-bit in the process. She confounded the slave catchers, who considered her long gone, by hiding in a tiny garret above a shed behind her grandmother's house. This bit of space—nine feet long, seven feet wide, and three feet high—became Harriet's home for seven years. She suffered from the heat, from the cold, and from poor ventilation. She had a tiny peephole in the wall that allowed her to occasionally catch a glimpse of her children. Because she could not stand up or walk around, she could barely use her legs after she finally emerged. Her story, her trials and tribulations, and the difficulties she later had in getting a publisher for her saga, all tell a very rich tale of life in the antebellum era (Yellin 1987, 98–99, 100–101, 114, 125, 148).

THE CIVIL WAR

North Carolina was one of the last slave states to leave the Union and seceded only after President Abraham Lincoln called for a levy of troops from each state to put down the Southern rebellion when the Ft. Sumter, South Carolina, crisis erupted into a shooting war. Except in the western counties, North Carolina public opinion evinced a decidedly pro-slavery attitude, although support for the Confederacy varied from family to family and from community to community. For example, John Gibbon, the original commander of the Army of the Potomac's famous "Iron Brigade," hailed from the Tarheel state (North Carolina's nickname) but chose to stay with the Federal army. Additionally, at least two regiments of white troops were mustered into the Federal army and formed the Union First and Second North Carolina Infantry. Some of these soldiers had originally been Confederates. When Rebel troops under Major General George Pickett of Gettysburg fame, trying to capture Washington and Plymouth on the Carolina coast in 1864, captured a number of these Union Carolinians, the Confederates tried and executed a few for desertion. In some circles, this eventually became a "cause célèbre." Nevertheless, more soldiers from North Carolina were mustered into the Confederate army than from any other seceding state. At the same time, Carolina politicians protested the implementation of Confederate conscription most vociferously. The Tarheel state's white population probably opposed forced conscription more thoroughly than in any other seceded area.

Much of North Carolina escaped Union army incursions until the final few months of the war. Federal forces occupied regions only along the coastline from early 1862 onward. Hence, African Americans from North Carolina who wished to fight for the Union and for their freedom had more obstacles to face than blacks from many other areas. In 1860, the state included more than sixty thousand African American men of military age.

Members of "Wild's African Brigade," which was recruited and organized at New Bern, North Carolina, by General Edward Augustus Wild, are shown here freeing North Carolina slaves. (Library of Congress.)

Just over five thousand eventually were mustered into the Union army. The approximately 8 percent who enlisted from North Carolina paled in comparison to the numbers joining from Louisiana or Mississippi or from the nonseceding border tates of Maryland and Kentucky. Yet the North Carolina black muster compared favorably with Virginia and Alabama. Thus, where large portions of a slave state were captured and occupied early in the war, black enlistment proved much higher. Proximity to the Union army likewise greatly increased the tendency of blacks joining (Berlin 1982, 12).

Slaves also experienced the war in various ways. Bob Jones of Warren County wanted to go with his master's son as his body servant when the young white man was mustered into the Confederate army, but Bob was thought to be too young. General Robert E. Lee's Confederate Army of Northern Virginia often had as many as three to four thousand blacks serving as body servants or as camp servants marching along with the ranks, some of these undoubtedly from North Carolina. Amy Penny's father was taken to Manassas to help dig field fortifications in the summer of 1861. Working as impressed slaves, digging fortifications for sixty days at a stretch, also typified many North Carolina African American experiences in the war years. In contrast to Bob Jones, Simuel Riddick of Perquimans ran off at the Civil War's onset and eventually found his way into the Union army as General Nelson Miles's personal body servant (Rawick 1941, 24, 160, 209).

Most slaves hoped for freedom and waited for the day when the Yankees would finally arrive. Clara Littlejohn remembered praying for the Yankees to come. A North Carolina freedwoman presented a regimental flag to the Thirty-fifth United States Colored Infantry (USCT) in 1863, which had a background of blue satin with gold trim. On one side, the goddess of liberty trampled a serpent; on the other, the word "LIBERTY" was emblazoned in bold letters. When the USCT soldiers marched through North Carolina in 1865, they came as an army of liberation. Isaac Johnson watched as "colored soldiers in Yankee uniforms marched by." An observer noted that when black soldiers trooped into Wilmington in March 1865, "they stepped like lords and conquerors" (Rawick 1941, 18, 55; Glatthaar 1990, 80, 206).

When the armies moved across the farms and plantations of North Carolina, looting posed a problem. Clara Cotton McCory of Orange County noted that when Sherman's army marched through, "the Yankees took about everything . . . very difficult to survive." Henrietta McCullers of Wake County remembered, "The Yankees really cleaned us out." The Confederate troops also posed problems for slave families. James Turner McLean of Buies Creek said that when Joe Wheeler's Rebel cavalry came through, "Wheeler's Cavalry took what they wanted and left . . . the Yankees took chickens" (Rawick 1941, 65, 75, 87).

Law and order also suffered. Jane Lee remembered that at the end of the war, "the Yankees came through . . . it was very dangerous to walk out . . . the woods were full of Rebs who deserted and runaway slaves." Anna Mitchell of Raleigh recalled, "Wheeler's Cavalry was worse than the Yankees. The Yankees kept the town from being torn apart. The Yankees with their blue uniforms just covered the town. They were like ants" (Rawick 1941, 52, 118).

At the end of April 1865, Joseph E. Johnston followed up Lee's capitulation at Appomattox by surrendering his Confederate army, the second primary Rebel field force, to General William T. Sherman at Durham Station. The Civil War had ended. Freedom for thousands of North Carolina slaves became an immediate reality.

EMANCIPATION AND RECONSTRUCTION

The sudden freedom for all African Americans, although a joyous occasion, also created the problem of how to survive, how to keep body and soul together while everything was sorted out. Tina Johnson remembered, "We came to Raleigh before things were settled after the war, and black folks lived on kush, cornbread, molasses, and what they could beg and steal from the white folks. Them days were surely bad." Jane Lassiter said her family "stayed on after the surrender . . . we had no where else to go." After slavery, Roberta Manson's family became "share-croppers for the old master." Patsy Mitchner found work as a laundress in Raleigh. Lily Perry said that her family stayed on the old plantation and "worked for wages" (Rawick 1941, 22, 41, 103, 119, 165).

Former Confederate soldiers began to use vigilante justice to impose their authority on former slaves. They dressed as hooded "night-riders" and eventually became connected with the Ku Klux Klan. Ben Johnson of Durham remembered that before the war, Ed and Cindy lived on Mr. Lynch's place. After the surrender, Mr. Lynch wanted them off and told them to move with a month's notice. When they refused to leave, "the Ku Kluxes got them . . . drug them out of their beds, whipped them, and threw them in a pond. Ed lived and Cindy disappeared." He also remembered that the Ku Klux Klan "hung Bob Baylor on the Old Red Oak on Hillsborough Road." Baylor evidently was fooling around with a number of women and was murdered (Rawick 1941, 10–13).

In September 1865, white North Carolinians organized a new state government under the leadership of William N. Holden, editor of the *Raleigh Standard* and a secession opponent. Representatives to the convention included only white men who had opposed North Carolina's withdrawal from the Union. These delegates completely excluded the new freedmen. This provisional administration under new governor Holden passed legislation remembered as the "Black Code of 1866." Although granting considerable economic liberties, the legislation restricted the rights of African Americans in giving legal testimony and in serving on juries. This assembly rejected the Fouteenth Amendment and refused to pass resolutions instituting a system of public education in the state (Butler and Watson 1984, 292).

In 1867, Congress passed legislation that set up a military occupation of the former Confederacy to expedite a fuller, more complete "reconstruction" of the former slave states. Thus, North Carolina became part of Military District #2, commanded by Major General Daniel Sickles. Sickles was well-connected politically, had lost a leg at Gettysburg serving as III Corps commander, and enjoyed a scandalous reputation. An electorate defined by universal manhood suffrage subsequently chose a new state legislature that included twenty-one African Americans. This assembly in 1868 passed a new state constitution, ratified both the Fourteenth and Fifteenth Amendments, and created a public school system for all Carolinians. These progressive enactments would last only a few short years (Butler and Watson 1984, 292).

WHITE REDEMPTION AND JIM CROW

From 1870 to 1876 in North Carolina, white males, especially those who had supported the Confederacy, set out to regain the machinery of local government within the state. Supporters and political partisans backing the Democratic Party referred to the process as "redemption." The goal entailed taking away political power from the Republicans and from the freedmen who comprised a substantial portion of its voter base. The Ku Klux Klan provided an effective, intimidating extralegal force that Democrats widely deployed in the Tarheel state in the autumn elections of 1870 (Butler and Watson 1984, 292).

Klan violence mounted in many counties, especially in Alamance, Caswell, and Rutherford, where Democrats and Republicans waged tightly contested elections. The Klan employed the tactic of having its membership march through politically contested communities in military formations—an easy task for the former Confederate infantry that comprised the ranks. No one opposed these threatening extralegal formations that cowered many blacks and potential white Republican voters as well.

Additionally, the Ku Klux Klan terrorized black families and any politicians who attempted to speak out in their behalf. They hanged Wyatt Outlaw, the Republican leader of Alamance County in February 1870. In May, they murdered John Stephens, a state senator and former Freedmen's Bureau agent from Caswell County. They even attempted to murder Governor Holden but failed in the attempt. Federal troops and militia under Colonel George W. Kirk arrested some Klan leaders, but few were indicted and none was convicted. Thus, the Democrats regained control of the state legislature in the fall elections of 1870. Even one of the Ku Klux Klan's leaders who had attempted to assassinate the governor earned a seat in the assembly in Raleigh (Butler and Watson 1984, 293).

Eventually federal authorities sent in marshals who arrested some Klansmen and more vigorously sought prosecution. Congress also passed a series of laws that made Klan violence a federal offense. This quieted the "night-riders" and quashed the terror by the end of 1871. Furthermore, the governorship remained in Republican hands until 1876; however, the legislature began passing resolutions in 1873 and 1875 that limited black roles in local county affairs. Justices of the peace, who collectively dispensed local justice through the lowest county court and also formed the county supervisors, were to be no longer subject to popular election. They were to be henceforth appointed by the state legislature in Raleigh who removed or refused to select any blacks for these local positions. Eventually, North Carolina also adopted other election laws, such as literacy requirements that grandfathered-in most would-be white voters but demanded that any black who tried to register to vote had to read any selected part of the state constitution and then fully explain the meaning of that specific statute. The now all-white justice-of-the-peace committees subjectively evaluated freedmen on this literacy test. Soon a poll tax would be implemented. By 1876, North Carolina freedmen suffrage had precipitously declined; North Carolina, according to white Democrats, had been redeemed.

Jim Crow segregation laws henceforth governed social interaction between blacks and whites. In January 1877, racial segregation became the official policy for public schools. Statute law proscribed any interracial marriages. Moreover, many African Americans still toiled as day laborers or as sharecroppers. Attempts to get fair hearings over compensation disputes proved virtually impossible. Moreover, white posses continued to employ vigilante justice: North Carolinians lynched more than sixty African Americans between 1890 and the 1930s. The hopes for a more racially egalitarian society in the Tarheel state had to await the civil rights revolution of the 1960s (Powell 1989, 403–405, 448).

REFERENCES

Berlin, Ira, Joseph P. Reidy, and Leslie S. Rowland, eds. 1982. *Freedom: A Documentary History of Emancipation,* Series II, *The Black Military Experience.* New York: Cambridge University Press.

Butler, Lindley S., and Alan D. Watson, eds. 1984. *The North Carolina Experience: An Interpretation and Documentary History.* Chapel Hill: University of North Carolina Press.

Cathey, Cornelius Oliver. 1956. *Agricultural Developments in North Carolina, 1783–1860.* Chapel Hill: University of North Carolina Press.

Crow, Jeffrey J. 1977. *The Black Experience in Revolutionary North Carolina.* Raleigh: North Carolina Department of Cultural Affairs.

Frey, Sylvia R. 1991. *Water from the Rock: Black Resistance in a Revolutionary Age*. Princeton: Princeton University Press.

Glatthaar, Joseph T. 1990. *Forged in Battle: The Civil War Alliance of Black Soldiers and White Officers*. New York: Free Press.

Johnson, Guion Griffis. 1937. *Ante-Bellum North Carolina: A Social History*. Chapel Hill: University of North Carolina Press.

Merrens, Harry Roy. 1964. *Colonial North Carolina in the Eighteenth Century*. Chapel Hill: University of North Carolina Press.

Powell, William S. 1989. *North Carolina: Through Four Centuries*. Chapel Hill: University of North Carolina Press.

Quarles, Benjamin. 1961. *The Negro in the American Revolution*. Chapel Hill: University of North Carolina Press.

Rawick, George, ed. 1941. *The American Slave: A Composite Biography*, Volume 15, *North Carolina Narratives, Part 2*. Westport, Conn.: Greenwood Publishing.

Tadman, Michael. 1989. *Speculators and Slaves: Masters, Traders, and Slaves in the Old South*. Madison: University of Wisconsin Press.

Yellin, Jean F., ed. 1987. *Harriet Jacobs: Incidents in the Life of a Slave Girl*. Cambridge, Mass.: Harvard University Press.

WEB SITES

Allen Parker Slave Narrative: http://core.ecu.edu/hist/cecelskid/nctime.htm

Anti-Slavery Leaders of North Carolina—E-text: http://docsouth.unc.edu/nc/bassett98/bassett98.html

Harriet Jacobs—*Incidents in the Life of a Slave Girl*—E-text: http://docsouth.unc.edu/jacobs/menu.html

Thomas H. Jones Slave Narrative—E-text: http://docsouth.unc.edu/jones/menu.html

Wilmington in the 1890s: http://www.spinnc.org/spinsites/1898/education/chapter–.1.htm

South Carolina

TIMELINE

1526: First Africans arrive in what will become South Carolina

1663: King Charles II of England grants the Carolina region to friends and political allies

1670: First permanent settlement is established in South Carolina region

1729: Separate royal colonial governments are established for North and South Carolina

1739: Stono Slave Rebellion exposes need for black codes to control the slave population

1740: South Carolina Assembly enacts the Negro Act establishing South Carolina's slave code

1788, May 23: South Carolina ratifies the Constitution and joins the Union

1800: Act of 1800 strengthens the South Carolina slave code

1819: Black anti-immigration laws are further strengthened

1822: Denmark Vesey slave revolt rocks South Carolina—36 conspirators are hanged

1860, December 20: South Carolina becomes the first slave state to secede from the Union, setting in motion the steps leading to the Civil War

1861, April 12: Confederate forces commanded by General P.G.T. Beauregard bombard Ft. Sumter, beginning the Civil War

1865, April 26: Surrender of Confederate General Joseph E. Johnston at Durham Station, North Carolina, ends the Civil War in the east; slavery officially ends in South Carolina; the Freedmen's Bureau soon controls 300,000 acres of abandoned lands

1868, June 25: South Carolina is readmitted to the Union; South Carolina Assembly establishes the Land Commission to finance land distribution

1868–1877: South Carolina is subjected to congressional reconstruction; federal military units occupy the capital of Columbia

1877, April 10: President Rutherford B. Hayes withdraws the remaining federal troops from Columbia and former Confederate General Wade Hampton becomes governor; white "redemption" in South Carolina is complete

Slave and Free Black Population

Census Year	Slave Population	Population Percentage	Free Black Population	Population Percentage
1790	107,094	43	1,801	under 1
1800	146,151	42	3,185	under 1
1810	196,365	47	4,554	1
1820	258,475	51	6,826	1
1830	315,401	54	7,921	1
1840	327,038	55	8,276	1
1850	384,984	57	8,960	1
1860	402,406	57	9,914	1

**Net Slave Entries and Exits, by Decade
(Tadman 1989, 12)**

1790–1799: + 4,435	1830–1839: – 56,683
1800–1810: + 6,474	1840–1849: – 28,947
1810–1819: + 1,925	1850–1859: – 65,053
1820–1829: – 20,517	

ORIGINS OF SLAVERY

In 1526, the first Africans arrived in South Carolina with Spanish explorers. Over the next one hundred years, as nations battled for new world dominance, Africans would continue to arrive in small numbers with Spanish, French, and eventually English explorers. In 1663, King Charles II of England granted the Carolina region to eight friends and political allies, who established the first permanent settlement in 1670. Settlers to the region arrived from England and Bermuda, with the vast majority arriving from Barbados with their slaves. By the time the English crown established separate royal governments for North and South Carolina in 1729, blacks constituted a clear majority of the population in South Carolina. Slaves imported to South Carolina predominately originated from the Gold Coast, the Windward Coast, from the Angola region, and from the area between the Senegal and Gambia rivers. In addition, many bondsmen were brought into the colony from Virginia.

GROWTH AND ECONOMICS OF SLAVERY

The South Carolina economy as a whole first flourished from the production of rice and indigo from the seventeenth to the early nineteenth centuries. This was especially true of the sea islands of South Carolina, where indigo and rice cultivation accounted for the increased reliance upon slave labor beginning in the mid-eighteenth century. Rice planting and cultivation was a difficult task, and an owner's profits depended on the market prices, the health and welfare of the slaves, and the weather. In good years, planters could expect a 20 to 30 percent return on their investment; however, in other years, they might suffer a loss of 15 to 20 percent. In the long run, though, a rice planter using slave labor could expect a 15 percent annualized return on his initial capital investment.

Farmers and planters in the eighteenth century also grew wheat and tobacco. Only in the early nineteenth century would cotton replace tobacco and rice as the cash crop of choice. With 80 percent of the South's cotton crop going to Great Britain for its manufacturing, South Carolina, especially the upcounty region, became one of the largest cotton producing states in the South. On many farms and plantations in the nineteenth century, cotton production accounted for close to 50 percent of the total production output.

As elsewhere, slavery provided the backbone of the labor force and slave owners profited handsomely from the product of slave labor. Slaves also proved profitable as a type of expensive human commodities. Although cotton and slave prices fluctuated with the swings of the economy in the nineteenth century, on the whole, slave prices continued to rise, and bondsmen increased in value. By 1857, a good male field hand cost between twelve hundred and fifteen hundred dollars, and a good female slave cost between one thousand and thirteen hundred dollars. Teenage boys and girls sold for only slightly less than these amounts, and the least expensive slaves were those between the ages of ten and fourteen, who sold for five hundred to six hundred dollars.

Hiring out slaves in the eighteenth and nineteenth century appeared commonplace and proved to be a third avenue of profitability for slave owners. In many cases, an owner could expect to receive a 20 percent

annual dividend on his initial investment. No set arrangement for hiring
out servants existed. Some owners rented out their unskilled labor on a
yearly basis; others, according to the specific task and need of the lessee.
Skilled slaves, such as blacksmiths and carpenters, were hired out according to specific tasks. Furthermore, contracts for hiring out varied from case
to case. Oftentimes, however, it was the lessee who had responsibility for
the general welfare of the bondsman and was required to furnish food,
clothing, and shelter (Olwell 1998, 158–166).

SLAVE LIFE

In South Carolina, slave labor was used primarily for rice cultivation,
which dominated the eighteenth century economy, and for cotton production, which dominated the nineteenth century economy. In the rice fields
of South Carolina, the women had the responsibility for most of the fieldwork. They planted, cultivated, harvested, and processed the rice while the
men spent time with heavier work, such as clearing land, building fences,
and other manual labor. In this capacity, owners often employed the system of gang labor. Pregnant women, nursing mothers, the ill and aged, and
young teenagers all worked in the field. Women field workers often experienced some of the worst conditions. Work in the rice fields meant that
slave women often spent many days knee deep in water. Many slaves who
worked in the rice swamps lost their lives during the fever season, often
standing in water all day long while subjected to insect-borne diseases,
primarily cholera and malaria. Oftentimes, in the early part of the year,
while they were preparing the fields for planting, the ground would be
frozen, and women would have to break up the ice with their hands or their
hoes, a grueling task. In addition to the harsh conditions of work, field
hands also had to keep a constant eye out for snakes, rats, and alligators
(Schwalm 1997, 19–22).

Not all women worked the fields; some worked as nurses or as house
servants, and some tended the livestock. Domestic servants on the larger
plantations spent a significant amount of time cleaning, dusting, ironing
clothes and draperies, and cooking meals. Although some historians have
suggested that house servants lived an easier existence, this was not always
the case. Although house servants might have been better clothed and fed,
they were also under the constant watch of the owner or his wife, and, thus,
subject to constant ridicule and physical or sexual abuse.

On the cotton farms and plantations, work did not differ from other slave
states. Bondsmen woke well before sunrise, ate a small breakfast if possible,
and headed to the fields for a grueling day's work. In some areas, owners
used the allotment or task system. This meant that a slave was responsible
for a specific task or a specified amount of land to work that day. Once fin-
ished with the task, a slave was free to tend his or her own small plot of

land, or to spend the time as he or she wished. Different masters adopted different tactics. Some chose the task method, some chose the allocation method, others the gang system of labor. Regardless, slaves generally toiled from sunup and worked at least ten-hour days. Slave children too were required to work. They performed daily chores, tended the livestock, and carried food to their parents in the field. Children usually did not enter the fields until they reached puberty. Children also found time to play. John Davenport, an ex-slave, remembered that "[c]hillun had games like marbles and anti-over. Dey played anti-over by a crowd gitting on each side of de house and throwing a ball from one side to de other. Whoever got de ball would run around on de other side and hit somebody wid it; den he was out of de game" (Rawick 1972, 2:241).

Likewise, punishment was part of the work routine. Slaves received whippings for a variety of reasons including working too slow, feigning illness, breaking tools, talking back to the master, and for no reason at all; they were constantly subject to the whims of the master. On the larger farms and plantations, an overseer often meted out the punishment. Furthermore, on some farms and plantations, black men served as foremen or slave drivers and extended the lash to fellow bondsmen. While black overseers might have enjoyed better working conditions and an apparent higher status among whites, slaves viewed this in a different light. Oftentimes, the elevation of a slave or free black to the position of overseer caused a rift in the slave community as general field hands resented one of their own administering punishment and placing himself in a higher position. Women too had a role in the treatment and punishment of slaves. Ex-slave Victoria Adams recalled, "De massa and missus was good to me but sometime I was so bad they had to whip me. I 'members she used to whip me every time she tell me to do something and I take too long to move 'long and do it." Such situations not only reveal that punishment was not gender-specific, but also they underscore the uncertainty of a servant's daily existence and the fear that many slaves lived in, not knowing if they would be beaten from one moment to the next (Rawick 1972, 2:10–11).

While work exhausted slaves on a daily basis, many bondsmen were allowed Saturday afternoons off to tend their own piece of land or to do with as they wished. Furthermore, slaves generally received Sundays off from fieldwork, except during harvest season. The task system of labor employed by slave owners and the time off on weekends allowed slaves a measure of autonomy over their economic and social life by giving bondsmen ample time to grow their own agricultural produce, raise small animals, and socialize with family members in private. Generally, slaves grew vegetables or fruits to supplement their diet. Oftentimes, they also traded these goods, or the cotton they might have grown, with their masters for additional products such as sugar, molasses, flour, coffee, clothes, and utensils. While slave owners generally kept servants away from the outside market unless they had a special permit, an intricate internal slave economy developed and some slaves even prospered materially. As the reins on slavery were tightened, however, masters began their attempt to thwart such activities (Hudson 1997, 18–19; Schweninger 1992, 103).

Slave owners, with few exceptions, were concerned first and foremost with profit. As such, masters often fed their slaves the bare minimum to ensure constant productivity. By law, masters were required to feed and care for the general welfare of their servants, but in reality there was no way to monitor this when it came to the slave diet, and this too remained subject to the character of the owner. One ex-slave, William Ballard, recalled, "We was allowed three pounds o' meat, one quart o' molasses, grits and other things each week—plenty for us to eat." Some masters, though, did make sure their slaves were adequately fed on a weekly basis, realizing that well-fed slaves might work better and produce more. Millie Barber, another ex-slave, recalled, "All de old slaves and them dat worked in de field, got rations and de chillun were fed at de kitchen out-house. What did they git? I 'members they got peas, hog meat, corn bread, 'lasses, and buttermilk on Sunday, then they got greens, turnips, taters, shallots, collards, and beans through de week" (Rawick 1972, 2:26, 39).

When slaves became sick, oftentimes they resorted to herbal remedies administered by their masters or concocted themselves. Ex-slave Victoria Adams remembered that "Missus Martha sho' did look after de slaves good when they was sick. Us had medicine made from herbs, leaves and roots; some of them was cat-nip, garlic root, tansy, and roots of burdock. De roots of burdock soaked in whiskey was mighty good medicine. We dipped asafetida in turpentine and hung it 'round our necks to keep off disease." Only when it was absolutely necessary did owners consult for an outside physician (Rawick 1972, 2:12).

The harsh daily existence for slaves was certainly a factor. Many bondsmen resorted to flight, and the fear of punishment proved a strong motivating factor. Slaves oftentimes fled to the swamps in South Carolina and hid out for years in fugitive slave camps. They stole and gathered food, supplies, guns, and ammunitions to survive. A hunt for fugitive slaves often resulted in the discovery of such settlements, and fugitive slaves were rounded up, whipped, and either returned to their owners or sold back into slavery. Ex-slave Victoria Adams recalled, "De grown-up slaves was punished too. Whey they didn't feel like taking a whippin' they went off in de woods and stay 'till massa's hounds track them down; then they'd bring them out and whip them. They might as well not run away. Some of them never came back a-tall, don't know what become of them." Although punishment was almost an inevitable result of flight, bondsmen did seek to control their own lives, even if for just a day (Rawick 1972, 2:11).

In a few instances, slaves went further than simply fleeing from their masters and took a step toward outright rebellion. For example, slaves and free blacks in South Carolina paid careful attention to white reaction during the revolutionary era and took lessons from the dominant white society. In Charles Town in the 1760s, after the Sons of Liberty protested publicly against the Stamp Act, slaves took to the streets and also began to cry out for liberty. Whites reacted with fear and violence to put down this potential uprising. In the 1820s, slaves again attempted a rebellion. In 1822, whites uncovered a plot organized by Denmark Vesey, a free black man who had spent years involved in the slave trade, to seize local armories and to arm the black population for a takeover of Charleston. Although the rebellion never materialized, the conspiracy to do so was real and sent shockwaves of fear down the spines of white South Carolinians (Olwell 1998, 225; Lofton 1964, 144–154).

As was common throughout the South, the family unit and religion provided an outlet for slaves and served as the basis for a rich and vibrant culture that gave meaning to their lives, allowing them at times to escape the confines of their environment. Marriage, however, was a difficult task for slaves if they could not find a suitable mate on their own plantation. Oftentimes, masters discouraged slaves from marrying outside the plantation since that meant the slave men might be absent to visit their spouse, and owners worried that such an arrangement would give slaves a feeling of independence and freedom, something that owners did not want to encourage.

The economic status of an individual slave was an important factor in some cases, for it influenced a servant's ability to court and win the hand of any eligible female slave. Oftentimes, a female slave might have the attention of several men, and the economic status of the male bondsman might have played a factor in the women's choice. The better dressed a man was, especially having good shoes, the more his chance improved for a potential mate. Manners and strength also were significant factors. How a man would potentially treat his mate, and whether he could defend her, played a role in the decision process. Courting, though, was not necessarily the norm and, more often than not, slaves simply married because it met their immediate needs. Bondsmen fully understood the vulnerability of their union, which could be threatened with possible sale from their spouse and their children, and thus many slaves did not take the time nor care to emulate white society by spending time with courting rituals. Slaves who did marry generally performed the traditional broom jumping ceremony and might have been wed by a black preacher if one was available. Some masters even gave their slaves wedding presents in cash or goods. Afterward, on some plantations, the slaves might enjoy a large social gathering and dance. Marriage was a serious undertaking, even more so for some slave owners who counted on the union to produce a child. For example, some masters, such as James H. Hammond publicly whipped his slaves, one hundred lashes, if the marriage ended in divorce. The slave family in South Carolina was subject to the same intrusions experienced by slaves in other states. Some masters did not respect the bonds of marriage, and, even worse, some masters did not respect the humanity of their slaves. There were countless cases in which owners sexually assaulted their female servants; the male bondsman could do little but stand by and watch (Hudson 1997, 154–159).

Religion too played a significant role in the lives of slaves. Protestant Christianity made inroads into the slave community, and bondsmen received baptism into the various denominations including the Anglican, Methodist, and Baptist churches. For many slaves, their involvement in the white Christian churches was an avenue of acceptance into the larger white society, a mode of escape, and an attempt to gain control over their own lives. Many slaves who converted to Christianity felt that they possessed grounds to stand against their masters and to demand better treatment; some even used their entrance into white Christianity as the basis for refusing to work on the Sabbath and likewise spent extra time in devotions, prayer, or in reading scriptures. Thus, conversion afforded some slaves the opportunity to become literate and even to distinguish themselves from other bondsmen in the plantation community. Nevertheless, many owners, due to the history and fear of slave rebellion, criticized attempts to teach the slaves to read, even if it related to the scriptures. Oftentimes, as well, these slaves received ridicule from the majority of nonliterate slaves, thus creating division in the slave community. As elsewhere, though, slaves took what they needed from white Christianity and blended it with their own African traditions to create a living and vibrant culture. For example, an integral part of many slaves' religious experience included the ring shout. This highly emotional practice involved slaves joining in a circle, dancing, praying, shouting, and singing aloud (Olwell 1998, 128–131).

FREE BLACKS

Slaves could earn their freedom in a variety of ways: from their service in the American Revolution, from their devotion and years of service to their masters, from their status as mulattos as a result of racial mixing, and, most commonly, from the death of a master whose last will provided for their manumission. Although private manumission was outlawed in 1820, slaves did continue to receive their freedom.

From 1790 to 1830, free blacks enjoyed their highest point of prosperity, and some even earned considerable financial standing. Free blacks worked in more than thirty various occupations including carpenters, tailors, shoemakers, contractors, merchants, coal and wood dealers, and seamstresses. Furthermore, free blacks could own property, but they could not vote. They could testify in court against other blacks but not against whites. Some free blacks did have the opportunity of education. For example, in Charleston, the Brown Fellowship Society maintained a school for free black children. Nevertheless, education for free blacks was extremely rare due to laws that prevented their freedom of assembly. Thus, free blacks occupied a space between slavery and freedom (Lofton 1964, 85).

A phenomenon not yet fully explored or understood is the existence of black slave owners. In South Carolina, it was not uncommon for free blacks, who themselves emerged from the confines of bondage, to own slaves. Evidence suggests that many of these black slave owners had once been skilled slaves, not general field hands. Many blacks purchased slaves for their own labor, realizing that slaveholding presented a road to economic security. In many cases, free blacks struggled to buy their family members. Although, after 1820, slave owners could not legally manumit their slaves without legislative approval, it is doubtful that family members in bondage served in the same capacity as those slaves purchased for labor and skills. In these cases, it was not uncommon for the free blacks to pay above market price for their kinfolk. Many white slave owners took advantage of the situation and charged exorbitantly high prices. Likewise, there were those masters who did take pity on the circumstance and sold the slaves to their kinfolk for a nominal fee. At times, however, this whole process became problematic for these new black slave owners. Their enslaved kinfolk, by law, were property and subject to taxation. Oftentimes, black owners were not able to pay their taxes and were forced to sell their own children. While more likely than not they sold their children to friends or other relatives to ensure the sanctity of kinship networks, the mere fact of selling their loved ones reinforced in their minds the reality of their situation and the confines of the peculiar institution that kept them bound; they could never truly be free (Koger 1985, 31).

In addition, many black slave owners did purchase bondsmen as a means to prosper economically. They understood the dominant culture in which they lived and realized the avenue to financial security lay down the path of private property ownership of human chattel. Some free blacks even entered the elite slaveholding ranks of South Carolina society. For example, Reuben Robertson had been a slave owner throughout much of the antebellum era, and by 1850 was reported to own fifty slaves. Robertson even married a white woman, Sarah, and had children with her. While Robertson's case is extremely rare, it does reveal that the door to economic prosperity was not completely closed to blacks and that racial mixing, while looked down upon, was a small established part of society. Nevertheless, the Civil War and Southern defeat meant an end to black slave ownership, and Reconstruction threatened the economic security that many black owners might have enjoyed (Ware 1990, 264).

BLACK CODES

In September 1739, in the Stono River region of South Carolina, south of Charleston (Charles Town), an estimated twenty slaves or more gathered for a rebellion. These slaves stole guns and ammunition to use against merchants, planters, and their families. Beating drums, singing, and shouting cries of liberty, they marched toward Florida while killing slave owners and torching plantations. The rebellion, however, was met and crushed by the colonial militia, who killed many of the participants. Those who survived the massacre were later executed. The Stono rebellion was significant because it raised the issue concerning the lack of slave codes to regulate the peculiar institution and, thus, gave birth to the slave codes in South Carolina.

On May 10, 1740, Lieutenant Governor William Bull signed into law the Negro Act. This act established the black codes for South Carolina, influenced the Georgia black codes, and remained virtually unaltered throughout the slave years. The Negro Act established the death penalty for plotting insurrections, running away, committing arson, murder, concocting poisons, poisoning someone, and teaching another to make poisons. In the colonial era, slaves guilty of committing arson, poisoning people, or convicted of other heinous crimes were often sentenced to death by burning. Accounts exist that confirm that this method of execution survived until the 1830s. As a more humanitarian approach to execution emerged in the wake of increasing national abolitionist influence, and the need to justify slavery increased, South Carolinians abandoned the practice of burning a slave to death in favor of hanging, which was deemed less barbaric. Owners, however, did receive compensation for their executed slaves, except in the cases in which a slave murdered a white person or took part in a rebellion (Ware 1990, 106).

In addition to establishing the death penalty for specific crimes, the Negro Act also made it illegal for a slave to travel off the master's land without a pass, to own firearms, to own livestock, or to trade publicly on his own account. Furthermore, the Negro Act banned the practice of slaves hiring themselves out. Any slave guilty of violating the law in one of these or other instances was subject to a whipping and often branded on the cheek to mark the administration of the punishment. Such brandings could have a negative financial impact for the owner if he desired to sell the slave at a later date. The general fear of slave uprisings, and the daily problems of slave management, forced politicians to pass legislation that required white slave owners to have one white man reside on the plantation if there were ten or more slaves. This was significant for it led to the hiring of overseers who generally had the responsibility of meting out punishment to slaves (Olwell 1998, 62–64).

As slavery gained a stronger foothold in South Carolina and the free black population simultaneously increased, legislators passed additional legislation affecting the lives of whites, slaves, and free blacks. The Act of 1800 attempted to regulate manumissions and the growth of the free black community by allowing only those slaves who could take care of themselves to be manumitted. Thus, children and the elderly were not set free. Furthermore, law prohibited all assemblies of free and enslaved blacks for educational instruction, even if whites were present. It also forbade all free blacks from meeting for religious reasons between sunset and sunrise. Due to pressure from the Baptists and Methodists, however, this law was amended in 1803 to allow for religious assemblies, with the provision that a majority of those assembled be white. This was repealed in 1819 and restated that religious assemblies were lawful as long as one white man was present. Often, though, this might have been overlooked and enforced only during periods of heightened anxiety among whites (Lofton 1964, 91–92).

In 1819, the South Carolina Assembly outlawed the entrance of free blacks. Anti-immigration laws reflected the fear of a growing black presence that brought with it the possibility of revolt. This fear was evident even before the Denmark Vesey revolt. The 1819 resolution was a restatement of previous anti-immigration laws that originated in 1794 and were restated in 1800 and 1803. The 1819 law was restated in 1820, however, with a new resolution. The 1820 law carried with it a provision that any free black caught entering the state was to be arrested and brought before a magistrate, whereupon he would be ordered to leave the state within fifteen days or face a twenty-dollar fine. Failure to leave would result in a repeat of this procedure. Furthermore, in 1820, private manumissions were outlawed unless an owner received permission from both houses of the state assembly; the legislature, however, rarely granted manumissions. Nevertheless, owners quite often illegally manumitted their slaves.

As the peculiar institution grew, along with the abolitionist threat and a fear of uprisings, legislators continued to pass additional black codes. In 1834, it became illegal to teach a slave to read or write. This law came under fire from many Protestants, especially members of the Associate Reformed Presbyterian church, who petitioned the legislature to repeal the law that slaves might be taught to read the scriptures and pursue the word of God to live productive lives. The small minority of Protestant reactionary reformers failed in their attempt to have the law repealed and simply represented a minor voice of dissent (Kellison 2002, 218).

THE CIVIL WAR

On April 10, 1861, Brigadier General P.G.T. Beauregard, commander of the provisional Confederate forces at Charleston, South Carolina, demanded the surrender of Ft. Sumter, the Union garrison in Charleston Harbor. When the Union refused to capitulate, Confederate forces opened fire on the fort on April 12. The next day, Union forces surrendered and the American Civil War commenced.

In South Carolina, as elsewhere, it has often been assumed that all blacks sided with the Union cause. This is not necessarily true. In many areas, free blacks sided with the Confederacy in an attempt to drive the Union out and safeguard their land. White and black individuals understood that war meant destruction of their property, looting of their homes, and the loss of life. Thus, many free blacks sought to aid Southern whites in the Confederate cause, drive out Union forces, and protect their home and property. Free blacks in Charleston, for example, gathered and collected four hundred fifty dollars for the war effort. Ironically, the Confederacy snubbed such offers of assistance. It would not be until after President Abraham Lincoln issued the Emancipation Proclamation, taking effect on January 1, 1863, that Confederate forces would seek to recruit free blacks and organize them into militias for the war effort. Prior to this, and throughout the war, however, the Confederate government did allow for conscription of slaves to serve the Southern cause. The Confederacy used slaves in numerous capacities, such as cooks, teamsters, scouts, lumbermen, spies, and dockworkers. Nevertheless, numerous South Carolina slave owners rebuffed the attempt to conscript their slave property for the war effort. The loss of a slave meant the loss of property and profits, and ran counter to the Southern ideology of private property ownership that Southerners held dear. In many cases, though, slaves served their masters best at home, especially when the Union began to make inroads into Confederate territory. When the Union soldiers came through an area, slaves generally hid all the valuables and food in holes dug in the ground to keep them out of Union hands. In some cases, slaves aided their masters in physically defending their farm or plantation.

In the beginning stages of war, the Union spurned the use of runaway slaves to aid the Northern cause. In many instances, they turned the fugitive slaves away. Simple circumstances dictated this course of action. The Union simply did not have the necessities to care for vast numbers of runaway slaves. With the passage of the Second Confiscation Act in July 1862, which declared rebel-owned slaves free within sixty days, and the Emancipation Proclamation, however, the situation changed. Immediately, Union forces began to use free blacks and fugitive slaves for the war effort. Doing so not only was an attempt to undercut Confederate manpower but was also a means by which the Union did not have to draft white factory workers in the North. Regardless of the Union justification for using black soldiers in time of war, free blacks and fugitive slaves viewed service in the Union army, in whatever capacity, as the proper course of action. Although in many cases, their situation might have been worse than during slavery, blacks participated in the war effort in an attempt to free kinfolk, to enact revenge against Southern whites, and to help bring an end to the peculiar institution.

This 1862 Timothy O'Sullivan photo, taken possibly at the Smith plantation in Port Royal, South Carolina, shows African American slaves preparing cotton for the gin. (Library of Congress.)

Furthermore, South Carolina African Americans made up one of the first black units to be included among the Union troops. The First South Carolina Volunteers became effective in mid-October 1862 and joined the Union forces who served along the South Carolina coast and among the sea islands. The First South Carolina was commanded by the radical white abolitionist Thomas W. Higginson, who thought blacks who had worked as slaves would make excellent soldiers; he was not disappointed. Two more African American South Carolina regiments soon followed. Altogether, 5,462 South Carolina blacks joined the Union army. Thus, in South Carolina, free blacks and slaves played a significant role in the American Civil War, for both the Confederate and Union cause (Morrill 2002, 291–292, 300; Berlin 1982, 12, 37–41).

EMANCIPATION AND RECONSTRUCTION

In 1863, the U.S. Congress declared that all property abandoned by an owner who supported the Confederate cause was subject to seizure by the federal government. At the war's end, all property seized was turned over to the Freedmen's Bureau. In 1865, the bureau had control over some three hundred thousand acres of land in South Carolina, which it sought to sell or lease to freedmen. Lease agreements would last for three years with the option to buy within that period. From this emerged the dream of freedmen that the federal government would provide them with forty acres and a mule. Conflicting federal legislation, disputed land titles, and outright hostile opposition from South Carolina whites made this more of a dream than a reality. In addition, many ex-slaves simply did not desire to take part in the land distribution but rather chose to stay with their master, work the land for wages, and remain in the only place they knew as home. For example, ex-slave Frances Andrews recalled, "I heard about the 40 acres of land and a mule the ex-slaves would get after the war, but I didn't pay any attention to it. . . . I think this was just put out by the Yankees who didn't care about much 'cept getting money for themselves." Another ex-slave, Granny Cain, recalled, "I don't know nothing about 40 acres of land for the slaves after the war. We just stayed on with the master 'til he died, for wages; then we hired out to other people for wages. I don't know nothing 'bout slaves voting after the war" (Rawick 1972, 2:18, 168).

In 1868, however, the South Carolina legislature created the Land Commission to finance the redistribution of land to freemen. The Land Commission used confiscated land and was authorized to purchase land from whites to sell to blacks. Between 1868 and 1880, the Land Commission was responsible for distributing land titles to more than fourteen thousand black families in South Carolina. The efforts of the commission led directly to the establishment of black communities such as Promise Land, which eventually established a school and church, elected local officials, and actively supported the Republican Party. Nevertheless, the vast majority of blacks simply fell upon hard times and found their conditions sometimes worse than that of slavery as they were forced into tenant farming and sharecropping contracts with whites who often did not abide by the agreements. For those who chose to stay with their masters, conditions were often much better. Ezra Adams, an ex-slave, recalled, "You ain't gwine to believe date de slaves on our plantation didn't stop workin' for old marster, even when they was told date they was free. Us didn't want no more freedom than us was gittin' on our plantation already. Us knowed too well dat us was well took care of, wid a plenty of vittles to eat and tight log and board houses to live in" (Rawick 1972, 2:5).

Efforts to extend education existed during the antebellum era. These were isolated cases and not the norm. After the Civil War, though, with the aid of the American Missionary Association, schools and teacher training programs were established in an attempt to extend education to freedmen. As elsewhere, though, the vast majority of free blacks could not afford private education and thus were relegated to the poorly maintained schools established for African Americans. The quality of education was paltry, with few supplies and poorly trained teachers. In addition, outright hostility from angry whites thwarted efforts to aid freedmen in any manner.

Violence in South Carolina was the norm during Reconstruction. Nowhere else in the entire South was the Ku Klux Klan more active, especially in York County, South Carolina. In 1868, white anger and fear gave birth to this hooded organization of men and women who terrorized blacks almost on a daily basis. Their targets were black leaders who took an open stance politically, black militia leaders who patrolled the roads of the county, and oftentimes just ordinary citizens who happened to be in the wrong place at the wrong time. The Klan was responsible for numerous and various types of attacks, such as burning the houses of black men suspected or guilty of miscegenation. They terrorized blacks in their own homes. In one instance, fifty to seventy-five Klansmen surrounded the house of Thomas Roundtree. They fired shots into his house, forcing him to flee; they then shot him on the spot and cut his throat from ear to ear. Ex-slave Frances Andrews recalled that the Klan often rode to brutalize newly freed slaves. "After the war, the 'bush-whackers,' called Ku Klux, rode there. Preacher Pitts' brother was one. They went to negro houses and killed the people. They wore caps over the head and eyes, but no long white gowns." Blacks were suspected of virtually every crime that occurred, and Klansmen took that as an opportunity to engage in their own form of justice, often by lynching African Americans. Aunt Millie Bates, an ex-slave, recalled one of her experiences as a child: "De worsest time of all fer us darkies wuz when de Ku Klux killed Dan Black . . . he won't no mo' kaise de took dat nigger and hung him to a simmon tree. Dey would not let his folks take him down either. He jus stayed dar till he fell to pieces." The Klan was also was guilty of threatening white Republicans who they believed acted too much for the benefit of the blacks in society. In addition, they burned stores and homes of whites who were sympathetic to the freedmen as a means to reduce or drive out the military presence (West 2002, 5, 49–55, 60–65; Rawick 1972, 2:17, 46).

South Carolina began to establish Jim Crow laws immediately after the Civil War. The Constitution of 1865, passed only a few months after the Civil War ended, failed to grant African Americans the right to vote. It also retained racial qualifications for the legislature. Consequently, freedmen had little course for redress against unfair laws and abuse. In addition, Jim Crow laws sought to regulate the immigration of blacks into the state, forcing them to enter into a bond as a testament to their conduct. Furthermore, free blacks were forbidden from some occupations and could work only as artisans, shopkeepers, and mechanics after obtaining a license from a judge, which often cost as much as one hundred dollars.

Free black women, though, played a significant role in South Carolina reconstruction and fought against the injustices of white society. For example, one of the most prominent black women of South Carolina, Frances Ann Rollin, filed a lawsuit against a ship captain who refused her first-class passage aboard a steamboat. Rollin and other leading black women activists also secured a charter for a branch of the American Woman Suffrage Association in South Carolina. Black women were among the vanguard in fighting for equality during the Republican-controlled era. Nevertheless, even partial equality for the majority of South Carolina African Americans during Reconstruction would remain only a dream as the most radical Southern state fought to maintain its system of white supremacy (Gatewood 1991, 172, 184).

The violent reaction by South Carolina whites to the initial attempts of freedmen to exercise their new status led directly to congressional reconstruction and military occupation. From 1867 until 1877, federal troops occupied Columbia. During this decade, the Republican Party, supported by the freedmen, was able to push through the passage of the Fourteenth and Fifteenth Amendments. The U.S. Congress agreed to readmit the reconstructed state in June 1868. The presence of federal troops, however, was the only means by which the Republicans maintained state control. In April 1877, President Rutherford B. Hayes removed the federal forces occupying Columbia. Immediately, the Democrats installed their governor, former CSA cavalryman, General Wade Hampton. The "redeemed" assembly quickly enacted Jim Crow segregationist laws that the reconstructed legislature had proscribed. The freedom and liberties that South Carolina Africa Americans enjoyed for the few years following 1868 became only a fleeting memory (Foner 1988, 427–431, 542–544, 571–599).

REFERENCES

Berlin, Ira, Joseph P. Reidy, and Linda S. Rowland, eds. 1982. *Freedom: A Documentary History of Emancipation*, Series II, *The Black Military Experience*. New York: Cambridge University Press.

Dusinberre, William. 1996. *Them Dark Days: Slavery in the American Rice Swamps*. New York: Oxford University Press.

Foner, Eric. 1988. *America's Unfinished Revolution, 1863–1867*. New York: Harper & Row.

Gatewood, Willard B., Jr. 1991. "'The Remarkable Misses Rollin': Black Women in Reconstruction South Carolina." *South Carolina Historical Magazine* 92 (July): 172–188.

Hudson, Larry E., Jr. 1997. *To Have and to Hold: Slave Work and Family Life in Antebellum South Carolina*. Athens: University of Georgia Press.

Kellison, Kimberly R. 2002. "Toward Humanitarian Ends? Protestants and Slave Reform in South Carolina, 1830–1865." *South Carolina Historical Magazine* 103 (July): 210–225.

Koger, Larry. 1985. *Black Slaveowners: Free Black Slave Masters in South Carolina, 1790–1860*. Jefferson, N.C.: McFarland & Company, Inc.

Littlefield, Daniel C. 1990. "The Colonial Slave Trade to South Carolina: A Profile." *South Carolina Historical Magazine* 91 (April): 68–99.

Lofton, John. 1964. *Denmark Vesey's Revolt: The Slave Plot that Lit a Fuse to Fort Sumter*. Kent, Ohio: Kent State University Press.

Morrill, Dan L. 2002. *The Civil War in the Carolinas.* Charleston, S.C.: The Nautical & Aviation Publishing Company of America.

Olwell, Robert. 1998. *Masters, Slaves, & Subjects: The Culture of Power in the South Carolina Low Country, 1740–1790.* Ithaca: Cornell University Press.

Rawick, George P., ed. 1972. *The American Slave: A Composite Autobiography.* Westport, Conn.: Greenwood Publishing Company.

Rose, Willie Lee. 1964. *Rehearsal for Reconstruction: The Port Royal Experiment.* Athens: University of Georgia Press.

Schwalm, Leslie. 1997. *A Hard Fight for We: Women's Transition from Slavery to Freedom in South Carolina.* Urbana: University of Chicago Press.

Schweninger, Loren. 1992. "Slave Independence and Enterprise in South Carolina, 1780–1865." *South Carolina Historical Magazine* 93 (April): 101–125.

Tadman, Michael. 1996. "The Hidden History of Slave Trading in Antebellum South Carolina: John Springs III and Other 'Gentlemen Dealing in Slaves.'" *South Carolina Historical Magazine* 97 (January): 6–29.

_____. 1989. *Speculators and Slaves: Masters, Traders, and Slaves in the Old South.* Madison: University of Wisconsin Press.

Ware, Lowry. 1990. "The Burning of Jerry: The Last Slave Execution by Fire in South Carolina?" *South Carolina Historical Magazine* 91 (April): 100–106.

———. 1990. "Reuben Robertson of Turkey Creek: The Story of a Wealthy Black Slaveholder and His Family, White and Black." *South Carolina Historical Magazine* 91 (October): 261–267.

West, Jerry L. 2002. *The Reconstruction Ku Klux Klan in York County, South Carolina, 1865–1877.* Jefferson, North Carolina: McFarland & Company, Inc.

Wood, Peter H. 1974. *Black Majority: Negroes in Colonial South Carolina from 1670 Through the Stono Rebellion.* New York: W.W. Norton & Company.

WEB SITES

Denmark Vesey Conspiracy: http://www.pbs.org/wgbh/aia/part3/3p2976.html

The Experience of a Slave in South Carolina: http://docsouth.unc.edu/jackson/menu.html

The Goodings Describe Reconstruction in South Carolina: http://lcweb2.loc.gov/learn/features/timeline/civilwar/recon/goodings.html

The Gullah Creole Language: http://lcweb2.loc.gov/learn/features/timeline/civilwar/recon/goodings.html

On the Old Plantation: http://docsouth.unc.edu/clinkscales/menu.html

Slavery in South Carolina: http://www.richland2.k12.sc.us/rce/slavery.htm

Stono Rebellion: http://www.pbs.org/wgbh/aia/part1/1p284.htm

Tennessee

TIMELINE

1766: "Mulatto Jim" accompanies Colonel James Smith on his explorations of the Cumberland River region

1796, June 1: Tennessee enters the Union as a slave state

1819: Death penalty becomes standard punishment for slaves convicted of murder, arson, rape, and robbery

1822: Tennessee outlaws miscegenation

1831: Tennessee Assembly passes laws barring free blacks from entering the state

1861, June 8: Tennessee secedes from the Union; Tennessee Senator Andrew Johnson continues to hold his seat in the U.S. Congress

1862: President Abraham Lincoln appoints Senator Andrew Johnson military governor of Tennessee

1864, April 12: Fort Pillow Massacre—Confederates kill black Union troops after they have surrendered

1864: Lincoln and the Republicans select Senator Andrew Johnson, a Tennessee Democrat, as Lincoln's vice-presidential running mate for the 1864 election—Lincoln and Johnson officially ran as National Union candidates

1865, March: Freedmen's Bureau is created by Congress and opened in Tennessee

April 14: President Lincoln is shot; Johnson becomes president the next day on Lincoln's death

1866, May 1–2: Memphis riots erupt when rumors spread that black
    Union troops tried to prevent white police officers from arresting a
    black man
        July 24: Tennessee is readmitted to the Union

1867: Fisk University in Nashville is established for the education of freedmen

1868: President Johnson is tried by the Senate under 11 articles of impeach-
    ment, but is acquitted by one vote

Slave and Free Black Population

Census Year	Slave Population	Population Percentage	Free Black Population	Population Percentage
1790	3,417	9	361	1
1800	13,584	12	309	under 1
1810	44,535	17	1,317	under 1
1820	80,107	19	2,737	under 1
1830	141,603	20	4,555	under 1
1840	183,059	22	5,524	under 1
1850	239,459	24	6,422	under 1
1860	275,719	25	7,300	under 1

**Net Slave Entries and Exits, by Decade
(Tadman 1989, 12)**

1790–1799: + 6,645	1830–1839: + 6,930
1800–1809: + 21,788	1840–1849: + 4,837
1810–1819: + 19,079	1850–1859: – 17,702
1820–1829: + 31,577	

ORIGINS OF SLAVERY

The first blacks to travel to what would become Tennessee accompanied
Spanish and French adventurers who explored as early as 1541 the Mississippi River up to the site of present-day Memphis. Exploration by En-
glish-speaking frontiersmen began shortly after the conclusion of the
French and Indian War. In 1766, Colonel James Smith traveled to the
Cumberland region accompanied by at least one black whom he noted
as a mulatto lad named Jim. Likewise, a "negro fellow" was part of
James Robertson's party, which explored the area that eventually became Nashville in 1779. Settlers, mainly from North Carolina, soon followed.

The region that would become the Volunteer State emerged out of land ceded to the federal government by North Carolina in 1790. Provisions excluding slavery in that territory did not exist, and Anglo settlers quickly moved into the area with their bondsmen. The population grew so rapidly that in just six short years Tennessee became a state in 1796. The state constitution of Tennessee, however, did not mention slavery. Instead, the state operated under laws that guided North Carolina regarding the peculiar institution. Because no restrictions existed on bringing slaves into the territory, in the first decade of settlement, the number of slaves increased more than three-fold from 3,417 to 13,584, and in the second decade enslaved African Americans again increased more than three-fold to 44,535 by 1810. Middle Tennessee would eventually have the most number of slaves in the state, but the western region would hold the highest concentration or density of slaves.

ECONOMICS OF SLAVERY

In antebellum Tennessee, slavery emerged as the cornerstone of an economically diverse state. Chattel slavery was profitable for whites both as a measure of wealth and as income derived from the products of slave labor. In 1790, the average value of a slave ranged from one hundred fifty to two hundred dollars. This increased to nearly four hundred dollars in 1795, six hundred dollars in 1803, and close to one thousand dollars in 1818. Slave prices in the 1830s fluctuated with the downturn in the economy, but by the 1840s rose once again. In 1846, skilled slaves sold for an extremely high price. For example, carpenters sold for twenty-five hundred dollars, blacksmith aides for eleven hundred dollars, painters for one thousand dollars, and field hands for one thousand dollars. As the dependency on slave labor increased, the price for bondsmen continued to rise. On the eve of the Civil War, fifteen-year-old males sold for a minimum of fourteen hundred dollars, twenty-one-year-old males for seventeen hundred dollars, thirty-four-year-old males for thirteen hundred dollars, and seven-year-old girls for one thousand dollars. Considering the devaluation of the dollar by the time of the Civil War, the real value of the slave was less than the selling price. Nevertheless, slaves remained an expensive commodity, and owners made certain that they purchased only the best slaves possible. One ex-slave, Millie Simpkins, recalled her experience at a slave auction that punctuates this reality: "A Mr. Chandler would bide de slaves off," she recalled, "but 'fore dey started biddin' you had ter tek all ob yo clothes off en roll down de hill so dey would see dat you didn't hab no bones broken, or sores on yer" (Mooney 1957, 37; Rawick 1972, 16:66).

As elsewhere, whites profited from the product of slave labor. In Tennessee, the primary crop production consisted of cotton, tobacco, and corn. In 1801, Tennessee produced 2,500 bales of cotton. This increased to 50,000 bales in 1820, 194,532 bales in 1850, and by 1860, the state produced 296,464 bales of cotton. Tobacco production also was an extremely important part of the state's cash crop that relied on slave labor, especially in the western counties. In 1840, the state produced 29,550,432 pounds of tobacco, and by 1860, the state produced 43,448,097 pounds of tobacco with the aid of slave labor. Corn also was a staple part of the economy. Tennessee produced 44,986,188 bushels in 1840, and this amount increased to 52,089,926 bushels in 1860. The dramatic increase, especially in cotton and tobacco production, can be attributed only to the unyielding reliance upon the institution of slavery, which in turn came to be seen as an economic necessity. The increased agricultural production along with the escalating price of slaves ensured that the peculiar institution would be profitable for slave-owning whites in Tennessee (Mooney 1957, 128, 134, 139).

SLAVE LIFE

Because slavery proved profitable, owners often worked their slaves for fourteen to sixteen hours a day in the summertime to maximize profits. The work life of slaves in Tennessee did not differ significantly from that in other slaveholding states. Slaves woke well before sunrise to the sound of a bugle or horn, if possible ate a small amount, and then headed to the fields. Oftentimes, an owner would give his bondsmen a break for lunch, and then slaves toiled in the fields until sundown, with a possible break for dinner. Usually the slave children had the responsibility of hauling food and water to their parents in the field. They were not to interfere with the work schedule, though; any slowdown or stopping of labor was not permitted by the owner or overseer. Any interruptions resulted in a whipping for a slave. Not all bondsmen worked the fields. Depending on the size of the farm or plantation, some slaves served their masters in a domestic capacity, and the older slaves who could not toil in the fields generally worked at other chores, especially tending livestock and gardens. Contrary to popular belief, though, the position of the slaves did not determine their treatment. A common belief is that household servants were treated better than were field hands. This was not always the case; the disposition and personality of the owner primarily determined the treatment of the slave. Cecilia Chappel, an ex-slave, recalled her days as a nurse and house servant. When asked about her experience, she recalled, "I wuz whup'd wid a bull whup, en got cuts on mah back menny a time. I'se not shamed ter say I got skyars on mah back now fum Marster cuttin' hit wid dat bull whup. Mah Missis also whup'd me. . . . Sum times she would lock us up in a dark closet en bring our food ter us. I hated bein' locked up" (Rawick 1972, 16:6).

An integral part of work life involved the practice of owners hiring their slaves out, a common practice throughout the state. This also offered owners another way to profit through the labor of enslaved African Americans, especially during harvest season when the demand for extra labor increased. Usually, the hirer covered food, clothing, and shelter. Medical care varied according to each contract. Costs varied from place to place, but, generally, an unskilled slave hired out for ten dollars per month. Skilled labor, especially blacksmiths, commanded higher amounts. In the beginning stages of slavery, bondsmen were permitted to hire themselves out on their own free time. Beginning in 1823, though, as the desire to safeguard profits emerged with the flourishing cotton economy, it became illegal for a bondsman to hire himself or herself out.

In smaller towns, such as Franklin, slaves experienced less supervision over their labor and social life. The widespread practice of owners hiring out their slaves for domestic service, and slaves hiring themselves out, along with the presence of a small number of free blacks, provided these urban slaves with more control over their economic and social life. Furthermore, racial relations in such an environment were somewhat more relaxed, and whites did not necessarily enforce the letter of the law in this small-town environment (Tolbert 1998, 212).

To maximize their profits, slave owners provided only the bare necessities for their servants, often feeding a minimum amount of food. One ex-slave, Robert Falls recalled, "They didn't half feed us either. They fed the animals better. They gives the mules, ruffage and such, to chaw on all night. But they didn't give us nothing to chaw on." This, he later added, led the slaves to steal. They would lie about stealing, of course, but still received a whipping for the theft. Regarding such treatment, Falls remarked, "But it is easier to stand, when the stomach was full." Although the law required owners to care for and to feed their slaves, masters found ways to avoid possible persecution for any illegal infractions. Ex-slave Millie Simpkins recalled, "One marster we useter 'yer 'bout would grease his slaves mouth on Sunday mawnin', en tell dem ef any body axed ef dey had meat ter say 'yes, lots ob hit'" (Rawick 1972, 16:12, 67).

In the midst of their harsh environment, slaves sought the refuge of family and religion as an avenue of escape and hope, which gave meaning to their daily existence. As elsewhere, slaves often married from their own or adjoining farms and plantations. As was the custom, slave couples recognized their unions with the ceremonial broom jumping tradition. Nevertheless, many owners generally had little respect for upholding the bonds of marriage between slaves. In one sample case, it was found that 23 percent of the couples were separated by sale. There is no definite way to know the true percentage of broken families, but it remains clear that an owner's economic interests took precedent over the welfare and maintenance of black families. Nevertheless, slave families that did exist provided the foundation by which slaves transmitted their oral culture, taught their children the necessary lessons for survival, and formed the intimate bonds that al-lowed them to endure their harsh environment (Cimprich 1985, 10).

Religion likewise offered slaves an avenue of hope and temporary es-cape. This was most evident when camp meetings arrived in the area. Ex-slave Precilla Gray recalled, "Hab gon' ter lots ob camp-meetin's. Dey'd hab lots ob good things ter eat and fed eberbody. Dey'd hab big baptizin's down at de Cumberland Riber and many things." For blacks and whites alike, camp meetings served both a religious and social purpose. Religious revivals allowed bondsmen temporarily to escape the confines of their harsh environment and socialize with bondsmen from other areas.

Their religious experience, though, was not limited to the infrequent religious revival. Oftentimes, slaves would sneak into the woods at night, gathering for their own social and religious experience. There existed a widespread belief among slaves that if they turned a pot or kettle upside down on the ground, no one would hear their singing and praying. An ex-slave, Ann Matthews, recalled that "durin' slavery de white folks didn't want de niggahs ter sing en pray, but dey would turn a pot down en meet at de pot in de nite en sing en pray en de white folks wouldn't 'yer dem" (Rawick 1972, 16:25, 45).

FREE BLACKS

Free blacks posed a problem for white society in Tennessee. Their abil-ity to live free and self-sufficient lives ran as a counterpoint to pro-slavery ideology. Furthermore, the existence of a free black population in the bor-der states increased the fear and potential of slave uprising from abolitionist influence. Therefore, as with most of the slaveholding border states, such as Missouri, there did not exist a large free black population in Tennessee. Beginning in 1831, the assembly passed legislation that proscribed free blacks from moving into the state. Anyone caught doing so was subject to a fine of ten to fifteen dollars and a prison term of one to two years. Politi-cians amended the law regarding free blacks in the 1840s. In 1842, it be-came legal to allow manumitted and free blacks who had lived in Tennessee prior to 1836 to remain in the state, as long as they posted bond testifying to their good behavior. Politicians again amended this law in 1854, stating that if free blacks failed to post bond, they could be sold back into slavery. The proximity of Tennessee to free territory and the growing abolitionist campaign against slavery ensured that a significant free black population would not exist in the state. By 1860, only 2 percent of the en-tire black population in Tennessee lived free. Most Tennessee slave own-ers believed that the presence of a free black community potentially threatened to undermine the institution of slavery.

BLACK CODES

In the first ten years of statehood, slavery was not defined by any set of laws or codes but rather was viewed as an economic necessity and a privilege of property-owning whites. Thus, it was not necessary to create a multitude of legislative enactments regulating the institution. The law only required that owners feed and clothe their slaves and provide for their economic security and general well-being. In addition, owners were forbidden to maim or kill a slave. In 1819, however, politicians did repeal the law that made it illegal to kill a runaway slave (Apperson 2000, 4).

The black codes that eventually did emerge in Tennessee were largely shaped by North Carolina's slave codes and affected the lives of both whites and blacks. As elsewhere, laws existed to safeguard the institution of slavery and to produce a level of social stability to ensure economic profitability.

In 1803, regulations were passed that decreed that a ten-dollar fine should be the penalty for anyone attempting to incite a slave to rebel in any manner. There was also a ten-dollar fine chargeable to anyone who permitted slaves to congregate without a pass. These rules reflected white fears that slaves would plan and implement a rebellion. Thus, from the onset, whites exhibited a fear of potential slave revolts.

As the slave population increased in Tennessee, and slavery emerged as more of a perceived economic necessity, laws also regulated how whites treated chattel property. Beginning in 1813, anyone who unjustifiably harmed or abused a slave was liable to indictment. In the 1820s, a legal movement emerged to protect the social stability of slavery, and politicians declared that whites could not cohabitate with blacks. Many upper-class whites feared that miscegenation would undermine their patriarchal society by leading free blacks to demand social or political equality. Even worse, many whites feared racial mixing might lead slaves to revolt. In addition, it became illegal in 1826 to bring a slave, previously convicted of any crime, into the state. Rising concerns about safeguarding the institution of slavery led politicians in the 1830s to forbid owners from manumitting their slaves unless these bondsmen left the state. This 1831 law would be amended in 1852 to allow some freedmen to reside in the state under certain conditions. Similar to other states, Tennessee also had to deal with runaway slaves. To safeguard the return of their human property, in the 1830s, politicians decreed that a five-dollar reward should be the standard for returning runaway slaves. They increased this amount to twenty-five dollars in later years. By the 1840s, as a more humanitarian approach toward the treatment of slaves became popular as a means for justifying chattel slavery, a twenty-five dollar fine in 1842 would be inflicted on owners who did not supply their slaves with sufficient clothing. As elsewhere, the laws operated mainly in theory, and the prosecution of whites who violated the law occurred only in rare cases.

Legal codes not only were enacted to ensure the stability of the peculiar institution but also were designed to regulate the actions and personal habits of slaves. In 1753, slaves were not allowed to have a gun or permitted a certificate for hunting, unless the owner posted a bond for good behavior. If a slave hunted with dogs without a pass, he would be punished with thirty-nine lashes. If a slave forged a pass for hunting, this also resulted in a whipping of thirty-nine lashes. As the slave population and the fear of black violence increased, so too did the penalties. In 1819, any slave convicted of murder, arson, burglary, rape, or robbery received the death penalty. In the 1830s, it also became illegal for slaves to sell liquor without an owner's permission. Owners simply would not trust slaves with whiskey for they feared that slaves had the tendency toward violent behavior if they became intoxicated. Those who violated the law received five to ten lashes. In the 1830s, though, the fear of slave revolt did not seem paramount, and the penalty for rebellion became a matter dictated by local courts. As the abolitionist movement made more of a national impact and the fear of slave insurrections increased, the assembly, beginning in 1858, decreed that any slave in rebellion would in all cases be subject to the death penalty. Of course, each area had its own black codes. For example, in Memphis in 1856, it became illegal to teach a slave to read. Cecilia Chappel, an ex-slave, recalled, "I dunno how ter read or rite. De white folks didn' 'low us ter l'arn nuthin'. I declar' you bettuh no git kotch wid a papah in you han'." In Nashville, local authorities declared in 1857 that slaves could not travel after 7:00 P.M. The legal system safeguarding the institution of slavery in Tennessee was similar to that of other states and served to safeguard a system of labor that underpinned the state's racial, social, and economic system (Rawick 1972, 16:5).

THE CIVIL WAR

The outbreak of Civil War, however, disrupted the institution of slavery in Tennessee. The need for armed forces and laborers in the military conflict led the Confederate government to permit the impressment of slaves. Those slaves who did serve in the army worked as general laborers, built fortifications, and worked as personal body servants. Many slave owners in Tennessee, however, viewed the impressment of their slaves as a violation of their personal property rights and sought to keep their bondsmen out of the hands of the Confederate army. Flight by Tennessee slave owners with their African American chattel was a common occurrence. Wiley Childress, an ex-slave, recalled that "durin' de war mah Missis tuk mah mammy en us chillins wid her ter de mount'ins 'till de war wuz gon'." Slave owners often transported their bondsmen into the mountain region to protect them from the ravages of war, to prevent their possible escape into the Union lines, and to hide them from Confederate authorities (Cimprich 1985, 29; Rawick 1972, 16:9).

In the beginning stages of war, however, the Union did not officially attempt to disrupt the peculiar institution. Prior to 1862, Union forces in Tennessee operated according to the policy of exclusion, choosing not to interfere with slavery and forbidding runaway slaves from entering their camps. Much of this policy was out of practicality; the sheer numbers of possible runaways would have been too much for Union forces to feed and care for. Army commanders disobeyed the policy of exclusion only when it benefited their cause, and this was generally out of the need for labor (Cimprich 1985, 20, 35).

The Emancipation Proclamation, effective January 1, 1863, affected only those Tennessee slaves who still resided in areas controlled by the Confederacy. When black enlistment became available, Tennessee African Americans flocked to the mustering agents. Thousands of Kentucky blacks who crossed over into Tennessee to join the Union army in a bid to achieve their freedom joined them. Clarksville especially became a center for both Tennessee and Kentucky enlistments. By the autumn of 1863, five regiments had been organized from Tennessee black volunteers. All told, 20,133 Tennessee African Americans joined and served in the Union army. Lorenzo A. Thomas, the U.S. Army adjutant general, reported that the black troops along the Mississippi River had "proved a most important addition to our troops" (Berlin 1982, 11–12, 170).

On April 12, 1864, Confederate forces under General Nathan Bedford Forrest attacked and captured Fort Pillow, Tennessee, a Union encampment on the Mississippi River originally constructed by the Confederates. The fortifications were manned not only by white troops but also by black soldiers from Tennessee and Kentucky units, among others. A number of these black soldiers were summarily executed by the rebels after they had tried to surrender and had thrown down their weapons. This unsavory incident went down in history as the Fort Pillow Massacre (Berlin 1982, 539–548).

By the time the Civil War ended in April and May of 1865, nearly all of Tennessee had been overrun by the Union army. Part of the state had been under federal control from early 1862 onward. The few remaining Tennessee Confederate troops still in the field surrendered in April 1865 with General Robert E. Lee at Appomattox, Virginia, and with General Joseph E. Johnston at Durham Station, North Carolina. Other small rebel detachments quickly laid down their weapons as well. The Civil War was over and slavery had ended in Tennessee.

EMANCIPATION AND RECONSTRUCTION

In Tennessee, the push for freedom and equality for blacks actually began during the Civil War. In many urban areas, especially in Memphis and

Nashville, blacks gathered to protest their condition. At these rallies, black leaders often read the Declaration of Independence, waved banners with slogans such as "Free and Equal," and marched in protest. Blacks, thus, did not wait patiently in their struggle for freedom. Despite such occurrences, the general experience for freedmen was typical of other states. Many freedmen stayed on their farms or plantations devoted to their masters and homes. Others fled quickly when they learned of their freedom, venturing into the unknown with little or no belongings. Robert Falls, an ex-slave, recalled, "I remember so well, how the roads was full of folks walking and walking along when the niggers were freed. Didn't know where they was going. Just going to see about something else somewhere else. Meet a body in the road and they ask, 'Where you going?' 'Don't know.' 'What you going to do?' 'Don't know'" (Cimprich 1985, 104, 198; Rawick 1972, 16:15).

When Andrew Johnson took over as military governor of the liberated part of Tennessee in 1862, the state began the task of reconstruction. Unlike many areas in the Confederacy, this process in the regions long occupied by the Union army had already begun by the time the Confederates finally surrendered.

The Freedmen's Bureau first appeared in Tennessee in the spring of 1865. The state was part of a larger district that included Kentucky and northern Alabama. In 1866, though, Tennessee became a separate region divided into several subdistricts. One of the primary goals of the Freedmen's Bureau in Tennessee was to extend education to African Americans. In some areas of Tennessee, there existed a movement during the Civil War to extend education to blacks, and historians estimate that nine thousand blacks had some rudimentary education by 1865. In 1866, the Freedman's Bureau opened several schools across the state. In addition, with aid from the American Missionary Association and the Western Freedmen's Aid Commission, a school opened in Nashville to train black teachers for the freedmen's schools. The goal of the program was to train black teachers and reduce the high student-teacher ratio (66:1) in the freedmen's schools. The school in Nashville would eventually become Fisk University, named after Clinton B. Fisk, the first director of the Freedmen's Bureau in Tennessee. At the same time, the legislature supported the creation of a statewide public school system. Opportunities for higher education were also available to some extent. For example, Virginia Walker Broughton, who graduated from Fisk University in 1875, became the first African American woman in the South to obtain a college degree.

In addition to organizing and managing schools, the Freedmen's Bureau negotiated labor contracts between the ex-slaves and white employers, organized orphanages, hospitals, and offered legal advice. Such support for African Americans, however, outraged the white citizenry of Tennessee, and racial tensions soared. On May 1 and 2, 1866, in Memphis, the state experienced the worst racial uprising in its history. The Memphis riot broke

Tennessee freedmen line up for assistance at the Memphis office of the Freedman's Bureau. (Library of Congress.)

out after it was reported that black soldiers from Fort Pickering had killed several policemen attempting to arrest a black soldier. As a result, Union General George Stoneman locked the African American soldiers in their barracks, leaving nearby black communities vulnerable to attack. A mob of angry whites took advantage of the situation and attacked defenseless men, women, children, missionaries, and teachers. In the melee, churches, homes, and schools were burned and destroyed, women were raped, freedmen were robbed, hundreds of people were injured, and forty-six African Americans were killed. While many freedmen fled during the riot, officials also jailed hundreds of African Americans.

Despite the advances in education, the Memphis riots reflected the reality of life for freedmen—African Americans did not enjoy social equality. Tennessee passed some of the first Jim Crow segregation laws in the South that restricted the freedom of African Americans. Passing legislation that segregated schools, public accommodations, and transportation, however, forced African Americans to unite and build up their own black communities, where many rose to general positions of leadership in and outside of the black community. Significant in this process was the role of African American women. For example, Ida B. Wells, a teacher and journalist, owned her own newspaper, the *Memphis Free Speech*, which she used to launch a nationally recognized antilynching campaign in 1892.

In addition, black women played a significant role in many postwar Tennessee towns. For example, in Memphis, African American women formed many organizations, such as the Daughters of Zion, the Baptist Sewing Circle, and the Sons and Daughters of Canaan, for the social, religious, educational, and economic benefit of black women in specific and the black community in general. These women worked as seamstresses, laundresses, and in a general domestic capacity. These industrious women formed the organizations and became leaders in the postwar free black communities of Tennessee. One historian claimed that African American women "were the moral centers of their households, their communities, and the race as a whole." Their role in the black community challenged the racial stereotypes of the era and provided unity, a critique of white society run by Jim Crow laws, and the necessary moral leadership of a race struggling to find its place in a society largely ruled and dominated by the doctrine of white supremacy (Cimprich 1985, 129; Bond 2000, 261–265).

While the postwar restrictions on African American advancement in society might not have been as confining as in other states, the institution of slavery itself and the segregated postwar state left many blacks bitter and resentful. Robert Falls, an ex-slave, recalled, "If I had my life to live over, I would die fighting rather than be a slave again. I want no man' yoke on my shoulders no more" (Rawick 1972, 16:12).

REFERENCES

Apperson, George M. 2000. "African Americans on the Tennessee Frontier: John Gloucester and His Contemporaries." *Tennessee Historical Quarterly* 59 (Spring): 2–19.

Arroyo, Elizabeth Fortson. 1996. "Poor Whites, Slaves, and Free Blacks in Tennessee, 1796–1861." *Tennessee Historical Quarterly* 55 (Spring): 57–64.

Ash, Stephen V. 1988. *Middle Tennessee Society Transformed, 1860–1870: War and Peace in the Upper South*. Baton Rouge: Louisiana State University Press.

Berlin, Ira, Joseph P. Reidy, and Leslie S. Rowland, eds. 1982. *Freedom: A Documentary History of Emancipation, 1861–1867*, Series II, *The Black Military Experience*. New York: Cambridge University Press.

Bond, Beverly G. 2000. "'Every Duty Incumbent upon Them': African-American Women in Nineteenth Century Memphis." *Tennessee Historical Quarterly* 59 (Spring): 254–273.

Cimprich, John. 1985. *Slavery's End in Tennessee, 1861–1865*. Tuscaloosa: University of Alabama Press.

Edwards, Gary T. 1998. "'Negroes . . . and All Other Animals': Slaves and Masters in Antebellum Madison County." *Tennessee Historical Quarterly* 57 (Spring/ Summer): 24–35.

Howington, Arthur E. 1986. *What Sayeth the Law: The Treatment of Slaves and Free Blacks in the State and Local Courts of Tennessee*. New York: Garland Publishing, Inc.

Mooney, Chase C. 1957. *Slavery in Tennessee*. Bloomington: Indiana University Press.

Rawick, George P., ed. 1972. *The American Slave: A Composite Autobiography*. Westport, Conn.: Greenwood Publishing Company.

Tadman, Michael. 1989. *Speculators and Slaves: Masters, Traders, and Slaves in the Old South*. Madison: University of Wisconsin Press.

Tolbert, Lisa C. 1998. "Murder in Franklin: The Mysteries of Small-town Slavery." *Tennessee Historical Quarterly* 57 (Winter): 203–217.

WEB SITES

Aunt Dice: The Story of a Faithful Slave: http://docsouth.unc.edu/robinsonn/menu.html

Black History in Tennessee: Anderson County: http://www.geocities.com/brenfoster

Blacks in Tennessee: http://newdeal.feri.org/guides/tnguide/ch10.htm

Reverend J.W. Loguen, as a Slave and as a Freeman: http://docsouth.unc.edu/neh/loguen/menu.html

Tennessee Slave Narratives (26): http://memory.loc.gov/cgi-bin/query/S?ammem/mesnbib:@field(STATE+@od1(Tennessee))

Texas

TIMELINE

1790s: Slave families live in San Antonio and La Bahia

1821: Stephen F. Austin makes his initial proposal to the Mexican government for land grants in Texas

1823, January 4: Mexico passes the Imperial Colonization Law outlawing the slave trade in Texas

1824: First Black Codes are enacted in the region

1835–1836: Texas Revolution results in the independence of Texas from Mexico

1836–1845: Texas is an independent republic

1837: Texas Black Codes are strengthened

1845, December 29: Texas enters the Union as a slave state

1846: Texas creates a formal slave patrol system

1861, February 23: Texas secedes from the Union and joins the Confederacy

1865: Texas Governor Andrew Jackson Hamilton declares African Americans equal with whites before the law
    March: Freedman's Bureau is established in Texas
    June 19: Confederate resistance and slavery end in Texas

1867: African Americans cast 35,952 votes for a constitutional convention

1867–1870: Texas is administered by Union troops as part of Military District #5

1870, March 30: Texas is readmitted to the Union

1873: Democrats triumph in state elections and "redeem" Texas for whites

Slave and Free Black Population

Census Year	Slave Population	Population Percentage	Free Black Population	Population Percentage
1850	58,161	27	397	under 1
1860	182,566	30	355	under 1

Net Slave Entries and Exits, by Decade (Tadman 1989, 12)

1840–1849: + 28,622	1850–1859: + 99,190

ORIGINS OF SLAVERY

Bondsmen arrived in Texas in the mid- to late eighteenth century. In 1790, fifteen slave families lived in San Antonio and La Bahia (present day Goliad). Of these families, it is known that six had descendents living in the territory. Africans came to Texas as slaves. They were bought in New Orleans or along the Texas-Louisiana border. In the beginning, owners used their slaves primarily as "barter currency" in the cattle business (Robbins 1971, 153–162).

Before the Texas Revolution in 1835, however, slavery was in a tenuous position. Blacks lived as both freemen and as slaves. Evidence also suggests that during this era there was little segregation or discrimination. This was especially true during the late eighteenth and early nineteenth centuries when Texas was racially open and many blacks found it possible to improve their social, political, and economic standing. In fact, many fugitive slaves came to Texas to live as freemen where they found their existence somewhat more bearable than in their previous state of residence. Nevertheless, when Stephen F. Austin made his initial proposal for land grants in Texas in 1821, it included the provision of fifty acres per slave; he later increased that to eighty acres per slave. The major problem that early Anglo settlers in Texas faced was a barrage of antislavery measures from the Mexican government (Campbell 1989, 14; Tjarks 1974, 291–338).

During the 1820s, Mexico passed a number of antislavery measures that affected Texas, leaving the survival of the institution there in doubt. On January 4, 1823, Mexico passed the Imperial Colonization Law. This decree outlawed the purchase and sale of slaves. Furthermore, it directed that children born to slaves would be free at the age of fourteen. This law remained in affect for only one month. Mexico's President Augustine de Iturbide was overthrown in February 1823, and the law was soon annulled. With a three-man junta now governing the nation, Mexico produced a new constitution in 1824. This constitution explicitly forbade the traffic in slaves. Three years later, the state of Coahuila and Texas produced a state constitution stating that no person shall be born a slave in the region. Furthermore, it declared that the introduction of new slaves into Texas would cease by September 1827.

Settlers moving into Texas, however, evaded antislavery legislation by holding Africans as indentured servants instead of slaves, a mere technicality. Before moving to Texas, owners often took their bondsmen before a notary public or government official and drew up a contract between the owner and slave indicating that the slave wished to accompany his or her master to Texas. While all contracts varied, they generally included provisions stipulating that the owner would care for the indentured servant by providing clothes and other necessities. Furthermore, the owner would pay the servant a small wage. From this, indentured servants repaid the owner his cost, the cost of transportation, and the cost of clothes and living expenses. In addition, some contracts listed the specific number of years of service, often ninety-nine years. These tactics all but ensured that Africans in Texas would live a life of slavery.

Mexican officials realized that such technicalities allowed for the introduction of slavery and decided to act against this. In 1830, Mexican President Anastacio Bustamante issued a decree declaring that servants and day laborers could not be obligated by any contract for more than ten years. While this theoretically threatened the institution of slavery, reality reveals that Anglos in Texas disregarded all antislavery legislation. Stephen F. Austin and the early settlers instead supported the peculiar institution on the grounds of economic necessity. They argued that if the region were to grow and prosper economically, slavery was a vital necessity. While they did hold racist beliefs regarding Africans, moral and theoretical issues surrounding slavery took a backseat to economic concerns.

In the early 1830s, the slave trade in Texas exploded, despite Mexico's efforts to thwart the existence of the institution. Slaves were shipped from Africa to Texas, via Cuba. In addition, established ventures in Texas sought to import slaves from the Caribbean. With these early arrivers determined to extend a hard grip on slavery, the institution was almost inevitably secured (Campbell 1989, 33; Lack 1985, 185).

In 1835, Texans cast their lot for revolution. The Texas Revolution represented a turning point for slavery in Texas. The revolution itself offered slaves an opportunity to escape. Some found refuge in serving Mexican soldiers as guides and messengers; others fled to Mexico to live free. On the other side, slaves were used to build fortifications, and some even took up arms in Texas's defense. Many others, though, aided their owners in moving eastward to escape the war. While the chaos of war offered several avenues for bondsmen, Texas's independence from Mexico doomed African Americans to their position as slaves. With the defeat of Santa Anna's forces by Sam Houston at the Battle of San Jacinto on April 21, 1836, Texans secured slavery for the Lone Star state. Even before the revolution ended, Texans held a convention to declare their independence and to write a constitution for the Republic. Texas citizens and politicians provided clear constitutional guidelines supporting the peculiar institution. Article Nine of the Texas constitution legally sanctioned slavery on the same basis that it existed in the United States. Furthermore, Texas independence and the new constitution threatened free blacks, who now were permitted to live in the Republic only by special permission from Congress. With new constitutional guidelines in place, the Republic of Texas squarely secured the institution of slavery (Campbell 1989, 46–47; Lack 1985, 185).

THE GROWTH OF SLAVERY

From the days of the Republic to the Civil War, slavery grew rapidly in Texas. Most of the slaves who arrived in Texas came with their owners. A good number, though not a majority, arrived in Texas as merchandise, sold in the slave trade. Although the Texas constitution outlawed this practice, some individuals continued to carry out the trafficking of slaves. Generally, these slaves would arrive from Africa via numerous other places, especially Cuba. African males were brought into Texas for labor. African women also were brought to Texas, not only for labor but also for their reproductive value. Owners often encouraged their slaves to have as many children as possible, often enticing them with lighter work loads, cash payments, clothing, and passes. Only in rare cases did owners force two individuals together for the purpose of "stock improvement." This involved placing together a male and female slave who had the best physical attributes.

Regardless of why slaves came to Texas, they arrived in large numbers after 1836. Statistics reveal that the tenuous situation of slavery ended once Texas won its independence from Mexico. From 1835 to 1860, a steady increase appears every decade. While the growth in slavery is due in part to Texas's independence, which meant freedom from Mexico's antislavery laws, slavery would not have increased to such a degree if the institution was not in some way valuable to slave owners (Campbell 1989, 56; Malone 1983, 38–40).

THE ECONOMICS OF SLAVERY

The majority of individuals who lived in the Lone Star state were neither slaveholders nor plantation owners. In 1850, for example, only 30 percent of all Texas families owned slaves. Of that, only a little more than 2 percent owned more than twenty slaves. With slavery on the increase in the antebellum era, and only a minority of the population owning slaves, slavery must have been profitable in some fashion.

Examining the peculiar institution, evidence suggests that slavery was economically profitable in numerous ways. First, slavery was profitable in terms of the production of slave labor. This was especially true regarding cotton production. As slavery increased in Texas, so too did cotton production. Although it cost slave owners to feed, clothe, and house their slaves, historians have revealed that slave owners who grew cotton in Texas enjoyed at least a 6 percent return on their investment. Many larger farms and plantations that used slave labor, though, were self-sufficient in their food supply, which allowed them larger profits from slavery. A second manner in which slavery was profitable resulted from the hiring out of slaves. Many of the bondsmen were urban slaves or from larger plantations who were hired out when a labor surplus existed. Slave hiring in antebellum Texas was rather expensive. Throughout this period, hirers generally paid ten times the amount for what it would cost them to purchase a single acre of land. Hired slaves generally worked to produce cotton, thus making the production of slave labor valuable even for those who did not own slaves. Slavery also was profitable as a valuable capital investment. In 1843, the mean value of a slave was approximately $345. By 1858, this value increased to $765. These dollar amounts, though, are only the mean figure, and many slaves, such as field hands who were in good shape, brought in an excess of a thousand dollars. Finally, slavery was valuable as a measure of wealth. Owners sold bondsmen for cash or used their value as collateral for loans whenever the need arose (Campbell 1989, 74, 85–90; Lack 1981, 10).

Slavery not only was valuable for individuals in Texas but also for the state. Slave property existed as an important source of tax revenue. The state taxed slaves in the same fashion as land and livestock. Slaves were also a valuable source of labor for the state. Internal improvements, such as the upkeep of roads, were a state responsibility requiring a great deal of labor. Thus, in many areas throughout Texas, county court commissioners designated a number of slaveholders each year to be responsible for the building and maintenance of local roads. The profitability of slavery, in such numerous ways, to the state, slave owners, and non-slave-owners helps to account for the increase in slaveholding in Texas from the Republic era to the Civil War (Campbell 1989, 68–73, 95).

SLAVE LIFE

Because the use of slave labor was profitable in so many ways, and the number of slaves increased in Texas, a number of questions regarding the material condition of slaves, their work, physical treatment, and personal issues arose. Lee Pierce was a slave in Marshall and Sulphur Springs, Texas. Recounting his days during slavery, Pierce's statement reveals a great deal about the uncertainty, harshness, and impersonal nature of the peculiar institution in Texas.

> When I was 'bout eleven year old, Marse Spencer done got in debt so bad he had to sell me off from mammy. He sold me to a spec'lator named Buckley, and he taken me to Jefferson and drapped me down there with a man called Sutton. I had a hard time there, had to sleep on the floor on hot ashes, to keep warm, in wintertime. I nussed Marse Sutton's kids 'bout a year, den Buckley done got me 'gain and taken me to de nigger trader yard in Marshall. I was put on de block and sold jes' like a cow or horse, to Marse Henry Fowler, what taken me to Sulphur Springs. I lived with him till after surrender. (Rawick 1972, 5:185)

The material condition of enslaved African Americans varied from place to place and according to the disposition of the owner. This was especially true before 1845 when no legal guidelines existed directing owners to provide even the minimum sustenance for their slaves. The Texas Constitution of 1845, however, mandated that owners provide the necessary clothing and food for slaves. The clothing stipend was hardly adequate. The law required owners to furnish their male slaves with a pair of shoes and two pairs of pants over the course of the year. Female slaves received two dresses over the course of a year. In the summer, slaves rarely wore shoes; these were used more during the winter to keep their feet warm. Because the clothing allotment was inadequate, many slaves, especially on the larger farms, made their own clothes, with the owner's permission. Generally, the black women spun the yarn and made all necessary items of clothing for their slave families.

The slave diet was adequate to provide them with the basic nutrition and daily energy to work. While corn and pork were primary foods, numerous masters also provided their slaves with wild game, vegetables, and poultry. Oftentimes owners permitted slaves to have a small plot where they grew their own vegetables. In the frontier region, slaves generally lived at the same level of subsistence as their owner, because farmers there essentially grew what they needed to eat. Slaves were valuable assets, and masters realized the necessity of keeping their slaves fed, at least on a subsistence level (Harper 1985, 398).

Slave quarters usually consisted of one room cabins with no floors and no windows, or if windows existed they did not open. These cabins were not adequate for extreme weather conditions. Generally, each cabin contained only a bed or two, usually attached to the wall by two long poles. The slaves, if they so desired, supplied additional furniture. While the housing conditions varied from place to place, and the wealthier owners generally provided more adequate shelter, it was the slaves themselves who had the responsibility for building their cabin; this was especially true in the early stages of slavery on the frontier.

Due to the cycle of cotton and corn production, slaves kept busy most of the year. Add to that the daily chores, such as taking care of the livestock, mending fences, clearing new ground, killing and butchering hogs, gathering and splitting firewood, and slaves generally worked from first light until very dark—twelve- to sixteen-hour days depending on the time of year. Women also worked the fields, but their work was not done at nightfall. They also had the responsibility of feeding the children, spinning, and sewing. Anna Miller, a slave in Palo Pinto, Texas, recalled, "I'se helps card, spins and cuts de thread. We'uns makes all de cloth for to make de clothes, but we don' git 'em. In de winter we mos' freeze to death. De weaven' was de night work, after workin' all de day in de fiel'" (Rawick 1972, 5:82).

Some slaves on larger farms and plantations, and in the city, also worked as blacksmiths, carpenters, brick masons, tanners, and cobblers. On the frontier, where cotton was not the primary crop, many frontier farmers did own slaves, albeit a minority of the total white population. Most likely, these slaves worked the same jobs as white men at the time. They engaged in cattle herding, corn and wheat harvesting, carpentry and other necessary skilled jobs. In some parts of Texas, slaves worked as cowboys, spending a majority of the time herding and driving cattle. Owners were very careful to entrust a slave with a horse for this only meant the risk of flight. The slave-master relationship on the frontier also tended to be more informal than in other parts of the state or the South. Oftentimes frontier slaves traveled freely, shared the same food as their owners, and worked and hunted alongside their masters. On the frontier, though, bondsmen also shared the same enemy as their master—the Indian. Numerous accounts throughout the nineteenth century reveal that Indians did not discriminate in their attacks and often killed many slaves. Nevertheless, this was not true in all cases. There are some instances where runaway slaves found a new home among the various Indians tribes and in some circumstances rose to positions of leadership (Harper 1985, 398–400; Porter 1949, 151–163).

When it came to work and responsibility, slave children often engaged in the same tasks, regardless of sex. They tended livestock, milked cows, carried food and water to the other slaves working in the fields, spun thread, weeded, took care of babies, and ran errands for the master and mistress. As a boy, Lee Pierce recalled that "the first work I done was herdin' sheep. I never done much field work, but I was kep' busy with them sheep and other jobs round the place." More often than not, slave children were not assigned difficult tasks and were granted some degree of freedom. This generally ended when puberty set in, and they made the transition to the field and more arduous tasks. In some cases, though, slave children who lived on larger farms or in the city learned skilled tasks. Adult slaves knew how important it was to learn a skill, for this often meant escape from the fields. In these special instances, children learned through apprenticeship or merely by watching. On the smaller farms, children did not have the luxury of being taught even the basics of unskilled labor and were often forced into the fields with little knowledge of how to work basic equipment. Though all men, women, and children worked, for the most part, the majority of slaves did have Sundays off, except during harvest season. On these days, they tended their own patches of cotton or vegetables, engaged in social activities, and might have even hired out their labor (Rawick 1972, 5:186; Malone 1983, 34).

A significant aspect of slave life involved the practice of hiring out for labor. Slave hiring in Texas began almost from the onset of the peculiar institution. In 1823, Stephen F. Austin himself contracted out to hire three slaves for a one-year period. In the beginning stages of slavery, settlers often contracted out their slaves to obtain the necessary funds to purchase land. In these cases, the cost of the labor would be credited against the cost of land. Slave owners generally hired out their slaves when a surplus of labor existed or if difficulty supervising all the slaves arose. The most common reason for hiring out slaves, however, was due to estate probates. Oftentimes, when the head of the household died, he left a widow and minor children who needed financial care. In addition, the farm or plantation also needed constant tending. Estate guardians, thus, often made the practice of hiring out slaves to pay for necessary estate costs, the maintenance of the land, and the support of the family. This, of course, had a double beneficial effect by aiding those individuals who had the money to rent a slave but not enough yet to purchase and keep their own slave.

Specific rules governed the hiring of slaves. By law, anyone wishing to rent a slave had to advertise the hiring in at least three places, one of those locations being the front door of his county courthouse. Slaves generally were hired for one year. In early January, people would gather at the county courthouses where slaves were rented in a public auction. Slaves hired out at this time worked for a year and were returned to their owners on December 25 of the same year. Renters, though, could avoid the cost of advertising and paying for an auctioneer by petitioning a county judge to permit a private hiring. In this case, the owner and renter would work out their own contract. Due to the huge demand for slave labor, only in rare circumstances was an owner unable to hire out a slave. While most slaves hired out went to one renter, there were cases where two or more individuals pooled their money to share the bondsman. In all cases, the hirer was responsible for the slave's food and clothes. More often than not, he also was responsible for the medical expense incurred in case a slave became sick or injured. In some cases, though, this amount could be deducted from the cost of hiring the slave, due to time lost. If a slave happened to die while hired out, the hirer's cost was reduced in proportion to the time the slave served. If a slave ran away, however, the loss was incurred by the hirer (Campbell 1989, 82–90).

A slave's physical treatment depended upon a variety of circumstances: the number of other slaves on the farm or plantation, the jobs he or she performed, and the personality and character of the owner. Beginning in 1840, slaves were protected by law from cruel and unusual punishment by their owners. Any owner found guilty of abuse or maiming a slave, potentially reducing his or her value, received a fine or jail sentence. The existence of physical abuse was common knowledge. Nevertheless, few individuals were indicted for cruelty against slaves. Though charges against owners were rare, in one case, Elizabeth Slack of Hunt County was indicted in 1863 for cruelty to a slave. Of course, bringing charges against cruel owners was somewhat problematic because slaves could not testify against whites or against each other. Furthermore, few whites were willing to bring charges against their neighbors. Only in cases where death resulted from abuse was an owner likely to find himself in trouble with the law. Such laws, attempting to protect slaves, reveal that on some level whites did recognize the humanity of slaves. Any cognizant recognition of this, however, most likely was superceded by the fact that such laws protecting slaves aimed more at protecting the condition of slaves to ensure their value and productivity. Though slaves in theory were protected from cruel and unusual punishment, practice reveals uncountable instances of physical abuse through whipping. Most owners did not view this method of punishment as cruel or unusual. Thus, slaves everywhere either witnessed or were subjected to the lash. One slave in Texas recalled, "Day sho whups us. I'se gits whupped lots a times. Marster whips de men and missus whups de women. Sometimes she whups wid de nettleweed. When she uses dat, de licks ain't so bad, be de stingin' and de burnin' afterm um sho' misery" (Harper 1985, 400; Rawick 1972, 5:82–83).

The physical treatment, labor conditions, and uncertainty from hiring out all served to attack the slave's psychological well-being. Although slavery was harsh beyond our current imagination, it was not so binding that it left slaves without a sense of self, family, and community. That is not to defend slavery, but only to say that enslaved African Americans were not completely defeated in the harshest of circumstances. Family life and religion provided two necessary means to keep legal slavery from becoming psychological slavery.

Slave families tended to be large and were means to aid slaves in enduring the hardships of bondage. Family members gave each other necessary love and support to endure their hardship. Though slave families provided immense personal value to slaves, they were at the same time sources of hardship and frustration because bondsmen had no control over the breakup or treatment of family members. While the majority of owners recognized the sacred bond between mother and child, fathers often were sold with little or no regard to the family. The same held true of sons in instances where the males were old enough to work hard labor and could bring a decent amount of money on the auction block. The practice of hiring out also undermined the slave family, as fathers and sons were absent for long periods. Thus, the slave family had a tendency to be matrilineal.

The maintenance of familial units, of course, depended upon the character of the masters and how they treated their slaves. There is no easy way to characterize slave life when it comes to familial relations. In some cases, slaves did join together out of mutual feelings. In some instances, their masters allowed them to celebrate the occasion. Many times this was done with the traditional broomstick ceremony in which the joining couple would jump over a broomstick in front of witnesses, symbolizing their unity and willingness to join together. While most masters did not interfere in the sexual lives of their slaves, there did exist some instances of sexual contact between master and slave. In these cases, slave women were almost helpless against the sexual advances of their masters, and husbands were powerless to defend their wives. Any type of resistance certainly would incur the physical wrath of the owner. Some evidence also suggests there were instances of breeding. In these cases, a master would simply order two slaves to move into the same cabin together. This was done for procreation whereby a master hoped that women would produce bigger and stronger sons capable of more work. Some owners also used exceptionally strong slaves as studs, hiring them out for breeding purposes. Though slave marriages might not have been the most stable, being undermined by all these factors, their importance was tremendous. The family unit and family ties remained exceptionally strong and provided the slaves with a necessary foundation that gave meaning to their lives and allowed them to endure the most difficult circumstances (Malone 1983, 47).

Religion also proved vital in giving slaves meaning to their lives. Though some masters prevented their slaves from going to church out of fear that they would hear the message of equality before the Lord, it remained virtually impossible to prevent slaves from exercising religious activity. At night, slaves stole away to the woods to partake in their own private ceremonies.

In some instances, congregations did allow slaves to form their own churches and worship freely. Although rare, such instances were more likely to occur for the urban slaves. The Baptists did make some inroads in preaching to slaves. Some Baptist slave owners encouraged their slaves to attend services, and records do reveal that many slaves were baptized into the white Baptist churches and attended service with whites. Most likely, slaves attended church and involved themselves in church-related activities because they afforded them outlets from the dull and difficult routine of fieldwork. In addition, they knew that attendance would please their master and they understood that a happy master meant an easier time for them. On the frontier, where the slave institution was less formal, slaves often were allowed to attend religious meetings and even attend church with their masters (Harper 1985, 401; Lack 1981, 10; Palm 1976, 3–8).

As the Civil War grew closer, antislavery sentiment in northern Texas increased, which in turn led to many civil disturbances. These were especially pronounced from 1858 through 1860. In part, activities of the Methodist Episcopal church in north Texas fueled the unrest. This branch of Protestantism aimed at "extirpating slavery," but its preaching did not necessarily encourage slaves to revolt or to break the law. Nevertheless, evidence suggests that the sermons and teachings of these ministers did lead slaves to rise up and in some cases they were charged with murder and arson (Norton 1965, 322, 332–333).

Slave uprisings were especially frequent in northern Texas from July to September 1860. Slaves were suspected of violence, of starting numerous fires, and of destroying property, especially in the Dallas and Henderson areas. Whites suspected that those slaves who did revolt were encouraged by Northern abolitionists who promised slaves that these actions would procure their freedom. Northern abolitionists and members of the Methodist Church North allegedly promised to take the slaves to the North or to Mexico. Although officials obtained voluntary and forced confessions from blacks, the precise circumstances surrounding the events of 1860 are not fully known. Confessions revealed that both the upcoming election of Abraham Lincoln and the work of abolitionists promising freedom to the slaves had an impact on the peculiar institution. Furthermore, the revolts, whether by individuals or groups, did represent outlets for slaves. They were means for them to protest their unjust condition. Nevertheless, the series of events preceding the Civil War were not full-scale rebellions and therefore hardly put slavery in Texas in any jeopardy (White 1949, 259–285).

BLACK CODES

The peculiar institution would not be complete without legal guidelines and Black Codes. Legal guidelines provided a sure foundation on which this controversial institution could operate in an orderly manner. The first Black Codes were passed in 1824. These codes forbid the stealing or luring away of a slave or the harboring of a runaway slave. Any person who found a runaway slave was to administer ten lashes and return the bondsman either to the rightful owner or to the proper authorities. Furthermore, individuals could not buy produce from a slave without the owner's permission. In addition, slaves who stole received ten to one hundred lashes, unless spared by the owner who made restitution, three times the value, to the offended party (Campbell 1989, 18–19).

During the Republic and statehood eras, the law of slavery in Texas became more comprehensive. It affected both slave owners and slaves. Rules governed the right to own slaves, criminal acts against slavery, slave conduct, the problem of runaways, and free blacks. Until Texas declared and won its independence from Mexico, there did not exist a legal right to own slaves. With independence secured, Texans legally sanctioned and safeguarded the institution of slavery in the state constitution. Because slaves were valuable in so many ways, laws were also necessary to govern criminal acts against slave property. In Texas, it was a crime to entice a slave to leave his or her master. Anyone doing so, and anyone harboring a runaway slave, was subject to a fine and possible jail sentence. Furthermore, the laws forbid any person from conducting unauthorized trade with a slave. In addition, to ensure that slaves would not get out of line, it became a crime to sell liquor to a slave. In the city, Black Codes also prevented slaves from congregating unsupervised, from gambling, or from acting in a disorderly fashion (Lack 1981, 9).

While many laws affected the actions of whites, laws did exist that affected the conduct of slaves. Beginning in 1837, the laws forbid insurrections, raping white women, poisoning people, physically assaulting whites, and arson, murder, and burglary. Each of these acts was a capital offense punishable by death. Punishments against slaves, though, were not uniform throughout the state. It would not be until 1860 that the law clearly distinguished between two types of punishment: whipping and death. Capital offenses were punished by death and all other offenses were punished by whipping. The problem, however, was that slave masters often punished their slaves without regard to the law and often punished them when no crime was committed.

The problem of runaways was also an important issue regulated by law. In 1841, the law gave the right and responsibility to apprehend runaway slaves and to return them to the justice of the peace or proper owners. In cases where runaway slaves were not claimed, they were sold at auction. In 1846, Texas created a formal slave patrol system to aid in the enforcement of laws and to regulate slave activity. Bondsmen feared the patrols, and there are numerous known instances where slave patrols took the law into their own hands. One slave in Texas recalled, "If us slips off dem patterrollers gits us. Patterrollers hit 39 licks with de rawhide with de nine tails. Patterroller gits 50 cents for hittin' us 39 licks" (Rawick 1972, 5:222).

FREE BLACKS

From the beginning, Texas law recognized the existence of free blacks on Texas soil and permitted them to remain in the Lone Star state, as long as they abided by all laws and obtained permission from Congress to reside there. Many Texans feared that the existence of a free black population would undermine the institution of slavery. Nevertheless, the law forbidding emancipation was more often than not overlooked, as countless owners, upon their death, freed their slaves. In addition, the Constitution of 1836 barred slave owners from emancipating their slaves unless they sent them out of the Republic.

Sam Houston, the first president of the Republic, supported the early laws existing at the founding of the Republic. In 1840, however, newly elected President Mirabeau B. Lamar repealed all previous laws and commanded that all free blacks leave the state of Texas by January 1, 1842. In 1842, however, Sam Houston won re-election as president. He remitted this law and allowed free blacks to remain in Texas if they registered with the chief justice of the county in which they resided. Though Texas law during the days of the Republic allowed free blacks to remain, legislation did make it unlawful for the importation or immigration of additional free blacks. Furthermore, free blacks who violated the law could find themselves sold into slavery. These laws remained in effect until 1845.

At that point, when Texas entered the Union, it became illegal for free blacks to remain in Texas unless the Texas legislature provided a specific relief. In reality, free blacks often ignored the law or moved to other places in Texas that did not uphold this law. Free blacks who remained in Texas did receive some legal protection. The state ensured that free blacks could not be sold into slavery. Whites found guilty of doing so received hard labor in the state penitentiary. Free blacks who did remain in Texas were subject to strict codes of conduct. For example, if a free black was found guilty of verbally insulting a white person, the penalty received was between twenty-five and one hundred lashes. Most other crimes of a more heinous nature, such as physical threats, attempted murder, and poisoning, were punishable by death. Furthermore, free blacks were not permitted to socialize with whites. In addition, an act approved in 1846 forbade free blacks from hiring out slaves. Ironically, though, no provision existed to prevent free blacks from owning slaves (Muir 1943, 215).

Blacks who remained free, however, had to justify their value economically. Many free black women were heads of households and justified their freedom by the services they performed. They were most useful to white males by serving as cooks, laundresses, and seamstresses. Some black women owned their own farms, and some even owned slaves themselves. Before 1836, free black women enjoyed a higher status than they would in later years. Before the era of the Republic, they often intermarried with white males and associated freely in society. In addition, not to be over-looked, was the important role of friend played by both free and slave women. This was especially true on the frontier where the existence was often isolated and lonely (Malone 1983, 28).

The life and conditions of free blacks varied from place to place and over time. While some individuals might have carved out a respectable life, in most cases their situation was extremely difficult. In many instances, conditions were so bad for free blacks that they would sell themselves into slavery, taking a master of their own choice. Such actions were supported by the Texas legislature.

THE CIVIL WAR

With the election of Abraham Lincoln in 1860, and what appeared subsequently as an impending civil war, politicians in Texas were forced to justify the peculiar institution. They did so on an economic and racial basis. Texas politicians armed themselves with economic arguments to support the institution of chattel slavery. For example, Texas and Confederate politician John Henniger Reagan argued in the U.S. House of Representatives that setting the slaves free would be disastrous for northern and foreign manufacturing; it would hurt their shipping and commerce. Texas and Confederate politician Louis Trezevant Wigfall also put forth an economic argument before the U.S. Senate. He emphasized that abolition would be a threat to the merchant of the north and abroad, sailors, and shipping and manufacturing interests. On a racial basis, Texas Supreme Court Judge Oran Milo Roberts argued before a crowd in Austin that slaves were not capable of self-government and therefore should not be set free. Freedom, he argued, would cause that race to "descend into the vilest barbarism" (Jewett 2002, 11–27).

With the onset of the Civil War, the institution of slavery and the situation of free blacks faced potential disruption. Few slaves in Texas, however, actually fought in the Civil War. Enslaved African Americans who did go off to war most likely served their masters in some capacity, such as a nurse, a horse tender, or as a personal servant. Slavery in the Lone Star state would not face hazard from Union forces, but rather its severest threat came from those politicians who fought so hard to protect the institution. In March 1863, the Confederate Congress passed a law that allowed for the impressment of slaves, primarily to build fortifications and perform other necessary duties, but also to fight if need be. Texas owners were hesitant to abide by the law. They generally refused to risk danger or loss of their vital property. While the institution in Texas as a whole was not bothered by war, some slaves did use the crisis as an opportunity to flee. With so many men gone, and the care of land and labor left in charge of overseers, women, and children, slaves used the chaos as an excuse to leave; others stayed and simply acted out in rebellious ways (Marten 1990, 29–36).

In the Confederate states that had been overrun by the Union military, as well as in the nonseceded border states, numerous blacks joined the Union army when enlistment became available in 1863. In Texas, this option was virtually closed to almost all Texas slaves, since the Union army had no presence in the Lone Star state. Fewer than fifty blacks from Texas enlisted in the Union forces (Berlin 1982, 12).

EMANCIPATION AND RECONSTRUCTION

After the Civil War ended, blacks reacted in various ways to the news that they were now free. Some sang songs of jubilation, some wept, others were shocked, many did not understand, and some remained silent. Whatever the reaction, blacks did share the same postwar expectation. They expected the same freedoms as whites and the same opportunities; they desired political and social equality. This meant an access to education and the freedom to form their own institutions. After the war, many freedmen did begin to organize their own schools, and they too withdrew from white churches and formed their own black churches. While blacks sought to improve their conditions in life, the majority did so in the same vicinity. A massive black exodus out of the state did not happen. Many stayed with their former masters; others left if they had a place to go; and a majority, if they moved, traveled only a few miles away to work for someone else. Although blacks had renewed expectations, it did not take long for the realization to set in that some aspects of life were now more difficult. Finding food, clothing, and shelter became a burden that some could not shoulder. Due to the difficulties, therefore, many freedmen found their way back to their masters' farms (Smallwood 1976, 16–17).

To aid blacks in their plight, the federal government established the Freedman's Bureau in March 1865, as a part of the Department of War. The federal government wanted to help the ex-slaves in the transition to freedom. In Texas, though, the bureau was extremely limited in its accomplishments. For the most part, it distributed food rations of corn, pork, peas, coffee, and tea. Beginning in October 1866, these rations where confined to hospitals and asylums. The judicial power of the bureau was also limited and finally ended in November 1867 when general orders from Winfield Scott Hancock closed bureau operations. The bureau simply did not have the manpower to cover all of the state; in fact, it only covered approximately one third of Texas. While bureau agents attempted to improve labor relations between former masters and former slaves and to accelerate the education of the freedmen, the bureau in Texas virtually failed in nearly all aspects (Neal and Kremm 1989, 25–26).

Texans themselves further hindered the plight of the freedmen. Texans opposed political equality for African Americans and believed that the

Frederic Remington's depiction of the Buffalo Soldiers, African American cavalrymen who served in Texas and other western states and territories after the Civil War. (Library of Congress.)

temporary rights granted after the Civil War would not be permanent. Due to these racist beliefs, emancipation, in reality, was not immediate. Many Texans clung to slavery as long as possible, believing that servitude benefited the black race. Due to these underlying racist assumptions, as well as their economic investment in black servitude, many Texans held on to their slaves well after the Civil War ended. Even though the Republican Party sent the military into the state to ensure freedom for African Americans, Texas was simply too large geographically for the army to control or to cover thoroughly.

Not all Texans, however, held to a racist ideology. The appointed provisional governor of Texas, Andrew Jackson Hamilton, attempted to usher in some semblance of equality after the Civil War. On September 8, 1865, he declared that blacks and whites were equal before the law, especially in terms of punishment for crimes committed. Three days later, Hamilton declared that blacks should have the right to be called for jury duty (Ledbetter 1979, 253–263).

The Texas Assembly resisted the ratification of the Fourteenth Amendment and was subject to congressional and military reconstruction beginning in 1867. For the next few years, many African Americans actively participated in Texas politics. Freedmen cast 35,952 votes for delegates to a constitutional convention and even elected nine black representatives to the convention. These delegates made a significant contribution to the convention and constitution. For example, African American delegates offered resolutions, which were eventually passed, on matters dealing with allowing blacks to run for office, for allowing black marriages, and for allowing offspring full legitimacy. In addition, five African Americans signed the new Texas constitution. Those who did not, opposed the new constitution on the grounds that allowing ex-Confederates the opportunity to vote might let the ex-rebels regain enough power and control to violate the will of Congress and the rights of blacks (Pitre 1988, 36–45).

Whatever gains freedmen made, however, often came with a high price. Though legally protected, there were no means to deal effectively with violence, and many officers of the law were the actual perpetrators, involved in the fraternal organization of the Ku Klux Klan. One slave in Palestine, Texas, recalled that "[a]fter freedom we'uns see de Klux and dey is round our place but dey not come after us. Dey comes across de way 'bout a nigger call Johnson, and him crawls under him house, but dey makes him come out and gives him some licks and what de bellow come from dat nigger! Him had git foolishment in him head and day come to him for dat." African Americans, though, did not sit passively by when trouble arrived. In some parts of Texas, freedmen organized themselves against the Klan. For example, in Jefferson, Texas, a man named Dick Walker "got up a cullud militia to keep the Klux off the niggers. The militia met here in the old African Methodist church" (Rawick 1972, 5:153, 186).

Operating under the rules of the new state constitution, the Texas Assembly eventually ratified the Fourteenth and Fifteenth Amendments. Congress allowed Texas to be readmitted to the Union on March 30, 1870, having fulfilled the requirements of a successfully implemented, reconstructed state government that included political rights for the freedmen.

After Texas once again became a full-fledged member of the United States, the whites in the Lone Star state began a three-year campaign to "redeem" the state. This referred to a political campaign to place the control of the Texas state government once again in the hands of the Democrats. By 1873, Texas had been redeemed and, over the next decade, state leaders systematically deprived African Americans of the freedom to participate, without threats or intimidation, in the political process. The white-dominated "redeemed" assemblies subsequently passed segregation and Jim Crow laws, which created a legal, second-class citizenship for Texas's African Americans, a status that remained current until the civil rights era of the 1950s and 1960s. Although slavery had been successfully cast aside, full political and legal equality between whites and blacks in Texas would be deferred for another eighty years.

While slavery in Texas did not exist as long as in other states, the institution did not differ significantly. Reflecting upon the plight of African Americans in Texas, former slave Margrett Nillin put it best: "What I likes be, to be slave or free? Well, its's dis way. In slavery I owns nothin' and never owns nothin'. In freedom I's own de home and raise de family. All dat cause me worryment and in slavery I has no worryment, but I takes de freedom" (Rawick 1972, 5:153).

REFERENCES

Berlin, Ira, Joseph P. Reidy, and Leslie S. Rowland, eds. 1982. *Freedom: A Documentary History of Emancipation, 1861—1867,* Series II, *The Black Military Experience.* New York: Cambridge University Press.

Cain, Jerry Berlyn. 1975. "The Thought and Action of Some Early Texas Baptists Concerning the Negro." *East Texas Historical Journal* 13 (Spring): 3–12.

Campbell, Randolph B. 1989. *An Empire for Slavery: The Peculiar Institution in Texas 1821–1865.* Baton Rouge: Louisiana State University Press.

Harper, Cecil, Jr. 1985. "Slavery Without Cotton: Hunt County, Texas, 1846–1864." *Southwestern Historical Quarterly* 88 (April): 387–406.

Jackson, Susan. 1980. "Slavery in Houston: The 1850s." *Houston Review* 2 (Summer): 66–83.

Jewett, Clayton E. 2002. *Texas in the Confederacy: An Experiment in Nation Building.* Columbia: University of Missouri Press.

Lack, Paul D. 1985. "Slavery and the Texas Revolution." *Southwestern Historical Quarterly* 89 (October): 181–202.

———. 1981. "Urban Slavery in the Southwest." *Red River Valley Historical Review* 6 (Spring): 8–27.

Ledbetter, Billy D. 1979. "White Texans' Attitudes Toward the Political Equality of Negroes, 1865–1870." *Phylon* 40 (September): 253–263.

Malone, Ann Patton. 1983. *Women on the Texas Frontier: A Cross Cultural Perspective.* El Paso: Texas Western Press.

Marten, James. 1990. "Slaves and Rebels: The Peculiar Institution in Texas, 1861–1865." *East Texas Historical Journal* 28 (Spring): 29–36.

Muir, Andrew Forest. 1943. "The Free Negro in Harris County, Texas." *Southwestern Historical Quarterly* 46 (January): 214–238.

Neal, Diane, and Thomas W. Kremm. 1989. "What Shall We Do with the Negro? The Freedmen's Bureau in Texas." *East Texas Historical Journal* 27 (Fall): 23–33.

Norton, Wesley. 1965. "The Methodist Episcopal Church and the Civil Disturbances in North Texas in 1859 and 1860." *Southwestern Historical Quarterly* 68 (January): 317–341.

Palm, Rebecca W. 1976. "Protestant Churches and Slavery in Matagorda County." *East Texas Historical Journal* 14 (Spring): 3–8.

Pitre, Merline. 1988. "The Evolution of Black Political Participation in Reconstruction Texas." *East Texas Historical Journal* 26: 36–45.

Porter, Kenneth. 1949. "Negroes and Indians of the Texas Frontier, 1834–1874." *Southwestern Historical Quarterly* 53 (October): 151–163.

Rawick, George P., ed. 1972. *The American Slave: A Composite Autobiography.* Westport, Conn.: Greenwood Publishing Company.

Robbins, Fred. 1971. "The Origin and Development of the African Slave Trade in Galveston, Texas, and Surrounding Areas from 1816 to 1836." *East Texas Historical Journal* 9 (October): 153–162.

Smallwood, James. 1976. "Black Texans During Reconstruction: First Freedom." *East Texas Historical Journal* 14 (Spring): 9–23.

Tadman, Michael. 1989. *Speculators and Slaves: Masters, Traders, and Slaves in the Old South*. Madison: University of Wisconsin Press.

Tjarks, Alicia V. 1974. "Comparative Demographic Analysis of Texas, 1777–1793." *Southwestern Historical Quarterly* 77 (January): 291–338.

White, William W. 1949. "The Texas Slave Insurrection of 1860." *Southwestern Historical Quarterly* 52 (January): 259–285.

Woolfolk, George R. 1976. *The Free Negro in Texas, 1800–1860: A Study in Cultural Compromise*. Ann Arbor, Mich.: University Microfilms International.

WEB SITES

Jack Black Slave Narrative: http://www.claudeblack.com/slavery

Slave Narrative of J. Vance Lewis: http://docsouth.unc.edu/neh/lewisj/menu.html

Slavery in Texas: http://austin.about.com/library/weekly/aa061902a.htm

Slavery in Texas—Correspondence: http://www.tamu.edu/ccbn/dewitt/slaveryletters.htm

Texas Slavery Project: http://www.texasslaveryproject.uh.edu/

Virginia

TIMELINE

1619: First enslaved Africans are sold to Virginia settlers in Jamestown

1662: Colonial Virginia House of Burgesses defines slavery in statute law

1680: House of Burgesses requires that any slave away from home must carry a pass or be subject to arrest and punishment

1698–1775: Between 75,000 and 100,000 African slaves are brought to Virginia

1705: Virginia slave statutes are consolidated into one comprehensive enactment—human chattel are defined as property, the same as real estate

1754: Slave patrols are established

1775, November 7: Lord Dunmore, whom the patriots had previously run out of the colonial capital at Williamsburg, proclaims that slaves belonging to rebels will be freed if they run away and join British forces

1776: Dunmore departs Virginia, taking with him a large number of former Virginia slaves
    Thomas Jefferson, a Virginia slaveholder, composes the basic draft of the Declaration of Independence

1788, June 25: Virginia ratifies the U.S. Constitution and joins the Union

1800: Gabriel's slave rebellion is discovered in the Richmond suburbs

1831: Nat Turner's slave insurrection in Southampton County terrifies white Virginians

1859: Abolitionist John Brown attempts to incite a slave insurrection at Harper's Ferry; Brown is hanged at Charles Towne, Virginia

1861, April 17: Virginia secedes from the Union and joins the Confederacy; northwestern Virginia sets up its own government, remaining loyal to the Union; Confederate capital is moved to Richmond in June; Federal General Ben Butler at Fort Monroe in Hampton, Virginia, declares slaves escaping from masters supporting the rebellion to be "contraband" of war

1863: West Virginia becomes a separate state

1865, April 9: General Robert E. Lee surrenders the main Confederate army at Appomattox Courthouse, Virginia, effectively concluding the Civil War in Virginia; slavery ends in the commonwealth

1867: Virginia becomes Military District #1 under the Reconstruction Acts; Virginia voters elect blacks to serve in the Constitution Convention

1868: Two dozen African Americans serve in the Virginia General Assembly

1869: Freedmen's Bureau leaves Virginia

1870, January 26: Virginia is readmitted to the Union; military reconstruction ends; white "redemption" of the state is begun by Virginia Democrats

Slave and Free Black Population

Census Year	Slave Population	Population Percentage	Free Black Population	Population Percentage
1790	292,627	39	12,866	1.7
1800	345,796	39	20,124	2.2
1810	392,516	40	30,570	3.1
1820	425,148	40	36,883	3.5
1830	469,757	39	47,348	3.9
1840	448,987	36	49,842	4
1850	472,528	33	54,333	3.8
1860	490,865	30	58,042	3.6

Net Slave Entries and Exits, by Decade
(Tadman 1989, 12)

1790–1799: − 22,767	1830–1839: − 118,474
1800–1809: − 41,097	1840–1849: − 88,918
1810–1819: − 75,562	1850–1859: − 82,573
1820–1829: − 76,157	

ORIGINS OF SLAVERY

In 1584, English explorer Sir Walter Raleigh, one of Queen Elizabeth I's favorite courtiers, designated a largely undefined portion of the middle Atlantic seaboard of North America "Virginia," after England's "virgin" queen. Spanish, French, Dutch, and British captains and crews had landed at various places along this coastline throughout the sixteenth century. No extant records provide information on the likelihood that some crewmembers or impressed sailors may have been Africans. The Spanish, for a brief time around 1570, even attempted to place a settlement within the Chesapeake Bay of present-day Virginia. Whether this nonpermanent lodgment included any Africans is unclear. The first recorded visit of Africans, or at least Caribbean Creoles of African descent, occurred in 1586. English explorer Sir Francis Drake brought along captured slaves from a West Indies raid to Roanoke Island on the coastline of present-day North Carolina, although the island was then included as part of the newly named Virginia. He stopped by to check on a nascent colony organized by Raleigh and sited there by Sir Richard Grenville, the captain of Raleigh's naval expeditions, the year before. Ralph Lane, whom Grenville had left in charge, begged that his beleaguered group be rescued. Drake offloaded his captured human cargo and embarked Lane's band. Drake's and Lane's weary adventurers returned to England. No ship's logs left by Drake record what happened to the former slaves (see North Carolina chapter; Morgan 1975, 26, 34–42).

Enslaved Africans arrived to stay within the boundaries of present-day Virginia in 1619, a dozen years after the first settlers had founded Jamestown. John Rolfe, an early settler, had helped the colony survive by marrying Pocahontas, an Indian princess and daughter of Indian chief Powhatan, and by successfully growing tobacco for export: The first act brought a temporary truce with the Powhatan Indians, the latter offered a way for settlers to generate needed income. Rolfe noted that a Dutch man-of-war stopped by the new English settlement in the autumn of 1619 and sold twenty African slaves to the original white survivors, now known as the "early planters" (Morris 1996, 38–39).

The legal classification of these new "Virginians" remains unclear. Some scholars contend that blacks were initially treated similar to indentured servants, who had time-defined contracts usually of three, five, or seven years, rather than as individuals whose servitude had no limit. As natives of Africa, however, whatever their official legal status, they appear to have been treated as a separate category of personal property. Governor George Yeardley's will of 1627 split his livestock, his indentured servants, and his blacks into different categories of personal property. Moreover, few Africans in Jamestown during the 1620s appear to have had last names or at least last names known by the white inhabitants (Morris 1996, 39).

Up until the 1660s, however, few Virginians of African lineage resided in the colony. Less than four hundred lived in Virginia in 1650. The numbers began swelling in the 1660s and increased to around two thousand by 1670. During the decades of the English Civil Wars, the Cromwellian conquest of Ireland, and the restoration of King Charles II, the 1640s and the 1650s, a great deal of the populace of England and of the British Isles suffered through periodic episodes of political, economic, and religious turmoil, unrest, and warfare. These events created a pool of potential white indentured servants who often had little other financial option. Some indentured servants escaped to Virginia to avoid prison or the gallows. By the 1660s, however, with the easy-going Charles II ensconced on the throne and entertained by a bevy of winsome mistresses, the trip out to the virgin wilderness under an indentured contract became less desirable. Horrible tales of life in Virginia, as well as the frequency of the early deaths of many white farm laborers, filtered back to England and further dampened the ardor of would-be British servants (Morgan 1975, 158–180).

By the 1660s, the death rate for newcomers to Virginia had dropped precipitously, and African slaves had become a better buy economically. For example, if an indentured servant survived, he or she would return to England in seven years; however, an African slave, as well as that slave's offspring, even if initially slightly higher in cost, would provide a permanent labor force. Thus, once the death rate for newcomers dropped, slaves became a more popular option. At the same time, African slaves were more available than individuals in the dwindling pool of white indentured servants. Moreover, since the few remaining tidewater Indians now lived peacefully on reservations, added land could be safely put under cultivation. Additionally, white/Indian warfare on the frontier, eventually leading to Bacon's Rebellion of 1676, significantly reduced the threat of attacks from Native Americans living in the piedmont area south of the James River. Thus, the way was open from the late 1660s to the 1720s for Virginians to increasingly exploit the wilderness along the tidal estuaries by using labor provided by Africans brought as slaves across the Atlantic or transported as second-generation bondsmen from the Caribbean (Morgan 1975, 180–181, 250–270, 297–299).

THE FIRST SLAVE CODES

As the number of Africans in Virginia gradually rose, the local county courts began defining the financial worth of human chattel held as personal property in order to evaluate and to probate estates. By the 1640s, wills typically separated white indentured servants and blacks as different categories of property with far different valuations. In William Burdett's inventory, Mary Vaughn, noted as a white servant with eleven months to serve, received a property valuation of four hundred pounds of tobacco.

On the other hand, the probate committee, usually an ad hoc group of local justices of the peace, valued two African Americans at three thousand pounds and two thousand pounds of tobacco, respectively. No notation was made about their length of servitude. The committee appeared to assume that the court understood that the bondsman's tenure of indenture was permanent; hence, they were slaves. Additionally, sales of blacks from one white owner to another became more frequent. Most extant contracts from the 1640s included no length of service clauses and also were typically calculated in pounds of tobacco. The assumption that both white parties made about the sale of an African appeared to be that this human property was a chattel of lifetime servitude, or a slave. Nevertheless, few Virginians of African ancestry enjoyed free status at this time. Anthony Johnson, a free black, purchased property including slaves of African ancestry (Morris 1996, 40–41).

In 1662, the colonial Virginia House of Burgesses adopted a law that further refined the rather murky legal status of newborns: "all children borne in this country shalbe [sic] held bond or free only according to the condition of the mother." Henceforth, in Virginia, all children born of a slave mother would also be categorized as slaves (Morris 1996, 43).

In 1669, the House of Burgesses further defined the difference between servants and slaves of African ancestry by adopting a law that proscribed the punishments of slave owners in the same way as masters who abused indentured servants: "if any slave resist his master . . . and by the extremity of the correction should chance to die, his death shall not be accompted [sic] Felony . . . since it cannot be presumed that prepensed malice should induce any man to destroy his own estate." This law assumed slaves were estate property and allowed masters to physically correct and discipline their human chattel with little worry about legal recourse (Morgan 1975, 312).

In 1670, the House of Burgesses began offering rewards, paid in pounds of tobacco, for captured runaways. In 1680, Virginians demanded that all slaves carry a pass when off their home place or be subject to arrest. In 1691, the Burgesses redefined runaways as "negroes, mulattoes, and other slaves." The assembly then passed a comprehensive code in 1705 that consolidated past laws and defined slaves as property, held the same as real estate. Slaves could be used to collateralize debts and could be passed along to future generations in wills, the same as land (Hadden 2001, 26–29; Morris 1996, 66).

Virginia's slave codes drew on precedents from laws passed by assemblies in both the British Caribbean on Barbados and in South Carolina. In turn, Virginia law regarding African Americans greatly influenced slave codes being adopted in other Upper South areas such as Maryland and Delaware. Virginia codes also largely defined slave law in Kentucky when that commonwealth split off as a new state out of Virginia (the Old Dominion) in 1792.

Judges and courts in the southern section of the District of Columbia likewise used Virginia statutes and codes from 1800 to 1846 (see Kentucky chapter and District of Columbia chapter; Morris 1975, 66–67).

THE COLONIAL SLAVE POPULATION

Initially, slave traders sold to the Virginians mostly Africans who had
sojourned in the Caribbean or who had been born there. These Caribbean
Africans had already been forced to adapt to life on plantations in the West
Indies. Most had some knowledge of their masters' language and had also
been forced to accept the work discipline expected of enslaved plantation
laborers. After 1690, however, slave traders took blacks directly from Africa to the Chesapeake region. These individuals had no idea what awaited
them. They were further confused by not being able to comprehend the
language of their new masters. Many of the slaves could not even commu-
nicate with their fellow shackled sufferers, as a proliferation of tongues and
dialects abounded in the regions from where the slaves had been taken
(Kulikoff 1986, 40; Minchinton 1984, xiii).

From the 1690s until the eve of the American Revolution, thousands of
Africans had to withstand the brutal "Middle Passage" across the Atlantic to Virginia, had to endure further indignities while being sold, and, finally, had to somehow acclimatize themselves to their new world. That
only three out of four survived the first year in Virginia is probably not
surprising given the obstacles confronting each terrified transport.

The middle passage began along the African coast. Slave traders and
captains of "slavers," ocean-going ships built to carry human cargo, traded
for humans up and down the West African coast. Most Africans bound for
Virginia originated from villages and settlements along the coastal rivers
that ran inland. They typically had been captured by other Africans in wars
or were imprisoned during raids specifically sent into the interior to gather
up human cargo to trade to the Europeans. The prisoners were chained and
taken to the holding pens at trading depots sited at river mouths or on islands just off the coast. Traders and captains purchased their human cargo
bound for Virginia from these depots, called factories. These slave factories extended from the Gambia River (Guinea) in the north to the Congo
River in the south. After captains acquired a full load of chattel, the slave
ship's crew would drag each shackled individual below decks into an open
cargo hold. There they were chained to wooden planks that would be their
berth for the trip across the Atlantic.

Deaths among the transported Africans typically ran from 2 to 20 percent and could reach as high as 40 percent. The below-deck cargo holds
quickly became pestilential pits overflowing with vomit and human waste.
Some captains occasionally ran seawater through the lower decks to give
some relief from the stink. Others regularly brought their human cargo

above deck and subjected each individual to a drenching of cold seawater. The ship's crew routinely checked for any dead; bodies were discarded over the side of the ship without formalities. One Virginian noted, "The ship . . . several days before had come from Guine [*sic*] with 230 slaves. . . . They get them there for a small sum . . . but a hundred died on the voyage to Virginia" (Kulikoff 1986, 321–322; Minchinton 1984, xiii).

To increase market returns on their inventory, slave ship captains often "laid over" on a West Indies island to give their human cargo a chance to recover and to regain a more healthful countenance. The slavers then made their way up the coast to the Virginia settlements where the ships stopped at Jamestown. They also stopped at the larger plantations sited along the tidal rivers: the James, York, Rappahannock, and Potomac. Captains displayed the would-be slaves to potential buyers, neighboring planters, as well as local slave traders. These individuals bought slaves in the hopes of recouping their investment plus a profit by carrying the bondsmen inland to sell to farmers who lived at a distance from the wide tidal estuaries. Virginians generally had the first pick of the slave cargos. Unsold inventories of Africans were taken farther up the Chesapeake Bay to Annapolis and other Maryland plantations. Furthermore, most slaves had to undergo the humiliation of being displayed and examined three or four times before a sales contract could be finalized. Captains could expect to unload an entire cargo in a season (two or three months) (Kulikoff 1986, 323).

Slavers doing business in Virginia were required to report sales to naval officers who kept port records, or "naval lists," of imports into Virginia. (The British navy handled enforcement of the Navigation Acts that regulated colonial trade.) The colony operated six port districts at the time: Lower James, Upper James, York, Rappahannock, South Potomac, and Accomack (Eastern Shore). Their incomplete records indicate that from 1699 to 1775, 1,185 slave ships transported 83,825 enslaved blacks to Virginia. Colonial era demand for slaves peaked in the years from the 1720s to the 1750s when tobacco sold for good steady returns. Thus, overall, upward of one hundred thousand blacks involuntarily entered Virginia during the colonial days (Kulikoff 1986, 65, 80, 134; Minchinton 1984, xii–xiii).

COLONIAL SLAVE LIFE AND BREAKING IN

The new arrivals, still in shock from the travails of the brutal Middle Passage, confronted additional hardships as they attempted to survive in Virginia. They had to live as slaves, a condition most had not previously experienced. They also had to learn the commands of their new masters rendered in a language that few could initially understand. Finally, they were subjected to much colder weather than they were used to in their native habitat as well as to communicable diseases to which they had not previously been exposed. About a fourth would not live through the initial "seasoning" months (Kulikoff 1986, 324–326).

Furthermore, new masters often began calling them by names unfamiliar to their ears. Few Virginians were concerned with the given African names of their new human possessions. Other masters sent their new chattel to rough overseers who specialized in "breaking in" new slaves. These men instilled obedience and work discipline by the liberal use of the whipping lash. If the new slaves survived the Middle Passage, the new diseases, the cold winters, and breaking in, they were then ready to labor in the tobacco fields (Kulikoff 1986, 6, 319, 324).

By the 1720s, the number of Africans in Virginia had increased. Newly imported slaves henceforth would have a somewhat easier time. They could frequently find individuals who knew at least some words in their native dialects. Thus, instead of being thrown into a completely alien environment, newcomers could expect aid in acclimating to their new surroundings. Also, as the number of women rose, the likelihood that men could have partners and live in coupled relationships dramatically increased. Family life helped create a buffer to ward off the discontent brought on by the monotonous tasks filling the daily lives of most slaves. By the middle of the eighteenth century, enslaved males living in the tidewater region could generally find women to share their lives. This likewise held true in the piedmont area. After 1750, most newly imported slaves were sold directly to planters and farmers who grew tobacco in the piedmont area, which was largely settled by tidewater region families moving onto new lands from 1720 to 1770 (Kulikoff 1986, 335–337).

Slaves housing in the Chesapeake generally encompassed two types of buildings: log cabins and duplexes. Cabins generally had packed dirt floors, one or two rooms, a fireplace, a window, and a door. An entire family would be expected to occupy this type of residence. Duplexes were adjoining cabins which had doors at opposite ends and a shared main wall separating the living spaces. Two families occupied this form of housing. Most masters grouped slave housing together in one location. These cabins or duplexes were designated the "quarters." Larger slave owners often had more than one grouping of slave quarters while other slaveholders with multiple landholdings would build a separate living area on each farm. Slaves could be shifted among the different farms as labor needs dictated. The better-liked (by the slaves themselves) masters transferred complete families when moves became necessary. These slave families provided the primary setting for enjoyment, entertainment, and emotional fulfillment. Without family life, the slave experience in Virginia would probably have been quite dismal and even more unbearable for the blacks who endured it (Kulikoff 1986, 348, 368).

The primary hindrance from even more fulfilling lives resulted from the problems of "broad" wives and husbands. A "broad" husband or wife was a marriage partner who lived on a different home place. Most Virginia farmers and planters worked their labor force a five and a half day week, from sunup to sundown. This allowed husbands with "broad" wives the opportunity for family visits on Saturday night and Sundays. Visiting husbands, however, had to be careful to have signed passes and to not overstay their allotted time and risk punishment. Some masters used the threat of not allowing a husband with a "broad" wife visitation rights as a way of compelling a greater effort at work and of achieving better standards of obedience (Kulikoff 1986, 371–372).

RUNAWAYS, MAROONS, INSURRECTIONS, AND PATTEROLLERS

Many African-born slaves frequently ran away as soon as an opportunity arose. In 1705 and again in 1722, the Virginia House of Burgesses passed resolutions that stipulated the procedure whites should use when they captured a black who could speak no English and who could neither identify himself nor his owner. In the 1720s, groups of runaways attempted to set up maroon settlements in the Great Dismal Swamp south of Norfolk and on the then-frontier near current-day Lexington in the Shenandoah Valley. Eventually, Virginia colonial officials put into place a system of white slave patrols, the infamous patterollers (Kulikoff 1986, 328).

Small-scale plots, conspiracies, and planned attempts for groups to make off into the wilderness also happened with some regularity in Virginia's early days. This reflected three converging circumstances: the desire by newly arrived Africans, who had been born free, to get away from new master and slave discipline; the proximity of the frontier and the wilderness; and the unorganized or nonexistent efforts by whites to enforce resolutions passed by the assembly to control slave behavior. Local slave owners and residents uncovered and broke up escape plots and slave conspiracies in 1663, 1672, and 1680 (Hadden 2001, 28).

White residents in the Northern Neck, the peninsula bounded by the Rappahannock River and lower Potomac River, uncovered an even larger potential uprising in 1687. Slaves attempted to organize a widespread insurrection in the Northern Neck counties while meeting together at the outdoor public slave funerals, common to the period. Most owners allowed bondsmen from all neighboring home places to congregate in tribute to the passing of one of their own. Slave conspiracy ringleaders used these occasions, when most of the crowd was under less overt white scrutiny than usual, to plan an uprising. Eventually white slave owners found out some of the rough details, thwarted the attempt, and arrested and punished the leaders. The House of Burgesses soon added statutes that proscribed large outdoor public slave funerals and prohibited slaves from bearing arms or hunting weapons (Hadden 2001, 28).

From the late 1720s to the early 1750s, Virginia's lieutenant governors, especially William Gooch, persuaded the House of Burgesses to install an enforcement mechanism to carry out resolutions circumscribing slave behavior. These new procedures grew out of responses to continuing attempts by slaves to runaway, escape, and conspire. A small-scale plot uncovered in 1721 led to a statute barring all unsupervised slave meetings. In 1727, the Burgesses authorized the lieutenant governor and local county commanders to use the militia as slave patrollers. Gooch used this law and the militia in 1729 to destroy the attempt by some runaways to set up a maroon community near present-day Lexington in the Shenandoah Valley. A maroon community was a semipermanent settlement of runaways that lasted over a period of years. Gooch noted that more than a dozen escaped bondsmen had already begun clearing land and setting out crops when the militia broke up their settlement and returned the runaways to lives of servitude (Hadden 2001, 29).

Gooch also used the militia, organized as slave patrols, to disperse another attempt at organized conspiracy in the rural area south of Norfolk and in adjoining Princess Anne County. Approximately two hundred blacks gathered while their white owners gathered for Sunday church services. Slave patrols quashed the insurrection and arrested the leaders. That same year, militia, organized as slave patrols, destroyed an attempted conspiracy in King George County, east of Fredericksburg. Gooch, in 1736, ordered all county militia leaders to designate squads from their musters to patrol and check passes, especially on holidays, such as the Christmas–New Year's week, Easter, and Whitsunday (Hadden 2001, 30–31).

In 1754, the Burgesses passed enactments that formalized the slave patrols. Patrollers, henceforth, were excused from militia musters and would be paid for each day of service. From this time onward in Virginia, until the end of slavery in 1865, slave patrollers would be paid positions appointed and overseen by the county justices of the peace, who, as a committee, operated as county magistrates. The patterollers, as blacks referred to these white slave patrollers, had become a permanent fixture in the social fabric of Virginia's everyday world. Patterollers also quickly emerged as the most feared thorn under the blanket for most slaves and the bane of existence for most broad husbands.

THE AMERICAN REVOLUTION

The onset of the American Revolution created innumerable problems for Virginia's slaveholders. White Virginians had to handle the following: competing demands for manpower that affected the policing success of slave patrols; the freedom proclamation of Lord Dunmore; marching armies disrupting the commonwealth's countryside and loosening the reins of masters' authority over enslaved African Americans; and, perhaps worst of all, the liberal creed contained in the Declaration of Independence: "that all men are created equal, that they have been endowed by their Creator with certain unalienable Rights, that among these are Life, Liberty, and the Pursuit of Happiness."

At the start of the Revolution, many rumors abounded among the white community about slave conspiracies and uprisings and, throughout the slave quarters, about the possibility of freedom. Local counties wished to increase their slave patrols but at the same time faced militia levies used to supply Virginia troops to George Washington's Continental army. Some counties, like Richmond on the Northern Neck, began paying slave patrollers a better wage. In Amelia County, overseers, who had been exempted from military service, became more active in the patroller ranks (Hadden 2001, 158–160).

Lord Dunmore, Virginia's last colonial governor, created the primary necessity for increased patrolling. After being run out of the colonial capital at Williamsburg at the beginning of the Revolution, Dunmore remained offshore in the Chesapeake Bay plotting revenge. He put forth rumors that the British would free the slaves of Virginia rebels. This created turmoil among both whites and blacks. Eventually, on November 7, 1776, Dunmore issued a proclamation offering freedom to any slave who could bear arms, who belonged to an owner in rebellion against the British Crown, and who joined Dunmore's troops. Thousands of blacks in the tidewater region attempted to reach Dunmore's forces. Slaves in nearby North Carolina also tried to run away to freedom by joining Dunmore. On the Patriot side, slave patrols attempted to keep fleeing blacks in check (Hadden 2001, 160; see North Carolina chapter).

Slave patrols successfully captured hundreds of runaways, and many of them were then impressed as a labor force to work in Virginia's lead mines that produced ore that could be used to make bullets. Many captured blacks succumbed in these dangerous, unhealthy mines. Others who made it to the British did not fare well either. Dunmore organized approximately eight hundred Virginians of African ancestry into an "Ethiopian regiment" but provided these men with scant supplies. A majority perished from diseases running rampant in the camps. Dunmore appeared to be more interested in disrupting the slave owners than in offering a true opportunity for freedom for thousands of black Virginians. Dunmore finally left Virginia for good in July 1776, taking along those blacks still alive. Historians estimate that from three to five thousand slaves escaped to Dunmore, but far fewer survived to sail away with the former colonial governor (Kulikoff 1986, 418; Hadden 2001, 160–161).

As for the patriot military, Virginia free blacks could be mustered into the Continental army, but slaves could not. A few slaves, however, made

it into the ranks as substitutes for their masters. The final campaign leading up to the Yorktown surrender in the autumn of 1781 found army divisions marching across the Virginia countryside. The presence of British
troops already encumbered with many black camp servants led some Virginia slaves to try to get away. Some joined the British. Others simply took
the opportunity to escape. A large group of several dozen lived in a maroon community in the Dismal Swamp for a decade or more. The presence
of the British, as well as the plundering Loyalist cavalry seeking supplies
along the marching routes, also acted to loosen the reins of authority controlling slaves and to render the slave patrols invisible for considerable
periods of time. The Revolution upset slavery in Virginia but probably had
a smaller effect than in North Carolina, South Carolina, or Georgia (Kulikoff
1986, 419; see North Carolina chapter).

The liberal rhetoric promulgated in the Declaration of Independence and
other revolutionary era documents that used human rights language to
support rebellion against the British Crown challenged the underlying assumptions of slave owners of holding any humans in permanent bondage.
Historians have spent careers trying to figure out Thomas Jefferson, the
Declaration's primary author, who also pushed to make sure the Great
Lakes states (the Old Northwest) would be forever slave-free. Yet, Jefferson
numbered his slaves in the hundreds and became increasingly pro-slavery
as he aged. James Madison also grew more pro-slavery in outlook as time
passed. Patrick Henry, whose "Give Me Liberty or Give Me Death" speech
began Virginia's revolutionary journey, ranked as a very large slaveholder
in his later years (http://www.jmu.edu/madison/eliteandslave.html).

George Washington freed his own slaves at his death as did his wife
Martha, but many slaves managed by the Washingtons and their descendants did not obtain freedom until 1863. Neither Washington nor his wife
owned a large number of the human chattel living on Martha's lands, who
were acquired from her first husband. These enslaved blacks had been left
in trust to Martha's children and grandchildren. Eventually, Martha
Washington's grandson, George Washington Parke Custis, freed all these
slaves by will at his death. The future Confederate general and Custis's son-
in-law, Robert E. Lee, was engaged in carrying out these testamentary provisions at the Civil War's onset. He completed the process in 1863 (see
District of Columbia chapter).

Nevertheless, the Virginia trend in slave manumissions during and after the Revolution increased. Some took many years to complete, as previously shown. Many of the Virginians who decided to free their slaves
tried to use wills as freedom instruments and waited to divest themselves
of their human property until their own lives had ended. By 1806, the rules
had been tightened and the era for widespread manumissions in Virginia
had largely ended (Dunn 1983, 49–82; Kulikoff 1986, 419–422).

THE ANTEBELLUM SLAVE POPULATION
AND THE GREAT EXODUS

By the time George Washington took office as the new nation's first president in 1789, Virginia slavery had undergone some alterations as a result of the American Revolution. The Virginia Assembly closed the door to further slave importations even though the slave trade from Africa would be legal in the Southern states for almost twenty more years. Nevertheless, in the first census, local enumerators counted more than two hundred ninety thousand slaves in Virginia, or 39 percent of its denizens as noted in the opening summary. Virginia ranked as having more enslaved African Americans in its population than any other state, as well as the state with the greatest number of slaveholders, and would remain that way throughout the Early National era (1790–1820) and the antebellum era (1820–1860). In 1860, Virginia had more than four hundred ninety thousand African American slaves and more than fifty-two thousand white slave owners as part of its population (Dunn 1983, 51–52).

Up through 1830, the slave population in Virginia grew at the same pace as the white populace and remained a constant 39 to 40 percent of the total number of residents within the commonwealth. This consistent percentage in the number of enslaved African Americans living in Virginia, however, masked an enormous demographic shift that had begun as early as 1780.

As the Revolution wound down, restless Virginians had begun moving west of the Appalachian Mountains into Kentucky, taking their slaves along as well. Kentucky received a flood of immigrants during the 1780s including an avalanche of Virginians with human chattel. Kentucky joined the infant United States as a new state in 1792. The Commonwealth of Virginia agreed to split off the new commonwealth from its territory but demanded that the new Kentucky constitution legalize and protect slavery. Moreover, Virginia slaveholders dominated the statehood convention and argued for the necessity of bonded labor. Virginia in this way was responsible for the path Kentucky took in becoming a major domicile for African American slaves (see Kentucky chapter).

As other western areas opened up, Virginians continued to move out in search of adventure, virgin lands, and new riches. Many also carried along their African American chattel. Virginians took part in the land rushes to Alabama, Mississippi, and Texas. Many slave owning families in the tidewater and piedmont regions, where most Virginia slaves resided, had members who went west. This trend continued throughout the Early National and antebellum eras. The "exodus" peaked in the 1830s.

It has been estimated that Virginians carried out, sold, or distributed about five hundred thousand slaves from 1790 to 1860. The largest export years, the 1830s, coincided with the land rush to new acres opening up in

Texas and Mississippi. During this decade, so many slaves left that the total population of human chattel declined for the decade (Tadman 1989, 12).

Slaves were transferred in three primary ways. Masters who moved out of the commonwealth to new lands most often took their slaves with them. The Virginia Historical Society recently (2000–2001) estimated that about a third of all the white children born in Virginia in 1800 eventually left the state. Many went south to plant cotton, taking along their mobile labor force.

Other slave owners took advantage of the cotton boom and the demand for labor by selling excess chattel to slave traders. Richmond, during the antebellum years, ranked as the largest Upper South market for traders buying slaves for carrying south. Each autumn, coffles of African American slaves shuffled along the roadways from Virginia to the Gulf States.

As the number of former Virginians living in other slave states grew, an increasing number of blacks found themselves moved out of Virginia to other locations by the acts of wills and testamentary provisions. An older family member who died often split his property among his heirs. The great white exodus from Virginia meant that many families had branches in other Southern states. Because Virginia land could not be transported, slaves were most often used to equalize out-of-state inheritances.

As noted, the free black population received a fillip due to the increased trend toward manumissions during the revolutionary era. This grew out of the liberal human rights rhetoric abounding in the revolutionary days, which influenced a number of masters and mistresses to free their slaves. From 1806 onward, however, manumissions decreased. The free black population continued to grow through natural means and also through blacks who were able to earn enough money for self-emancipation. Many hired-out slaves lived and worked in Richmond, Petersburg, and Norfolk. Some masters allowed these slaves to remit a portion of their wages and to make their own living arrangements. These workers often could accumulate enough to buy themselves and family members. Richmond's antebellum population included thousands of free blacks and hired-out slaves who worked in the warehouses, the wharves, and the factories.

SLAVE LIFE

Virginia's antebellum economy closely resembled other Upper South areas. Slaves worked tobacco and grain fields and lived much as they had in colonial era. The most notable exception to this agrarian lifestyle occurred in Virginia's cities and towns. All had significant numbers of free blacks or hired-out slaves living in these communities. Substantially more free blacks and hired-out slaves worked in Richmond than in other comparable Upper South cities, such as Baltimore, Maryland, or Louisville, Kentucky. In Lynchburg in the piedmont tobacco region, a majority of the laborers in the tobacco factories and warehouses were slaves or hired-out slaves. Virginia had more factories, and more blacks working as factory laborers, than any other Southern state (Tripp 1997; Lebsock 1984; Takagi 1999; see Maryland chapter and Kentucky chapter).

The great fear among Virginia slaves was being sold south, either to pay off a master's debts or to go to another branch of the owner's family. Slave families were often wrenched apart, and no one knew if the new master would be good or mean. Since more than half a million slaves from Virginia were transported out of the state between the founding of the United States and the Civil War, this exodus touched just about every slave in Virginia in one way or another.

Virginia Hayes Shepherd, an ex-slave of Norfolk, remembered a particularly moving occurrence. An older slave owner and his wife died. The trustee had to sell slaves to pay off heirs. One enslaved woman who was to be sold had an infant.

> On auction day they were put on the block and sold her to one of those greedy Richmond traders. She begged him to buy her baby, but he [the trader] refused. She just had fits right there. . . . But she was taken to Richmond just the same and sold down South. (Perdue 1976, 258)

Jane Pyatt was born in Middlesex County and she and her mother were sold to new owners in Portsmouth when she was a baby. Pyatt recalled,

> Previous to 1861, there weren't any policemen . . . were patterollers instead. . . . If the slaves had a corn shucking party, or a prayer meeting, and if they made too much noise, the patterollers would arrest them. . . . These patterollers took two of my brothers. . . . I have never seen them since. (Perdue 1976, 235)

Reverend Ishrael Massie, who grew up as a slave in Emporia in Greensville County, remembered,

> Some nights house servants would come down to the quarters with long faces . . . they gonna sell some slaves. . . . Then such praying, honey. . . . Nobody wanting to be sold; but Marsa he ain't ask you nothing about wanting to be sold; he gwine sell you, and you got to go where they take you. . . . [M]y sister Sadie was sold . . . twas for right much money. . . . We didn't see her no more till Lee's surrender. (Perdue 1976, 211)

Nancy Williams of Norfolk recalled,

> Member one morning old white man rode up in a buggy and stopped by a woman what was working in the yard. . . . "Come on get in this

buggy, I boughtcha this morning." She wanted to tell her baby and husband goodbye . . . but he say "Naw! Hell!" I was so afraid they gonna
take me. God bless your soul. Halleluiah! (Perdue 1976, 319)

Virginia slaves had to put up with the same treatment as elsewhere in
the slave states: patterollers, whippings for no apparent reason, and some
very difficult masters and mistresses; however, the one fear that weighed
on everyone's heart was to be picked out to be sold south and separated
from family and friends.

GABRIEL PROSSER, NAT TURNER, AND JOHN BROWN

Slave owning whites in the commonwealth had endured numerous
small-scale plots, conspiracies, and failed insurrections during the colonial
days. Their slave owning descendants also experienced three major slave
eruptions in the Early National and antebellum eras. Two were locally
planned and one represented a major incursion from without.

In 1800, an African American slave, Gabriel Prosser, attempted to organize a slave insurrection in the area immediately surrounding Richmond,
Virginia's capital. He made use of the frequent travel in and out of Richmond by hired-out slaves and free blacks who worked in the city but lived
on farms a few miles away from downtown. He tried to organize and co-
ordinate a large-scale mass uprising of all slaves and free blacks who lived
and worked in Richmond and its suburbs. Whites uncovered information
about the plot and thwarted the attempt. James Monroe, the future president and current Virginia governor, called out the militia. Local companies
guarded the capitol and other government buildings, including the penitentiary that held incarcerated blacks. "For days, Richmond resembled an
armed camp with a small standing army in its midst." Monroe also organized the "Public Guard of Richmond," which would henceforth function
as a citywide slave patrol. Norfolk followed suit (Hadden 2001, 57, 61, 115,
149–150; Takagi 1999, 51–53, 61–69).

In August 1831, slave Nat Turner organized and implemented a slave
insurrection in Southampton County a few miles from the North Carolina
border. As a young boy, Turner had received special treatment from his
master because he had been so bright. Nevertheless, when he reached the
appropriate age, he was banished to the fields. Turner evidently never
overcame the shock of going from pampered star (relative to other slaves)
to field hand. He subsequently became a mystic and a noted slave exhorter
who was often referred to as Preacher Nat. His owner allowed him to travel
to other home places to hold services on weekends. This freedom and his
mystical reputation among the local blacks gave him the widespread contacts and influence he needed to plan the uprising. He hoped that all the
local Southampton slaves would rise up, kill their owners, and join him

on a march to the Dismal Swamp where they could set up a maroon (black runaways) community strong enough to defend itself. Unlike the many Virginia slave plots that were found out and thwarted, Turner's insurrection actually took place (Oates 1975, 7–66).

Turner and his cohorts unleashed their attack on the white Southampton County slaveholders late on a Sunday night (or early Monday morning) when whites were used to blacks moving around. Many regularly hunted and trapped on Sunday evenings and broad husbands returned from family visits. Sundays were likewise days of less supervision by white masters and overseers. With a half a dozen cohorts, which soon increased to forty but never many more, Turner started his rampage. His band traveled through the local countryside, butchering whites in their homes. Eventually, armed white militia caught up with parts of Turner's group and in a few days had killed or captured most of them. Turner hid for a few weeks but eventually gave up. He pleaded "not guilty" because he did not "feel that he was guilty." After trials in Jerusalem, Southampton's county seat, throughout late October and November, he and his partners were hanged. Turner's group had murdered about five dozen whites. Retribution was handed out to more than two hundred blacks, including many in the surrounding counties of Virginia and North Carolina, who had done nothing but looked "suspicious" (Oates 1975, 67–143).

This lethal insurrection led many Virginians and other Southerners to blame outside radical abolitionist groups for poisoning slaves' outlooks. In the same year, New England abolitionist William Lloyd Garrison began publishing *The Liberator*, perhaps the most famous antislavery publication in antebellum America. In strident prose, Garrison and his contributors demanded that the South immediately and unconditionally free all slaves. A full-fledged literary and political battle grew up between the abolitionists and pro-slavery apologists that continued until the Civil War and further heightened political tensions between the two sections, one slave and one free (Oates 1975, 147–151).

Within Virginia and nearby North Carolina, slave patrols took on a whole new meaning. Some masters and counties began clamping down on the travels of black preachers, further circumscribing their activities. Laws limiting black meetings were more rigidly enforced. Passes became more difficult to obtain, and blacks without passes or identification became more frequently subject to immediate punishment and possible incarceration. This most deadly insurrection put fear into the hearts of southern slaveholders; a fear that had not entirely disappeared by 1861 (Oates 1975, 152–166; Hadden 2001, 145–148).

The final rebellion within Virginia took place on its northernmost border adjoining Maryland; its primary planner and perpetrator haled from outside Virginia. In October 1859, abolitionist John Brown led eighteen followers into Harper's Ferry, a Virginia border town that contained a rail depot and a United States arms factory. He hoped to instigate a widespread slave uprising in Virginia and to use the Blue Ridge Mountains as a redoubt for a slave army. After some initial success in getting into the village, Brown's group was driven into an armory, surrounded, and killed, wounded, or captured. On December 2, Brown was hanged in the local county seat, Charles Towne, named for George Washington's brother Charles, an early settler (Oates 1984, 290–337).

Brown, who had enjoyed an unsavory reputation in Kansas as a brutal captain in the on-going guerilla war between pro-slavery and antislavery factions, struck a heroic pose as he calmly listened to his executioners at his trial and as he approached the gallows. His last message to his countrymen proved powerfully prophetic:

> **Charlestowne, Va, 2nd, December, 1859**
> I John Brown am now quite *certain* that the crimes of this *guilty land will* never be purged *away*; but with Blood. I had *as I now think: vainly* flattered myself that without *very much* bloodshed; it might be done. (Oates 1984, 351)

Brown became a hero and cause célèbre for many Northern antislavery and abolitionist groups. Meanwhile, a coterie of six well-known abolitionists hoped their previous financial support of Brown would not become known. In Virginia and other Southern states, politicians grew more adamant in supporting pro-slavery attitudes. Within a year and a half, the nation would be rent asunder and, within a few more months, Brown's prophecy would become all too real when the war began (Oates 1984, 353–361).

CIVIL WAR

Virginia delayed its secession until after President Abraham Lincoln called for a levy of troops to put down the shooting war that started with the firing on Ft. Sumter. This decision split Virginia asunder. The eastern two-thirds of the commonwealth, containing most of the slaves as well as most of the slaveholders, voted overwhelmingly to secede. The residents of the western counties, with few slaves, preferred not to leave the Union. Eventually, antisecession delegates met in Wheeling in the northwestern corner of Virginia and set up the Union state of Virginia. This eventually became, in 1863, the separate state of West Virginia (Shade 1996, 287–291; Wakelyn 1999, 56–57, 82–83, 273–274).

The Confederate capital moved to Richmond in the early summer of 1861. The primary Union strategy from then until the spring of 1865 involved trying to capture Richmond or attempting to defeat the Confederate army that guarded it. As in other parts of the South, those counties overrun by the federal army saw former slaves flee to freedom. Many runaways from Northern Virginia migrated into the District of Columbia. They lived in camps and worked on the docks moving military supplies, as cooks and laundresses, and digging entrenchments. Some former Virginia slaves eventually joined the Union army through District units (see District of Columbia chapter).

When the hostilities first commenced, the federal military still occupied Fort Monroe, a virtual island fortress adjoining Hampton where the James River entered the Chesapeake Bay. Benjamin F. Butler, a political star from Massachusetts who commanded the facility in the opening days of the war, was almost immediately overwhelmed with runaway slaves seeking freedom. When a local slaveholder demanded that the federal officer return his property, Butler replied that the slaves were "contraband" of war and thereby confiscated. This allowed the blacks to stay within the Union lines. For the next year and a half, until the Emancipation Proclamation took effect on January 1, 1863, escaped slaves were generally referred to as "contrabands" (Litwack 1979, 52).

Virginia contrabands served as laborers, cooks, mess attendants, hospital workers, and teamsters. Many became body and camp servants for federal officers. When the Union army began recruiting blacks in 1863, 5,919 from Virginia were mustered in. This number did not include those credited to the District. These enlistees represented about 6 percent of the black men of eligible military age in Virginia at the last census. The African American participation rate for being mustered into the Union army was substantially less than that of the other Upper South and border states (Litwack 1979, 52; Berlin 1982, 10).

Runaway slaves who reached Union lines became "contraband" of war and were not returned to their Confederate owners. In this photo, a group of contrabands, their possessions loaded in a wagon, follow the Union army across the Rappahannock River in Virginia. (Library of Congress.)

Cornelius Garner enlisted in Norfolk and joined the Thirty-eighth USCT (United States Colored Troops) in February 1864. He remembered, "We had colored soldiers and white officers. I fit [*sic*] in the Battle of Deep Bottom. We licked the Confederates good . . . made them retreat to Chaffin's Bluff. . . . Our regiment was the first in Richmond and we was the first to plant our colors on the capitol." He later went with the regiment to Texas and left the army in 1867 to return to the tidewater region (Perdue 1976, 103).

African Americans from Virginia also marched with the Confederate army. Officers carried along personal body servants to act as orderlies and cooks. Hundreds of Virginia blacks traveled the dusty trails with General Robert E. Lee's Confederates. During September 1862, an observer of Lee's first invasion of the North said that he counted around three thousand blacks marching with the rebel troops in the Army of Northern Virginia as it passed through Frederick, Maryland (Litwack 1979, 39–45).

Confederates also impressed Virginia slaves into work digging trenches, especially around Richmond and Petersburg in 1864. In the spring of 1865, as the fires stoking an independent Confederacy ebbed, General Robert E. Lee and Jefferson Davis, the rebel president, supported legislation in the Confederate Congress that would allow the Southerners to conscript blacks into the Confederate army with the promise of freedom as a reward. Many Confederate supporters refused to grasp at this final emergency lifesaver. Senator Robert M.T. Hunter of Virginia, a friend and supporter of Lee, nevertheless, felt that this had gone too far. He reached the most disturbing conclusion: If slavery had caused the war, and if the Confederacy had abandoned the war goal of the preservation of slavery, then how could it justify the loss of so many lives to save it? How could one justify the expenditure of so much blood and treasure? "Who would answer before the bar of heaven?" The end of the war arrived before the issue's ramifications were fully felt. Lee gave up Richmond and surrendered at Appomattox on April 9, 1865. Confederate resistance in Virginia ceased, and slavery had finally ended in Virginia after 246 years (Allen 1998, 191; Litwack 1979, 44–45).

EMANCIPATION

Most Virginia African Americans celebrated fiercely when freedom finally arrived. Ex-slave Annie Harris of Petersburg recalled, "we was dancing and prancing and yelling with a big bonfire . . . everybody for miles around was singing freedom songs." One song Harris heard contained the following lyrics:

> I's free, I's free, I's free at last!
> Thank God Almighty, I's free at last!
> Once was a moaner, just like you.

Thank God Almighty, I's free at last!
I fasted and I prayed til I came through.
Thank God Almighty, I's free at last!
                (Perdue 1976, 128–129)

Many new freedmen immediately began trying to put their families back together; however, the widespread dispersal caused by the large-scale exodus of Virginia slaves in the years before the war caused problems. Others moved. Charles Crawley, who was born a slave in Lunenburg County, remembered,

> We come to this town of Petersburg after Lee's Surrender . . . came here to Petersburg the second week after Lee's Surrender. The Marster and Mistess . . . was good to us . . . didn't want us to leave . . . but we comed to make a home for ourselves. (Perdue 1976, 78)

Freedmen began setting up churches and schools and attempting to make a living. Those who had jobs in the cities as hired-out blacks often kept the same positions. In the countryside, the whole system of wage labor and sharecropping had to be worked out. White farmers were less than forthcoming until the Freedmen's Bureau stepped in. Yet even these officials were frustrated with the enormity of the problem. Allen Wilson, a former slave, recalled, "The very first colored school in Petersburg was taught by Mrs. Elam of the Freedmen's Bureau at the Oak Grove on West Street." In Northampton County, whites belonging to the "Home Guard" shot three freedmen who refused to return to their former owner's home place after agreeing to work elsewhere (Morgan 1992, 128, 135; Perdue 1976, 329; Litwack 1979, 304).

Major General John M. Schofield, who had headed the Freedmen's Bureau in Virginia for nine months, took over as head of Military District #1 as the Reconstruction Acts of March 1867 dubbed the commonwealth. By October, more than one hundred thousand blacks had registered to vote in Virginia elections. More than a dozen blacks were selected for a new constitutional convention. In the contest for seats in the general assembly of 1868, more than twenty blacks won elections (Morgan 1992, 160–168).

While African Americans had achieved at least partial political power, they continued to suffer economically. Additionally, by the spring of 1868, the Ku Klux Klan had appeared in a few counties to terrorize black leaders. In 1869, the Freedmen's Bureau left the state to the disappointment of many former slaves. By late 1869, the African American gains under congressional reconstruction began eroding (Morgan 1992, 167–170, 210–211).

As soon as the federal military left in 1870, signaling the end of military reconstruction, and with the splintering of the Republican Party at the same time, white "redemption" began. This phrase defined the campaign by the white-dominated Democrats to reassert political control over the commonwealth. By the 1890s, African Americans in Virginia lived in a segregated commonwealth and had to accept a second-class status politically, socially, and economically. They had successfully put together families, had established communities, and had built many churches and schools, including Hampton Institute, yet they had not achieved full citizenship in their nation or in their state. This step would have to wait until the civil rights struggles of the 1950s and 1960s.

REFERENCES

Allen, John O. 1998. "Robert Mercer Taliaferro Hunter." In *Leaders of the American Civil War: A Biographical and Historiographical Dictionary*, ed. Charles F. Ritter and Jon L. Wakelyn. Westport, Conn.: Greenwood Press.

Berlin, Ira, Joseph P. Reidy, and Leslie S. Rowland, eds. 1982. *Freedom: A Documentary History of Emancipation*, Series II, *The Black Military Experience*. New York: Cambridge University Press.

Dunn, Richard S. 1983. "Black Society in the Chesapeake." In *Slavery and Freedom in the Age of the American Revolution*, ed. Ira Berlin and Ronald Hoffman. Charlottesville: University Press of Virginia.

Hadden, Sally E. 2001. *Law and Violence in Virginia and the Carolinas*. Cambridge, Mass.: Harvard University Press.

Kulikoff, Alan. 1986. *Tobacco and Slaves: The Development of Southern Cultures in the Chesapeake, 1680–1800*. Chapel Hill: University of North Carolina Press.

Lebsock, Suzanne. 1984. *The Free Women of Petersburg: Status and Culture in a Southern Town, 1784–1860*. New York: W.W. Norton.

Litwack, Leon F. 1979. *Been in the Storm So Long: The Aftermath of Slavery*. New York: Random House.

Minchinton, Walter, Celia King, and Peter Waite, eds. 1984. *Virginia Slave Trade Statistics, 1698–1775*. Richmond: Virginia State Library.

Morgan, Edmund S. 1975. *American Slavery, American Freedom: The Ordeal of Colonial Virginia*. New York: W.W. Norton.

Morgan, Lynda J. 1992. *Emancipation in Virginia's Tobacco Belt, 1850–1870*. Athens: University of Georgia Press.

Morris, Thomas D. 1996. *Southern Slavery and the Law, 1619–1860*. Chapel Hill: University of North Carolina Press.

Oates, Stephen B. 1975. *The Fires of Jubilee: Nat Turner's Fierce Rebellion*. New York: Harper & Row.

———. 1984. *To Purge this Land with Blood: A Biography of John Brown*. Amherst: University of Massachusetts Press.

Perdue, Charles L., Jr., Thomas E. Barden, and Robert K. Phillips. 1976. *Weevils in the Wheat: Interviews with Virginia Ex-slaves*. Charlottesville: University Press of Virginia.

Shade, William G. 1996. *Democratizing the Old Dominion: Virginia and the Second Party System, 1824–1861*. Charlottesville: University Press of Virginia.

Tadman, Michael. 1989. *Speculators and Slaves: Masters, Traders, and Slaves in the Old South*. Madison: University of Wisconsin Press.

Takagi, Midori. 1999. *Rearing Wolves to Our Own Destruction: Slavery in Richmond, Virginia, 1782–1865*. Charlottesville: University Press of Virginia.

Tripp, Steven Elliott. 1997. *Yankee Town, Southern City: Race and Class Relations in Civil War Lynchburg*. New York: New York University Press.

Wakelyn, Jon L., ed. 1999. *Southern Unionist Pamphlets and the Civil War*. Columbia: University of Missouri Press.

WEB SITES

Bethany Veney Slave Narrative: http://docsouth.unc.edu/veney/menu.html

Francis Fedric Slave Narrative: http://docsouth.unc.edu/fedric/menu.html

James Madison, the Virginia Elite, and Slavery: <http://www.jmu.edu/madison/eliteandslave.html

Nat Turner's Rebellion: http://www.pbs.org/wgbh/aia/part3/3p1518.html

Virginia's Domestic Slave Trade: http://fisher.lib.Virginia.edu/slavetrade

Appendix 1:
Number of Slaveholders
in 1860, by State

Alabama	33,730
Arkansas	11,481
Delaware	587
District of Columbia	1,229
Florida	5,512
Georgia	41,084
Kentucky	38,645
Louisiana	22,033
Maryland	13,783
Mississippi	30,943
Missouri	24,320
North Carolina	34,658
South Carolina	26,701
Tennessee	36,844
Texas	21,878
Virginia	52,128

Appendix 2: Dates of Admission to, Secession from, and Readmission to the Union

State	Admission	Secession	Readmission
Alabama	Dec. 14, 1819	Jan. 11, 1861	June 25, 1868
Arkansas	June 15, 1836	May 6, 1861	June 22, 1868
Delaware	Dec. 7, 1787	did not secede	
Florida	Mar. 3, 1845	Jan. 10, 1861	June 25, 1868
Georgia	Jan. 2, 1788	Jan. 19, 1861	July 15, 1870
Kentucky	June 1, 1792	did not secede	
Louisiana	Apr. 30, 1812	Jan. 26, 1861	June 25, 1868
Maryland	Apr. 28, 1788	did not secede	
Mississippi	Dec. 10, 1817	Jan. 9, 1861	Feb. 23, 1870
Missouri	Aug. 10, 1821	did not secede	
North Carolina	Nov. 21, 1789	May 21, 1861	June 25, 1868
South Carolina	May 23, 1788	Dec. 20, 1860	June 25, 1868
Tennessee	June 1, 1796	June 8, 1861	July 24, 1866
Texas	Dec. 29, 1845	Feb. 23, 1861	Mar. 30, 1870
Virginia	June 25, 1788	Apr. 17, 1861	Jan. 26, 1870

Appendix 3: Economic Statistics

Cotton and tobacco ranked as the major cash crops produced by slave field hands in the antebellum South. Slaves also labored to grow rice in the Atlantic coastal counties of North and South Carolina, hemp in Kentucky and Missouri, and sugar cane on a few large plantations in Louisiana. Cotton ranked as the most important U.S. export. Together with tobacco, these Southern staples accounted for more than half the value of all American exports during the antebellum decades.

1. Tobacco and Cotton Exports

Year	Cotton Exported (pounds)	Dollar Value	Tobacco Exported (hogsheads)*	Dollar Value
1800	18,000,000		79,000	
1810	93,000,000	$15,000,000	84,000	$5,000,000
1820	128,000,000	$22,000,000	84,000	$8,000,000
1830	298,000,000	$30,000,000	84,000	$6,000,000
1840	744,000,000	$64,000,000	119,000	$10,000,000
1850	635,000,000	$72,000,000	146,000	$11,000,000
1860	1,768,000,000	$192,000,000	167,000	$21,000,000

*Hogsheads held approximately 1,400 pounds of tobacco leaf.

Cotton and Tobacco (Percentage of Total U.S. Exports)

Year	Dollar Value of Cotton and Tobacco Exported	Dollar Value of Total U.S. Exports	Cotton and Tobacco Export Percentage
1820	$30,000,000	$70,000,000	43
1830	$36,000,000	$72,000,000	50
1840	$74,000,000	$124,000,000	60
1850	$82,000,000	$144,000,000	57
1860	$213,000,000	$333,000,000	64

2. U.S. Cotton Production, in Bales*

	1850	1860
Total U.S.	2,470,000	5,400,000
Alabama	565,000	990,000
Arkansas	65,000	367,000
Florida	45,000	65,000
Georgia	500,000	700,000
Louisiana	178,000	778,000
Mississippi	484,000	1,202,000
North Carolina	74,000	145,500
South Carolina	301,000	354,000
Tennessee	194,000	297,000
Texas	58,000	431,000

*In antebellum America, cotton bales averaged approximately 400 pounds of fiber.

3. U.S. Tobacco Production, in Pounds

	1850	1860
Total U.S.	200,000,000	434,200,000
Kentucky	58,000,000	109,000,000
Maryland	21,500,000	38,500,000
Missouri	17,000,000	25,000,000
North Carolina	12,000,000	33,000,000
Virginia	57,000,000	124,000,000

4. Average Farm Size, 1860

State	Average Farm Size in Acres
Total U.S.	200
Alabama	346
Arkansas	245
Delaware	158
Florida	346
Georgia	430
Kentucky	211
Louisiana	536
Maryland	190
Mississippi	370
Missouri	215
North Carolina	316
South Carolina	488
Tennessee	250
Texas	590
Virginia	340

In addition to supplying the labor to grow staple crops and exports, slaves also affected the relative wealth and farm size within the United States during the antebellum era. The slaveholding states typically included farms that averaged larger numbers of acres. Additionally, slaveholders were substantially wealthier than non-slaveholders because the market value of individual slaves comprised a part of a slave owner's net worth. While the average American head of household had an estate net worth of slightly under $2,500 in 1860, the average slaveholder was worth in excess of $9,000 (approximately $9,400). Any Southerner with two slaves was worth the same as the average Northern farmer. Within the South, slave owners were also substantially wealthier than their non-slaveholding counterparts. Gavin Wright estimated that the slaveholders in the "cotton" states averaged a net worth of nearly $25,000 ($24,748) in 1860. Non-slaveholders, on the other hand, had estates that were valued on the average at less than $2,000 ($1,781) (Wright 1978, 35–36).

REFERENCES

Dodd, Donald B., and Wynelle S. Dodd. 1973. *Historical Statistics of the South, 1790–1970.* Tuscaloosa: University of Alabama Press.

Fogel, Robert W. 1989. *Without Consent or Contract: The Rise and Fall of American Slavery.* New York: W.W. Norton.

Historical Statistics of the United States, Colonial Times to 1957. 1962. Washington, D.C.: United States Bureau of the Census.

Wright, Gavin. 1978. *The Political Economy of the Cotton South: Households, Markets, and Wealth in the Nineteenth Century.* New York: W.W. Norton.

Bibliography

BOOKS AND ARTICLES

Abernethy, Thomas P. *The Formative Period in Alabama, 1815–1828*. Tuscaloosa: University of Alabama Press, 1965.

Allen, John O. "Robert Mercer Taliaferro Hunter." In *Leaders of the American Civil War: A Biographical and Historiographical Dictionary*, edited by Charles F. Ritter and Jon L. Wakelyn. Westport, Conn.: Greenwood Press, 1998.

Allen, Richard. *The Life Experiences and Gospel Labors of the Right Reverend Richard Allen*. New York: Abingdon Press, 1960.

Allen, William B. *A History of Kentucky*. Louisville: Bradley & Gilbert, 1872.

Anbinder, Tyler. *Nativism and Slavery: The Northern Know Nothings and the Politics of the 1850s*. New York: Oxford University Press, 1992.

Andrews, Matthew Page. *History of Maryland: Province and State*. New York: Doubleday, 1929.

Apperson, George M. "African Americans on the Tennessee Frontier: John Gloucester and His Contemporaries." *Tennessee Historical Quarterly* 59 (Spring 2000): 2–19.

Arroyo, Elizabeth Fortson. "Poor Whites, Slaves, and Free Blacks in Tennessee, 1796–1861." *Tennessee Historical Quarterly* 55 (Spring 1996): 57–64.

Ash, Stephen V. *Middle Tennessee Society Transformed, 1860–1870: War and Peace in the Upper South*. Baton Rouge: Louisiana State University Press, 1988.

Atherton, Lewis E. "Missouri's Society and Economy in 1821." *Missouri Historical Review* 93 (October 1998): 2–25.

Bedinia, Silvio A. *The Life of Benjamin Banneker*. New York: Scribner, 1971.

Berlin, Ira. *Slaves Without Masters: The Free Negroes in the Antebellum South*. New York: Pantheon Books, 1974.

Berlin, Ira, Joseph P. Reidy, and Leslie S. Rowlands, eds. *Freedom: A Documentary History of Emancipation, 1861–1867*, Series II, *The Black Military Experience*. New York: Cambridge University Press, 1982.

———. *Freedom's Soldiers: The Black Military Experience in the Civil War*. New York: Cambridge University Press, 1982.

Berlin, Ira, and Leslie S. Rowland, eds. 1997. *Families and Freedom: A Documentary History of African American Kinship in the Civil War*. New York: The New Press.

Blassingame, John W., ed. *Slave Testimony: Two Centuries of Letters, Speeches, Interviews, and Autobiographies*. Baton Rouge: Louisiana State University Press, 1977.

Bolton, Charles S. *Arkansas, 1800–1860: Remote and Restless*. Fayetteville: University of Arkansas Press, 1998.

Bond, Beverly G. "'Every Duty Incumbent upon Them': African-American Women in Nineteenth Century Memphis." *Tennessee Historical Quarterly* 59 (Spring 2000): 254–273.

Boyett, Gene W. "The Black Experience in the First Decade of Reconstruction in Pope County, Arkansas." *Arkansas Historical Quarterly* 51 (Summer 1992).

Bradford, Sarah H. *Harriet Tubman: The Moses of Her People*. 1869. Reprint, Secaucus, N.J.: The Citadel Press, 1974.

Brown, Cantor, Jr. "Race Relations in Territorial Florida, 1821–1845." *Florida Historical Quarterly* 73 (January 1995): 287–307.

Brown, Titus. "Origins of African American Education in Macon, Georgia, 1865–1866." *Journal of Southwest Georgia History* 11 (Fall 1996): 43–59.

Brugger, Robert J. *Maryland: A Middle Temperament, 1634–1980*. Baltimore: Johns Hopkins University Press, 1988.

Bryan, W.B. *A History of the National Capital*. 2 vols. New York: Macmillan, 1914.

Butler, Lindley S., and Alan D. Watson, eds. *The North Carolina Experience: An Interpretation and Documentary History*. Chapel Hill: University of North Carolina Press, 1984.

Cain, Jerry Berlyn. "The Thought and Action of Some Early Texas Baptists Concerning the Negro." *East Texas Historical Journal* 13 (Spring 1975): 3–12.

Campbell, Randolph B. *An Empire for Slavery: The Peculiar Institution in Texas 1821–1865*. Baton Rouge: Louisiana State University Press, 1989.

Cathey, Cornelius Oliver. *Agricultural Developments in North Carolina, 1783–1860*. Chapel Hill: University of North Carolina Press, 1956.

Channing, Steven A. *Kentucky*. New York: W.W. Norton, 1977.

Christensen, Lawrence O. "Black Education in Civil War St. Louis." *Missouri Historical Review* 95 (April 2001): 302–316.

Cimbala, Paul A. "A Black Colony in Dougherty County: The Freedmen's Bureau and the Failure of Reconstruction in Southwest Georgia." *Journal of Southwest Georgia History* 4 (Fall 1986): 72–89.

———. *Under the Guardianship of the Nation: The Freedmen's Bureau and the Reconstruction of Georgia, 1865–1870*. Athens: University of Georgia Press, 1997.

Cimprich, John. *Slavery's End in Tennessee, 1861–1865*. University: University of Alabama Press, 1985.

Claiborne, J.F.H. *Mississippi, as a Province, Territory, and State*. Jackson: Powers & Barksdale, 1880. Reprint, Baton Rouge: Louisiana State University Press, 1964.

Clark, Thomas D. *The Kentucky*. New York: Farrar & Rinehart, 1942.

Coleman, J. Winston. "Lexington's Slave Dealers and Their Southern Trade." *Filson Club Historical Quarterly* 12 (January 1938): 1–23.

———. *Slavery Times in Kentucky*. Chapel Hill: University of North Carolina Press, 1940.

Crow, Jeffrey J. *The Black Experience in Revolutionary North Carolina*. Raleigh: North Carolina Department of Cultural Affairs, 1977.

Curtin, Philip D., ed. *Africa Remembered: Narratives by West Africans from the Era of the Slave Trade*. Madison: University of Wisconsin Press, 1967.

———. *The Atlantic Slave Trade: A Census*. Madison: The University of Wisconsin Press, 1969.

Davenport, F. Gavin. *Antebellum Kentucky*. Oxford, Ohio: Mississippi Valley Press, 1943.

Davis, Harold E. *The Fledgling Province: Social and Cultural Life in Colonial Georgia, 1733–1776*. Chapel Hill: University of North Carolina Press, 1976.

Din, Gilbert C. *Spaniards, Planters, and Slaves: The Spanish Regulation of Slavery in Louisiana, 1763–1803*. College Station: Texas A&M University Press, 1999.

Donald, David Herbert. *Lincoln*. New York: Simon & Schuster, 1995.

Donald, Henderson H. *The Negro Freedman: Life Conditions of the American Negro in the Early Years after Emancipation*. New York, 1952. Reprint, New York: Cooper Square, 1971.

Drago, Edmund L. *Black Politicians and Reconstruction Georgia: A Splendid Failure*. Baton Rouge: Louisiana State University Press, 1982.

Duncan, Russell. *Freedom's Shore: Tunis Campbell and the Georgia Freedmen*. Athens: University of Georgia Press, 1986.

Dunn, Richard S. "Black Society in the Chesapeake." In *Slavery and Freedom in the Age of the American Revolution*, edited by Ira Berlin and Ronald Hoffman. Charlottesville: University Press of Virginia, 1983.

Dunnigan, Alice Allison. *The Fascinating Story of Black Kentuckians: Their Heritage and Tradition*. Washington, D.C.: Associated Publishers, 1982.

Dusinberre, William. *Them Dark Days: Slavery in the American Rice Swamps*. New York: Oxford University Press, 1996.

Edwards, Gary T. "'Negroes…and All Other Animals': Slaves and Masters in Antebellum Madison County." *Tennessee Historical Quarterly* 57 (Spring/Summer 1998): 24–35.

Essah, Patience. *A House Divided: Slaves and Emancipation in Delaware, 1638–1856*. Charlottesville: University of Virginia Press, 1996.

Fehrenbacher, Don E. *The Dred Scott Case: Its Significance in American Law and Politics*. New York: Oxford University Press, 1978.

Fields, Barbara J. *Slavery and Freedom on the Middle Ground: Maryland During the Nineteenth Century*. New Haven: Yale University Press, 1985.

Filler, Louis. *The Crusade Against Slavery: 1830–1860*. New York: Harper & Row, 1960.

Finley, Randy. *From Slavery to Uncertain Freedom: The Freedmen's Bureau in Arkansas, 1865–1869*. Fayetteville: University of Arkansas Press, 1996.

Fleming, Walter L., ed. *Documentary History of Reconstruction*. Cleveland: Arthur Clark, 1906.

Flynn, Charles L., Jr. *White Land, Black Labor Caste and Class in Late Nineteenth-Century Georgia*. Baton Rouge: Louisiana State University Press, 1983.

Fogel, Robert W. *Without Consent or Contract: The Rise and Fall of American Slavery*. New York: W.W. Norton, 1989.

Foner, Eric. *Free Soil, Free Labor, Free Men: The Ideology of the Republican Party before the Civil War*. New York: Oxford University Press, 1995.

———. *Reconstruction: America's Unfinished Revolution, 1863–1877*. New York: Harper & Row, 1988.

Foner, Philip. *Frederick Douglass, A Biography*. New York: Citadel Press, 1964.

Franklin, John Hope. *From Slavery To Freedom: A History of Negro Americans*. New York: Knopf, 1947.

Frey, Sylvia R. *Water from the Rock: Black Resistance in a Revolutionary Age*. Princeton: Princeton University Press, 1991.

Fuke, Richard P. "Land, Lumber, and Learning: The Freedmen's Bureau, Education, and the Black Community in Post-Emancipation Maryland." In *The Freedmen's Bureau and Reconstruction*, edited by Paul A. Cimbala and Randall M. Miller. New York: Fordham University Press, 1999.

Garner, James Wilford. *Reconstruction in Mississippi*. New York: Macmillan, 1901. Reprint, Gloucester, Mass.: Peter Smith, 1964.

Garvin, Russell. "The Free Negro in Florida before the Civil War." *Florida Historical Quarterly* 46 (July 1967): 1–18.

Gatewood, Willard B. "'The Remarkable Misses Rollin': Black Women in Reconstruction South Carolina." *South Carolina Historical Magazine* 92 (July 1991): 172–188.

———. "Sunnyside: The Evolution of an Arkansas Plantation, 1840–1945." *Arkansas Historical Quarterly* 50 (Spring 1991).

Genovese, Eugene D. *Roll, Jordan, Roll: The World the Slaves Made*. New York: Pantheon Books, 1974.

George, Carol V. *Segregated Sabbaths: Richard Allen and the Rise of Independent Black Churches, 1760–1840*. New York: Oxford University Press, 1973.

Glatthaar, Joseph T. *Forged in Battle: The Civil War Alliance of Black Soldiers and White Officers*. New York: Free Press, 1990.

Greene, Evarts B., and Virginia D. Harrington. *The American Population before the Federal Census of 1790*. New York: Columbia University Press, 1932.

Hadden, Sally E. *Law and Violence in Virginia and the Carolinas*. Cambridge, Mass.: Harvard University Press, 2001.

Hall, Gwendolyn Midlo. *Africans in Colonial Louisiana: The Development of Afro-Creole Culture in the Eighteenth Century*. Baton Rouge: Louisiana State University Press, 1992.

Hamilton, Virginia Van der Veer. *Alabama*. New York: W.W. Norton, 1977.

Hancock, Harold B. *Delaware During the Civil War*. Wilmington: Historical Society of Delaware, 1961.

Harper, Cecil, Jr. "Slavery Without Cotton: Hunt County, Texas, 1846–1864." *Southwestern Historical Quarterly* 88 (April 1985): 387–406.

Harris, J. William. *Plan Folk and Gentry in a Slave Society: White Liberty and Black Slavery in Augusta's Hinterlands*. Middletown, Conn.: Wesleyan University Press, 1985.

Harrison, Lowell H., and James C. Klotter. *A New History of Kentucky*. Lexington: University Press of Kentucky, 1997.

Harvey, Charles M. "Missouri from 1849 to 1861." *Missouri Historical Review* 92 (January 1998): 119–134.

Hietala, Thomas R. *Manifest Design: Anxious Aggrandizement in Late Jacksonian America.* Ithaca: Cornell University Press, 1985.

Higgins, Billy D. "The Origins and Fate of the Marion County Free Black Community." *Arkansas Historical Quarterly* 54 (Winter 1995).

Hoffecker, Carol E. *Delaware: A Bicentennial History.* New York: W.W. Norton, 1977.

Howington, Arthur E. *What Sayeth the Law: The Treatment of Slaves and Free Blacks in the State and Local Courts of Tennessee.* New York: Garland Publishing, Inc., 1986.

Hudson, Larry E., Jr. *To Have and to Hold: Slave Work and Family Life in Antebellum South Carolina.* Athens: University of Georgia Press, 1997.

Hurt, R. Douglas. *Agriculture and Slavery in Missouri's Little Dixie.* Columbia: University of Missouri Press, 1992.

Hutchinson, Louise D. *The Anacostia Story, 1608–1930.* Washington, D.C.: Smithsonian Institute Press, 1977.

Jackson, Susan. "Slavery in Houston: The 1850s." *Houston Review* 2 (Summer 1980): 66–83.

Jewett, Clayton E. *Texas in the Confederacy: An Experiment in Nation Building.* Columbia: University of Missouri Press, 2002.

Johnson, Guion Griffis. *Ante-Bellum North Carolina: A Social History.* Chapel Hill: University of North Carolina Press, 1937.

Jones, Jacqueline. *Soldiers of Light and Love: Northern Teachers and Georgia Blacks, 1865–1873.* Chapel Hill: University of North Carolina Press, 1980.

Kellison, Kimberly R. "Toward Humanitarian Ends? Protestants and Slave Reform in South Carolina, 1830–1865." *South Carolina Historical Magazine* 103 (July 2002): 210–225.

Kennedy, Thomas C. "The Rise and Decline of a Black Monthly Meeting: Southland, Arkansas, 1864–1925." *American Historical Quarterly* 50 (Summer 1991).

King, Norma, ed. *A Northern Woman in the Plantation South: Letters of Tryphena Blanche Holder Fox, 1856–1876.* Columbia: University of South Carolina Press, 1993.

Koger, Larry. *Black Slaveowners: Free Black Slave Masters in South Carolina, 1790–1860.* Jefferson, N.C.: McFarland & Company, Inc., 1985.

Kolchin, Peter. *American Slavery, 1619–1877.* New York: Hill and Wang, 1993.

Kulikoff, Alan. *Tobacco and Slaves: The Development of Southern Cultures in the Chesapeake, 1680–1800.* Chapel Hill: University of North Carolina Press, 1986.

Lack, Paul D. "Slavery and the Texas Revolution." *Southwestern Historical Quarterly* 89 (October 1985): 181–202.

———. "Urban Slavery in the Southwest." *Red River Valley Historical Review* 6 (Spring 1981): 8–27.

Land, Aubrey C. *Colonial Maryland: A History.* Millwood, N.Y.: KTO Press, 1981.

Land, Aubrey C., Lois Green Carr, and Edward C. Papenfuse, eds. *Law, Society, and Politics in Early Maryland.* Baltimore: Johns Hopkins University Press, 1977.

Landers, Jane. *Black Society in Spanish Florida*. Chicago: University of Illinois Press, 1999.

Lebsock, Suzanne. *The Free Women of Petersburg: Status and Culture in a Southern Town, 1784–1860*. New York: W.W. Norton, 1984.

Ledbetter, Billy D. "White Texans' Attitudes Toward the Political Equality of Negroes, 1865–1870." *Phylon* 40 (September 1979): 253–263.

Lesko, Kathleen M., Valerie Babb, and Carroll R. Gibbs. *Black Georgetown Remembered: A History of Its Black Community from the Founding of "The Town of George" in 1751 to the Present Day*. Washington, D.C.: Georgetown University Press, 1991.

Levine, Lawrence W. *Black Culture and Black Consciousness: Afro-American Folk Thought from Slavery to Freedom*. New York: Oxford University Press, 1977.

Lewis, David L. *The District of Columbia*. New York: W.W. Norton, 1976.

Littlefield, Daniel C. "The Colonial Slave Trade to South Carolina: A Profile." *South Carolina Historical Magazine* 91 (April 1990): 68–99.

Litwack, Leon F. *Been in the Storm So Long: The Aftermath of Slavery*. New York: Random House, 1979.

Lofton, John. *Denmark Vesey's Revolt: The Slave Plot that Lit a Fuse to Fort Sumter*. Kent, Ohio: Kent State University Press, 1964.

Logan, Rayford W. *Howard University: The First Hundred Years, 1867–1967*. New York: New York University Press, 1969.

Lovett, Bobby. "African Americans, Civil War, and Aftermath in Arkansas." *American Historical Quarterly* 54 (Autumn 1995).

Macdonald, Robert R., John R. Kemp, and Edward F. Haas, eds. *Louisiana's Black Heritage*. New Orleans: Louisiana State Museum, 1979.

Madaras, Larry, and James M. SoRelle, eds. "Did Booker T. Washington's Philosophy and Actions Betray the Interests of African Americans?" In *Taking Sides: Controversial Issues in American History*, Volume II, *Reconstruction to the Present*. Guilford, Conn.: McGraw-Hill, 2000.

Malone, Ann Patton. *Women on the Texas Frontier: A Cross Cultural Perspective*. University of Texas at El Paso: Texas Western Press, 1983.

Marten, James. "Slaves and Rebels: The Peculiar Institution in Texas, 1861–1865." *East Texas Historical Journal* 28 (Spring 1990): 29–36.

McGowan, James A. *Station Master on the Underground Railroad: The Life and Letters of Thomas Garrett*. Moylan, Pa.: Whimsie Press, 1977.

McLemore, Richard A., ed. *A History of Mississippi*. Jackson: University Press of Mississippi, 1973.

McNeilly, Donald P. *The Old South Frontier: Cotton Plantations and the Formation of Arkansas Society, 1819–1861*. Fayetteville: University of Arkansas Press, 2000.

Merrens, Harry Roy. *Colonial North Carolina in the Eighteenth Century*. Chapel Hill: University of North Carolina Press, 1964.

Meyers, Christopher C. "'The Wretch Vickery' and the Brooks County Civil War Slave Conspiracy." *Journal of Southwest Georgia History* 12 (Fall 1997): 27–38.

Middleton, Arthur Pierce. *Tobacco Coast*. Richmond: Whittet & Shepperson, 1953.

Minchinton, Walter, Celia King, and Peter Waite, eds. *Virginia Slave Trade Statistics, 1698–1775*. Richmond: Virginia State Library, 1984.

Mohr, Clarence L. *On the Threshold of Freedom: Masters and Slaves in Civil War Georgia*. Athens: University of Georgia Press, 1986.

Moneyhon, Carl H. *The Impact of the Civil War and Reconstruction on Arkansas: Persistence in the Midst of Ruin*. Baton Rouge: Louisiana State University Press, 1994.

———. "The Slave Family in Arkansas." *Arkansas Historical Quarterly* 58 (Spring 1999).

Mooney, Chase C. *Slavery in Tennessee*. Bloomington: Indiana University Press, 1957.

Morgan, Edmund S. *American Slavery, American Freedom: The Ordeal of Colonial Virginia*. New York: W.W. Norton, 1975.

Morgan, Lynda J. *Emancipation in Virginia's Tobacco Belt, 1850–1870*. Athens: University of Georgia Press, 1992.

Morrill, Dan L. *The Civil War in the Carolinas*. Charleston, S.C.: The Nautical & Aviation Publishing Company of America, 2002.

Morris, Thomas D. *Southern Slavery and the Law, 1619–1860*. Chapel Hill: University of North Carolina Press, 1996.

Morrison, Michael A. *Slavery and the American West: The Eclipse of Manifest Destiny and the Coming of the Civil War*. Chapel Hill: University of North Carolina Press, 1997.

Muir, Andrew Forest. "The Free Negro in Harris County, Texas." *Southwestern Historical Quarterly* 46 (January 1943): 214–238.

Munroe, James A. *Colonial Delaware: A History*. New York: KTO Press, 1978.

Naglich, Dennis. "The Slave System and the Civil War in Rural Prairieville." *Missouri Historical Review* 87 (April 1993): 253–273.

Neal, Diane, and Thomas W. Kremm. "What Shall We Do with the Negro? The Freedmen's Bureau in Texas." *East Texas Historical Journal* 27 (Fall 1989): 23–33.

Norton, Wesley. "The Methodist Episcopal Church and the Civil Disturbances in North Texas in 1859 and 1860." *Southwestern Historical Quarterly* 68 (January 1965): 317–341.

Oakes, James. *Slavery and Freedom: An Interpretation of the Old South*. New York: Knopf, 1990.

Oates, Stephen B. *The Fires of Jubilee: Nat Turner's Fierce Rebellion*. New York: Harper & Row, 1975.

———. *To Purge This Land with Blood: A Biography of John Brown*. Amherst: University of Massachusetts Press, 1984.

Olwell, Robert. *Masters, Slaves, & Subjects: The Culture of Power in the South Carolina Low Country, 1740–1790*. Ithaca: Cornell University Press, 1998.

Otto, John Solomon. *Cannon's Point Plantation, 1794–1860: Living Conditions and Status Patterns in the Old South*. Orlando, Fla.: Academic Press, Inc., 1984.

Ouzts, Clay. "Landlords and Tenants: Sharecropping and the Cotton Culture in Leon County, Florida, 1865–1885." *Florida Historical Quarterly* 75 (Summer 1996): 1–23.

Palm, Rebecca W. "Protestant Churches and Slavery in Matagorda County." *East Texas Historical Journal* 14 (Spring 1976): 3–8.

Perdue, Charles L., Jr., Thomas E. Barden, and Robert K. Phillips. *Weevils in the Wheat: Interviews with Virginia Ex-Slaves*. Charlottesville: University Press of Virginia, 1976.

Perdue, Robert E. *The Negro in Savannah, 1865–1900*. New York: Exposition Press, 1973.

Pitre, Merline. "The Evolution of Black Political Participation in Reconstruction Texas." *East Texas Historical Journal* 26 (1988): 36–45.

Poole, Stafford, and Douglas J. Slawson. *Church and State in Perry County, Missouri* Lewiston, N.Y.: The Edwin Mellen Press, 1986.

Porter, Kenneth. "Negroes and Indians of the Texas Frontier, 1834–1874." *Southwestern Historical Quarterly* 53 (October 1949): 151–163.

Powell, Mary G. *The History of Old Alexandria, Virginia: From July 13, 1749 to May 24, 1861*. Richmond: William Byrd Press, 1928.

Powell, William S. *North Carolina: Through Four Centuries*. Chapel Hill: University of North Carolina Press, 1989.

Provine, Dorothy S. *Alexandria County, Virginia: Free Negro Registers, 1799–1861*. Bowie, Md.: Heritage Books, 1990.

Quarles, Benjamin. *The Negro in the American Revolution*. Chapel Hill: University of North Carolina Press, 1961.

Rainwater, Percy Lee. *Mississippi: Storm Center of Secession, 1856–1861*. New York: Da Capo Press, 1969.

Ransom, Roger L., and Richard Sutch. *One Kind of Freedom: The Economic Consequences of Emancipation*. New York: Cambridge University Press, 1977.

Rawick, George P., ed. *The American Slave: A Composite Autobiography*. 19 vols. Westport, Conn.: Greenwood Publishing Company, 1972.

Reidy, Joseph P. *From Slavery to Agrarian Capitalism in the Cotton Plantation South, Central Georgia, 1800–1880*. Chapel Hill: University of North Carolina Press, 1992.

Riordan, Patrick. "Finding Freedom in Florida: Native Peoples, African Americans, and Colonists, 1670–1816." *Florida Historical Quarterly* 75 (Summer 1996): 24–43.

Ripley, C. Peter. *Slaves and Freemen in Civil War Louisiana*. Baton Rouge: Louisiana State University Press, 1976.

Rivers, Larry Eugene. *Slavery in Florida: Territorial Days to Emancipation*. Gainesville: University Press of Florida, 2000.

Robbins, Fred. "The Origin and Development of the African Slave Trade in Galveston, Texas, and Surrounding Areas from 1816 to 1836." *East Texas Historical Journal* 9 (October 1971): 153–162.

Rodrigue, John C. *Reconstruction in the Cane Fields: From Slavery to Free Labor in Louisiana's Sugar Parishes, 1862–1880*. Baton Rouge: Louisiana State University Press, 2001.

Rose, Willie Lee. *Rehearsal for Reconstruction: The Port Royal Experiment*. Athens: University of Georgia Press, 1964.

Schwalm, Leslie. *A Hard Fight for We: Women's Transition from Slavery to Freedom in South Carolina*. Urbana: University of Chicago Press, 1997.

Schweninger, Loren. "Slave Independence and Enterprise in South Carolina, 1780–1865." *South Carolina Historical Magazine* 93 (April 1992): 101–125.

Sellers, James B. *Slavery in Alabama*. University: University of Alabama Press, 1950.

Shade, William G. *Democratizing the Old Dominion: Virginia and the Second Party System, 1824–1861*. Charlottesville: University Press of Virginia, 1996.

Shields, Jerry. *The Infamous Patty Cannon in History and Legend*. Dover, Del.: Bibliotheca Literoria Press, 1990.

Smallwood, James. "Black Texans During Reconstruction: First Freedom." *East Texas Historical Journal* 14 (Spring 1976): 9–23.

Smock, Raymond W. *Booker T. Washington*. Jackson: University Press of Mississippi, 1988.

Solomon, Irvin D., and Grace Erhart, "Race and Civil War in South Florida." *Florida Historical Quarterly* 77 (Winter 1999): 320–341.

Sydnor, Charles S. *Slavery in Mississippi*. 1933. Reprint, Gloucester, Mass.: P. Smith, 1965.

Tadman, Michael. "The Hidden History of Slave Trading in Antebellum South Carolina: John Springs III and Other 'Gentlemen Dealing in Slaves.'" *South Carolina Historical Magazine* 97 (January 1996): 6–29.

———. *Speculators and Slaves: Masters, Traders, and Slaves in the Old South*. Madison: University of Wisconsin Press, 1989.

Takagi, Midori. *Rearing Wolves to Our Own Destruction: Slavery in Richmond, Virginia, 1782–1865*. Charlottesville: University Press of Virginia, 1999.

Taylor, Joe Gray. *Negro Slavery in Louisiana*. Baton Rouge: Louisiana Historical Society, 1963.

Thompson, Ernest Trice. *Presbyterians in the South*, Volume One: *1607–1861*. Richmond: John Knox Press, 1963.

Tjarks, Alicia V. "Comparative Demographic Analysis of Texas, 1777–1793." *Southwestern Historical Quarterly* 77 (January 1974): 291–338.

Tolbert, Lisa C. "Murder in Franklin: The Mysteries of Small-Town Slavery." *Tennessee Historical Quarterly* 57 (Winter 1998): 203–217.

Tremain, Mary. *Slavery in the District of Columbia: The Policy of Congress and the Struggle for Abolition*. New York: Putnam's Sons, 1892. Reprint, New York: Negro University Press, 1969.

Tripp, Steven Elliott. *Yankee Town, Southern City: Race and Class Relations in Civil War Lynchburg*. New York: New York University Press, 1997.

Tunnell, Ted. *Crucible of Reconstruction: War, Radicalism and Race in Louisiana, 1862–1867*. Baton Rouge: Louisiana State University Press, 1984.

Wagandt, Charles Lewis. *The Mighty Revolution: Negro Emancipation in Maryland, 1862–1864*. Baltimore: Johns Hopkins University Press, 1964.

Wakelyn, Jon L., ed. *Southern Unionist Pamphlets and the Civil War*. Columbia: University of Missouri Press, 1999.

Ware, Lowry. "The Burning of Jerry: The Last Slave Execution by Fire in South Carolina?" *South Carolina Historical Magazine* 91 (April 1990): 100–106.

———. "Reuben Robertson of Turkey Creek: The Story of a Wealthy Black Slaveholder and His Family, White and Black." *South Carolina Historical Magazine* 91 (October 1990): 261–267.

West, Jerry L. *The Reconstruction Ku Klux Klan in York County, South Carolina, 1865–1877*. Jefferson, N.C.: McFarland & Company, Inc., 2002

Wharton, Vernon L. *The Negro in Mississippi, 1865–1890*. Chapel Hill: University of North Carolina Press, 1949.

White, William W. "The Texas Slave Insurrection of 1860." *Southwestern Historical Quarterly* 52 (January 1949): 259–285.

Whitman, T. Stephen. *The Price of Freedom: Slavery and Manumission in Baltimore and Early National Maryland*. Lexington: University Press of Kentucky, 1997.

Willis, John C. *Forgotten Time: The Yazoo-Mississippi Delta after the Civil War*. Charlottesville: The University Press of Virginia, 2000.

Wood, Peter H. *Black Majority: Negroes in Colonial South Carolina from 1670 through the Stono Rebellion*. New York: W.W. Norton & Company, 1974.

Woolfolk, George R. *The Free Negro in Texas, 1800–1860: A Study in Cultural Compromise*. Ann Arbor, Mich.: University Microfilms International, 1976.

Works Projects Administration. *Kentucky*. Lexington: University Press of Kentucky, 1939.

Yellin, Jean F., ed. *Harriet Jacobs: Incidents in the Life of a Slave Girl*. Cambridge, Mass.: Harvard University Press, 1987.

Yentsch, Anne Elizabeth. *A Chesapeake Family and Their Slaves*. New York: Cambridge University Press, 1994.

WEB SITES

Abolitionists, Free Blacks, and Runaway Slaves: http://www.udel.edu/BlackHistory/abolitionists.html

African American Civil War Memorial: http://www.afroamcivilwar.org

African American Experience: http://www.aristotle.net/persistence/index.html

African American Mosaic: http://www.loc.gov/exhibits/African/intro.html

African Americans and Native Americans: http://users.multipro.com/whitedove/encyclopedia/African-americans-and-american-indians.html

African Union Methodist Protestant Church History: http://www.aumpchurch.org/history.htm

Alabama Slave Code of 1833: http://www.wfu.edu/~zulick/340/slavecodes.html

Alabama Supreme Court and Slaves: http://www.lib.auburn.edu/archive/aghy/slaves.htm

Allen Parker Slave Narrative: http://core.ecu.edu/hist/cecelskid/nctime.htm

Antebellum Slavery in Georgia—Fanny Kemble: http://www.pbs.org/wgbh/aia/part4/4narr1.html

Anti-Slavery Leaders of North Carolina—E-text: http://docsouth.unc.edu/nc/bassett98/bassett98.html

Arkansas Resources: http://arkedu.state.ar.us/africanamerican/arkres.htm

Aunt Dice: The Story of a Faithful Slave: http://docsouth.unc.edu/robinsonn/menu.html

Autobiography of Frederick Douglass: http://odur.let.rug.nl/~usa/B/fdouglas/dougxx.htm

Bethany Veney Slave Narrative: http://docsouth.unc.edu/veney/menu.html

Black History in Tennessee: Anderson County: http://www.geocities.com/brenfoster

Blacks in Tennessee: http://newdeal.feri.org/guides/tnguide/ch10.htm

Booker T. Washington: http://www.spartacus.schoolnet.co.uk/USAbooker.htm

Central Alabama Slave Narrative: http://xroads.Virginia.edu/~UG99/brady/Albama.html

Charles Thompson's Slave Narrative: http://docsouth.unc.edu/neh/thompson/menu.html

Daniel J. Russell. History of the African Union Methodist Church: http://doc. south.unc.edu/church/Russell/menu.html

Denmark Vesey Conspiracy: http://www.pbs.org/wgbh/aia/part3/3p2976.html

Dred Scott Case: http://www.pbs.org/wgbh/aia/part4/4h2933.html

Experience of a Slave in South Carolina: http://docsouth.unc.edu/jackson/menu.html

Federal Writers Project—Narratives of Former Slaves—Georgia, 4 parts: http://memory.loc.gov/ammem/wpaintro/wpahome.html

Florida 1821–1845: http://www.floridahistory.org/floridians/territo.htm

Florida 1845–1865: http://fcit.usf.edu/florida/websites/links004.htm#slavery

Francis Fedric Slave Narrative: http://docsouth.unc.edu/fedric/menu.html

Frederick Douglass National Historic Site: http://www.nps.gov/frdo/freddoug.html

Frederick Douglass Papers: http://memory.loc.gov/ammem/doughtlm/doughome.html

Freedmen and Southern Society: http:// www.history.umd.edu/Freedmen/home.html

Geographical Distribution of Slavery in Missouri: http://www.missouri-history.itgo.com/slave.html

Georgia Slave Workplaces: http://www.rootsweb.com/~afamerpl/plantations _ usa/GA/GA_ plantations.html

Georgia's African American History: http://www.gavoyager.com/GLCfiles/blackhist1–.html

Goodings Describe Reconstruction in South Carolina: http://lcweb2.loc.gov/learn/features/timeline/civilwar/recon/goodings.html

Guide to the Microfilm Primary Source Material for African Americans, Mississippi, and Southern History in the J.D. Williams Library at the University of Mississippi: http://www.olemiss.edu/depts/general_library/files/media/mfguide.html

Gullah Creole Language: http://www.ccpl.org/ccl/gullahcreole.html

Harper's Weekly Reports: http://blackhistory.harpweek.com/3CivilWar/CivilWarLevelOne.htm

Harriet Jacobs—*Incidents in the Life of a Slave Girl*—E-text: http://docsouth.unc.edu/Jacobs/menu.htm

Harriet Tubman and the Underground Railroad: http://www.americaslibrary.gov/cgi-bin/page.cgi/aa/tubman

Harrison Berry Georgia Slave Narrative: http://docsouth.unc.edu/imls/berry/menu.html

Henry Bibb's Narrative: http://docsouth.unc.edu/neh/bibliography.html

Heritage of Slavery: http://www.arkansasheritage.com/peoplestories/africanamericans

Jack Black Slave Narrative: http://www.claudeblack.com/slavery/

James Madison, The Virginia Elite, and Slavery: http://www.jmu.edu/madison/eliteandslave.html

Jefferson County: http://freepages.genealogy.rootsweb.com/~ajac/arjefferson.htm

Josiah Henson and the Canadian Underground Railroad: http://www. uncletomscabin.org/

Kentucky Slave Chronicle, Isaac Johnson: http://docsouth.unc.edu/neh/ bibliography.html

Life of Benjamin Banneker: http://www.math.buffalo.edu/mad/special/ banneker-benjamin.html

Life of Harriet Tubman: http://www.nyhistory.com/harriettubman/life.htm

Louisiana Slavery: http://www.rootsweb.com/~afamerpl/plantations_usa/LA/ LA_plantations.html

Macon County Slave Narrative: http://www.dollsgen.com/slavenarratives.html

Man Who Sold His Wife: http://docsouth.unc.edu/oneal/menu.html

Mississippi Delta: http://xroads.virginia.edu/~UG99/brady/miss.html

Mississippi Plantation Life: http://www.blackokelleys.net/mississippi_ history.htm

Nat Turner's Rebellion: http://www.pbs.org/wgbh/aia/part3/3p1518.html

Nile of the New World: http://www.cr.nps.gov/delta/underground/slave.htm

On the Old Plantation: http://docsouth.unc.edu/clinkscales/menu.html

Pike County: http://homepages.rootsweb.com/~xrysta/research/blacks.htm

Reverend J.W. Loguen, as a Slave and as a Freeman: http://docsouth.unc.edu/ neh/loguen/menu.html

Role of the Negro in Missouri History: http://www.umsl.edu/~libweb/ blackstudies

Slave Narrative of J. Vance Lewis: http://docsouth.unc.edu/neh/lewisj/ menu.html

Slave Narrative of James Robert: http://docsouth.unc.edu/neh/roberts/ menu.html

Slavery and West Florida: http://www.geocities.com/Heartland/Bluffs/3010/ slavery.htm

Slavery in Early Louisiana: http://www.dickshovel.com/slavery.html

Slavery in Missouri and Little Dixie: http://www.rootsweb.com/~mocallaw

Slavery in North Georgia: http://ngeorgia.com/history/antebel.html

Slavery in Savannah: http://www.kingtisdell.org/Slavery.htm

Slavery in South Carolina: http://www.richland2.k12.sc.us/rce/slavery.htm

Slavery in Texas: http://austin.about.com/library/weekly/aa061902a.htm

Slavery in Texas—Correspondence: http://www.tamu.edu/ccbn/dewitt/ slaveryletters.htm

Slavery Petitions: http://history.uncg.edu/slaverypetitions/video/cowgill.html

Slavery Timeline: http://www.africanaonline.com/slavery_timeline.htm

Stono Rebellion: http://www.pbs.org/wgbh/aia/part1/1p284.html

Tennessee Slave Narratives (26): http://lcweb2.loc.gov/cqi-bin/query/ S?ammem/mesnbib:@field[STATE+@odl(Tennessee))

Texas Slavery Project: http://www.texasslaveryproject.uh.edu/

Thomas H. Jones Slave Narrative—E-text: http://docsouth.unc.edu/jones/ menu.html

Timeline of the Lincolns: http://www.pbs.org/wgbh/amex/lincolns/politics/ es_shift.html

Underground Railroad: http://www.nps.gov/undergroundrr

Underground Railroad in Delaware: http://www.lb.udel.edu/ud/spec/exhibits/
    undrgrnd.htm
Underground Railroad in Kentucky: http://www.ket.org/underground/history/
    questionof.htm
Underground Railroad Tour: http://www.dovermuseums.org/itineraries/
    undergroundrr.htm
Virginia's Domestic Slave Trade: http://fisher.lib.Virginia.edu/slavetrade
Wilmington in the 1890s: http://www.udel.edu/BlackHistory/blacklabor.html

Index

About the Authors

CLAYTON E. JEWETT is Adjunct Professor at Austin Community College, Austin, Texas.

JOHN O. ALLEN teaches at the Catholic University of America, Washington, D.C.